Roddy Doyle

Love

JONATHAN CAPE

LONDON

1 3 5 7 9 10 8 6 4 2

Jonathan Cape, an imprint of Vintage,
20 Vauxhall Bridge Road,
London SW1V 2SA

Jonathan Cape is part of the Penguin Random House group of companies
whose addresses can be found at global.penguinrandomhouse.com

Penguin
Random House
UK

First published in the United Kingdom by Jonathan Cape in 2020

penguin.co.uk/vintage

A CIP catalogue record for this book is available from the British Library

ISBN 9781787332270 (hardback)
ISBN 9781787332287 (trade paperback)

Typeset in 12.4/15.1 pt Plantin Std
by Integra Software Services Pvt. Ltd, Pondicherry

Printed and bound in Great Britain by Clays Ltd, Elcograf S.p.A.

Penguin Random House is committed to a sustainable future for
our business, our readers and our planet. This book is made from
Forest Stewardship Council® certified paper.

Love

Fiction
The Commitments
The Snapper
The Van
Paddy Clarke Ha Ha Ha
The Woman Who Walked Into Doors
A Star Called Henry
Oh, Play That Thing
Paula Spencer
The Deportees
The Dead Republic
Bullfighting
Two Pints
The Guts
Two More Pints
Smile
Charlie Savage
Two for the Road

Non-Fiction
Rory & Ita
The Second Half (with Roy Keane)

For Children
The Giggler Treatment
Rover Saves Christmas
The Meanwhile Adventures
Wilderness
Her Mother's Face
A Greyhound of a Girl
Brilliant
Rover and the Big Fat Baby

For Belinda

There stands the glass –

Fill it up to the brim –

'Til my troubles grow dim –

It's my first one today –

'There Stands the Glass' by
Russ Hull, Mary Jean Shurtz,
Audrey Greisham

He knew it was her, he told me. He told me this a year after he saw her. Exactly a year, he said.

—Exactly a year?

—That's what I said, Davy. A year ago – yesterday.

—You remember the date?

—I do, yeah.

—Jesus, Joe.

He saw her at the end of a corridor and he knew. Immediately. She was exactly the same. Even from that far off. Even though she was only a shape, a dark, slim shape – a silhouette – in the centre of the late-afternoon light that filled the glass door behind her.

—She was never slim, I said.

He shrugged.

—I don't even know what slim means, really, he said.

He smiled.

—Same here, I said.

—I just said it, he said. —The word. She was a tall shape – instead.

—Okay.

—Not a roundy shape.

—She's aged well, I said. —That's what you're telling me.

—I am, he said. —And she has.

—Where was the corridor? I asked him.

—The school, he said.

—What school?

—The school, he said again.

—We didn't know her in school, I said.

I knew he didn't mean the school we'd both gone to. We'd known each other that long. I'd said it – that we hadn't known her in school – to try to get him to be himself. To give back an answer that would get us laughing. He was the funny one.

—My kids' school, he said.

—Hang on, I said. —It was a parent–teacher meeting?

—Yeah.

—The woman of your dreams stepped out of the sun and into a parent–teacher meeting?

—Yep.

—Thirty years after the last time you saw her, I said. —More, actually. Way more. Thirty-six or seven years.

—Yeah, he said. —That's it, more or less. What did you say there? That she stepped out of the sun.

—I think so, yeah.

—Well, that's it, he said. —That's what happened. She did.

I didn't live in Ireland. I went over to Dublin three or four times a year, to see my father. I used to bring my family but in more recent years I'd travelled alone. The kids were grown up and gone and my wife, Faye, didn't like flying, and she wasn't keen on the drive to Holyhead and the ferry.

—Your dad never liked me, so he didn't.

—He did.

—He did not, she said. —He thought I was a slut. He said it, sure.

—He didn't say that.

—More or less, he did. You told me that, yourself, remember. I'm not making it up. He never liked me, so I won't be going around pretending I like him. I hate that house. It's miserable.

—She kissed me, Joe said now.

—In the school?

The man I knew – I thought I knew; I used to know – would have answered, 'No, in the arse,' or something like that.

—Yes, he said. —She remembered me.

I didn't know Joe well.

I used to.

We left school for good on the same day. He got work; I went to college, to UCD. He had money, wages – a salary. I had none until after I'd graduated. But we kept in touch. We both lived at home, a ten-minute walk from each other. We listened to records in my house about once a week, in the front room. He bought most of the records; mine was the house where we could blast them out. We played them so loud we could put our hands on the window glass and feel the song we were hearing. My mother was dead and my father didn't seem to mind. He told me years later he just wanted to see me happy. He endured the noise – the Pistols, Ian Dury, the Clash, Elvis Costello – because he thought it made me happy. I'd have been happy if he'd hammered at the wall with a shoe or his fist and told me to turn it fuckin' down. I'd have been happy if I'd felt I had to fight him.

We went drinking, myself and Joe, when I had the money. At Christmas and in October, when I came back from working in West Germany and London, before I had to spend the money I'd earned on books and bus fares. We'd get quickly drunk and roar. I rushed straight into anger. I thumped things, and myself. I let myself go, glimpsed the man I could become. I pulled back, and copied Joe. He drank, I drank. He laughed, I laughed. I roared when he roared.

—She remembered you?

—Yeah, he said. —She did. Immediately. Like I said.

I looked at him again. I could see why she'd have recognised him. The boy – the young man – was still there. His head was the same shape. He'd worn glasses back then and he still did – or, he did again – the same kind of black-framed glasses. He still had his hair. It was grey now, most of it, but it had never been very dark. He'd put on weight but not much, and none of it around his face and neck.

—Where were you? I asked him.

—In the school, he said. —I told you.

—Where, though?

—Outside the maths room, he said. —Waiting.

—For your turn with the teacher.

—Yeah, he said. —There were four or five people – mostly mothers – ahead of me. And I'd no one else to see – I'd seen all the others. We divided the list.

—Hang on, I said. —Trish was there as well?

Trish was his wife.

—Yeah, he said. —She was somewhere else. Queuing up for another teacher.

—You kissed the love of your life while Trish was in the building?

—Big building, he said. —It's a fuckin' school – in fairness.

That was more like the man I thought I knew. The man I'd wanted to be.

—You kissed her, I said.

—She kissed me.

—Where was Trish, exactly?

—Exactly, Davy? *Exactly?* Is this a murder investigation?

—Okay.

—For fuck sake, Davy.

—Okay – sorry. Go on.

—The home economics room, he said. —Or woodwork. Somewhere else. We took four teachers each, to get it over with as quickly as possible. Even at that, it took all afternoon. It's the only chance the teachers get to talk to adults. So, they fuckin' grab it. I was lucky.

—How come?

—I got to meet the maths teacher, he said. —A gobshite, by the way. But I was outside his door. I just happened to be there.

—And she walked in while you were waiting.

—Right place, right time. Yeah. Like I said – I was lucky.

—One of your kids does home economics and woodwork?

—What?

—You said home economics or woodwork. Trish was in one of those rooms.

—You're being Columbo again, Davy.

—Lay off.

—I just meant – like, for example. The rooms. Trish was somewhere else, in one of the other rooms, you know. Way off somewhere in the building.

—Which kid was it?

I'd never met his children and I didn't know their names. We told each other about the kids, brought each other up to date whenever we met, and then forgot about them. I hadn't seen Trish in twenty years.

—Holly, he said.

—You sure?

—Yeah, he said. —Of course, I am. Fuck off.

—Okay.

—You're being a bit of a prick, Davy.

—I'm not.

—You are.

—It's a bit of a shock.

—Why does it even matter?

—Okay.

—To you.

—I know.

I'd never seen him with his children but I knew he was a good father. And I knew what that meant. He was reliable. He'd given them their routines. He'd come home at much the same time every evening. He'd picked them up from football or gymnastics and he'd always been there on time. They'd seen him filling the dishwasher and the washing machine. They'd seen him cooking at the weekends; they'd probably preferred his cooking to Trish's. He'd served them Fanta in wine glasses on Saturday nights. He'd told them he loved them, twice a day, start and end. He'd read to them – the same book, again and again – gone swimming with them, slept on a chair beside them when they'd been kept overnight in Temple Street Children's Hospital. He'd read about asthma, eczema, OCD, intersexuality. He wasn't a man who didn't know what subjects his kids had done in school. He would never have pretended that he was that man.

He was right. It shouldn't have mattered. I shouldn't have cared. But it did. And I did.

We saw her there the first day, at a table under one of the windows.

6

We'd found a pub that liked us. We'd wandered the city centre for months, every weekend, starting after work on Friday and ending ten minutes before the last bus home on Sunday night. This was after I graduated and had new money in my pocket. We'd escaped from my front room and the record player. I could buy my round. We were peers now and we could become the lifelong friends we hadn't really been before. Getting drunk together, sneering at the world together, aching for the same women, denying it. We became the same man for a couple of important years. Before I left. Before he met Trish. Before I met Faye.

That day, the day we saw the girl who became the woman he saw years later, we got lost in the basement of Mercer's Hospital. We'd left Sheehan's on Chatham Street at the start of the holy hour – the pubs used to shut for an hour in the afternoon – and we'd wandered up to the Dandelion Market. But we were already too drunk – not drunk, exactly; more oiled – to flick through second-hand books and records. So we left, went back out on to South King Street. We got a bowl of chilli in a tiny place long gone and without a name; I'll never remember what it was called. It was so small, it didn't have a toilet. That was fine back then, normal, a restaurant or café without a loo. We were on South King Street again. We were the same man and we admitted we were bursting for a piss, really bursting, half an hour before the pub doors would open. Mercer's Hospital rose before us and we went in, trying to look like young men visiting a sick relative, and – I don't know why; I don't think I ever knew – we went down the stairs to the basement, instead of up to the wards. I remember the ceiling being low, just above our heads. There was no one else down there, no charging men or women in scrubs. There were no stretchers or abandoned wheel-chairs – I can't remember any. One corridor became two corridors, and another two – and no toilet. We ended up pissing into an enamel bucket in a broom cupboard, first him, then me; there was only room for one of us at a time.

We passed a toilet on our way back out. We didn't laugh. We were quickly ashamed – *I* was. The pubs were open when we got out into daylight, through a different door.

It was right in front of us. We'd never noticed it before. It had its own corner. We must have walked past it once or twice but we hadn't seen it.

—Looks okay, said Joe.

And it did.

We were sober again. It was early winter, afternoon. The sky was clear and the sun was making blocks of yellow and grey – the last few hours before night, the perfect time for drinking. Mercer's Hospital was behind us. Literally behind us. A pint would cure us, drown the shame. We'd start laughing again after the second.

We were twenty-one.

We looked in the window. It was plain inside, but a bit more than the standard Dublin pub. There was less wood, more light. There was one man sitting at the bar, his back to us. He was wearing a suit and there was a grey ponytail resting on the back of the jacket. It was the first time I'd seen a ponytail on a man who wasn't on *The Old Grey Whistle Test*. There were tables along the other wall, under a line of windows. Only one of them was occupied, by four people – a man and three women. There was a cello leaning against the wall between two windows, and three violin

8

cases sat on the table beside them. The women were drinking pints.

She was one of those women.

—Do we go in?

—Definitely, said Joe.

The double door was on the corner, under a porch. He went for the right side, I took the left. Both doors opened when we pushed, then walked in side by side – and sideways. The doors swung back into place behind us. We heard them creak, and rest.

There was no television, no horse racing. No radio, no music.

No one looked our way.

The man with the ponytail was reading a magazine. It sat on the counter between his gin and tonic and an ashtray. The musicians were talking quietly. I didn't know it then but the College of Music was around the corner, on Chatham Row. I heard strings and a trumpet coming from an open window the next time I passed it, the following Monday, when I was off on a wander during the lunch break. I'd been walking past the building for months.

There was no barman.

We stepped closer to the counter. We passed the musicians, went further – deeper – into the room, and took two stools at the end of the bar. We sat, and saw him. He was down on his hunkers, filling the lowest shelf with bottles of Britvic Orange. He heard us and turned, stood up, groaned, and smiled. It was the first time a barman had smiled at us.

—Gentlemen, he said.

He was happy to see us.

We stayed there for months.

★　★　★

9

She walked right through the thirty-seven years as she got nearer to him. The age crept across her face. Her back took a very slight stoop.

—But she was beautiful, he said.

Beautiful wasn't a word we'd ever used. The women we'd liked were always gorgeous. But we saw her the first time and she was beautiful.

—And she knew me, he said. —She came right up to me.

—Was it the first time you'd seen her?

—What do you mean?

—It wasn't the first parent–teacher meeting you've been to, I said. —Was it? And the school concerts, the football, hockey – all that stuff. All your kids went to that school, didn't they?

—I know what you mean.

—You've been going up there for years then. Was this the first time you saw her?

—Yeah, he said. —Yes.

He said Yes; he'd changed Yeah to Yes. He was in the witness box.

—How come? I asked.

—How come what?

—All those meetings and matches and you never saw her.

—You don't know the school, he said. —It's huge. There's over a thousand brats go to that place.

—Yes –, I said.

I was at it now, playing the prosecutor.

—Yes, but parent–teacher meetings aren't convened for the parents and guardians of every child in the school, are they? This one, when you saw her, it would have been just a form – a year group. Am I right? What class is Holly in?

10

—It was a year ago, he said. —She was in Transition
Year.

—What's that again? I asked.

He looked at me.

—I don't live in this country, I reminded him.

—She was sixteen, he said.

—Four years' worth of meetings and sports and cake
sales and sponsored walks.

—And I never saw her.

—How come?

—Maybe I wasn't looking, he said.

Now I stared at him. Was he making this up?

He shrugged.

—There's no answer, he said. —I don't know. It's a
big school. It's possible.

—But improbable.

—Okay.

—Was it the first time she saw you? I asked.

—It's not really –.

He stopped. And started again.

—It's not really the point, he said. —The fact is, she
saw me and it was like she'd seen me the day before.
The way she behaved, the way she spoke to me. Like
it was 1981, or whenever.

—Okay, I said. —But had she ever kissed you before?
In 1981?

—Back off a bit, Davy, he said. —Just listen. She
came up to me and kissed me.

—How?

—The cheek.

—One cheek?

—You didn't hear me, he said.

—I did, I said. —What do you mean?

—She kissed *me*, he said. —She didn't – whatever – offer her cheek for me to kiss. She kissed mine.

He was right; I hadn't been listening.

—Lips, he said. —Her lips kissed me – made actual contact with my skin. Not the air near my skin. Do you remember her well?

—Yes, I said. —I do.

—Do you remember her smile?

—Yeah, I said. —I think I do.

—Well, she smiled – while she was kissing me.

—Did she not smile when she saw you?

—She was smiling when she got there, like we'd arranged to meet – like she'd expected me to be there when she arrived, leaning there against the wall.

—Did that not worry you – a tad?

—No, he said. —Why would it have?

—Well, it was so – like – out of nowhere.

—I felt the exact same way, he said. —It made complete sense.

—Well, I said. —No offence. But it makes no fuckin' sense at all.

We were in a newish restaurant on the Clontarf Road, close to the Wooden Bridge. It was six months since the last time we'd met. We emailed each other occasionally, or texted, usually about music or football or dead friends and neighbours. We didn't crawl the pubs in town, the old places, like we used to when I came home. I'd always added an extra day's recovery before I went back – home – to England. I didn't drink now. I'd stopped. A glass of wine, the occasional bottle of craft beer at home – that was me. I stayed out of pubs. I don't think he drank much either. It was Monday night, this time. The restaurant was half empty. We weren't loud men. There was no one sitting too near

12

us. The waiter was young but old-school. He stayed away between courses and didn't keep passing, to ask us how we were getting on or if everything was perfect.

—Well, that was how it felt, he said. —Like we'd never been apart.

—But –.

—I know, he said. —I know. We'd never been much together. But I'm talking about feelings here, not facts. Feelings. The feel of the thing.

It sounded like something he'd said before. More than once.

He looked different, I decided. He looked bad – torn. In crisis. He was picking at his food. There wasn't much left on the plate – he must have been eating. But he looked too thin. The skin under his neck had become loose, wattled. I'd told him he was looking well, when we'd met an hour before, and I'd meant it. But now I was actually looking at him. He was scratching the palm of one of his hands. He'd been doing it since we sat down. He kept putting his fork down to do it. He'd been scratching his neck too. There were pink tracks under his ear. I'd almost been enjoying the car crash – man meets old flame and ruins his life. He'd been helping me. It was almost like he'd been sitting back, relating his misadventures, an arm resting on the back of the chair. But I saw it now, he wasn't like that. He was leaning forward, looking down at the table – examining what had happened.

He was sweating. But so was I. It was late May, and hot. The grass outside was brown. I'd cut my father's grass and the bucket behind the mower had filled with dust. The sweat on Joe was like a mask a footballer might have worn to protect a facial injury. He ran an

arm, a sleeve, across his face and became Joe again,
just Joe; the mask was gone.

I copied him. I rubbed my forehead with my
napkin.

—The heat.

—It's not too bad in here, he said. —But we're not
built for this, are we?

—No, I said. —There are forest fires – I saw it –
inside the Arctic Circle. In Sweden.

—There you go, he said. —The end of the world.

—Bring it on.

—Yeah – fuck it.

He scooped some rice onto his fork.

—Look, he said. —Davy. I know it sounds a bit mad.
What I'm telling you.

—Well –

—No, I know. It's okay. But it wasn't – it isn't. Mad.
It felt normal. Perfectly – yeah. Normal. Not the event
itself, I mean. The way it felt. At the time. It felt normal. Do you understand?

—Kind of.

—Is it boring?

—No.

—Trish said it was.

—You told Trish? What you've been telling me?

—I didn't get the chance, he said. —I didn't get far
with Trish, I'm afraid.

—That's understandable, I suppose. Is it?

—Absolutely, he said. —No – I understand. Her
position, like. I'm guessing I'd feel the same.

It was what I wanted to hear, Joe explaining what
had happened with Trish. How he'd met this timeless
beauty while Trish was on the next corridor, in the
queue outside home economics.

14

He put the fork to his mouth. I watched him chew, then swallow. He picked up his glass.

—The food's good.

—Yeah.

—We'll come here again.

—Yeah.

—Anyway –.

They stood beside each other in the queue outside the maths room. He didn't ask her if it was a daughter or a son she had in Transition Year. It didn't feel like they had to catch up, rattle off the list of kids, and he didn't want to waste the time they had until he was called in to meet the teacher.

—So you did feel it was a bit unique, I said.

—No, he said. —No. But the queue was getting shorter. I was there to hear what the teacher had to say. That was why I was there – I hadn't forgotten that. And I'd have to go in.

—Okay.

They talked about the school, about the weather. The everyday stuff. It was raining out there and the shoulders of her jumper – a big, baggy thing – were wet. Her hair was wet too, a bit. The hair was long, unusually long for a woman of her age. It was the length it had been when we'd first seen her, he told me, maybe just an inch or two shorter. It was the same colour – he thought. She was the same woman. He asked her nothing and she asked him nothing. They just talked. Two parents ahead of him, a couple with matching runners, went in. He was next. The time was running out. She took her phone from her jeans pocket.

—I'm 087 –, she started.

—You knew something was up.

—What?

—Something was happening, I said.

—Of course something was happening, he said. — Have I been denying anything?

—Well, look, I said.

I felt like I was leaning forward, inviting him to thump me, pushing my face at him. But I wasn't. I was sitting back and I knew I was making him angry. Goading him – because I wanted to.

—A woman takes her phone out, I said. —And starts reciting her number to the man beside her. She's not married to him, he's not married to her.

—Come here, he said. —Do you have to watch the end of a film before you decide if you'll watch the rest of it? Is that how it works in your house?

—No.

—Do you get my point?

—Do you get mine? I said. —She took out her phone. She wanted your number. She wanted to give you hers. She wanted to see you again. You knew that – you must have. And you're saying it was all perfectly normal?

—What's abnormal about falling in love? he said.

—At a parent–teacher meeting?

He smiled. He was looking at it, looking at himself in it, what had happened a year before, and it suddenly made him happy.

—For the first time in the history of mankind, he said. —In the history of the Irish education system. What do you think, Davy? A man and a woman in a queue and they end up falling for each other. Has it happened before?

—I'd say so, yeah.

—I agree with you, he said. —One broken marriage for every parent–teacher meeting is my estimate. I don't have the statistics to back that up, mind you. Will I go on?

—Yeah.

—It *is* different, he said. —I promise you that.

—Okay.

—So anyway, I took my phone out.

He went to Contacts and tapped as she recited the rest of her number. Then he gave her his. He put the phone back into his pocket. There was no deal; neither of them said they'd be in touch.

—Then I couldn't remember her name, he said.

—Ah, Jesus.

—Blank, he said. —Fuckin' blank. Nothing.

—For fuck sake.

—Do you remember it? he asked me. —Now?

—No, I said. —What is it?

—Wait, he said.

He wasn't even sure if he'd ever known her name – when he was outside the classroom.

—I could've asked her, I suppose.

—That might have been a bit strange, I said.

—True, he said. —But, anyway.

—Did she know yours?

—She did.

—Are you sure?

—I think she did.

—Was the maths teacher happy with Holly? I asked.

—Very, he said. —Holly's great.

He had her number but not her name. He decided she'd have to phone or text him first. If it was going to happen, it was up to her. What *it* was, he didn't know.

—Some sort of hole to be filled, he said. —No – that sounds wrong. I don't mean it crudely.

—Okay.

—An emptiness or something, he said. —Four wasted decades.

17

—You're joking.

He shook his head. The grin – the fun in his eyes as he looked over his lenses – was gone.

—Just because you saw her?

I watched his face as he pushed back words that wouldn't do.

—No, he said, finally. —Not just that.

He was trying to put the words together, the right words in good order; I could see him doing it. He wanted to hear himself say exactly what had happened, what he'd thought – how he'd felt.

—If –, he started. —If I'd seen her – just seen her. It would have been nothing. Just nice – or –. Nice to have seen that she was still around and looking so well, you know. But that's all. I think. I'd have texted you – for example. That kind of reaction. If I'd seen her from the car, say. Or if she was in here and we saw her leaving. A bit of a buzz – but nothing. I wouldn't have dashed after her. Or, even if she saw us and came over to say hello, that would have been it. But.

He picked up his knife and fork and cut at a piece of his peri peri chicken.

—That wasn't how it was, he said.

I expected him to fill his mouth and keep me waiting while he chewed. But he didn't. He wasn't entertaining himself now, or me. He was trying to understand. He was trying to be me, on the other side of the table, listening to his story, his version of events – the only version – for the first time. I'd been over for a few days between Christmas and New Year's, six months before – but he hadn't mentioned anything then. When I'd asked him how things were – and I'm sure I did ask him – he'd answered, 'Grand.' And nothing more. It was the response I always had ready too when I came

18

over to Dublin. *I'm grand. We're grand. Everything's grand.* He must have left Trish by then; he must have walked out of the house.

He was listening, examining his own words.

—She expected me to be there, he said. —And I was expecting her.

—Is that true? I asked.

I believed what he was telling me. I could see that he was pushing aside other possibilities, resisting the urge to add or amuse.

—Which? he asked back.

This time he put the chicken into his mouth.

—That you expected her, I said. —Is that actually true? Is that how you felt?

He swallowed.

—Yeah.

—Then, I said. —There? In the school.

—Yes, he said. —Definitely.

—Your long lost love suddenly appeared in front of you, I said.

—No, he said.

I was there to listen, not to cross-examine him. I was there so he could see me listening. He hadn't noticed my sarcasm, or he hadn't cared. And, immediately, I was glad. I didn't want to hear it either.

—That wasn't it, he said. —It wasn't like that. I'd imagine that would be huge. A heart thing, you know. Thump, thump. Like terror. When you think there's someone following you. To mug you. Did that ever happen you?

I nodded.

—You were mugged?

—No, I said. —I thought you meant the feeling, when you know you've a heart in your chest. Pumping away. It happened to us, remember?

19

—I do, yeah, he said. —Near Fairview.

—Yep.

—I'll never forget it.

—No.

—The fuckers.

—Yep.

—But, anyway, he said. —This wasn't that – when I met her. It wasn't like that at all.

There is a reason why men don't talk about their feelings. It's not just that it's difficult, or embarrassing. It's almost impossible. The words aren't really there.

—That – you know – that 'Oh Jaysis' feeling, he said. —It wasn't like that. It was calm.

—Calm?

—Yeah, he said. —I think. It's a year ago. But, yeah – I think that's how it was.

—Well, it hasn't been that calm since, I said. —Judging by what you've been telling me.

—No, he agreed. —That's true.

He cut more chicken.

—It's not a mid-life thing either, he said. —So don't even mention it. I'm fuckin' sick of it.

—I don't go in for that shite, I told him.

'Shite', 'grand', 'Jaysis' – I packed the words with my clothes and toothbrush when I was coming to Dublin for a few days.

—I didn't fall for some young one, he said.

—I know that, I said. —I was there when she was a young one, remember.

—Yeah, sorry. I think –. I don't know.

—Don't know what?

—I think it might have been easier if she had been a young one. If I'd made an eejit of myself running after someone half my age.

20

—With your dick in your hand.

—That's exactly –, he started.

He was whispering now, leaning over his plate.

—You've no idea how many times I've had to listen to that phrase in the last twelve fuckin' months.

He gave me four different voices.

—With your dick in your hand, with your *dick* in your hand, with your *dick* in your *hand*, with your fucking *dick in your hands*.

—Was Trish the last one? I asked.

—No, he said. —No. That was my son. Gareth. Trish was the first. And the second.

He laughed first, and I followed.

—Hang on, he said.

He put the chicken into his mouth. He looked at me, raised his eyebrows as he chewed. He was pale – a mid-winter face in very hot weather. He looked like he was starving. My own plate was empty. I remember looking down at it and being surprised. I'd eaten the salmon, the broccoli – I must have; I remember ordering them – but I'd tasted nothing.

He rested his fork on the side of his plate.

—I think they'd have understood, he said. —It would have made sense. If I'd been caught with a younger woman. Or even a neighbour, you know. The mad one next door.

I nodded.

—A bit of stupidity through the garden hedge, he said. —They'd have got that.

He sighed, smiled.

—But –, he said.

—But what?

—I'm – I don't know. Here we are and I'm still trying to explain it. I looked at her and it was like

21

nothing much had happened since the last time I'd seen her.

—And again, I said. —I'm going to ask you. Is that actually true?

He looked down at his plate. He looked up.

—I don't know.

She was the girl with the cello. But we didn't know that until later, in a different place. We sat at the bar that first day and felt accepted. One of my children is the age I was then – he's older – and I look at him when he lets me and I see a child, a kid trying to be an adult. He has a beard and a boyfriend; he lives in London, in Peckham. He's up and running, as they say. But he looks so young. The beard is a disguise.

We must have looked like that. We were working and twenty-one but we must have looked like two boys chancing their arms, hoping to get served in a real pub, in daylight. Served by a grown-up. That was how I felt, even though we'd already been drunk once that day and had had no problem being served in any pub in Dublin; I hadn't been refused service since my second-last year in school. But this one was different. This one felt like a club. Its lack – no radio, no television, music, no framed Doors of Dublin poster – seemed like more.

It was quiet.

—I love this, Joe said – he whispered.

—Me too, yeah.

I hadn't read a newspaper in a pub before but this was where I was going to do it. I hadn't sat by myself and drunk a slow pint; I'd never had a pint alone. I would now, here. I'd sit and look in front of me. I wouldn't shift on my stool or look over my shoulder. I'd be a man.

I didn't say this. I didn't think this. I felt it. For a while, I noticed no one else. I didn't see the women and the man pick up their instrument cases and leave. I must have heard them, I suppose, and I probably turned and looked at them as they left. It's not that I don't remember; I didn't care – that was what mattered. I remember how I felt. I'd entered a new state. I'd put on a man's jacket. I was a man. Because I'd walked into this particular pub. The boys who'd pissed in the bucket across in Mercer's Hospital were gone.

The place emptied and filled, and emptied again. The man with the magazine – it was *Private Eye* – stayed. But after the musicians had left, the place quickly filled again, this time with people with shopping bags. Previously, even earlier that day, we'd have sneered. Fuckin' shopping. Now we smiled. These were adults. Having a drink like us. It was women with shopping bags, and men with women. They were damp – it was raining out there – and happy. There were bursts of quiet laughter. There was no one trying to lasso the room. They all knew the barman. He was the landlord and, that afternoon, he ruled alone; he'd no help behind the bar. He beamed at the customers, greeted them all like they were fresh off the mailboat. And they beamed back. They'd known him for years, and he'd known them. He served them drink but it seemed incidental. They'd come in for a chat and approval, and he gave it. He really knew who they were. He liked them and they loved him.

He was called George. The name was in the air, never out of it. *George?* It was in the smoke. *George.* It was never a demand, always a greeting. He never rushed but he was always there. He smiled at us whenever he passed.

—Gentlemen, he said.

He wasn't being sarcastic, or snide. This was the thing: he respected us. And this is true: no adult male – no man older than me – had ever respected me before. Except, perhaps, my father. But he was my father, and a widower. There were just the two of us in the house and we got on fine without having to try too hard; I loved my father and I hated him. George didn't know us but he gave us the time he gave everyone else. There were generations of his customers there, in that hour between five and six. Some came in earlier, and some stayed longer. But they were all there in that hour, every Saturday. It became my favourite time of the week. There was no television or radio to give us the football results but I didn't miss them. We were going to become those people; we already were those people. There was a handsome man who hadn't shaved for a few days, with a bit of good grey in his hair. He was with a great-looking woman with a Switzer's bag. I'd be that man in ten years, maybe fifteen. I'd be here at teatime every Saturday. It would never be teatime in this world.

—How long've we been here? Joe asked me, that first afternoon.

—Don't know, I said.

I looked at my watch.

—Two hours? More? Three, maybe.

—How many pints have we had? he asked.

I had to think about it.

—Two, I said.

I looked at my pint. I wasn't ready for a fresh one.

—One an' a half.

—Jesus, said Joe. —That's fuckin' amazin'.

Ordinarily, we'd have been on our fifth, becoming just us, closing off the world around us. Protecting and building ourselves. We'd been drunk already that day, so we were just topping up what was already there. But it was different. We were here. We didn't need to cower or snarl, turn our backs on people who wouldn't have noticed. We didn't have to make our own noise. It was a dream; it had all the qualities of a good one. It was the drink, I know, the holes and fuzz it could give to the surroundings. Nothing was sudden or unwanted; there was nothing beyond the afternoon. It was the perfect state and I know now, decades later, it was only possible on a Saturday afternoon, in George's. I don't think I'm being sentimental, or *just* sentimental.

I smiled at George.

—Two, please, George, I said.

I don't recall smiling but I must have. I was twenty-one. In the ten years before that afternoon I'd smiled only when I'd decided to. This, again – *here* – was different. I watched George fill the glasses and leave them on the towel, beside four other waiting pints. He smiled at the line of six, then turned to fill glasses with gin and vodka. I looked at Joe. He was smiling, so I must have been too. It wasn't a grin. It wasn't because I'd been cheeky, because I'd called a middle-aged man I didn't know George. I hadn't been cheeky. Cheek was a thing of the past, as were anger and resentment, stupidity, exclusion. That was why Joe was smiling. We were in a new, unexpected life and we were at home in it. Adulthood wasn't too bad at all.

There was another thing too, another ingredient. We were being shown a new life; we were observing the middle-class world, an ease, a grace we'd never seen before. It could be ours if we wanted it.

—Gentlemen, said George when he put the pints down in front of us.

—Thanking you, George, said Joe.

It was his turn to call a grown man George.

—They look the business, he said.

George chuckled and accepted the money. He brought back the change – 'Now, sir' – and left it beside my pint.

—Thanks, George.

We were pissed, of course. Rat-arsed. I knew that when I stood up and went downstairs to the Gents. I was counting the steps down. I heard myself and stopped. But even that, the trip to the jacks, was different. My feet on the wood gave back the self-assured taps of a man who knew where he was going. I even looked back to see who was coming down behind me. There was no one; it was me who owned the self-assurance.

I came back up from the toilet and the place was emptying. The shoppers were heading home, and so was the man with the *Private Eye* and ponytail. For a minute – a minute – it was just us and George. It was thrilling.

—It's quiet now, said Joe.

—Yes, said George.

He was gathering the empty and half empty glasses and bottles from the three tables behind us. He put them on the counter.

—The calm before the storm, he said.

He was still smiling. He loved the storm, he loved the calm.

I looked around. It was a black and white world. White walls, black window frames, black counter, the white shirt on George.

—The jacks, I said quietly.

—Wha'? said Joe.

—You should see it.

—I will.

—It's clean, I said.

—Fuck off.

—It's well lit, I said. —There's a fuckin' bulb.

—My God.

—I'm tellin' yeh now, I said. —You'd eat your fuckin' dinner off the floor.

The room was warm and the cold that rushed in when the door opened was dramatic and welcome. But the intruder wasn't. We'd had George to ourselves and now we didn't. It was a small young man who'd come in – he wasn't a man at all; he was just a boy, a Dickensian kind of kid – and he took off his anorak while the door was still swinging shut. He was wearing a white shirt. He was staff, the apprentice.

—William, said George.

—George, said William.

—Did you have your dinner? George asked him.

—Liver, said William.

George clapped his hands and rubbed them.

—Lovely, he said. —With onions.

—I don't like onions, said William.

He'd disappeared behind a door and he came back out without the anorak. He looked at us and nodded. I didn't like it. He was seventeen, maybe eighteen, and he was nodding at his peers, two lads from across the river. He didn't see what he should have been seeing. George would look at us now and see kids.

—Did your mother put the onions on your plate? George asked William.

—She did, yeah, said William.

27

—Then I hope you ate them, said George, and he winked at us.

And that was it. We were still adults. William absorbed the lesson and George put the last of the glasses and bottles onto the counter. Then he went back behind the bar and started to wash them. George washed, William dried. He dropped the bottles that George rinsed into a crate and carried the crate away, downstairs. I expected George to look at us again, and smile. But he didn't. I was yearning – dying – to say something softly cruel about the kid. But I didn't. It wouldn't have been welcome; I knew that. It would have been childish.

—Good man, George, said Joe. —The lad should know his onions.

George laughed. He dried the last glass and put it on a shelf below him. His laughter wasn't loud or con-spiratorial, or diplomatic or forced. He'd heard something amusing and he'd laughed. Joe wasn't asking him to betray his apprentice, or to give us permission to tear into him when he came back upstairs. He'd said something funny – onions were always good for a laugh – and, while he was at it, he'd asserted our right to a vote in the land of the grown-ups. And George's response had affirmed that right.

—Two more, please, George.

The door swung open, and open, and open, and a new population slid in and took over the room, younger than the shoppers from earlier but two or three signifi-cant years older than us. We were at the back, near the coat hooks and the two flights of stairs, down to the Gents and up to the Ladies. People flowed in so quickly, it was as if one big gang of friends was arriving at once. They occupied the area near the door, then seemed to send out scouts to the remaining corners. Passages opened and two or three stepped in and took the remaining stools at the bar and the tables and benches along the walls. They were all at home, all of them linked, somehow. Although I could see now, it wasn't just one polite mob. There were men in twos and threes, there were two men alone, there were couples, and couples with couples, and two bigger, looser groups of friends. But there was something about them. Confidence, perhaps. Physical ease – they stood and leaned and sat, crossed their legs like they'd been trained to do it properly. It wasn't Christmas or coming up to Christmas but they all seemed like returned emigrants who'd picked up ways, notions, a body language that they could never have learnt in Ireland.

They were gorgeous.

William topped up our pints and placed them in front of us.

—Did you get the results? I asked him.

I needed a blast of familiarity and William was the nearest thing to us in the shop.

—Which do you want? he asked.

—Leeds.

He smiled.

—Lost.

—Liverpool, said Joe.

—Won.

He gave Joe his change.

—Now, sir.

That was enough; it steadied us. I'd felt the urge to leave or get plastered. I'd been panicking a bit and Joe, I knew, had too. But we said nothing. We sat and watched, and listened. It wasn't the fact that most of these people had a few years on us. I wasn't sure about that now, either. I was looking at young faces around me, and in the long mirror behind the bar. I reminded myself: I'd be twenty-two before the end of the year. I was educated; I had a degree. Joe had been working for more than three years. These people were at home; that was it. At home here, with George. At home everywhere, I suspected. We'd just arrived. We were only in the door. We'd none of their blood.

Joe was better at it than I was. I was good in my head; I was debonair, polished, ready to talk. But – I see it now; I see myself – I sat there. I looked at them all in the mirror. I didn't feel excluded. That was the big advance. But I was shy.

Joe wasn't. Or, I don't think he was. He didn't turn on his stool, to join in with the group of men and women behind us. He didn't offer anything on Ronald Reagan or the state of Irish rugby. He didn't, as my father would have put it, butt in. But he was lighter, somehow – looser. He sat on his stool side-saddle and helped pass back pints and change. He joked with people he'd never seen before. He smiled at women. He was *there*, much more than I was or could be. I loved him for it, and I didn't.

She was there. The woman we'd noticed earlier, the girl we'd find out played the cello – she was back. I saw her properly now. I realised first that I'd seen her before and I was a bit slow grabbing the fact that I'd seen her here, once, just three hours before. She – the sighting of her – seemed much more important. She felt long lost and suddenly found. I even thought I'd know her name.

She was beautiful. Something about her was beautiful. Gorgeous was our usual word but there was something about her: she wasn't real; she was more than real, or less – *too* real.

She'd changed her clothes and done something with her hair. It had been in a ponytail earlier – I think – maybe even a bun. Now it was free and long, like a veil or a scarf. She was wearing a black leather jacket, a biker's jacket. I hoped she'd look at me; she'd see me in the mirror, over her friend's shoulder, and she'd smile. I'd smile back at her reflection. I'd turn in my stool and smile at her. Then something magic would happen. She'd come to me or I'd get off the stool without deciding to; I'd go over there and I'd make her laugh. I'd stop being drunk but the courage would stay with me. She just had to look. To smile.

But she didn't do either. I remember nothing else. But we were there again the following Saturday.

—So she phoned you, I said.

He looked at me. He hesitated.

—Yes.

He seemed happy with the answer. We were back to facts, events.

—Not immediately, he said. —Not, like, that night or the next day.

—How long after?

—End of the week, he said.

—Friday?

—Thursday.

—I'd have guessed that, I said.

—Why – how?

—She'd phone you on Thursday, arrange something for Friday. End of the week. TGIF. That kind of shite.

—Don't get fuckin' snide, he said.

He meant it. He was hurt.

—Sorry, I said. —I was just imagining the start of something – an affair, I suppose. A fling.

—And have you ever had an oul' fling, yourself, Davy? he asked.

The anger was gone. For the first time that evening he was curious. The question was defensive but he wanted to know the answer.

—No, I said. —I haven't.

—Okay.

—What about you? I said. —Have you? Before –.

—Yeah, he said. —Yeah. Once – one. A woman in work. The Christmas party, believe it or not. All the fuckin' clichés. A good while ago though – ten years. More. It was stupid.

—Did Trish find out?

—No, he said. —No, she didn't. Thank God. It was –. Ah, Christ. She was unhappy.

—The woman?

—The woman – yeah. She was getting married.

—Jesus. And did she?

—Yeah, she did, he said. —But, no, it didn't last long.

—The marriage?

—No, the fling, he said. —The whatever. I don't know about the marriage – I'd have my doubts. But it was just, really – we needed some sort of a justification for the sex. I think. We couldn't admit that we did it because we were drunk. Too old for that or something. So we met up again twice after Christmas. Three times – yeah, three. And we were drunk then as well. It was fuckin' terrible, really. Jesus, when I think about it.

—Did she invite you to the wedding?

—No, he said. —God, no.

—Anyway.

—Yeah.

—She phoned you, I reminded him. —Your woman. After the parent–teacher meeting.

—Yeah. Yeah – she did.

He smiled now.

—She did.

—What's her name? I asked. —She must have said it when she called – when you answered.

—Jessica.

Nothing happened. Nothing rolled in my head, clicked into place. I couldn't remember her being called Jessica.

—How long did it take? I asked.

—What?

—To find out her name.

—You're asking strange questions, he said.

The wrong questions, he meant. Her name didn't matter.

—Just curious, I said. —These things can be awkward, I suppose. And you said it, yourself – you didn't know her name. I'm always forgetting people's names. Especially these days.

Six months before, the last time we met, we'd have had a laugh about the indignities of ageing, the list of daily humiliations. *Especially these days.* What I'd half intended telling him about this time was the sheer scale, the limitless variety of the surnames I had to deal with at work, and the first names too – never the *Christian* names, how the names accompanying the English accents had changed, or been added to, since I'd moved to England. I was good at it, in fact. I made sure I knew the names – Okeke, Igbinedion, Anikulapo-Kuti, Sargsyan, Dewab, Ali, Smith, Bautista, Chan.

I enjoyed it. I made sure there was never the hesitation before the name, or a little question mark after it – *Mr ... Okeke?* More important things, vital things I forgot – completely. But not at work, not the names. I made lists. I conquered the names and voted Remain. I'd intended – half intended – telling him that.

—Same here, he said. —It's shocking. Head like a fuckin' sieve. But yeah – she said, Hi, it's Jessica.

—And you knew it was her.

—Yeah, he said. —I'd put *George* into the address book. Temporarily. Till I found out her name. If she phoned.

—And she did.

—She did.

—Where were you?

—At home, he said.

—What time?

—Nine? he said. —A bit later – half-nine. We were watching – actually.

He sat up straight. He smiled – he grinned. He became himself.

—D'you know what we were watching? he said.

—What?

—*The Affair.*

—Really?

—Can you fuckin' believe it? You've seen it, yeah?

—No.

—Watch it, he said. —It's brilliant. Filthy. The first series, anyway. We were watching the second series.

—What episode?

He laughed.

—Four.

He shrugged.

—I don't know, he said. —But it might have been four.

—And she was Jessica.

—Yeah.

—Did the name ring a bell?

—Yeah, he said. —It did.

—You remembered she was called Jessica?

—Are we in a police station again, Davy? he said.

—Sorry, I said. —It's just, I've no recollection of her name at all.

—But you remember it now, he said.

—Yes, I said. —Yeah, I do. At least –.

—What?

—I don't know. I think I do. Yeah, yeah – I do remember it.

But I didn't. Not then.

George smiled as if he'd been expecting us. William came out of the room in the back and gave us the half time scores. The man with the ponytail looked up from his copy of the *New Statesman* and stared at us.

She wasn't there – and that was when I remembered her. I hadn't thought of her all week but now I missed her so much I wanted to go home. There were two women and a man, three violin cases. I didn't know if they were the same women and the same violins, but they were at the same table and under the same window. Three violins, two women, no cello.

We parked ourselves on our stools and watched George put the glasses under the Guinness taps. He put the pints on the towel to settle.

—Gentlemen, he said.

—Thanks, George.

The door swung open and he went down to meet the men who'd just walked in.

—No cello today, I said.

—No, said Joe.

I knew then that he'd noticed her too and that, like me, he was happily suffering.

—She might be in later, I said.

—Yeah.

We were sober. We hadn't seen each other during the week. We'd met at the bus stop down from Joe's house. We hadn't bothered with the Dandelion Market; we'd gone straight to George's. We hadn't said much. We were afraid to talk, I think, afraid that we'd find the place altered, or ordinary. Not once, though, did I think of her. It was the stool, the counter, the pint in front of me, my friend beside me, the night ahead of us. But then she was there, or her absence was there, and I was devastated and so was Joe. The other women didn't interest us. There could be no compensation. We watched them leave with their instruments. We watched the arrival of the shoppers, and the departure of the shoppers and the man with the ponytail. We got the final scores from William. We watched George at work. Joe went out to the phone box at the foot of the stairs to the Ladies, to tell his mother that he wouldn't be home for his tea.

—Why d'you do tha'? I asked him when he got back.

—Wha'?

—Phone home.

—Just to tell her.

—Tha' you won't be home?

—Yeah.

—You're never home.

This was for George. He was at the taps, filling glasses. Listening – not listening – smiling, taking orders.

—Yes, I am.

—On Saturdays, I said. —When was the last time you went home for your tea?

—A while ago.

—Months ago.

—Okay. She just likes me to phone. She likes answerin' the phone. We've only had it a couple o' years.

We were waiting. Holding our breath. Waiting for her. Praying for her. The woman I now know was called Jessica. *Is* called Jessica.

—Wha' d'you think? he asked me.

I knew exactly what – who – he meant. The place was filling again. The day was over; we were sitting in the night. We were looking at women. There was always the ideal woman but there were all the other women too. We were recovering. Starting to feel the buzz of the previous week. These would be our people now and this was still our future, with or without the woman. We were laughing again, chatting. Soaking it in, soaking in it. I could feel myself melting – it was good – flowing slowly into the noise, the accents, the jokes, the stories, the geography. Listening. Hoping someone would say something to me. Male, female – a way in. The start. It was why we'd been coming into town. To make the break. To live up, somehow, to the music we loved, the books we read. To walk streets instead of roads, cross a real river, sit in the pubs that Behan and Flann O'Brien had sat in, find the women who'd see, who'd understand, who'd hold us, who'd do things to us. Who'd come up to us and start it. Let us in. Let us soar.

She was there.

I think I knew it before I saw her. But I've no idea why I think that. It's a long time ago; I'm a different man. I'd forgotten she existed. Her sudden resurrection – Joe pushing back the stone – was unsettling.

37

She was there.

Over at the door, behind a group of men and women at the other end of the bar. She'd asked for a pint of Harp and I watched George carry it from the tap to that group and I saw her hand, her arm, her shoulder, her face, as the bodies made way and she leaned in and paid for the pint, took it and smiled at George. Then the curtain closed and she was back behind the gang. But I knew she was there before I saw that. I knew the pint that George was pouring was for her. I might have heard her voice through the other voices – although I hadn't heard her speak the week before. But I knew the hand was hers, the arm, the shoulder. I saw the curtain open, I saw the curtain close.

We were at the wrong end of the bar.

That was what we were, it was what we did. We anticipated rejection, we guaranteed it. Outsiders – and we made sure it stayed that way. Honest, vital, yearning, pure. One woman – that woman – would see it. She'd come and take my hand.

My hand.

Our hand.

—What did you tell Trish?

—What?

—When she phoned – when Jessica phoned you. When you were watching *The Affair*. What did you say to Trish?

I wanted it to fall apart. I wanted to delay it – their second meeting.

—Nothing, he said.

—Nothing?

He shrugged.

—Work, he said. —Something like that.

—Were you sitting beside each other? I asked him.

—I think so.

—Hang on, I said. —Joe.

—What?

—So far, like – so far. You've been really precise. Seeing her in the school. Watching *The Affair*.

—I don't remember which episode.

—Don't start, I said. —You know what I mean. You know exactly where you were sitting. You know exactly what happened. You might regret starting to tell me, okay. But it's too late for that.

I think he'd heard himself and he didn't like it. He was belittling Trish – inevitably. He was being cruel. His kids were in the house, somewhere near. He was about to destroy his family and, in the telling, he'd laughed.

He looked at me.

—I don't –, he said. —I actually don't know why I'm telling you.

I didn't respond. He was talking to himself. He knew exactly why he was telling me.

—I was sitting beside her, he said.

I said nothing but he heard the next question, anyway.

—Close, he said. —We watch – watched, fuck it – a lot of box sets. Sky Atlantic and Netflix, you know. Some great stuff. We –.

He stopped. He put down his fork. He picked it up.

—We always went to bed early after *The Affair*.

He sighed.

—It's a bit shit, isn't it?

I didn't answer. I didn't nod or shake my head.

—So, yeah, he said. —The phone went. It was in my pocket.

He smiled, slightly.

—I had it on vibrate, you know. Trish felt it before I did. She nudged me – that's your phone. And –

—It was Jessica.

—Yeah. So. I – well – I put the phone to my ear.

—You knew who it was.

—Yeah. I told you. I'd put *George* in the address book. I don't know any other Georges, except George from the pub. So – and yeah, I looked at the screen before I accepted the call. And, anyway – yeah. It was short.

—Did you go out into the hall or anything?

—What? No – no. Trish put the telly on pause. And it was very short, you know – the call. She asked me how I was. I said fine or grand. She said she'd like to meet up.

—Did you ask her how she was?

—No. I just said I'd phone her in the morning.

—You made it sound like work.

—Well – yeah. Yeah. But I didn't plan it, like. It's – what? – it's sneaky or something. I know – I *knew*. But I didn't have lines prepared in case she phoned me when I was with Trish – or at work. Or anywhere. It just seemed the easiest thing to do. But really, I could've just told Trish that it was someone I used to know and we'd met at the parent–teacher meeting, and we'd swapped numbers.

—As it had happened.

—Yeah – exactly. As it happened.

—Why didn't you tell Trish then?

—Honestly? he said. —I'm not sure. And honestly – I didn't want to.

—You could have told her that day – the day you met. On your way home together.

—That's true, he said. —And I didn't. I never even thought about telling her. That's not true, though. I didn't want to tell her. So, there you go. It's all out, Davy. I told Trish it was a woman from an ad agency. A pain in the arse, I said. I showed her the screen – George – the name, you know. And we laughed. Trish thought it was a bit hilarious, a woman called George. Like Enid Blyton.

—What?

—There was a girl called George in the Enid Blyton books. The Famous Five, or the something Seven. D'you remember?

—Think so.

—So, he said. —She was supposed to be a lesbian.

—What?

—George in the Enid Blyton books. I heard that, or read it somewhere. I think it was Trish told me. Yeah, she was gay, apparently. Or maybe it was the actor who played her on the telly – doesn't matter.

He looked at me. He wanted me to take over, to ask him. But I didn't.

—We watched the rest of the episode, he said. —And went up to bed.

He looked out a window, at the road and the bay and Bull Island. He had to turn to do this. I was the one facing the windows. He spoke as I looked at the side of his head. I half expected to see Trish's face on the other side of the glass, staring in at us.

—Same as always, he said.

He turned back to face me, although he looked down at his plate.

—Yeah, he said, as if answering a question. —Same as always.

—Really?

—Yeah, he said. —Yeah – no. I knew –. At least I think I knew. I felt –. I felt it was the last time we'd have sex. I felt – it's hard to – I don't know. Be honest, I suppose. Candid – is that the word? I imagined it was going to be the last time.

—Was it?

—No, he said. —Like I said – the same as always. There was nothing sudden or anything.

He looked at me.

—Okay.

—Life went on, he said.

—And that was –. Was that a good thing?

—What?

—Life, I said. —The sex. You weren't suffering, pretending? Feeling violated.

—No, he said. —Not at all. God, no.

He'd missed my sarcasm and I was glad now that he had. We rarely spoke about sex in any kind of detail, especially since we'd got married. We wouldn't be starting now. I didn't want the details. I didn't want to hear myself making up moments to match his.

—But, he said. —I definitely felt something was happening. And I don't just mean I'd be phoning Jessica in the morning and whatever might have come from that. The possibility of cheating – the idea. I don't mean that. It was like I'd remembered something.

—What?

—Something, he said. —Something important that I'd forgotten I'd needed.

—Your keys.

—Don't start, he said, and smiled. —I've thought about this. To try and explain it to the kids some time. If they ever want to hear it. And to myself, to be honest.

—Do they talk to you?

—The kids? he said. —No. No, they don't. It's shite.

—Must be.

—Yeah.

—Sorry, I said. —Go on.

—I think, he said. —The easiest way – the clearest way. Say you suffer from amnesia.

—A blow to the head.

—That'll work, he said.

I checked my phone. I took it from my pocket, had a quick look. The screen was blank – no missed calls or messages.

—You forget everything, said Joe. —Absolutely everything. But bit by bit things come back. Colours, say. The names of the colours of things that you can see from your bed in the hospital. It's a gradual thing, day by day. The names of things come back to you at random. You realise you're lying on a bed, you're looking out a window.

—You've thought about this.

He ignored that.

—There's a seagull out there, he said. —And a plane. You're slowly filling up with words. And the images that come with them. But there's still a huge hole. You don't know why, but you know there's something missing. And it – the hole, I mean – the knowledge, the lack of it. It becomes more important than the other discoveries. Your son comes in and you know him – you *know* him. He's not just the moody kid who comes in to see you. You know his name because you've always known it, not just because you were told it. You gave him his name – you know that. And you know what a son is – really is. And what a father is. And what it feels like. It's like your life, all your living, your

43

experiences, are filling you, pouring through you again. Your wife, your other kids, your mother. Your job. Everything's becoming sharper. Feelings are making sense. You wake up with an erection and you know why. The word erection is there for you. And it's great – although maybe not in a hospital bed. But it's great. You hold the thing in your hand and you know what it's there for and you know you remember what women are like and why they excite you. And skin. And breasts and all the other things you've loved – skirts, hair, laughter. And babies and birth, and you're beginning to feel complete. But not. You're certain there's something important missing. Something's still lost and you haven't a clue what it is. You just know it's there – and it's not. And say you get out of the hospital and things stop being fresh and new and life is normal again, and it's as if you never had the accident or whatever it was in the first place. It's as if you never lost your memory. Day to day, everything seems back in place. Like footballers' names, say, when you see them on the telly. And knowing exactly where to put your hand, how far you have to lean across, so that it lands exactly on your wife's hip when you're both in bed and falling asleep. Your day to day life smothers the ache, the sense that there's something missing. You're back in your life. And then bang.

—Jessica.

He blinked.

—You understand, he said.

—I think so, I said. —Yeah, I think so.

I'd forgotten he spoke like that, that he'd once been capable of speaking like that. That I'd sit back while he rolled out the story. I'd forgotten, completely. I'd often wondered – I'd just been wondering – why I kept in touch with this man. I'd forgotten who he was. I understood exactly what he meant.

—What about Trish? I said.

—What?

He looked annoyed, and a bit stupid. For a second.

—Sorry, he said. —What about Trish?

—Jessica filled the gap, so to speak. Like you just said. And I'm not trivialising what you said, by the way. I *do* know what you mean. I think I do. But what about Trish? Did she – I don't know – did she just stop being there? Jessica arrives and –

—Are you serious? he said. —Davy – are you fuckin' serious? Trish?

He was alive again, glad to be speaking.

—Did she stop being there? he said. —Did, she, stop? You don't know Trish.

—No, I agreed. —I don't know her.

—You do.

—Not really, no, I said. —I don't. And you don't know Faye.

—Okay, he said. —You don't know her well, we'll say. But Trish is a force of nature. That sounds like shite but it's true. She's amazing, Davy. Believe me. Like, to be clear here. Davy? To be clear. I love Trish.

—Okay.

—I love her. The fuckin' ground she walks on.

—Okay, I said. —I hear you. But when you followed her up to bed. After *The Affair* and the phone call.

—Davy, he said. —This isn't about sex.

—You had sex with Trish.

—Yes.

—You'd just spoken on the phone with Jessica.

—Yes.

—You brought that upstairs with you. You must have, surely.

—Okay, he said. —Yes.

—And this isn't about sex – you said.

—Now, he said. —Now it isn't. Now. It's misleading.

—Well, I'm feeling misled.

—We're jumping the gun, he said. —That's the problem. It's my fault, I think. So – being blunt. I had sex with Trish that night.

—But you were thinking about Jessica.

—No, he said. —No. Honestly, though – a bit. But Trish is Trish. Trish –. I'm not going into detail – it'd be wrong.

—Yes.

—I'll just say. Actually – two things. I'll say two things. One is that, with Trish. There was only the two of us in the bed – really. Okay? And the other thing is, and I only thought of this later. I think she knew.

—Trish knew?

—I think so, he said. —I think she did.

I watched him. He was looking at a corner of the room, above me, to my left. Then he looked at me.

—It was like she was doing her driving test, he said.

He burst out laughing. He did – the noise charged out of him. A woman sitting near the front, at a window, turned and looked our way, squinted at Joe's back, then turned back to her plate. It was the first time we'd been loud. I was laughing too.

—Sorry, said Joe. —Fuck – that sounds terrible. But it came into my head. Remember when you were doing your test and you were told – well, I was, anyway. By my da. Not just to remember to look in the rear mirror and the side mirrors but to make sure the inspector

46

saw you doing it. The inspector or the instructor or whatever his job description is. Make sure he saw you doing all the correct things.

I was still laughing.

—Well, Trish was doing her driving test that night, he said. —If she heard me, Davy – fuckin' hell. I can hear her. *At least I fuckin' passed it.* But anyway – yeah. I think she knew. At some level she knew. And now that I think of it, I was probably the one who was doing the test. And Trish was the inspector.

—Did you pass?

—Probably not. No.

—She'll have to go to the jacks, said Joe. —And this is fuckin' Thermopylae.

We were sitting right at the doors, down to the Gents and up to the Ladies.

—She's drinkin' pints, he said.

—Harp.

—She'll have to pass this way.

And she did. Jessica, or the woman – the girl – I know was called Jessica. Her hair passed us. And her back. And we saw her legs for a second from the knees down, her jeans, as she went up the stairs.

I waited for Joe. He didn't let me down.

—God, Davy, I wish I was a toilet seat.

—Tha' particular toilet seat.

—Yeah – Christ. Only tha' one. Or the jacks itself, I'd prefer tha'. The fuckin' flush – the whole shebang.

—I'm not so sure.

—I fuckin' am, he said. —She'll be done by now.

—Washin' the hands.

—Always, he said. —Here we go, she's comin' back.

47

Even when the place was full, you could hear the feet, you could feel them, on the stairs as the women came down from the loo. But never going up – a different journey, a different kind of weight. We heard her, then saw her feet, her legs, and we turned away just as she got to the foot of the stairs and opened the door, back in.

At least, I turned away. Joe didn't.

—She smiled at me, he said, and we watched the back of her head as she pushed her way – and she did push; I remember that – back to her friends at the front of the shop.

—Did she?

—Yeah.

—Have you witnesses?

—Myself, he said. —An' her.

—That's not enough, I said.

—It fuckin' is.

—Did you phone her back? I asked him.

—She phoned me, he said.

—Before you did.

—Yeah.

—I mean the second time, I said. —The day after.

—I know, he said. —No, I was going to but then I wondered about it, you know. What was I letting myself in for. I wasn't sure if –. I was perfectly happy, Davy, you know. That's true – really. I don't know –. I kind of decided. I'd wait till lunch time, or whatever. I'd wait.

—Put it off.

—Or forget about it – yeah. But –.

He sat back, then sat back up. He put his elbows on the table. He looked down as he did it, made sure he was well clear of his plate.

—I love her, he said. —I always loved her.

—What?

I waited for him to grin, become Joe.

—I loved her, he said.

He nodded, slightly. He was listening to himself, and answering himself.

—Yeah, he said. —So –

—Sorry, Joe, I said. —I'm being stupid here. You loved who?

He looked at me.

—Jessica, he said.

He looked around, like he was looking for a waiter; he wanted to get the bill and go. But he didn't. He settled down again, looked back at me.

—It sounds mad. I know.

He was still listening, talking to himself.

The waiter was beside the table.

—More beers, gentlemen?

—Yes, please, I said. —Thanks.

—It's true, said Joe.

He was looking at me again. He sounded different, more convinced. Less pale. I didn't want to say anything now. I didn't know why I'd let the waiter go off for the beers. I wanted to go. Back to my father. Back to something I understood. I half hoped I'd feel the phone in my pocket, a text or a call. But I couldn't resist.

—How can you say that? I asked him.

—What?

—You loved her.

—Because it's true, he said.

—For fuck sake, Joe, I said. —Thirty years. Thirty-five years – no, thirty-six.

—Asbestos can incubate for forty years, he said.

—Sorry?

—Inhale asbestos, he said. —It can still get you forty years later. It happened a friend of mine – you didn't know him. Jim Cahill – a carpenter.

—Are you saying she's asbestos?

I was hoping he'd sit up and glare at me, laugh, hit me or the table.

—No, he said. —I'm only saying.

—What? I said.

I was furious now. I wasn't sure why. What he was saying was ridiculous. That was fine; I don't think I minded that. But he expected me to follow him, to nod and believe. So I kept going. My own elbows were on the table.

—You're saying – what? Your love was incubating? Fuckin' hibernating, in your fuckin' heart? Is it a song? My love is incubating.

The waiter arrived back and put the bottles on the table, picked them up again one at a time, took the tops off them, and put them back down. He picked up my glass.

—That's grand, I said. —Thanks. We'll pour them ourselves.

—No better men, said the waiter.

He smiled and was gone.

—Go on, I said to Joe.

—You go on, he said.

—Well, I said. —This. You see the woman for the first time in – we'll say thirty-five years.

—It's thirty-seven years.

—Grand, I said. —And you can't remember her name. You might not ever have known her name.

—I did.

—Okay, I said. —And – it's not that you fell for her. I could understand that. Not that it matters if I

50

understand anything. But I'd understand it. She's well-preserved. The ageing beauty – and she sails down the corridor at you. You're feeling low, unloved.

He was looking straight back at me. He nodded slightly.

—Redundant, I said.

—Are you? he said. —Do you feel redundant?

—God, yeah, I said. —So. Yeah. I can imagine being excited. And a bit smitten. There's nothing in me that wouldn't understand that. If it was me. If she asked me for my number or whatever. If she kissed me and stayed close to me, so I'd feel her breath on my face. I'd go home imagining being with the younger version, half hoping she'll phone me. Half hoping she won't. And seriously – Joe. Joe. I *can* imagine phoning her back and falling in love. If I saw her doing the same. Or I thought I did. Falling for me – even enjoying my company. If we met for lunch or a drink and the chat wasn't too awkward. It would be great, I'd say. Brilliant. The same age, like. None of the guilt – calculating that she's nearer your daughter's age than your own. You'd have plenty to talk about. Especially if the years have been kind to her. She'd be a bit of an upgrade – I don't know.

I'd run out of words; I didn't want to be crude. *A bit of an upgrade.* I wished I hadn't said it. His expression hadn't changed. He looked like a man who was interested in what he was hearing.

—But, I said. —Saying you've always loved her. That I don't get. I don't understand it. Sorry.

I poured the beer into my glass.

—That living a lie thing, I said.

—What?

—All these years I've been living a lie.

—Did I say that?

—No.

—Did I suggest it?

—Yeah.

—How?

—Of course you did.

—How?

—You said it there. You always loved her.

—I did.

—But you hadn't seen the girl for most of your life.

I could feel myself wanting to shake, wanting to get up and go, or just move.

—It's like what I said about it incubating, he said.

—That's fuckin' idiotic.

—Fuck you, Davy.

—You can't take asbestos – or anything else, right. And compare it to human emotion, and expect to go unchallenged. No fuckin' way, Joe. The argument, if it's even an argument, has no validity at all. It explains absolutely nothing – sorry.

—Okay.

He shrugged.

—Maybe that's the problem with honesty.

—What?

—No one really believes it, he said.

—Jesus, Joe.

I'd give it another five minutes.

—What's happened to you? I asked him.

—Nothing.

—Joe.

—Nothing, he said again. —A lot – obviously. If you look at it one way. My life has changed completely. Fuckin' completely – Jesus, Davy.

He picked up his bottle.

—But I'm still the same, he said. —Same man.

—You're not.

—Oh, I am.

—Okay.

I watched him fill his glass. It was easier than watching him.

—But, I said. —Tell me.

—What?

—Your amnesia theory.

—It beats the asbestos theory, he said. —Or, so it seems.

He smiled. He was going to laugh; I hoped he was. He'd been having me on. He'd met a good-looking woman. They'd been having a fling. It had gone past that, too far. He was a fuckin' eejit – it would be a boast. He was where he was. For fuck sake.

I decided to give him a nudge.

—What's the sex like? I asked.

—There isn't any.

He smiled again. He should have shrugged. But he didn't.

—I told you already, he said.

—You didn't. When?

—I told you it wasn't about sex, he said. —Will we stay here or move on?

—We can finish these first, I said.

I held up my glass.

—Okay, he said. —Grand.

I wasn't a drinker. I dreaded having to drink two or three pints. I'd tell him I had to get back to my father. It wouldn't be a lie.

—You met her, I said.

It seemed like days since this had started.

—Yeah, he said. —So, anyway, she phoned me. Again, like. The day after.

—Where were you?

—The toilet, he said. —In work. I swear to God, the glamour. I was washing my hands, drying them. A Dyson, or one of those jet engine ones.

—Give me a towel any day.

—Or the sides of my trousers, yeah. Anyway. I felt the phone in my pocket, just in time. I nearly dropped it.

—You knew it was her.

—No – yeah. No. It could have been anyone – any one of dozens of people. I've got the thing stuck to the side of my head half the day. And non-stop in the car.

—You'd said you'd phone her back.

—What?

—The night before, I said. —When she phoned you the first time. When you were watching *The Affair*. You told me you told her you'd phone her in the morning. You showed Trish your phone. *George.*

—Yeah.

—But you didn't.

—Because she phoned me first, he said. —Are you trying to catch me out here?

—No.

—Okay, he said. —But I told you already. Like – I had serious fuckin' misgivings, Davy. I told you.

—Did it not worry you? I asked him.

—What?

—That she phoned you again, I said. —That she couldn't wait.

—Are you serious?

His face was back; he was Joe again.

—When was the last time you felt that a woman couldn't wait to meet you? he asked. —Never mind everything else? When?

—Never, I said. —If I'm being honest.

I wasn't. Being honest.

My wife decided I was going to be her husband three minutes after she met me. Or so she's always said.

She was someone's daughter, some old friend of my girlfriend's mother. We were sitting beside each other at a wedding. At my girlfriend's brother's wedding. The friend, the mother's old friend, had recently died.

—I'm sorry.

—Ah, thanks.

—It's hard, I said.

I was about to tell her that my own mother was dead.

—Oh, good, she said. —Let's see if we can keep it that way.

She looked up from her prawn cocktail. She stared at me, and smiled, and changed her fork from her right to her left hand, and put her hand right under the table, on my leg. She walked her fingers backwards, up my thigh, and she leaned out, in front of me, against me, so she could chat to my girlfriend.

—You've a fab boyfriend here, Cathy, so you do.

—You watch yourself now, said Cathy.

She said it cheerfully, for the table. But she didn't like Faye. That was very clear.

—Don't worry, said Faye. —I'm only here for the grub, so I am.

She patted my leg goodbye and put her fork back in her right hand.

—First time I've ever eaten these yokes, she said.

—Prawns?

—Yeah.

—D'you like them?

—They'll do, she said. —I like the pink stuff. The sauce, like.

I watched her eat.

—Actually, I said. —Now that I think of it. Faye.

I gave Joe time to remember that Faye was my wife.

—What?

—She was all over me, I told him. —When we met each other the first time.

He smiled.

I wanted to talk to him for a change, and not have to listen. I wanted to entertain him.

—She terrified me, I said.

He laughed.

—It was at a wedding, I said. —Do you remember Cathy?

—No, he said. —Do I?

—We went with each other for a while.

—Hang on, he said. —The garda.

—That's right.

—She was nice.

—Yeah, she was, I said. —I really liked her.

—What happened?

—Well, I said. —Faye.

—Do I know this? he asked. —Did you tell me before?

—Don't think so, I said. —I don't think I'd have been able to tell anyone back then.

—Great, he said.

—It was too fuckin' –.

—Embarrassing.

—No, I said. —Unimaginable.

—Great – go on.

56

He was glad we'd swapped places, and so was I. And
I told him about the wedding, why I was there, why
Faye was there, what she'd said when I started to offer
my condolences.

—She said that?

—Yeah.

—With Cathy right beside you?

—The other side of me, yeah.

—And did you? he asked.

—What?

—Stay hard.

—More or less, I said.

It wasn't right, what I was doing. I knew it, and felt
it. It was crude and possibly cruel. And treacherous.
But I knew this too: I wanted to hear myself talking
about Faye. I wanted Joe to witness her. I was tired of
his no-sex fling.

—Love at first sight, said Joe. —Jesus.

—I didn't even have to see her, I said.

That was true, somehow. The day after the wedding
I couldn't have described her. I could have recited every
word she'd said but I didn't know what colour her hair
was, or her eyes. She overpowered me.

—I didn't have time to drink, I said.

He laughed again.

—Let's go and get one now while we're at it, he said.
—A drink in a pub. Can we cope with the excitement?

—If we're careful, I said.

We paid the bill, gave the waiter two credit cards,
left him a real fiver each for the tip, and went outside.
It was still hot, shockingly hot.

—It's like we're stepping into a different country,
said Joe.

—Yeah.

—I'm a bit sick of it.

—Yeah – same here. A bit.

—No more weather talk.

—Grand, yeah. Where'll we go?

There were two pubs we could walk to, the Sheds and the Pebble Beach.

—I was in the Sheds a while back, said Joe. —A funeral – the afters. It was fine.

—Grand.

We headed that way.

—Or we could go in to George's, said Joe.

—No.

—Come on.

He'd turned around, and I looked back too. There was a taxi coming towards us, heading towards town.

—We'll have one in the Sheds, I said. —And then decide.

He looked at his watch. It was more than three hours to closing time.

—Okay, he said. —That'll work.

I'd have the one in the Sheds, then head back to my father. I'd tell that to Joe when we were there with the pints in front of us.

—Go on, anyway, he said, as we walked through the heat, as we got used to it again. —What happened then?

—I'm not sure if I can tell it that way, I said. — Chronologically – blow by blow. So to speak.

—Did she?

—What?

—Blow you.

—No. No – shut up.

His Jessica was some sort of ghost of Saturdays past but Faye was to be the slut who crawled under the table at a wedding and opened my zip.

It was my fault.

—When she put her hand on my leg, I told him.
—She was joking.

—What?

—She wasn't really – I don't know. She wasn't trying to seduce me.

—But, said Joe. —Her hand was still on your fuckin' leg. Was it?

—Yeah.

There were times when I could still feel the fingers marching up my thigh.

—But she wasn't –. Like I said, trying to seduce me – or tease me. In the conventional sense. It wasn't like that.

—Then what –?

—Shut up and listen, I said. —I shouldn't have told you about her hand.

—But you did.

—I know – shut up. It was everything about her.

I wanted to go home. I wanted to go now to the airport, get home and see Faye. Ask her to forgive me. For forgetting, being stupid, a coward. For being here. Away from her. For keeping her away.

—More than anything else, I said. —It was her voice. No, not her voice. Her words.

—Her words?

—The way she spoke, I said. —Yeah. She commentated on everything.

—Jesus, he said. —I'd hate that – no offence.

—You weren't there, I said. —It was incredible. The best thing ever. That sounds crumby, but it was. It was the sexiest fuckin' thing.

—Sexy?

—Ah, man, I'm telling you –.

I came from a silent house. My father and I passed each other and smiled. We spoke when we needed to, when we sat together at the kitchen table. My mother's death destroyed him. I remember laughter – his, hers. I remember long trips in the car, a black Ford Anglia, the two of them chatting while I stood between their seats. I was twelve when she died, and the radiators went cold. The bedroom was cold, the hall and the landing were cold. I used a can opener for the first time. I taught myself to make tea properly. I filled the washing machine and got it right. He put money in a cup and told me to take it when I needed food. Or anything. I wasn't unhappy. Once the shock of my mother's death passed. Although I'm not sure now that it ever did. Her voice still wakes me sometimes – I think. I took money from the cup and bought a shirt, a record, ten Silk Cut, and a packet of coconut creams. I watched television till the programmes stopped. He discovered me when I was fifteen – that was what it felt like. He stopped in the hall and asked me how I was. He booked a holiday for us, in Italy, a week in Rimini. We both flew in a plane for the first time. He asked me about school, my favourite subjects, what I wanted to do. One day, we passed a church.

—Do you go to mass? he asked me.

—No.

—Ever?

—Not really.

—Okay, he said. —Do you think about your mother?

—Yes.

—So do I, he said. —All the time. Literally all the time.

Neither of us had eaten pizza before.

—Do you like it? he asked me.

—It's brilliant, I said.

—You're right, he said. —I wonder can you get these things in Dublin.

—Don't know.

—Worth investigating.

He held his wine glass out to me.

—Give this stuff a go, he said.

He watched me, he smiled, as I took a sip. It was a big thing, his smile; it took over his face. It changed him.

—D'you like it?

—No, I said. —A bit.

—Oh, the slippery slope, he said.

He laughed, and so did I.

—She'd have liked you, he said.

I didn't know what he meant.

—She'd have liked the boy you are now, he said. —The man.

His eyes watered.

—Sorry.

I often lie awake and think of that week. I never saw him cry again. He never saw me cry. But I came home knowing he loved me. I've never forgotten the solidity of that. It's what kills me, sometimes.

We never became talkative. He left me alone. He checked on me.

—How are things?

—Fine.

—Alright for money?

—Yeah.

—How's the study going?

—Good.

—Grand.

★   ★   ★

Faye overwhelmed me. I'd never known a funny woman. Faye was funny and knew it, and she knew she was often hated for it. She was a smart alec, a bitch, too big for her boots. I saw that around the table at the wedding, before I really saw Faye. She spoke like a man, like she was entitled to speak. I saw eyes raised to heaven, elbows discreetly nudging ribs. I saw affection, envy, lust, hatred. I saw no one yawn.

I heard Cathy.

—For fuck sake. This one.

It wasn't cruel. It was an adult quietly assessing a precocious child, expressing an opinion she knew I'd share. But I wasn't sharing anything.

We were half the length of the banquet room away from the top table, our backs to the bride and groom. When the speeches started, we – myself, Cathy, Faye – turned our chairs to face the speakers and clap. It was the first wedding I'd been to.

—Is it yours? I asked Faye.

I was apprehensive asking her. I knew it wouldn't be a simple Yes or No, and she was going to attract attention. But I wanted to hear her; it was all I wanted.

—Jesus, no, she said. —I was at my parents' wedding, so I was.

This was 1986. Faye was nineteen.

I laughed. No one else did.

—How was it? I asked her.

—Oh, romantic as fuck.

—She was like Mícheál O'Hehir, I told Joe.

We'd reached the Sheds. We stood outside.

—You fell in love with a woman who looked like a racing commentator?

—You know what I mean.

—Not really, he said. —No. Did she sound like Mícheál O'Hehir? I'm puzzled here a bit, Davy. I don't think I remember what Faye looks like. Do you have a photo?

—No.

I wasn't lying.

—Let me be absolutely clear, I said. —Faye was nothing like – looked nothing like Mícheál O'Hehir. Or sounded like him.

—Grand.

—But she leaned against me and talked into my ear, non-stop, right through the speeches.

—Christ.

Joe pulled open the lounge door and I followed him in.

—That would do my head in, he said back to me.

We stood at the door.

—So, go on, he said. —Mícheál O'Hehir was trying to get off with you.

—Fuck off, I said. —And just listen.

—I am.

—Just fuckin' listen, I said. —Say – Jennifer Lawrence, let's say. Jennifer Lawrence sat beside you at a wedding. And she leaned right up against you, just as – like – it was dawning on you that it was her. And you're much younger than you are now.

—Why? he said. —Why does that matter?

—It just makes it a bit less unfeasible, I suppose. Slightly less. And it's more comfortable that way. And anyway, I was only twenty-seven when this happened, remember.

—Okay.

—So, she starts talking – Jennifer Lawrence. She starts talking – whispering into your ear, and you can feel each word. Like the tip of her tongue.

I was surprising myself.

—Right through all the speeches. And you're surrounded by people. Including your girlfriend, by the way. Would you object?

—Well –.

—Would you object?

—I was only going to ask – fuck off. Which one is Jennifer Lawrence? What's she been in? D'you want a pint?

I wasn't sure if I did. I don't drink Guinness, not since I moved to England. But there was something – a feeling, something behind my eyes. This might be the last time I'd spend with Joe. We both knew it.

—Okay, I said.

—Two pints, please, said Joe to a barman who stood behind his counter, waiting for us.

We sat at the bar. The place wasn't busy; we had a stretch of the counter to ourselves. The television above us was on – some sort of panel discussion on Sky Sports. But the sound was down – mute.

I was trying to think of a Jennifer Lawrence film.

—*The Hunger Games*, said Joe. —That's her, isn't it?

—Yes – yeah.

—I didn't see it, he said. —Hang on, though. *American Hustle*. She was hilarious in that one.

—There you go, I said. —A hilarious, gorgeous woman keeps talking into your ear. For what seemed like hours. And, actually, mightn't have been much less than an hour. Because the fuckin' speeches went on for ever.

—I'm beginning to get you, he said. —I can see how that might distract you, alright.

—Captivated me, I said.

I'd found the word I wanted.

—Good man, he said. —And was Faye gorgeous? Like Jennifer Lawrence?

I wanted to go. I wanted to stand up off the stool, turn my back, stop looking at him. Go.

—I thought so, I said.

—Good.

—He rides his housekeeper, so he does. And her sister.

She was talking about the priest holding the microphone at the top table.

—And he's been in the bride's mammy as well. Sure, there isn't a lady up there at that table that he hasn't serviced at some time or another. Usually in the morning, mind you. After mass and before confessions. A quick bang and the holy rosary, a drop of tea and a couple of Jaffa Cakes. He eats them off their arses, so he does.

I knew my life had changed when I noticed that I was leaning into her; I was the one doing the leaning. I still had a girlfriend and we had plans, hinted at, half formed. I was holding her hand. And she was holding mine. Cathy. But she got there ahead of me, a few days later. She phoned my father's house; she left a message. I'd a flat of my own but there was no phone there. I stayed with my father a few nights a week. I used the washing machine. I took food he left for me in the freezer. Cathy normally phoned me at work.

—She won't be around this weekend, my father told me. —She told me to tell you.

—Okay.

I liked Cathy. I liked being with her. I liked waiting to meet her, especially when she was coming off duty. She raced at me. I thought I'd loved her.

—I don't want to interfere, said my father.

I'd forgotten he was there; I'd forgotten where I was. I was surrounded by Faye, swallowed by her.

—What? I asked my father.

—I'm not sure you'll be seeing her any weekend, he said.

—Who?

—Cathy, son.

—Okay.

—The way she spoke.

—Okay.

—Is that for the best?

—Probably.

—She was brusque, he said. —On the phone.

—Okay.

He'd met Cathy. I'd brought her home to meet him. They'd chatted; they'd liked one another. But it seemed so far away. In another country, another life.

—I liked her, he said.

—Yeah, I said. —So did I. *Do.*

—You're not too heartbroken, anyway?

I didn't answer. I didn't know how to. I was sad, relieved. I wondered if he could smell Faye. Because I could.

I looked at Joe as he accepted the pints and handed a ten-euro note to the barman. He placed each glass on a beermat. He seemed to be measuring distance, making sure he got the calculation exactly right. I could tell: he'd forgotten what we'd been talking about, what I'd been telling him outside. What he'd said.

—Where are you living? I asked him.

He looked at me. He moved sideways on his stool so he could do it.

66

—At home, he said.

—Where's that?

And was Faye gorgeous?

—Jessica's, he said.

—Is that home now? I asked him.

—Yep.

He nodded, like he was examining what he'd said for truth, and found it.

—Yeah, he said. —I kind of think of it as home.

—What about the other one?

—Well, there you go, he said. —Fuckin' hell.

—What happened?

—We'll get there, Davy. Don't worry.

We made love, myself and Faye, the night before I went to see my father, the night he gave me Cathy's message. Faye clung to me. We were in my flat, a room without pictures except for the record covers stacked along the wall, beneath the window. Faye grabbed me tight to her. Her mouth was at my ear.

—Sanity, sanity, sanity, sanity.

I didn't know what she was saying. Whispering. Gasping. The word formed itself later, while I watched her sleeping. She was fast asleep, out for the count. I remember thinking that – *out for the count*. I'd fucked her to sleep. She'd fucked herself to sleep. Her face was deep in the pillow, under her hair. Her mouth was slightly open. Her breath lifted some strands of hair. They dropped, and shot up again. She was a cartoon, I thought, one of Disney's perfect females. She was the girl at the end of *The Jungle Book*, but she had all of Baloo's lines, and King Louie's lines, and some of Shere Khan's. I was afraid to sleep. I was afraid she'd stop being there. The light would come up and she'd be gone.

—What're you fuckin' looking at, David?

She was awake. I could see her eyes shining. She hadn't moved.

—You.

—Grand.

That was what I loved. She wouldn't let me fantasise, make more than was there. She was real. Everything – she did, she said, she didn't – was real.

They'd met.

—Where?

He looked annoyed. I'd interrupted him. It was like he'd been composing his story, alone, writing it. A minute ago, he'd been chatting to me. With her, with the idea of her, he didn't want me there. It surprised me. I thought he'd been showing her off earlier, in the restaurant. And I'd expected a bit of triumph, the bit of crack. I don't think I wanted it but it was what I'd been anticipating.

They'd met in a café in town, Wigwam, on Middle Abbey Street.

—Why there?

I wanted to irritate him now. To wake him up.

—Distance, he said. —And proximity.

—To what? I asked. —Who?

—Work, he said. —People in work. Wigwam's near to, and a safe distance from. I wasn't hiding anything, though.

—You were, I said. —You lied to Trish.

—Not really, he said. —I withheld information.

—Withheld the truth.

—Okay – fuck it, he said. —It was simpler that way. It wasn't malicious, or dishonest – I don't think. Although Trish might disagree. She'd tear my fuckin' eyes out. But look, I didn't want anybody seeing me. From work, I mean. Or anyone else. And as well, I didn't want it to seem like I was hiding. Seem to myself, I mean. Because I wasn't. I don't know –. It was near enough to work but not too near. And I needed the car after – after I met her, like. I don't know why I'm going into all of this.

He met her in Wigwam. One of his sons – I can't remember the name – had worked there before he'd moved to Cork, and that was why Joe had thought of it. No one he knew would be there and he'd never met any of his son's more recent friends. He wasn't worried about anything getting back to the son or to Trish.

—It's a hipster spot, he said. —The beardy lads.

—Tattoos.

—Tasteful ones, yeah, he said. —Middle-class tattoos. Art. Do any of your kids have tattoos?

—Yeah, I said.

—Same here. Does Faye?

I looked at him.

—No, I said. —Does Trish?

He shook his head.

—No, he said. —But you never know. She might have had *Joe Is a Cunt* tattoed to the back of her neck or something. In Mandarin or Latin.

—She was there, anyway, I said. —Jessica.

—She was, he said. —She got there before me. She was sitting at one of the tables, with a pot of tea.

—Did she stand up when you got there?

—What?

—Did she stand up?

—Why?

—Politeness, I said. —Tradition – formality. Although it's usually the man who does that – is it?

—No, he said. —She didn't. There was none of the formal stuff.

That was what he'd been trying to say.

—It was like we'd never been apart, he said.

—You were never together, I told him.

—Okay, he said. —And that's not strictly true either. And anyway, the woman doesn't have to stand, does she? It's the man's job – I think you're right. Holding the door open and stuff like that. Used to be, anyway. It might cause offence these days, though. Opening a fuckin' door.

It was a good place, Wigwam, a cool place. But they were easily the oldest people there; they had decades on everyone else. He noticed it; she said nothing. He ordered a coffee, an Americano, paid for it, and sat. He sat beside her. The table was too wide, so he wasn't going to sit opposite her. It would have been like a job interview.

—Or a parent–teacher meeting, I said.

—There you go, he said. —Love stories begin.

He got in behind the table and sat beside her. She kissed him. On the cheek.

—Now this sounds mad, he said.

—Go on.

He felt he was living his real life.

—Like, the minute I sat down, he said.

It wasn't that he was suddenly waking up. It was nothing as dramatic as that, nothing that made him angry or giddy. It was just that: he sat down. It was her weight beside him, and her warmth, beside him and against him. It felt familiar and right. It was an

70

emptiness filled; it had always been this way. This was how he felt. He was in the rest of his life.

I was looking at him. There was no twitching. He wasn't shredding a beermat. He looked well in the pub light.

—But, he said. —This is the gas bit.

—What?

—I couldn't remember her name.

—She told it to you – when she phoned you.

—Yeah, but I put George into my phone. I told you that. And I didn't change it. I never have. But – there – I couldn't remember her fuckin' name.

—That *is* weird.

—I know, he said. —In a way.

He had a theory: he didn't remember her name because he didn't have to. He was fairly certain he knew it all the way to the café. He'd parked in the Arnotts car park.

—I thought you said it was near where you work?

I'd no real idea what Joe did for a living. 'In the bank'. That job description described nothing any more. I knew he'd done a degree at night, ten years or so after we'd left school, and that he had a master's too. I knew he'd been 'in the bank' since 1977 but I didn't know what, or where, that meant. Or which bank, or what type of bank.

—What was near where I work? he asked.

—Wigwam.

—Yeah – true. But I needed the car. Immediately – immediately after. I was going to see Holly. She'd a match over in Booterstown. I can do a lot in the car – work, like. It's all talk – the phone. Anyway, let's not get bogged down in the car park. It doesn't matter.

That was one life. The job, the car, the daughter. He'd been in that life as he crossed Abbey Street and watched the Luas approach from the Jervis stop, as he walked into the café. He knew her name, the woman he was meeting. He knew her first name; he remembered it. Then he didn't. Because he didn't have to remember it. He was where he was supposed to be, beside this woman. This was his life.

Jessica.

The name was there. A few minutes later.

—But it didn't pop up in my head, he said. —Do you know what I mean?

—Yeah, I said. —I do.

—It was like my own name, he said. —Just there.

—Okay. Did you get to the match?

—Yes – yeah. Yeah. Of course.

He smiled.

—I was late. But I was always going to be. I was aiming for the second half.

—Did she win?

—You're a terrible bitch, Davy, he said. —Yeah, she did. She scored two goals. In the second half. So I got to see both of them.

They'd stayed in the café for an hour and a half. She had to get home.

—Is she married?

—No.

—Was she?

—Yeah. But years ago. Back around our time. That era, like.

—So she was young when she got married.

—Yeah, he said. —That wasn't unusual, though. Back then.

She'd lived with a man for years, after the marriage. Or, he'd lived with her; it was her house. She had a daughter.

—Is he the father?

—No, he isn't. That was a different guy, again.

—Okay.

—It's not as – what? – as frantic as it sounds, he said. —I don't think it was. We're talking about decades.

—Okay, I said. —And she's in Holly's class, is that right? The girl.

—Same year, he said. —Not the same class. Except for one or two subjects.

—And how's that?

—Not too good, he said.

—Hardly surprising.

—No, he agreed. —Holly refused to go to school for a while. And she wouldn't talk to me. It wasn't great.

—How is it now?

—Still not great. A bit better. I texted her a while back – last week, I think. And she answered. *Fuck off x.* But that's Holly – all over. She answered, that was the thing. First time in – Jesus. Months. Anyway, I look at the *x* a couple of times a day. Only one *x*, mind. It used to be two.

He wasn't joking. I wanted to ask him about Jessica's daughter. I wanted to dig away at him. But I didn't; I restrained myself.

—What did you talk about? I asked him.

—That's the thing, he said.

—What?

—We didn't, he said. —Talk. I mean, we did. But we didn't catch up, if you know what I mean. We didn't fill in the years. Kids, partners, jobs – there was nothing like that. Or the school – the girls' school, like. We didn't mention the place at all.

—What did you talk about then?

I wasn't believing him. This strolling in and out of different lives – I wasn't having it. He was sitting beside me and there was only one of him. He'd been having an affair, he'd been caught, and he was trying to make something mystical or inevitable out of it. It was boring.

—Like I told you, he said. —It was just like we'd always been together. I don't really remember what we talked about. Just – stuff.

—Fuckin' stuff?

I came back to Dublin to see my father but I knew I'd keep doing it after he died, a couple of times a year. I loved speaking like a Dubliner. It felt like physical exercise.

—I honestly don't remember, he said. —She was reading a book – when I came in.

—And you spoke about that?

—I think so, he said. —Although she said she'd got it in Eason's for her kid – the daughter.

—What's her name?

—Hanoi.

—Are you serious?

—Yep.

He shrugged; he grinned.

—The kid hates it, he said. —She tells everyone it's the Irish for brilliance.

—Bright kid.

—Yeah.

—Do you get on with her?

—I do, yeah, he said. —We –. I suppose we kind of keep a distance. But I like her.

—What was the book?

—What?

—The book Jessica was reading.

—A school book. Chemistry, I think.

—She was reading a fuckin' chemistry book?

—Flicking through it, he said. —Killing the time.

—Were you late?

—No, I wasn't, he said. —I was bang-on. I'm never late. Ever. Anyway, she said she'd been in Eason's and she'd bought a pen as well, and she showed it to me.

—For fuck sake.

—That's my fuckin' point, he said. —It was like we'd seen each other earlier and there wasn't much filling in to do. Somehow, like – I knew she'd have the book.

—Come on –

—Just calm down, he said. —I'm telling you, that was what it felt like. *Felt*, not facts. But there now – she knew what I do for a living.

—Facebook.

—I'm not on Facebook.

—You've always worked in the bank.

—Yeah, but she never knew that – I don't think. But she did. In Wigwam.

I told him what I was thinking.

—It's kind of boring, Joe.

—I know, he said. —That's my point as well. I think. It's boring if you're looking in the window at it but not when you're inside.

—So you swapped one kitchen for another one.

—You don't understand.

—No, I agreed. —Is she better looking?

—Ah, stop, for fuck sake.

—I don't fuckin' understand.

—She is, by the way.

He shut his eyes like he wished he hadn't spoken.

—It felt –, he said.

He picked up his pint, and put it back down.

—It felt like I'd come home, he said.

—In Wigwam?

—Fuck off, Davy, he said. —I'm wasting my fuckin' time. It's impossible.

He picked up the pint again and brought it to his mouth.

It was my round – I needed something to do, to get away from Joe's face and the urge to whack it. I was looking at the barman, waiting for him to look my way. He was in the passage between the lounge and the bar, hiding there, looking down at his phone. I wasn't a local; I didn't want to interrupt him.

The barman was standing to my left. Joe was on the other side of me and he took advantage of the back of my head; I wasn't looking at him as he spoke.

—I'd always been with her, he said.

The barman looked up. I lifted my glass. He nodded and took two empty pint glasses from under the counter.

—Okay, I said.

I didn't care. I knew Joe – or, I thought I knew Joe. We'd end the night with his story, not mine. I didn't care about either of his homes, the new or the old. Or him. I was here, listening, because I used to know him. Old times' sake. But it wasn't enough; I knew that. I looked at the barman filling our glasses. I took my phone from my pocket and checked it. I had it on vibrate but I was worried I'd miss a call or a message. There was nothing on the screen.

—There were two things she told me that kind of caught me on the hop, said Joe.

I put the phone away, leaned back to get it deep into my pocket, and looked at him.

—What were they?

—She's dyslexic, he said.

—Really?

—Yeah, he said. —She was flicking through the book, like, and she mentioned it.

—How? Should you not've known that already, if you'd been with her all along? Like you said.

—I didn't mean that literally.

—Okay.

—You know that.

—Okay.

—So, anyway, he said. —She said she envied Hanoi and I asked her why.

—That was brave.

—What d'you mean?

—Middle-aged women hate younger women, I told him.

—Their daughters, though?

—Oh, yeah.

He shrugged.

—Okay, he said. —But, no. It was the reading she envied. She can't really read.

—Faye can read, I told him.

—Yeah, he said. —So can Trish.

We laughed. It felt like the first time we'd laughed that evening; I thought it might have been. It was like a new sound, a new feeling.

—What was the other thing? I asked him.

The barman was approaching with the pints. I was rooting in my jacket for my wallet. It was stupid, bringing a jacket. The heat – the last thing I'd needed was a jacket. But I hadn't been thinking when I'd gone back to the house to shower, to change, after I'd phoned Joe earlier. I'd been given permission: I was escaping for a while, a couple of hours.

I'd stopped carrying cash in my trousers pockets. Some years back – maybe ten – I'd noticed that I was hitching my trousers every time I stood up, and often as I walked. I'd seen a woman at work looking at me, and looking away. I'd blamed the coins and the keys. So I'd banished them from my trousers, everything except the phone. Now, as I put my hand into the inside pocket of my jacket and found it empty, I was anxious enough to assume that the wallet was gone. Drink had never made me relax; it had never made a different man of me.

The wallet was in the second inside pocket. Joe waited while I took out a twenty. A bookshop loyalty card and a couple of petrol station receipts slipped out with the money. He tried to catch them but they fell onto the tiles. I gave the twenty to the barman.

I was drunk.

—Thanks.

Joe handed me the receipts and the loyalty card and sat back up on the stool.

—She has a son as well, he said.

—Jessica has?

—Yeah.

—Older, younger?

—What?

—Than the girl.

—Older.

—And what's his name? I asked. —Bangkok, Rangoon?

—He has a daughter, said Joe. —His name's Peter.

—Peter? I said. —That's a bit fuckin' conventional –.

There was something he'd just said; it had slipped away but it rolled back.

—He has a daughter – you said.

78

—Right.

—So, I said. —Your girlfriend's son has a child.

—Yeah.

—She's a grandmother.

He nodded.

—You left your wife and kids for a glamorous granny.

He nodded again; he was pleased. I'd been bored; I'd told him. He knew I wasn't bored now.

—Looks like it, he said.

—Same father?

—Sorry?

—Is what's-his-name's –

—Peter.

—Peter – is Peter's father the same as Hanoi's?

—No, he said. —There's a big age gap. He's much older.

He put his new pint on the beermat. He drew a line with a finger, down through the condensation on the glass.

—I think I might be, he said.

I knew what was coming. I'd known it – somehow – all night. I'd slipped into his new life too.

—Might be what? I asked.

—His father.

—Are you?

—I think so, he said. —I might be.

—For fuck sake.

—I will never, ever give you a grandchild, my daughter, Róisín, told me a few years ago.

She was eighteen, and joking. I'd just told her I wouldn't give her the money to go to Berlin for the weekend. I laughed – I always laughed when Róisín wanted me to laugh. But I believed her. I felt no loss; there was nothing being whipped out of my arms. I looked at Faye but I wasn't sure she'd heard.

—Your lovey-dovey thing with Róisín, she'd said once, a few years before. —What's that about?

—It isn't about anything, I'd said. —I don't even know what you mean.

—It gives me the sick, she said.

—I'm her father.

—You are.

—Fuck off, Faye.

—Nice.

—Well, yeah – fuck off. What are you even saying?

—Nothing, she said. —Me? Nothing. You're spoiling her.

Róisín was, I think, fifteen. We'd been watching *Mean Girls* together. She'd been watching; I'd been watching her watching. She leaned against an arm of the sofa and draped her legs across mine. She wouldn't let me look at my phone or iPad. I watched her getting ready to laugh; I watched her silently recite lines that were about to be delivered.

—How many times have you watched this thing?

—More times than I care to remember, she said.

Róisín is English, born here, in Wantage. She had only one living grandparent in Ireland, my father. But she liked the Irish phrases. She collected them. She liked her name – she liked the *fada*s, the accents on the 'o' and the 'i'. She liked the trouble they caused in school and elsewhere.

—The lady asked if I was an Arab, she told me one evening when I picked her up after swimming.

—What lady?

—The lady at the swimming pool. When she asked me to spell my name.

—The swimming teacher?

—The lady behind the glass.

—Why did she want to know your name?

—I had to give her the envelope.

—The swimming money.

—Yes.

—She thought your name was Arabic? Syrian or something.

—Yes.

She giggled.

—The fucking eejit, she said.

—Now now.

There was a rule: she was allowed to say 'fuckin' eejit' now and again, but only when she was alone with one of us and only when the situation – the fuckin' eejit – warranted it.

We laughed.

She made me laugh. Just as her mother had – and did. Although they were very different. Their senses of humour couldn't sit in the same room. It had been like that since Róisín had started talking, probably before. But I might be making that up. I *am* making that up.

—I love her when she's asleep, said Faye.

Róisín was the baby in the cot, beside our bed.

I thought Faye was joking. And she was. But she wasn't. That was Faye.

—It's when they're awake, she said. —Fuckin' Jesus.

—They're work, I said.

We had two children – a toddler and this baby.

—Do you have a photocopier in work, Dave, do you?

—We do, I said.

—Do you love it?

I laughed quietly.

She nodded at the sleeping baby.

—Then why should I love these yokes?

We lay back on the bed, still dressed.

—No squeaking now, David, she said. —She'll wake up on us.

I looked at Joe. I'm his father, he'd said. I might be. I was a character in his box set but I'd slept through a couple of episodes. I'd missed something – I hadn't heard something, when I'd been concentrating on grabbing the barman's attention.

He'd had sex with her, long ago. Or, he thought he had. He'd had a son he'd known nothing about. Or hadn't told me about. 'I might be'. The way he spoke, the way I'd heard him – it sounded like a decision he was thinking about making. I wanted to rush in. I wanted to pulverise the possibility. The betrayal. I wanted to leave, to get away from anything else I might hear.

And I didn't.

—Have you met him? I asked.

—No.

—How come?

—He lives in Perth, he said.

—Australia.

—Yeah.

That was handy, I thought. Borneo might have been better. Or way up the Limpopo. Away from Skype and Qantas. He wasn't confessing anything. I'm his father – I might be. It wasn't a statement. He was listening, testing the words – not on me, on himself.

I don't drink any more. I've given up, more or less. There was one night, I was having a fight, wanting a fight, with Faye and the phrase – that's the drink talking – introduced itself, nudged me, and I believed it.

—I'm sorry, I said.

—Are you?

—Yeah. I am. I – Christ – I don't even know how we started. It's me – I'm sorry.

—So, she said. —Just to be clear. In future, if there's going to be a row between us – unlikely as that might seem now – I'll be the sole instigator. Is that right?

—If you want.

—I do.

—Okay.

—Grand, she said. —And what do you want back, David? Let's play treaty negotiations. What are your proposals, tell us? What would you like?

—Nothing, I said.

—Ah, go on, spoilsport, she said. —Would you not like to ride Alison up the road? I've seen you looking at her.

—I didn't realise that was something you could organise, I said.

—I'm the queen of the madams in this town, so I am. And that one's a right hoor. Isn't she?

—Yes.

—A hoor. So, is that what you want, Kofi Annan, is it?

—No, Faye, it isn't.

—What, so?

—Nothing.

—Ah, go on, she said. —Not even me?

—I always want you.

—My eye, you do.

—I do.

—That's definitely the fuckin' drink talking.

—I want you now.

—I'm fuckin' here, look.

I didn't make a declaration. I didn't tell Faye or anyone else that I wouldn't drink again. I didn't go to AA; I'm not an alcoholic. I just stopped drinking once the fridge and the wine rack were empty. Faye buys a bottle of wine whenever she wants one. She's always said it: wine looks stupid lying on its side. I don't go to the pub; I don't have a local in Wantage. I drink very occasionally. I feel it – I feel it in my head, almost immediately. I can go months without a pint, yet feel drunk after a couple of gulps, like I'm topping it up, carrying on where I'd left off the night before.

I don't drink. But I was drinking with Joe. And the drink was going to talk. It already had; there'd been a nastiness in some of the things I'd said. I saw it – I'd heard it. I was being a prick. A prickless prick, Faye once called me, after I'd had a go at her, fooled myself into thinking that I could be as quick as she was.

I was never violent. Just stupid.

There was something I knew, or felt: this was the last time I was going to speak to Joe. He wasn't going to contact me again, and I wouldn't be contacting him. There wouldn't be a fight; nothing would come to a head. The pub would shut, and we'd leave – we'd go. I'd have one more pint and I'd leave. I wouldn't go into town with him, to George's. I wasn't going to let that happen. We'd go outside and talk for a few more minutes. We'd shake hands, probably hug, and go. Our separate ways. My father would die and I wouldn't come back to Dublin. Staying away wouldn't be too difficult.

I'd be careful now.

—How does that feel?

—What? he asked.

—Having a son you didn't know you had, I said. —A man. He must be – what? – mid-thirties.

—Yeah, he said. —Mad, isn't it?

—He's not far off middle age, I said. —When you work it out. You'll get to know him when his life is half over.

I wasn't being careful enough.

I wanted to kill Joe. I wanted to obliterate Joe. I just wanted to fuckin' kill him.

But I didn't. The fog opened – it wasn't me talking. I could hear Faye. That'll be the drink, will it?

I knew how he was going to answer.

—I wasn't –. I don't know, Davy – I wasn't that surprised. When she told me.

I was right.

—Does nothing surprise you, Joe?

—Good question, he said. —But no. No, I don't think so.

—I have a free house, she told me.

—Is that right? I said.

—It is.

She'd phoned me in work four days after the wedding.

—How did you know I worked here?

I needed to speak softly but I wanted to shout. I wanted the lads and girls around me to know that I was being chased by a woman – by this nineteen-year-old woman.

—I phoned every office in Dublin, she said. —And I told them, I need to talk to the ride with the hair.

She'd phoned Cathy's brother, on his honeymoon, and she'd asked him where I worked. She told me about it months later. Cathy never told me.

My boss was standing at his door, looking my way. I was chuffed. All eyes were on me.

—And the house, I said. —Could you tell me where it is, please?

—Gorey.

—Really? That's fine, yes.

—Not all the girls give a flying fuck about living in Dublin, she said. —Some of us can function perfectly well away from the bright lights.

—I'm sure you're right, I said. —Could I get your number, please, and I could phone you back later?

—No.

—No?

—I'm in a fuckin' phone box, she said. —Did you think I was lying back in bed or something, in my negligee? Are you holding your pen?

—Eh – yes, I am.

—I'm going to give you the address. I'll be expecting you on Friday night. What time do you finish work?

—Five – that's right.

—See you at eight and don't dare be fuckin' late.

—Thank you –.

She was gone.

—I'll get back to you when I have the details – bye bye.

I put the phone down and took the applause and the slagging.

—We're telling Cah-tee! We're telling Cah-tee!

I borrowed my father's car.

He looked at me. It was the day after Cathy had left the message; she wouldn't be meeting me at the weekend. We'd just been talking about her. He took the key off his keyring.

—I liked Cathy, he said.

I'd asked him for the car and told him I'd have it back on Sunday – or Saturday if he needed it. I hadn't told him I was meeting someone else.

He held out the key. Like he didn't want to do it, like it was going against his better judgement.

I was tempted not to take it.

He rarely spoke about my mother. He was younger than I am now. I don't think he saw other women; I never met any. There'd been none in the house. I used to dream of that – awake, and sometimes when I slept. I'd find a woman in the kitchen. She'd be lovely, when I was in charge of the dream. A bit too old to be gorgeous – she'd be handsome. One of the great-looking mothers. I'd sit in school thinking of her. When I slept she was warm; she was warmth – that was all.

I made it to Gorey with thirteen minutes to spare. The drive through Arklow nearly killed me. I didn't have a driving licence. I'd driven with my father on Dollymount Strand and, once, to Howth and back. Alone, I'd driven to Northside Shopping Centre, and home to my flat with a gas canister. The crawl through Arklow – my legs ached, the car cut out twice, I was afraid I'd go into the bumper in front of me. I was starving. I missed Cathy. I could feel the pint in my hand; I could feel her beside me as we found a bit of free wall and leaned back together in the full, Friday-night pub.

I couldn't remember what Faye looked like.

That's still the case. Her eyes are brown but I might be wrong. I'd be surprised if they aren't, but not that surprised. I could go downstairs now and check. But she'd see me looking and she'd want to know why. Or, much more likely, she'd know why.

—You're sticking me into your book.

I haven't told her I'm writing. I don't need to.

She wasn't exactly beautiful. There was nothing striking about her; I think that's accurate – except her eyes. Her eyes came from a silent movie – maybe that's why I can never be sure of their colour. They were huge and they moved so precisely, when she told them to. Always, to make me laugh. And she moved, she walked, like she was going to come straight at me. She touched everything, rubbed her fingers along walls as she went, tapped fragile things, pressed buttons, picked up phones, tried on coats and hats – women's, men's, children's. Stared at me, not smiling – but smiling. Not just her eyes – all of Faye was in a silent movie. But then there was her voice, her Wexford accent – the words, the stream of brilliantly managed madness. I don't think I ever fell in love with Faye. I don't think I had time to. I knew, when I sat with her at the wedding, she was dangerous. She'd have said anything – she didn't care, and she gave all of herself so you'd know that. Nothing she said or did was predictable. I don't think I ever successfully anticipated what Faye was going to say – I think that's true. There were two types of men. There were the men who encountered Faye, and backed away. Then there were the men who met Faye, and fell over. The latter outnumbered the former. Faye became the only woman in the room, on the train, at the table.

Her house was at the top of the town. I was in a town that had a bottom and a top. It stood alone – the doctor or the priest's house. It had its own wide gate and high stone wall. And a tree that leaned out over the street. I didn't know if I should drive right up to the front door; I didn't know if I was allowed to, if it was done.

I chanced it.

There were no lights on in the front of the house. The front door was deep inside a porch. There was no bell – I couldn't see one – just a brass knocker, a fox's head.

I gave it a tap.

And another.

The door opened. The hall light hadn't come on.

Her top teeth had trapped her bottom lip, like she was trying not to laugh – I could see that.

—Well, it's David, she said. —You're a bit early, aren't you?

—Will I wait?

I was pleased with myself; I'd managed to talk.

—You will in your hole, she said. —In you get. What's that yoke you have there?

I looked down at the thing she was looking at.

—My bag, I said.

—Oh, she said. —How's Cathy, tell us? She's not in the fuckin' bag, is she?

I was still outside the house.

—Hope not, I said.

—I like Cathy, she said.

—So does my father.

—Grand, so. They have each other.

She walked away from the door. I stepped into the dark of the hall and followed her.

—Shut the door, for fuck sake. I hope you love cats.

—I don't mind them.

—Grand.

I was there a night and most of a day before it occurred to me that I hadn't seen a cat. There was a dog sitting on my lap, licking my chin. I laughed.

—What?

She was sitting beside me.

—You don't have any cats, I said.

She sat up and turned, so she was looking straight at me.

—I will never be a cat lady, she said. —I swear to fuckin' God.

—Was your mother a cat lady?

—Are you fuckin' suggesting I got rid of the cats when my poor mammy died, are you? I threw them in after her, into the cold, cold grave – they bounced off the fuckin' coffin. Is that what you're suggesting?

She was naked under her father's dressing gown. He'd been wearing it when he died, she told me.

—Look, she said.

She took twenty Sweet Afton from a pocket.

—His fags, she said. —Exactly where he left them.

She put them back.

—There was a cat, actually, she said.

—Yeah?

—It disappeared after she died.

—Seriously?

—Just fucked off, so it did.

She leaned over me, and the dog; she was on her knees now. She was inspecting the arm of the sofa.

—Aha.

She picked up something.

—Exhibit A.

—What is it?

I couldn't see anything. She was pretending to hold something right in front of my eyes.

—Moggy hair, she said.

I could see something now.

—Could be a dog hair, I said.

There were three dogs in the room. There were more, out behind the house.

—I'm allergic to cats, she said. —If I put this anywhere near my face, my eyes will explode.

Her face was right up to mine. She'd shoved the dog off my lap. There was a fight going on now, down on the floor, with the other two. But I didn't look. I couldn't, and I didn't want to. I could see the hair now, clearly; it stood up between her fingernails like a pin. She held it right under her left eye.

—Cat or dog?

Her left eye was all I could see.

—Go on, she said.

I gave her the answer I thought she'd want.

—Cat.

The white hair divided the eye in half. Then I saw it move, slide, down the eye. She didn't blink.

The hair was gone.

—Anything happening?

—No.

She sighed.

—Ah, well – must only be a dog's.

She sat back.

—Next time maybe.

She pulled the dressing gown around her.

—I like being an orphan, she said. —It's kind of cool, isn't it?

—Yeah, I said.

I thought about it.

—It is.

—Men like riding orphans, she said. —Did anyone ever tell you that now?

—No.

—An orphan with a house and a shop and a vagina, she said. —Do you know what that makes me in the town?

—What?

—The catch with the snatch.

Neither of us laughed. The words sounded vicious – like she was hurting herself.

Faye didn't often laugh.

—Do you own a shop? I asked.

—I do, she said. —The name over the door and all. You have no idea how many mammies have called in to me since my own mammy went to her maker. Women, now, whose husbands slept with my mammy – or stayed awake while they gave her a seeing to. But the wives – they're more than willing to let bygones be bygones. Because they want me for their sons.

—Do they bring the sons?

—They've more sense, said Faye. —They bring cakes. Flans. And shepherd's pie and flowers. And they ask me how I'm holding up and how I'm managing, rattling around in this old place all on my own, and who do I have to look after the shop for me till I sell it, which would be a crying shame because – now – the town needs that shop, that shop, they tell me, was the making of the town.

—What's in the shop?

—Garments for the peasantry, she said.

—Clothes.

—Well done. Clothes. My mother was mad.

—What did she die of?

—Ah, sure. Well –. She kind of killed herself – accidentally, of course. But that's for another day. Cathy.

I couldn't keep up. (I still can't.) She seemed to be telling me that Cathy had been involved in her mother's suicide. I'd never heard of a woman killing herself before. It had always been men and boys – and not many of them.

—What about Cathy? I asked.

—Did you ever meet her dad?

—Well, yeah, I said. —He was at the wedding last Saturday, remember?

—But, I mean, you've met him. You've had a chat with him, have you?

—Yeah – a short one. When he was up in Dublin for a match. What about it?

—He's a nice man. He'd be number one on my list of the nice dads who've been in this house.

—Did your mother –?

—She did.

—I didn't know Cathy was from around here.

—You never met my mother, she said. —You wouldn't have just crossed the street to have a look at her. You'd have driven the length of the county and further. Can you think of one spectacular thing in Ireland? Name it – quick, quick.

—The Cliffs of Moher.

—My mammy was the Cliffs of Moher. I'm not like her.

—You're the Giant's Causeway, are you?

It was like she hadn't heard me. Nothing crossed her face.

—I will never be like her, she said.

—Okay.

—Listen, she said. —Listen to this. Listen.

—I am.

—I will only ever know the one man, she said. —Do you read your bible, do you?

—Not really, I said.

I was trying to understand what she'd just said.

—That's the *know* I mean, anyway, she said. —The biblical know.

We'd made love the night before. We'd made love half an hour before.

The eyes – they had me pinned. They were waiting for me to say something.

—Okay.

—She cried when they were late, she said. —And she cried when they left. She gave them the bum's rush if they were on time, she laughed at them if they wanted to stay. She threw all the little statues at them. Look at the mantelpiece, sure – there's nothing left on it.

—Were you here?

—I was only ten when Daddy died.

—Okay. Who managed the shop?

—She did.

—Did she?

—She reinvented the place. One of the shepherd's pie ladies told me. She said it was the best thing that ever happened the town. You could go shopping without having to go up to Dublin. She converted a big shop into a fuckin' department store.

—Well worth her husband's infidelity.

—Whose husband?

—The shepherd's pie lady.

—Well, God, she said. —Yeah, well worth it. All the major brands for the loan of the husband's mickey? Well worth it, boy. Cathy's mother tried to persuade the brother to start courting me.

94

—The brother that got married?

—That's him.

—You're messing.

—I don't think I am.

—When he was already engaged to your woman that he married?

—This was business, she said. —To be fair to her. I own a fuckin' department store and the fiancée's only an oul' nurse. His wife she is now, God fuckin' love her.

I waited a second.

—Did he call you? I asked.

—No, he did not.

—Then how do you know his mother was going to loose him on you, so?

I didn't know where the language – *loose him on you, so* – had come from.

—I turned on a lamp, she said. —When she was here, like. His mammy – in here. It was getting dark. But it didn't turn on. But she said, 'Cathal will fix that for you.'

—It was probably the bulb.

—I knew that. It was only the fuckin' bulb. And that's what I told her – it's only the bulb.

—And was it?

—No, she said. —It was banjaxed.

I looked around, at the three or four lights in the room.

—Where is it?

—You won't be fixing it either.

—I know.

—I flung it out the scullery door, she said. —That's where all the broken shite is going from now on – from here on fuckin' in.

It was quiet now. There was something about the air; I thought she was going to cry – was already crying. But she wasn't, she didn't. The dogs had gone off, wandering. I thought I heard them on the stairs. It was dark now, and cold.

—Are you an only child? I asked her.

—D'you think I'm a fuckin' child?

—No.

—I did the Leaving last year, she said. —I was a schoolgirl less than a year ago. Does that make you feel guilty?

—Not in the least.

—Or the opposite, she said. —Does it give you a horn?

—No.

—Grand, she said.

She sang a song I didn't recognise.

—I ain't got no sister, I ain't got a brother, I ain't got a father, not even a mother.

—How did you do in the Leaving?

—I'm a lonely girl, I ain't got a home. All honours. The genuine articles.

—College?

—Fuck it, she said. —I'm grand. I'm up past my fuckin' gills in expertise. Did you ever hear a stupider word than 'sibling'?

—No – I don't think so.

—Have you any of the sib-illings, yourself, David?

—No.

—Interesting, she said.

—Why is it?

—We're both only children – *only* children. With dead mammies.

—Why is that interesting, though?

—It just is, she said. —Things happen for a reason. Says I.

She looked straight at me.

—You'll do me, she said.

She wasn't smiling.

—Thanks, I said.

I was. Smiling.

We watched as she pushed her way to the front of the pub, to her friends.

—Did yeh get a good look at her arse?

—Perfect.

—Yeah.

—Fuckin' perfect.

—What'll we do?

We did nothing. We stayed where we were. We kept an eye out, in case the wall of shoulders and heads opened. We glimpsed her, we nudged each other.

—Did yeh see the way she leaned out there, to get her pint?

—The tit – the shape of it under her jumper.

—Ah, man.

—A hand on tha' thing.

—Ah, man.

—The weight of it – can you imagine?

—Ah, fuckin' man.

—Look, said Joe. —Your man up there is goin'. Will we grab his stool?

We'd get in there, closer to her. We'd start chatting to the lads on the edge of her crowd. We'd find something in common – there'd have to be something. Joe would get us started. Someone would shift, leave, go for his coat, and she'd be in front of us. Me. I'd talk – I'd think of something, something would happen.

—Is he goin' or wha'? He's sittin' down again, the cunt.

—Fuckin' arsehole – make your fuckin' mind up, for fuck sake.

—What'll we do?

Joe stood up. He picked up his pint and he grabbed his jacket.

—Come on, he said.

I watched him as he politely battled his way up the room. He smiled at the people he was pushing. I couldn't see his face but that was what he was doing. I knew Joe. I knew what was in him, and I knew I held him back.

I stood up and grabbed my own pint and jacket, and I went after him. He'd found room for his pint on the counter. He'd thrown his jacket onto a pile near the door. He was listening to two men and a woman. He was getting ready to speak when I got there.

That might be what happened, or something like it. I can see it happening; I've no problem describing it. Joe made the move, and I'd have followed him. I wouldn't have waited.

—The Ramones, he said later that night. —They never let yeh down, sure they don't?

We were walking home along the North Strand, towards Fairview. We had to walk that far every weekend before a taxi, going back into town, would stop for us.

The Ramones were what the two lads and the girl had been talking about when Joe had arrived and parked his pint. The two lads were thinking about going to see *Rock 'n' Roll High School*, later, after closing time.

—The best music film ever, said Joe.

They said nothing back. They didn't know him; they'd never seen him. They didn't turn away but they didn't really look at him.

—Better than *The Last Waltz*, even, said Joe.

It was the girl who spoke. —Really?

—I think so, said Joe.

I knew this: he hadn't seen *Rock 'n' Roll High School*.

—How did yeh know? I asked him on the way home.

—Know wha'?

—Tha' she liked *The Last Waltz*.

—I guessed, he said. —She'd hair like Emmylou Harris.

—No, she didn't.

—She used to, he said.

—How d'you know tha'?

—I just do.

—Fuck off, Joe, I said. —What're you on abou'?

—I could tell, he said. —She'd got her hair cut recently – a whole change o' style. She kept puttin' her hand up to it. Pattin' where it ended. An' it was black, like Emmylou Harris's.

—You're a spoofer, I told him.

—You really should've had a few sisters, Davy, he said. —The things you'd've learnt, I'm not jokin' yeh.

—Like?

—Like – tonigh'. One o' me sisters got her hair done a while back an' she cried for fuckin' days after it. She wouldn't come ou' o' their bedroom. An' when she did – when she started actually fuckin' starvin' – she kept touchin' her hair. Where her hair used to be. Like your woman tonigh'. I could tell. She was anxious about it. More, she was grievin' for it. Kind of. Even though she likes the new look. She's missin' the hair. Like me sister did. Panickin'. It must be a huge decision for a bird

99

with long hair. When her hair is the most spectacular thing abou' her. I'd say, anyway. The fairy tales are full o' women's hair.

—Which sister?

—Paula. I think. I can't remember. But I'd say Paula.

I wondered then, as I'd wondered before, why he hadn't had more success with women. He knew all about them, it seemed to me. How they worked, what they thought. What was important, what made them laugh. I remember once, when we were still in school, he'd stopped the life in the classroom with just two words.

—Girls wank.

No one doubted him. No one said 'No way' or 'Fuck off, Joe.' But what did they wank with? It was a question no one was going to ask. What did they pull or stroke? The teacher – I can't remember who it was; I can't remember the names of most of our teachers – he couldn't believe the silence, couldn't quite accept it, when he walked into the room and shut the door.

—What's going on? Out with it.

He opened the door again, in case he had to escape; that was what it was like. Hostile, anxious. A lad at the back, behind us, whispered.

—He's right.

The mothers liked Joe. The sisters liked Joe. The women and girls in the shops liked Joe. Or, they didn't dislike him. They were civil, sometimes even patient. They didn't see him as the enemy. And there'd been regular messages from other girls. *Mary wants to go with you. Tell your friend Joe that Jackie Salmon says he's a ride. I do not, you – fuck off.* I wondered why he hadn't gone from girl to girl to woman, why he hadn't lived

100

a different life. Maybe he had – he was claiming children now that I'd known nothing about, *he'd* known
nothing about.

—You're still a spoofer, I said that night, on the
North Strand. —Emmylou Harris, me hole.

—Well, you fuckin' explain it then, he said. —G'wan
ahead. Give us the benefit of your hard-earned fuckin'
expertise.

—She liked us, I said.

—Us?

—Me.

—Fuckin' you?

—Both of us, I said. —Doesn't matter.

—Hang on, he said. —This is Emmylou the skinhead
we're still talkin' about, yeah?

—She wasn't a skinhead.

—Grand, he said. —But she fancied us, you're sayin'.
Us.

—Yeah, I said. —Me, anyway.

—She fuckin' hid it well, he said.

He was never going to let her fancy me. He wasn't
going to let me think it.

We'd gone to *Rock 'n' Roll High School.* We'd tagged
along, not exactly welcome, but not unwelcome either.
We'd stood outside George's while they – we didn't
know who they were – convened, decided, left, stayed.
Our girl was there, moving among them. There were
ten or eleven going on to the film. We were in there
with them, and we got going; we set off. We moved
down South William Street, on the path, off the path,
onto the street, past the Hideout, past Grogan's.

She wasn't there. She'd gone; she'd left – she was
going somewhere else, with someone else.

—She's not with them.

101

—Doesn't matter, said Joe. —This is a long-term investment.

—What d'you mean?

—We're in the gang, he said.

It's how I remember it. This is what we said and did.

We lost them somewhere before College Green but caught up with them on O'Connell Bridge. I don't remember any names. I'm not sure I ever knew any. But I must have known some – there were parties later, conversations, sex. I can see faces. I can see a woman's hip, a smile, eyes. I can almost feel skin, and breath. I remember the Emmylou Harris girl. I think her name was Alice. But that was later; I learnt it later, another time. I didn't know Jessica's. I'm sure of that. But her name is there now, in the story. I remember things, events, and now she's become a woman I knew much better than I know I actually did.

O'Connell Street was wild. There was a fight at the rank outside the Gresham. There was blood on the ground, and a tooth. There was a screaming girlfriend and another girl who was trying to get at her hair. She was being held off by more girls and a man who was threatening to hit her.

We made it to Findlater Place, and into The Regent. The Emmylou girl was sitting in front of us. She turned and smiled, at Joe – then me.

—This better be good, she said.

—Wait an' see, said Joe. —It's great.

That seemed to be it: Joe had organised this adventure, even though she'd been looking at me as she spoke.

—It's brilliant, I said.

She smiled, and turned back to face the screen.

We were out of the seats the minute we heard 'Sheena Is a Punk Rocker'. We got into the narrow lane between the wall and the seats. We were still at it, pogoing and bashing into one another, long after Joey Ramone had stopped singing. Joe had his hand on Emmylou's back; they were gasping together, laughing. I'd be going home alone, I thought. The routes out of town at two in the morning – Summerhill, Seán McDermott Street, the North Strand – they terrified me.

But here we were an hour later, walking home, the two of us.

We'd convened again outside the cinema. They gathered, and moved. Emmylou was there, near Joe, then not. She moved – he didn't.

He was with me.

I was happy.

—Great fuckin' film, I said.

—A load o' shite, said Joe.

—You said it was the best music film ever.

—Tha' was before I saw it.

—It wasn't tha' bad.

—It served its purpose, he said.

We were in the gang – we hoped we were. Like Joe had said, as he'd predicted. But we'd have to wait and see. We never spoke about why we were doing this. Was it to know the girl, to sleep with her, to fall in love with her? Both of us – or Joe? I remember thinking – or, feeling: it was about acceptance. I remember wanting something more.

We were coming up to Newcomen Bridge and the blocks of flats. There was a gang of lads on the other side of the street. Seven or eight of them – they seemed too chaotic to be interested in us. Still, passing them, waiting for the footsteps, the shouts – I knew it would happen, I felt it, expected, almost wanted it. The need to stay quiet, the urge to speak. To run, and draw attention to ourselves. I'm almost sixty now, but I can still feel the pain in my chest – the exhilaration – when I ran as if my life depended on it. Because it did.

We were over the canal bridge when we heard the voice behind us.

—Here, lads, d'yis have a light?

It was too early to run.

Joe looked over his shoulder.

—No.

—Come here – what's your fuckin' hurry?

Now it was time to run.

—Fuckin' queers!

I thought we'd be okay. If they'd been waiting for us, they'd have been ready for the ambush, dispersed across the street. We ran under the railway bridge. We were close to the widest section of the street, and the fire station. (I don't remember if the station was there, if it had been built when we ran past where I know it is now.) We'd been drinking all night but we were fast and they weren't that fussed about catching us – that was the hope. There was Fairview Park now, to the right. A gay lad had been battered, murdered in there, for £4 and a watch. A few months before – for being gay. It might have been these guys – they might have done the kicking. I couldn't hear their steps now – I wasn't sure. I didn't look back and I wasn't going to. They'd kicked the poor guy to death – they'd been waiting for him. I could hear Joe beside me; his breath was mine. My legs were hurting, my chest was torn. I could hear them behind us, still there, still chasing. A taxi – a fuckin' taxi! Crawling back into town. On the opposite side of the road. Joe saw it too. We got out onto the road and dashed across to the park side. We stopped running – the taxi was coming up to us. If the driver saw us running he'd keep going. I tried not to bend over, to get my breath, to vomit. I didn't look behind me. Joe lifted his arm, his hand. The taxi approached – we were fucked if he didn't stop. They'd push us over the railings, drag us into the park. Kick us to death. The papers would suggest that we were gay. Last chance, the last second, the taxi halted just behind us. Back door open – Joe got it open. We were in. Safe, saved. Joe told the driver where we were going. He did a U-turn – the street was empty. The park was dark. We saw shapes back at the fire station. The lads, the queer-bashers. They'd given up before we'd stopped the taxi. It didn't matter.

The sweat was cold.

The taxi turned on to the Howth Road.

—The things we do for love, said Joe.

He started laughing.

—Next week, he said. —Wait an' see. It'll all have been worth it.

It made no real sense.

But it was great.

—Does he look like you? I asked Joe.

—Do your kids look like you? he asked.

I've been told that my children look like me. I've been told they look like Faye.

—A bit, I said. —People say it. Faye says it.

—A bit, said Joe. —That's the thing. We all look a bit like everybody. Seriously. Get a picture of Whitney Houston up on your phone there. And we'll find something that makes her look a bit like the barman. Go on.

He was trying to escape. But I did it. I googled Whitney Houston and chose an early photo, pre-*The Bodyguard*.

—God, she was lovely.

—And the barman fuckin' isn't.

We were close now, shoulder to shoulder; we leaned into each other to share the phone.

—His forehead, look.

—Okay, I said. —That's Whitney's.

—Look at the way he's standing – look. He's definitely one of the Houstons.

—It's weird, that, isn't it? I said. —How we inherit the way we walk or something like that. My Róisín walks exactly like my mother did. According to my father.

Joe nodded at the barman.

—Maybe he sings like Whitney, he said.

—It's not impossible.

—We could start singing 'I Wanna Dance With Somebody' and see if he joins in.

—And get ourselves barred.

—Maybe she never died, he said. —She's a barman in the Sheds.

—Does Peter look like you? I asked.

—Don't be a cunt, Davy.

—I'm not being a cunt, I said. —I'm trying to remember.

—What?

I shrugged. I sat up, away from his shoulder, from him. I tried to straighten my back – stay straight.

—Some of it's so vague, I said.

—What?

—Back then, I said. —There are things that are like yesterday.

He nodded.

—Same here – yeah.

—And other stuff, I said. —That must have happened at about the same time. But –. Like, for example. Faye says we did something and I haven't a clue. No recollection of it. Say, some place we went to. She'll talk about food we had, maybe – where and what. I can't remember it but I don't doubt it happened. Then she'll mention something else that happened on the same day, same place, and I'll be there – every detail.

I wanted him to see us both back then, back in George's, back on the stools – stools like the ones we were sitting on now. I wanted to be there. It was my story too. We'd adored the same woman. It had been a joint decision. A thing we'd made up together. In the space of an evening – food and a few drinks – he'd gone from reminding me of the existence of a woman we'd never got to know to telling me that he might have been the father of her grown-up son. I'd been there at the beginning and this ending wasn't acceptable.

There was a question I hadn't asked, a question so obvious I almost burst out laughing.

—Does she say you're the father?

—Not in so many words, he said. —No. She doesn't insist on it.

—So –.

He sighed, and I heard him inhale.

—It's tricky, Davy. Look – just tricky. I'm not doing it justice. The words are letting me down.

I understood what he meant – I think I did. I could feel the solidity of my marriage to Faye, although I couldn't have explained it. But my children were mine

107

– it was very straightforward. There were events I attended, events I took part in. I fucked my wife and she fucked me. We have two children. She's the mother; I'm the father. There were miscarriages and an abortion. I ache when I think of my children; they are beyond anything I could put words to. I think of their weight when I first held them, their cheeks, their first laughs, the fat little hands clutching my finger. But there was also blood and shit. My children are facts and Joe's phantom, middle-aged baby made me fuckin' furious.

—I have to go for a piss.

We walked down Main Street that first weekend. We weren't going anywhere in particular – I didn't think we were. We'd no goal, no destination. Gorey then wasn't Gorey now. Gorey today is windows full of wedding dresses. Gorey then was fewer and smaller windows, a country town in Wexford trying to be a bit more. Gorey today seems like a suburb of Southside Dublin, somehow cut off from the mainland.

—Just showing you the roots, said Faye as she shut the back door.

She didn't lock it.

—What'll you do with the dogs? I asked.

—They can go for their own fuckin' walk, she said.

—I meant, when you leave.

—Who says I'm leaving?

—You do, I said.

—Do I now?

—Yeah, I said. —You said as much.

—Said as much. Did I say I was leaving this place – in actual words?

—You implied it.

—And tell us, she said.

We were out on the street now.

—Did Gladys Knight sing, 'I'm *implying* on that midnight train to Georgia' – did she?

—Not really.

I loved being with her.

—No, she fuckin' did not. I never implied on a train in my life and neither did Gladys. Or any of the Pips. It's downhill all the way, this place, look.

She was right. We were walking down a hill, towards a crossroads.

—Even coming back up, it's fuckin' downhill.

—You're not happy here, I said.

She snorted.

She stopped.

—And do you think now, David, that if I leave – *if* I leave, pack a case and actually leave – it'll be because of you, and this will make me a happy girl?

—Yeah.

—God love you.

The town – this end of town – was quiet, although there were cars and vans passing us, slowly. I could see people down the hill, below us. It was late afternoon, getting dark, already cold. We were outside a shop that had a pyramid of jars of blackcurrant jam in its window.

She moved again. I went with her. She found my hand. That thrilled me.

—Where's your shop? I asked.

—Wait now – wait. Till you see.

She stopped again.

—I'm making a prediction, she said. —One day – one day – there'll be traffic lights at this crossroads. Watch out for the tractors now.

We ran across the street, although we didn't have to. The traffic wasn't moving.

She let go of my hand.

—Look now, she said. —There.

She pointed across the street. The shop was twice the width of the other shops, to the left and right. The name was big and red, above – across – both window displays.

—Your surname's Devereux, I said.

—There now, she said. —You've had your hand on my arse and only now you find out that the arse is called Devereux. It's shocking, so it is. What's the country coming to?

She took my hand again.

—What happened your mother? I asked.

—What d'you mean, like?

—How did she die?

She let go of my hand and pointed across the street again.

—The shop?

—It's not a shop, she said. —I told you. It's a department store.

—And it killed your mother?

—I'm blaming it, anyway, she said. —It's more interesting than cancer, sure, isn't it? A woman in a man's world, David. A woman takes over the man's world. She was made for the job – and she wasn't. It killed her – they killed her. She wasn't wired for it, so she wasn't.

She was holding my hand again.

—The cancer only came skipping along behind it, she said. —I could blame my dad for dying, I suppose. And leaving her with the fuckin' thing. Come on.

—We're not going in?

—I'll never go in, she said. —Which, now, is a pity. Cos I loved it in there. Being in there with Mammy. In under everything. Watching her. I loved it. But, sure.

—Will you sell it?

We were heading back up through the town.

—When the probate's sorted, I will, she said. —Sounds medical, doesn't it?

—Probate?

—Like something with veins.

I stood at the urinal, then at the sink. No one else came in. The toilet was near the back of the pub. There was a smoking area a bit further back; I'd seen the sign for it. I could go out there – there might be a gate, a way to escape without going back in and past him. I'd leave my jacket – and my wallet; I didn't care.

But I'd just needed the time. The minute alone. I hated what Joe was at, but it was intriguing, perplexing – familiar. The things we say and don't say, the things we tell and don't – I knew what he was doing.

I checked my phone. There was nothing.

I went back out – back in.

I separate us. I sit alone in George's. Joe isn't beside me. I watch her at the table. I see the cello case, leaning against the wall, under the window. I decide it's hers. She's beautiful. She shines. I don't know why I think that – *she shines*. It could be that there's nothing physically outstanding about her, except, perhaps, her hair. The words about her arse and tits – banter, bravado – frightened lads. I'm alone now. I'm not in competition. I'm not reining back jealousy or

111

desperation. But she *is* beautiful. She *does* shine. She has a pint of lager in her hand. Her fingers are long. She puts the pint down. She stretches – I want to shout. Her head goes back, her hands reach for the ceiling. I can see an inch of white tummy – it's not a stomach. Her head is back, she's not listening to her friends. She lowers her arms – she changes shape, becomes smaller, fuller. She smiles at her friends – she's back. *Sorry*. She grins. I see her teeth. And I've already heard her voice. Southside Dublin.

This didn't happen.

Nothing like this happened.

She sat at the table with her friends, the other musicians – the music students, whatever they were. She had her back to the window. She wasn't beautiful. She was gorgeous. And she didn't shine. She was human – she was gorgeous. I remember that. Flesh and blood – legs, arms, neck. I remember her lifting her arms to stretch. I remember groaning. It was theatrical but it was real. Joe was beside me – *Oh, for fuck sake*. He can fuck off; he's not there. I'm alone. I was alone. I was looking across at her; there was no running commentary. Thirty-seven years ago. She was gorgeous. I was in love with her. In love with what I made her. She stood – she wasn't tall – and came over to me. She stood beside me while she ordered her drink – *Point of Horp, George, please.*

—Point of Horp, Joe whispers beside me. —For fuck sake.

I push him away again – he's not there.

She was real. A great-looking woman. I wouldn't have called her a woman back then – a girl is what she'd have been, back when I was still a boy. She was one of a line of girls and women that myself and Joe declared ours in the years we hung around together. Gorgeous, real, but not for us – impossible. And that was the point – the impossibility. We invented them. We had the raw material, safely on the other side of the bar, the window glass, the road. We'd make them up, give them traits, habits, urges. We even gave them names. We'd been doing it for years.

After the girl in George's, we never did it again.

But my point is: I was there. I was there *too*. I saw her too. I fell for her too. I never even got to know her name – too.

—What happened after Wigwam? I asked him.

—More Wigwams, he said.

—You met her again.

—Yeah, he said. —Yeah. I did.

I was calm again; it didn't matter. I'd be going home soon, to England. I'd tell Faye all that had happened. She'd put down her book, she'd look at me over her reading glasses; she'd take them off, put them on her head. She hadn't really known Joe. But this was a story. She'd love it.

They'd met again.

—Four days after.

A pub this time – he couldn't remember which.

—How come?

—I just don't.

—You remember everything else, I said.

—Let's say it was Harry Byrne's, he said.

—Was it?

—Let's say it was, he said. —It probably was. It was, once – definitely.

—Does she still drink Harp? I asked.

—What?

—She used to drink Harp, I said.

—That's right, he said.

He laughed.

—I'd forgotten that, he said. —Jesus.

He looked down the bar, to the line of taps.

—Does Harp still exist? he said.

—They still drink it in the North, I think.

—Do they?

—I think so – yeah.

—That's gas, he said. —But anyway, no. She had a glass of Merlot. I think. Red – some sort of red. I don't think she drank it. She just had it in front of her.

—A point of Horp, I said.

—What?

—That was how she used to pronounce it.

—Is that right?

—Yeah.

—Okay, he said. —I can't remember that.

It was late afternoon, the second time, on his way home from work.

—I know what you're thinking, he said.

—You don't.

—Okay, he said. —But I think I do.

—Okay.

—You think we had a couple of drinks – for the Dutch courage. And then we went somewhere. Howth summit or somewhere – for a smooch. In the back of the car.

Earlier in the evening I'd thought exactly that. Or a hotel room – that was more likely. He'd slept with the woman of our dreams thirty-seven years after we'd put the thought into our heads. Now, before he spoke, I knew I was wrong. It hadn't happened – the hotel, the back of the car. But I didn't know what *had* happened. Nothing had happened. But that, I knew, wasn't it either. This was a different kind of story.

And that was it, I thought. It was a story. Not an account, or a long boast. Joe was telling me a story.

—How come I do it all? Faye said once, after she'd moved to Dublin.

—What d'you mean? I asked her.

We'd been living together for two months. We were lying on the bed. It wasn't housework and it wasn't money – I didn't know what she meant.

—I do most of the talking, she said.

—Yeah, I agreed. —You do.

She said nothing. I wasn't worried.

—If we were in a film, I said. —You'd get up on your elbow now. You'd make sure your tits were covered by the sheet and you'd stare at me before you said your next thing.

She laughed.

Faye rarely laughed. It was another thing I loved about her. It was always a surprise. And a victory.

—That's what I mean, she said.

—What?

—I'm the one who'd normally have said something like that, she said.

—True, I said.

—Why, though?

—It's you, I said.

—It's me?

—Yeah.

—So, then – what's you?

—I'm the one who loves you for it, I said.

—Is that right?

—Yeah.

—I like that, she said. —Oh, I do like that.

And she did. For a long time. Maybe she still does.

—I'll marry you now for saying that, David, she said.

—Will you?

—I will, she said.

—Good.

—And we'll see how it goes.

—Grand.

—You can kiss the bride now, David, she said. — Anywhere you want.

They met twice a week at first. She didn't ask about his family. Joe asked her nothing. He thought – the way she sat, the way she looked at him, and didn't look at him – he thought she thought, he already knew. There was nothing to ask, no years to fill in. He thought.

—She was a cheap date, so, I said.

The drink was talking. It was the night's second energy. I was enjoying myself again.

—Hang on, said Joe. —Hang on. Listen – I looked up the word salacious – a while ago there. I googled it. I've been hearin' the word all me life and I knew what it meant, and I didn't – exactly. If you know what I mean.

—I do.

—So I googled it and read the definitions and the synonyms and all that. And this isn't salacious or crude or prurient or indecent. Or anythin'. What I'm tellin' you. And it won't be.

—Great word, though.

—Granted. Brilliant word. Gives me the horn.

116

He burst out laughing.

—Why did you look it up? I asked him.

—Somethin' Trish said.

—You're still talking to Trish?

—Listenin' to her.

I saw his face. He regretted what he'd just said, he wanted to take it back.

—There's nothing necessarily salacious about having sex with a woman you're not married to, I said. —Or talking about it – more to the point. Is there?

—Not at all, he said. —Not at all.

The drink was talking for him too.

—Not at all. But what I'm sayin' is, it wasn't like that. We didn't – I don't know – paw each other.

—Did you want to?

—What?

—You said it, not me – paw her. I don't know – put your hands where you'd wanted to put them back in the day.

—No.

Where you'd wanted to, was what I'd said. Where *we'd* wanted to, was what I'd meant.

—Not really, he said.

—Not really?

—Stop it, Davy.

—Stop what, Joe?

—Just fuckin' stop it. You're not listenin'. You're like fuckin' Trish.

—I'm sorry?

—Lookin' for muck where there isn't any. Wantin' it to be about body parts.

I knew now why he'd been googling. I could hardly remember what Trish looked like but I could hear her saying salacious. And body parts.

—Okay, I said. —Sorry. I'm interrupting you. Go
on.

—Well, he said. —What?

—Go on with what you were saying.

—Well, all I was sayin' – all I wanted to clarify –.
Was that it wasn't about – like – the biology. Or just
biology.

—Okay.

—Just that. It was like we were friends. Lifelong
friends, I mean.

—Like you and Trish.

—Okay, he said. —Yeah.

—How did Trish take it? I asked.

—Oh, for fuck sake.

He seemed to be grateful. He was off the hook. He'd
have no problem relating this part.

—God, he said. —Jesus.

—Did you tell her?

—What d'you mean?

—Did you tell her? I repeated. —I mean, did you
get to tell her, yourself, or did she find out?

—Oh, he said. —No, no. I told her. I plucked up the
fuckin' stupidity. Jesus.

He laughed.

—I made sure the house was empty, he said. —But
I don't know, Davy. I didn't –. I thought it would be
grand.

—You didn't.

—I did.

—You can't have.

—I fuckin' did, he said. —We were gettin' on great,
me and Trish. We always have. But, I can see why that
might seem like a ridiculous thing to say, and I agree
– it's fuckin' daft. But I'll tell you what happened. The

way the unconscious works or whatever – fuckin' hell. I decided I'd better put me shoes on. Before, you know, I told her – don't ask me why.

I started laughing.

—I know, he said. —I thought I'd have to escape – I don't know.

—Probably.

—Yeah – but I don't know. It made sense – if anythin' made fuckin' sense. But they were in under the coffee table. I'd taken them off earlier. We were watchin' –

—*The Affair.*

—No – fuck off. Somethin' else – I can't remember now. But, anyway, here goes, I said to myself. Get it out there. It was Friday, the kids were all out. And I started puttin' one of me fuckin' shoes on. Why are you doin' that? she asks. And d'you know what I said? I'm just goin' to put the bins out. It was the first thing I thought of – instead of what I'd actually been goin' to tell her. Puttin' the fuckin' bins out. It's Friday, she says. I'd put the bins out the night before. And I'm still puttin' my other shoe on. I should've stopped – I don't know – and waited for another time. But she was lookin' at me like she might be witnessing early-onset Alzheimer's or somethin'.

He was loving this. He was telling a different, much easier story.

—I should've taken the fuckin' things off – the shoes, like. But –. This is where the madness kicks in or somethin'. I actually told her. I decided to go ahead and tell her. To reassure her, nearly. That I wasn't losin' the marbles.

—You told Trish you were seeing another woman so she wouldn't think you had dementia?

—Basically, he said. —Yeah.

—How did you word it?

He ignored my question, or he seemed to.

—The shoes were fuckin' awkward, he said. —I'll tell you that.

He looked down at his feet – he stuck a foot out.

—These aren't the same ones, he said. —They were more like boots, the ones I was wearin'. It was a bit of a fight gettin' them on – especially the way we were sittin' – back on the couch, you know. And so, anyway, I was puttin' the other one on – doin' the lace – and I said, I met someone I used to know, by the way.

—Like that?

—Yeah.

—And?

—Hiroshima, Davy. Fuckin' Hiroshima. She was straight in there, no warnin'. I knew it! I fuckin' knew it! You fuckin' bastard!

He looked around, to make sure he wasn't being heard. He looked at me.

—I expected her to say, Who?, or somethin' like that. I don't know – ease my way into tellin' her. But she went straight to the end. D'you know what she said?

—What?

He'd lowered his voice.

—I knew you weren't ridin' me.

—Jesus, I said. —That's brilliant.

—It is in a way, he said. —Isn't it? Not accurate. But deep – or somethin'. Astute. Would we ever guess that?

—Men?

—Yeah, he said. —Would we? That our partner was thinkin' of another man while –

—Or a woman.

—Better yet. But a man – keep it simple. A different man. While she's with you.

—Would we notice – is that what you mean?

—Yeah. Or care. Anyway, I wasn't. Ridin' a different woman.

—But you were thinking of her.

—No, he said. —No. I wasn't.

The fun was out of his voice, suddenly. He was remembering: he had something he'd been trying to tell me.

—It wasn't about sex, he said. —Jessica.

—Really?

—Yeah. Really.

—Is that an age thing? I asked him.

—What?

—Well, I said. —If you'd met her, say, twenty years ago – even ten. Would it have made a difference?

—She's a beautiful woman.

—I don't doubt you, I said. —I didn't say different. Just to be clear. I'm not saying that you weren't all over her because her tits have sagged or she has a couple of chins that she didn't have before.

I didn't like talking this way – but I was enjoying myself, now that Joe wasn't.

—And so do we, by the way, I said. —We all age, is what I'm saying. The urge mightn't be there – or it's different. Or subtle. Not based on erections.

—Take it easy, Davy, for fuck sake.

—No, listen, I said. —You see a middle-aged woman. Almost elderly, really. Statistically. You meet her again after years apart. But – here's the thing. She's contemplating an elderly man – almost. You. Late middle-age – very late middle-age. It has to – I don't know – influence how we behave. Somehow. Doesn't it?

I was denying him the integrity of his story. But I wasn't. I was with him. Still with him. Trying to stay with him. For old times' sake.

121

—I don't think so, he said. —Not the way you mean.

—What do I mean?

—We get older, we slow down, he said. —I'm with you there. I agree with you. We calm down. We're less impetuous. Unless –. But, okay, I see what you mean. Two people – man, woman – both of them nearly sixty. There'd be a different pace. The energy levels are different – it's only natural. But.

—But?

—I don't want to be – well – salacious. I already have been, just there, I know. But that was what Trish said. I was only quoting her. But. Me and Trish made love every night, for weeks. Months – before I left. Nearly every night now. Twice a fuckin' night, occasionally. Now and again.

He'd lowered his voice again. I was leaning over to him again, to hear.

—I couldn't get enough of her, he said. —And she was the same – just as bad.

—She didn't know you were leaving. Presumably.

—You're missin' the point, Davy, he said. —I think you are. And, actually, I think she did know. She sensed it. That's what she was sayin', anyway. And I wouldn't be disagreein' with her. Although I hadn't made the decision. And I never did. She threw me out, basically.

—Did she?

—I couldn't stay, he said. —It was fuckin' unbearable. But she knew all the time – so she said. But that's a different story – kind of. The point is, the sex was never better. Old and all as I am – we are. She is. She'd kill me if she heard me but it was fuckin' incredible.

I could see it again: regret.

—So, you're right, he said. —But you're wrong.

—Go on, I said.

—Well, he said. —I think I'm too drunk now. I've lost me thread. Or somethin'.

—Not really, I said. —It's my fault. I've been interrupting you. Distracting you. Go on.

—Okay, he said. —But I am drunk – a bit. I'm out o' practice. You're the same, I'd say – you must be.

—A bit, I said.

—We should have gone into trainin', said Joe.

—Go on, anyway, I said.

—Where was I?

—Sex or the lack, I said. —Trish versus Jessica.

—Fuck off, Davy.

—Sorry, I said. —I'm only jogging your memory.

—Right, he said. —Like –. Okay. This sounds –. This is what I've wanted to say all night. But it feels too late. I've missed the opportunity.

—You haven't.

—All the talk about sex. It wrecks everythin'. Always has. Tryin' to do your exams – back in the day. And all you could think about was tits. D'you remember that?

—I don't need to, I said. —But we're falling into the trap again.

—The tits trap.

—There are worse traps.

—There are. But Jesus. There now – did Jesus think about tits?

—Definitely.

—Up on the cross?

—Especially up on the cross, I said. —He was looking out over the crowd. Scoping the talent. Your woman at the back looks pleasant.

—There we go again.

—Go on.

—Avoidin' the issue.

—Go on then.

—Yeah – okay. But I'm goin' to ask your man for a glass of water. I'm not used to drinkin' any more, Davy.

—Same here.

—We're up for the sex but down on the drink, he said. —Excuse me?

The place was still quiet; the barman heard him.

—Could you give us a glass of tap water, please? said Joe.

The barman nodded.

—No problem.

—And two more pints, said Joe.

He sat back.

—While he's at it.

He sat up again, put a hand on his back.

—So, he said.

He waited until the barman had brought him the water.

—Thanks very much.

The pints would be another few minutes.

—So.

He knocked back half the water. He placed the glass behind his pint glass.

—This is –. I have to be careful here, Davy. How I express it. I'm not bein' cagey or whatever. But first of all – goin' back to Trish an' that. She was wrong. There was never another woman in the bed with us.

—Okay.

—I don't know why I'm tellin' you all this, by the way. Maybe cos Trish wouldn't listen to me. You're Trish for the night, Davy. How does tha' feel?

—I'll get back to you, I said.

We laughed.

—You were puttin' your shoes on, I reminded him.

—I was goin' to tell you about the other thing, he said.

—What other thing?

—How I felt about Jessica.

—Finish the Trish story first.

—It's not a story, he said.

—Oh, it is, I said. —It definitely is.

—Well, it's a true one, he said. —She caught me on the hop, anyway. And that's puttin' it mildly. What was I doin', puttin' my fuckin' shoes on, though?

—You knew you were going to have to leave, I said.

—But I didn't.

—Didn't know?

—Didn't leave.

—Oh.

—Not then, he said.

—But she attacked you.

—Well, yeah, she did, he said. —I told you what she said – I knew you weren't riding me. An' God, Davy – I hadn't been anticipatin' anythin' like that. Like I said, she skipped loads of pages an' went straight to the fuckin' conclusion. An' I think now, actually –. I think puttin' the shoes on, continuin' that – it helped. It gave me somethin' to do, if that makes sense. Does it?

—Yeah.

—I could kind o' stay calm, he said. —Because I was doin' somethin' else. She was standin' up over me. She'd stood up – that was the problem. Part of it. And another thing went through my mind. The things we think of – Jesus. In moments o' crisis. We've a stove in the room, a gas stove. We got it put in, it must be fifteen years ago – longer. But I was thinkin', thank Christ we did. Because we'd the coal fire up to that, you know.

So there would've been the poker there an' the coal tongs and she'd have fuckin' skulled me with the poker.

—Has she hit you before? I asked him.

—Trish? No, never – no. But this was kind of exceptional, in fairness. An' the way she exploded –. But, like I said, I stayed calm. Not calm – numb. Numb's better. I stayed where I was – sittin', I mean. An' I kept putting the shoe on. What're you on about? I said. It was only someone I used to know. But she wasn't havin' it. No way. Who is she, she wanted to know. An' I said, Who said it was a woman? An' she definitely wasn't havin' that. Did I take her for a complete eejit? And I probably had. An' the only eejit in the room was me.

He stopped. I watched him, thinking. I said nothing – I made sure I said nothing.

—I'm fallin' for it again, he said.

—What?

—I'm pretendin' it's about me bein' caught doin' the dirty on me wife. But it isn't. But Trish, I suppose, thought I was, so I got dragged into tha' – that interpretation, I suppose. But tha' wasn't what I'd intended at all. But I was back-pedallin' from the outset, so to speak, an' I never got the chance to say what I'd wanted to say.

—What did you tell her, though? I asked.

—Oh, he said. —Just, she's a girl I used to know, ages back.

—That's true.

—But it's not, he said. —It's not true. She's not just anythin'. But I told Trish it was – she was; Jessica – before her time an' I'd hardly known her then either. I dismissed it – her. Jessica. But funnily –.

—What?

126

—Trish didn't.

—Wha'?

—Dismiss it, he said. —She wanted to know every-thin'. Her name. An' I was blessed there. I didn't know her name – her surname. It's true. An' I must've looked honest when I said I didn't, because I didn't. But then she grabbed my fuckin' phone.

—Oh, Christ.

—Exactly. But then I thought, it's not too bad because I didn't have Jessica's name in the phone book.

—George.

—There you go – you remember. But Trish is racing through my phone – the fingers, you know – the way women can do it. An' I don't stop her. I don't try to get it back. But I'm lookin' at her an' I'm thinkin' she's done this before, she's searched through my phone before. I mean, she knew my password already. And that's grand – I know hers. Do you know Faye's?

It took me a second to realise he'd asked me a question.

—Yeah, I said. —I do.

—I'd have thought so, he said. —It's the same with most couples is my bet. But the way Trish was doin' it, scrollin' through whatever she was scrollin' through. I knew she'd done it before. When I wasn't there. An' I knew I was fucked. She'd been ready for me all along. You phone this George item a lot, don't you? she says. An' she phones you as well, look it. And she phones her.

—Trish phoned Jessica?

—Yep.

—On your phone.

—Yep.

—Fuckin' hell, Joe.

—Go on, he said. —Laugh. Get it over with.

He was laughing before I was.

—Jesus, Joe.

—I know.

—Your two worlds collided.

—Oh, they did, he said.

—What happened?

—Well, he said. —She phoned her. An' she answered. Is that George? she says – Trish – an' she doesn't wait to hear wha' Jessica is goin' to say. Is that George the lezzer from Enid Blyton? she says. I couldn't believe it – I nearly laughed. But then she says, Stay away from my husband, bitch, I know where you live. An' fuckin' hell, I wondered if she did.

—She said it with conviction.

—She fuckin' did, man, he said. —Then Jessica must've been talkin', because all Trish did was go, Yeah, yeah, yeah, yeah – drownin' her out, you know. Just you mark my words, she said. Stay away from him or I'll improve your face for you. I'd never heard her talk like tha' before – so brutally, like. An' then she deleted the number. She held it up to show me she was doin' it – Look.

—What did you do?

—Nothin', he said. —I just sat there. But then she was scrollin' through my photographs. Do you take many photographs, Davy?

—Not really – no.

—Same here, he said. —I don't think many of us do, men our age. It doesn't come natural. So all she found, really, was pictures she'd sent me, herself. The kids, an' sometimes somethin' she was thinkin' of getting' an' she was askin' what I thought, d'you know the way?

—Yeah.

128

—Curtains or a fridge, or whatever.

Faye had once sent me a photo of a single Weetabix, and the message: Will I buy the pack? I'd been telling her earlier about the busy day I had ahead of me, before I went to work.

—At least you haven't been sendin' her pictures of your penis, said Joe.

—Trish said that?

—Yeah, he said. —An' that gave me a chance to speak. Why the fuck would I do somethin' like that? To give the girl a laugh, she says. The poor miserable bitch. She wasn't lookin' at me – she didn't look at me the whole time. She was like Carrie from *Homeland*, totally concentratin' on the phone. An' the way she spoke – it was like she knew Jessica. Like she'd met her an' didn't like her.

He was running out of steam. He'd finished telling the story he hadn't wanted to tell, the event that was – he thought – beside the point. Jessica definitely existed; I knew that now. Trish had made her more real than Joe had been able to manage.

—What happened then? I asked.

—Nothin'.

—Nothin'?

—Nothin' much, he said. —Then. But, yeah.

—Yeah what?

—We had sex again, he said. —Me an' Trish.

—But not that night.

—Says who?

—Really?

—No, he said. —Not tha' night. But listen, Davy. I was sayin' earlier. Like, this isn't about two women fightin' over me or anythin' like tha'. Or me havin' the midlife crisis or somethin'.

—Midlife?

—Late midlife, he said. —Fuck off. It isn't. When I saw Jessica, when I met her again. I thought – I felt. It felt like I'd been livin' two lives. That's it, really. I've been livin' two lives. There was my life – the family, Trish, the job an' tha'. The – I suppose – the official life. An' there was a shadow life I've been livin' as well – that I've only become aware of. Since, like. Since I met her. Because I didn't really meet her, Davy. I'd been with her all the time. Tha' was how it felt. What I've been tryin' to say. Honest to God. I wasn't cheatin'.

—What did she think about Trish calling her?

—She didn't mention it.

—Did you?

—No.

—Come here, I said. —Did you ever tell Trish?

—Wha'?

—About Jessica, I said. —Did you ever manage to tell her what happened?

—Not in one sittin', he said. —No. Not really.

There were no other customers at the bar when we got there, at half-three, immediately after the holy hour. George was lifting the window blind in the far corner.

—Gentlemen.

We sat at our end of the bar, and looked whenever we heard the doors – pushed open by shoulders and shopping bags but not by instrument cases. She didn't come in. And no one arrived with a violin or cello, an advance party from the college around the corner.

—D'you get many comin' in from the College of Music, George? I asked.

—Oh, we do, said George.

—Especially on a Saturday.

—Not especially, no, said George. —But when there's an orchestra around in the Gaiety, they'd come in, a lot of them, between the matinee and the evening performance on the Saturdays.

—With their instruments?

—No, no.

George laughed – he chuckled.

—You'd never get a piano through that door.

He rubbed his hands and walked down to meet two lads who'd just come in. One of them was carrying a record bag.

—Spandau Ballet is my guess, I said.

—Duran Duran, said Joe.

—Fuckin' dopes.

—She might be in the orchestra in the Gaiety, said Joe.

—In the pit.

—But listen, he said. —There's no way she's playin' in a panto. I'm not havin' it.

—There wouldn't be a cello in a panto, would there? I said. —An orchestra.

—No, said Joe. —Probably not.

I'd never been to a pantomime. I've been to quite a few since then. There were seven or eight years when our kids loved going to the panto at Christmas, the trip to the Wyvern Theatre in Swindon, the dinner before, ice-cream during the interval. Faye loved it too.

—Timmy Mallett, she said once.

We were just home, in bed, after going to *Aladdin*.

—You wouldn't know whether to bring him home or kill him, she said.

She sighed, and put her hand on my back.

—Kill him for me, David, she said.

—Is that an order?

—I think it is.

—Now?

—No rush, no. Just, before next Christmas.

—Opera, maybe, I said to Joe.

—That'd make more sense.

—I've never been to an opera, I said.

—Same here.

—Will we go?

—What's the point? said Joe. —The best part of it will be under the stage.

—Our girl.

—Sawin' away in the dark.

—It can't be dark, I said. —They'd have to be able to read the music. Wouldn't they?

—Would they not just know it off by heart, like the singers?

—Don't think so.

—Our bird would.

—I kind of like the idea of her readin' the music, I said. —And turnin' the page.

—Okay.

—Maybe even wearin' reading glasses.

—Ah, no, said Joe. —Fuck that.

—No?

—Well, maybe. Okay – black ones.

—No lenses.

—Cool.

—Would she be smiling as she plays? I asked.

—No, he said. —No. Geniuses don't smile.

—She's a genius?

—Definitely.

—She's mad then.

—Grand, said Joe. —But she's not drinkin' this after-noon, so she can't be that fuckin' mad.

There was a short period, a few minutes at about half-four, when there were no women at all in the room, just men.

—What's the story?

—Don't know.

—Maybe it's the future, said Joe.

—Wha'?

—A world withou' women.

—Bleak.

—Uncomplicated.

—Fuckin' bleak.

We could pretend that women complicated our lives. There was no one there to sneer.

We'd started our second pints when I realised something.

—I haven't eaten since Thursday.

—Serious?

—Yeah, I said. —No breakfast yesterday. An' no lunch. I forgot me sandwiches an' I went to buy the Joe Jackson album, an' I had to leg it back to work by the time I'd stopped talkin' to your man in the Sound Cellar. Then a few pints after work an' I fell asleep in front o' the gas fire at home. An' then we came straight into town. An' no fuckin' breakfast.

I didn't tell him about the girl from work, the girl who'd smiled at me earlier in the day, or how I'd stood beside her in the pub – Hartigan's – and hoped she'd talk to me, say something and then I'd be able to talk to her; how I'd left after seven pints, five pints after she'd left.

—You slept in front o' the gas?

—Till abou' two. I woke up sweatin' – Jesus. Wringin'.
Then –

—Did your da not wake yeh?

—He never goes into the front room if I'm in there.

I'd often seen him – the darkness made by his feet
– on the other side of the door. The feet would stay
there a minute, then go.

—Does he think you're with a bird or something?
Joe asked.

—Don't think so, I said. —But anyway, I'm fuckin'
starvin'.

We left.

—Back in a bit, George.

—Ah, now.

We went to the Coffee Inn on South Anne Street, for
spaghetti bolognese. Food always felt like a waste of
money. But I liked the place – packed with more of the
people I wanted to be. We had two pints in Kehoe's, two
in Neary's, two more in Sheehan's. It was a different part
of the day, a different life, when we got back to George's.

I was alone, outside. Joe had been with me, beside
me, on Chatham Street. Then there'd been no room
on the path. I'd gone out on the road, back onto the
path. I'd lost Joe, but hadn't noticed.

I stood outside. I looked in the window. The door
glass – both doors, both panes – was frosted, with a
clear, round section just below eye level, a porthole. I
had to bend slightly to look in.

She was in there, among the friends. I looked at the
men around her. If I'd had a marker, I could have
drawn on the window, followed their eyes, mapped
them, circled where their gazes intersected. On her face,
all of them on her face. And – somehow – on my face,
my eyes reflected in the glass watching her.

She scratched her neck. She pulled the neck of her jumper down, slightly. She scratched a point above her collarbone with just one finger, then patted the jumper back into place. She looked at no one in particular – no man or woman. She was alone. She didn't see the map.

Joe was beside me. Looking through the other porthole. Seeing what I saw. We stayed out there. For minutes.

—Does she still play the cello? I asked.

His answer surprised me.

—Yeah.

—Does she?

—Yeah, he said. —Every day.

All women were mad. Faye told me that. And I believed her.

The sun was bright outside; the curtains seemed to have disintegrated. My father was downstairs, in the kitchen. He was making no noise. I pictured him sitting at the kitchen table, tea and Saturday's *Independent* in front of him, looking at the door to the hall or at the ceiling. He was smiling, shaking his head.

We were in my old bedroom because we hadn't been able to stop a taxi the night before and the house had been nearer than our flat, and I wanted him – I didn't tell Faye this – to see her. I think now too: I wanted to provoke him. To be difficult. To amuse him. I wanted to give him something to tell other men, if he spoke to other men. Give him the chance to smile and raise his eyes to heaven.

—A lot of the men are too, she said.

—Mad?

—That's what I'm fuckin' talking about, David.

She slapped my chest.

—You should be bloody listening.

—I am.

—Yes, she said. —Mad. A fair few men are. But not necessarily in a good way. Almost never.

Faye was at her funniest, her most interesting, most entertaining, before sex and after sex. I don't think I ever correctly anticipated what she'd say. But when she spoke, when she started giving it the full Faye, I knew there was going to be sex. I wanted it and she wanted it.

—Mad men are bad men, she said.

—Am I mad?

—No, she said. —But I'm working on it. But not really. I like you kind of sane, so I do.

Women were mad.

She'd point them out. The hints, the clues – the eyes, the clothes. The walk, the hair, the gaze. There was madness in them and on them all.

—And you're mad, I said.

—I'm the fuckin' Queen of the madness, boy, she said. —Or I will be, by the time I've finished.

It was mascara, or a pair of tights, or dark eyes behind a curtain of hair. The attempts to stand out or fit in. Madness was the destiny of all women, she said, so it was best to claim it before it claimed you.

—My mother tried not to be mad, she said as we lay in bed in my old bedroom. —She tried so hard, she ended up being some kind of a man. She beat the men at their own game. When Daddy died, they thought my Uncle Jim would step in. Daddy's little brother, a real

136

Devereux, like. It was in the blood and all that fuckin'
nonsense. But Mammy wasn't having it. She'd always
thought the shop was a bit shite and she wanted to
give it a go. Make a proper place out of it. And she
did. Uncle Jim and the rest could all fuck off.

I was listening for sound from downstairs. I wanted
my father to know that I wasn't alone, that there was a
naked girl beside me. That I was fine. That I was happy.

—Cathy isn't mad, I said.

—Oh, she fuckin' well is, said Faye. —And I haven't
finished telling you about Mammy.

—Go on.

—The good's gone out of it now.

—Go on.

—Well, said Faye. —You know about ladies' men?

—Yeah, I said. —Kind of.

—You wish you were one.

—I don't.

—Liar, she said. —You're a big fuckin' liar. You do
so.

—Am I not one already?

—You'll do me, David, she said. —Mammy became
a man's lady.

I'd no idea what my mother had been like, if men
had liked her or if she'd enjoyed the company of men.
I had nothing to help me. Just her with me. I couldn't
recall her out in the world.

—What d'you mean? I asked Faye.

—She was one of the lads, she said. —She really
took to it. And they let her – they loved it. She drank
with them, she went to the race meetings. She'd have
seduced their wives if she could've. And maybe she did
once or twice, I don't know. When I was out at school.
But no, not really – I don't think that. That wouldn't

have been on. So, she seduced the lads instead. And she lost it, somewhere.

—Lost what?

—The sanity.

—Oh.

—But, said Faye. —When was the last time you changed these sheets, by the way?

—Well, I don't live here.

—Ah, Jesus, she said. —It could be years.

—No, I said. —I don't think so – I don't know. A few months.

—They look worse.

—I slept here at Christmas.

—Fuckin' Christmas? That's nearly a year ago – Jesus. She slapped the bedclothes.

—Fuckin' dust, she said. —My God. But there's no girl smell off them anyway. So there's that, at least. You're the lady's man elsewhere, David, but not in this *leaba*. But Mammy. There was a time, a point, when she was happy mad.

—What's happy mad?

—In control of her own madness. She decided, I'll ride him – for the crack. Before he decides he's been riding me.

—Are you serious?

—I am, David.

—How d'you know this?

—I'm an observant lassie, so I am. And there was only the two of us in the house. After he died – Daddy. And she was happy.

—Because he died?

—No, she said. —Not really that. She cried a lot – I remember that. I'd hear her just before I'd walk into the kitchen or something. And she'd stop when she saw me.

She'd wipe her eyes, and smile, call herself an eejit. She was fuckin' devastated. I'm pretty sure she loved him.

—I never heard my father cry, when my mother died.

—Ah, sure, that's only natural, she said. —I could never like a blubbery man.

—I'll remember that.

—You'd better.

—I will.

—And it doesn't mean he didn't, she said.

—I don't think he did.

—Nevertheless. Mammy tried to hide it – kind of. Your dad might have succeeded.

—Okay.

—Anyway, I think it caught up with her or something, she said. —And she died, God love her.

—Was it not cancer?

—That's just the official version, she said. —She thought she was beating them at their own game – the lads. The best of Wexford's economic fuckin' wonders. But really, all she was doing was riding. It disappointed her, David. And then some.

She sat up.

—Let's go meet him, so.

She dropped off the end of the bed and found my jumper on the floor.

—Will he like me? she asked.

I watched her pull the jumper over her head.

—I like your stink, David, she said. —It's nice and manly.

—Thanks.

—Now get up, she said.

—He'll love you, I said.

*   *   *

—Is she any good? I asked Joe.

—I think so, he said. —Yeah, she is. It's one of those instruments though, isn't it?

—What?

—The cello, he said. —It's hard to tell if it's bein' played well or not.

—Is it?

—When it's alone, he said. —By itself. No violins or flutes or whatever.

—Is that right?

—Ah, yeah, he said. —Definitely. Like a bass guitar or somethin'. At a gig. Did you ever enjoy a bass solo?

—No.

—Same here. If he's good, grand. Just don't play a fuckin' solo to prove it.

—I'm that way with guitar solos too now, I said.

I hadn't been to a gig in years. I'd suggested to Róisín that we go to Arcade Fire together, in London, a few years ago. She didn't even laugh at me. Although she let me buy two tickets, for herself and a friend of hers who I never met.

—Fuckin' unbearable, said Joe. —Are solos even a thing any more?

—Good question.

—An' we don't know the answer, he said. —Which, in itself now, is a fuckin' answer.

The pints had arrived. I'd paid for them and the barman had gone back to his hiding place. The stools on either side of us were empty. We were still alone.

—But it sounds like music, he said. —When she plays. It's good. Not bad at all.

—I interrupted you, I said.

—Yeah, he said. —Again.

—Sorry.

—I don't blame you, he said. —It must seem a bit bizarre. What I'm tellin' you. I can hear tha' – I understand it.

—Did you tell Trish?

—Tell her wha'?

—What you just said. About livin' a shadow life.

—Well, I did, he said. —Or I tried to. But – not the night I was tellin' you about.

He picked up his new pint.

—She said somethin' about my shadow cock an' where it had been all these years.

I laughed.

—Fair enough, I said.

—I suppose so, he said. —I don't know if I want this pint.

I picked up my own.

—Has to be done, I said, although I didn't want mine either.

I tapped his glass with mine.

—The shadow life.

—Don't get fuckin' nasty, he said.

—I'm not.

—Okay.

—Sorry, I said. —Go on.

—Will we go in to George's after these?

—No, I said. —We won't. Tell me – go on.

—Right, he said. —Okay.

He brought his pint closer to him. He looked at it.

—Like, I felt that way when I saw her in the school – Jessica. The time when I saw her comin' down the corridor. I wasn't surprised – like there'd been no gap, no years in between. An' listen, I'm not addin' a gloss to it, significance or somethin', after the fact. But I know as well. It happens. It's happened to me.

—Me too.

—The head playin' tricks. The light in a room, or somethin'.

—Or a piece of music.

—Sometimes, yeah – I don't know, though. I don't mean nostalgia. Or the other one. Déjà vu.

—I know what you mean – go on. It's like wakin' up – a bit. As if your real livin' has been the dream.

—That's it, he said. —To an extent. But I'd some-times feel tha' way if I was at a meetin' an' I'd only been half listenin' to what was goin' on.

—That's my normal state, I lied.

—Yeah, he said. —Yeah. But this wasn't daydreamin' or dozin' off.

—I know.

—It was much –. It wasn't that at all.

—I remember once, I said. —We were away for a week, me and Faye. About five years ago. Portugal. Just the two of us. In Lisbon.

—Nice.

—It was. But I woke up and the light – at the edge of the curtains, around the edges. It wasn't that I knew I was somewhere different – the hotel room. I actually thought that it was my bedroom – that I always woke up to this light.

—Yeah –

—Hang on. When I turned in the bed, I didn't expect to see Faye. Faye was a shock. For a second – just a split second. I didn't know who she was. My real wife wasn't there. It felt like somethin' was pulled out o' me.

I heard it: my accent was changing, reverting. I was becoming the Dublin boy I'd been when we'd first seen Jessica. And so was Joe; he was well ahead of me. The drink was letting us pretend. The drink was making it easy, and honest.

—Did you know your real wife? Joe asked. —If you know what I mean. In the dream.

—No, I said. —No, I didn't. I wouldn't go tha' far. But it lingered – for days. I even resented Faye. Although I knew tha' was daft. I'm not sayin' the experience is the same as yours, by the way. But there are similarities. Aren't there?

—Absolutely, he said.

I had him going again. He wanted to shove both of my wives out of the way. He wanted to hear himself telling me his story.

—But I didn't reject Trish, he said.

—I didn't reject Faye, I told him.

—You forgot about her.

—Only because I was half asleep, and only for a couple o' seconds.

—I didn't forget Trish.

—Good man, I said. —Look, Joe – for fuck sake.

—I know, he said.

He grinned – gave me the old Joe.

—What're we fuckin' like? he said.

—It's the drink, I said. —Makes us fuzzy.

—It always did.

—We were better at it, though – back then.

—That applies to everythin', but – doesn't it?

—Except cookin'.

—Exactly, he said. —The shite tha' doesn't matter. D'you cook?

—A bit, yeah.

—Same here. It's messin', really, but, isn't it? Playin'.

—An excuse to drink.

—That as well, yeah.

An excuse to turn my back and hide, I could have said. An excuse to avoid talking.

—Go on, I said. —We'll be thrown out before you're finished.

—Right, he said. —So – anyway. I dismissed it. The feelin'. I kind o' did. I kept sayin' to myself, she's just a great-lookin' girl from your past – cop on. A well-preserved woman, as they say. We liked them, even when we were kids.

—True.

—D'you remember Missis Early?

—She was probably only thirty.

—Forty.

—A kid.

—Okay. But anyway, I kind of insisted tha' that was it. Tha' was what I was up to. Messin', really. The bit of excitement. I have the number but I won't be phonin' her, but I can if I want. An' it worked.

—Wha' d'you mean?

—Well – Trish. Jesus. I won't be salacious, Davy. But I was rock fuckin' hard. An' Trish –

—Can I stop you there? I said.

—Wha'?

He looked like a man who'd been delivering a very good TED Talk.

—Did you not do it, swap phone numbers and meet her, just to add spice to your life? That's what I'm hearin'.

—I thought so, he said. —That's what I'm tryin' to say. At the start I did. I was open to tha' theory.

—It wasn't conscious, no?

—Well, okay, yeah – it was. It *was* my fuckin' theory. To an extent. But I wasn't just actin' the bollix. I wasn't actin' the bollix at all.

144

—But it was workin' out well.

—Ah, man, he said. —D'you remember what it was like, when you'd fall for a girl. Like, after the first time you'd been with her. After the sex, I mean. The feelin' – how full you'd feel.

—Spunk eyes, we called it.

—I know, yeah – I remember.

He laughed.

—Spunk eyes, he said, and laughed again. —A head full o' spunk. But it was like tha'. Like there was milk behind your eyes. You'd drift through the day with an erection an' a sponge for a brain.

—Overwhelmed.

—Fuckin' literally. You couldn't think of anythin' except the woman. The smell of her – Jesus. Everythin'. You didn't even count the hours till the next time – it was too fuckin' mathematical. You were too stupid. There was just – yeh know, like. The cunt.

—Okay.

—It's funny how we use tha' word so casually these days, isn't it?

—I don't like it.

—Same here, he said. —But anyway, that's where I was. With Trish. Back in my glory days. I was in love with me wife, for fuck sake.

—Gas.

—Well –. It was brilliant. But it's exhaustin', man, I'll tell you that for nothin'. We were neglectin' the kids.

He thought about what he'd said – I saw him – and he burst out laughing.

—Jesus –.

He slapped my shoulder. It was a new one, a gesture – an act – that wasn't his. Or, it hadn't been.

The barman was looking across at us.

—Anyway, said Joe. —Back on track. Tha' was the drink talkin' again.

He took a breath, held it, let it go.

—But, he said. —I believed in it. The feelin'. I expected somethin' to happen.

—Wha'?

—I didn't know, he said. —Somethin'. I wasn't actin' the maggot – is what I'm sayin'. But, all the same, I felt I was cheatin'. When I was makin' love to Trish.

—Cheatin' on who?

—Trish, he said. —Jessica. Me, even.

—It didn't stop you, though.

—No, he said. —No, it didn't. I thought –. I think I thought. It was becomin' the new normal – or somethin'.

He wasn't smiling. He wasn't a rogue.

—I wish I'd agreed with Trish, he said.

—What d'you mean?

—When she said she knew I was ridin' someone else, he said. —I mean, it wasn't true. Wha' she said – it wasn't. But I wish I'd been brave. I denied every-thin'. An' here I am. If I hadn't denied it, where would I be?

—D'you know?

—No, he said. —But I shut the door too quickly.

—D'you think Trish wanted another woman in the bed?

—It's not about beds.

—I'm lost, so, I said.

I sounded like Róisín pretending to be Irish.

—What is it abou'?

—I don't know, he said. —Souls?

—Ah, for fuck sake.

146

He stepped down off his stool.

—I've to go to the jacks, he said. —Back in a minute. Stay there, Davy.

—Your bladder's the same age as the rest of you, at least.

—Fuck off.

He smiled at Faye – I thought he was smiling at her.

—I've heard all about you, he said.

He hadn't. I'd said nothing to him. I know now: he hadn't needed to hear anything. He'd have seen me, gazing at nothing, the times I'd been to see him. Looking at my watch, dying to get away.

I'd never been upstairs – in my childhood bedroom – with Cathy. I'd brought her home to meet him but we'd never sneaked in, shoes off, half pissed and giggling. I'd liked Cathy but I'd never had what Joe and myself called the spunk eyes. I'd gone through none of the time in a white daze. She'd needed a boyfriend and I'd do her. I thought that then – I think I did – and it had suited me too. I'd have married her; we'd been well on our way to saying something about it when I sat beside Faye at that wedding.

Faye said I'd do her too. But it was different. She'd actually said it, like no one else could – the crease at the left side of her mouth, the half shut left eye. Faye wanted me. When I was inside her, I knew it was me she wanted inside her. It was me on top of her. It was me she was pulling to her. It was never her face, her shape, an ankle, a hand. It was Faye.

—Nice to meet you, Mister Walsh, she said.

All she was wearing was my jumper.

147

Cathy had offered to put on the kettle. They'd spoken about their counties – she was from south Wexford, my father was from Waterford – and the people, the families, the farms, they might both have known. He'd said more to Cathy than he ever said to me. He'd chatted to her, with her. I'd watched him respond to the presence, and the attention, of a woman. I was getting to know him. I was making him happy.

—Was Cathy a lesbian? he asked me, a few years ago.

—Cathy?

—The girl you went out with that time, he said. —I've often wondered.

—No, I said. —Not as far as I know.

—I wondered, he said.

—Back then?

—No, he said. —No, no. The thought wouldn't have occurred to me back then.

—Same here, I said.

—Did you ever think it, yourself?

—No, I said. —No. I didn't.

—Would you think it now? he asked.

—Why would I?

—Well, he said. —With what we know now. And the same-sex marriage referendum and all that. And she was a *Bean* Garda too, remember. So, there's that as well.

—I don't think she was gay, I said.

—Right.

—I don't think wearing a uniform indicates you're gay – if you're a woman.

—Back then, though.

—I don't think so.

—Well, I liked her, anyway.

—So did I.

—Do you ever hear from her?

—No.

—I liked her.

—Yeah.

He sat up when he met Faye. That was the big thing. He sat up.

No – he stood up. My father stood when Faye stood in front of him in my blue jumper, at the opposite side of the kitchen table. He walked around to shake her hand.

—It's very nice to meet you too, he said. —I've heard all about you.

He turned, walked back around the table, and sat. He looked at Faye, the nineteen-year-old girl standing in his kitchen – my mother's kitchen. I thought his face was melting. It was shifting, sliding – something was happening to it. I thought he was going to do what I'd just told Faye I'd never seen him do: cry.

But that stopped.

He sat up. My father was a man and there was a woman in the room. He sat up – and I knew my father like I hadn't known him before. I could imagine him now with my mother – holding her, being with her, kissing the back of her neck. I saw what he'd lost and I loved him.

Then something happened. The man fell from his face – the admiration, the longing. He looked at me. He stared, then looked away. He pretended to read the paper. He waited for us to leave.

—You're crap at this, Joe, I told him.

He was back from the toilet, back beside me.

—Crap at wha'?

—Explainin' yourself.

—I'm not, he said. —Fuck off. Seriously, though –. Davy –.

He looked at his pint.

—I don't want this, he said.

I picked up mine. I drank, took an inch off it.

—I haven't been fair to Trish, he said.

—You left her.

—That's not the point, he said. —Fuck off. Although it is.

—Wha'?

He picked up his pint.

—Despite her anger, he said. —Whatever. I was the one tha' made the move. Left, you know. She didn't tell me to. But anyway –.

—Wha'?

—It's the salacious thing again, he said. —I've been makin' a bit of a joke of her, haven't I?

—I don't know, I said. —I don't think so.

—I have, he said. —Yeah, I have. It's not good. I love Trish.

—Okay.

—I do, he said. —Tha' doesn't stop. I tried to tell her.

—Did she listen?

He didn't answer. He didn't need to. He knocked back more of his pint than I thought he would.

—But when I met up with Jessica, he said.

—The first time?

—First, second, all the times. I knew this was my life. I felt at home.

—So you said.

—Literally, he said. —At home.

—Where were you?

—I told you, he said. —It doesn't matter. It was bein' with her. I was at home. Finally, Davy.

—Finally, Joe?

—Finally. Yeah – finally. I'm tellin' you how I felt. I know it sounds feeble – I can't do anythin' about tha'.

—What about your other home?

—Look, he said. —I'm just tellin' you what it felt like. It's not – I don't know – it's not a chessboard. Or Monopoly. Houses an' property. An' it's not logical, I know – believe me, I know. Or maybe even sane. But it's how I felt.

—What's home? I asked him.

—Wha'?

—What d'you mean by it? I asked. —Me – it's the house. Faye and the kids. The house and the people in it. And the years we've been in it. The whole history. My father's house – it's not home. Not now, any more. I hate bein' there.

That was true. I hated sleeping in that house. I hated waking up in it, knowing where I was. It was always a shock.

—It's a big word – home, I said.

—Yeah.

—So, wha' d'you mean by it?

—Well, it's hard, he said. —If we'd been here a year ago –

—Exactly a year ago.

—That's right, yeah. A year. If it was a year an' a day ago, then. I'd be agreein' with you. Every word. Trish an' the kids, in the house. Tha' was home.

—Not now?

He didn't answer. He took his phone from his pocket, looked at it, put it back in his pocket.

—No, he said. —I wish –. But I don't know.

I took my own phone out and looked at it.

Nothing.

—I don't know, he said now. —I used to think tha' was good.

—What was?

—Sayin' I don't know, he said. —I used to think it was a sign o' somethin'. Maturity. An' equality. Trish said it once. After one o' the kids asked me somethin' an' I said it. I don't know, I mean. She said, A man admits he doesn't know. We laughed. I thought it was great. Liberatin' or somethin'. An' it was. In work as well. Because I've been there so long. It doesn't really matter what I say, I'll do the job anyway. I said it at a meetin' once. Lads, never be afraid to admit you don't know. Their faces – Jesus.

—I can imagine.

—Trish said I was overdoin' it, he said. —Like I was claimin' it as a philosophy or somethin'. Some lifestyle bullshit. An' I was – in a way. But she said the kids were startin' to think I was just thick. An' a proper dad should be a cranky know-all. But, anyway. Now, it kills me.

—Does it?

—No, he said.

He rolled down one of his shirt sleeves.

—If I'm being honest, he said. —No.

—Drink talkin'.

—No.

He buttoned the sleeve.

—It's what I'd wish for, he said. —I think. Between ourselves – I wish I could feel tha', that it kills me, not feelin' tha' the house – Trish an' tha' – is home. But it doesn't kill me. So –.

He pulled down the other sleeve.

—So, there yeh go.

—Okay.

—It's not, though. Okay. Is it?

—No.

—No, it's not. Somehow. I don't know, Davy. Tha' part of it.

—Wha' d'you mean?

—The family, he said. —They just –. Look –. They don't seem there now.

—Joe.

—Wha'?

—Have you any idea how many men I know who've left their wives for other women? Men our age. An' you know them too – men who've done wha' you've done. We could spend the night countin' them.

He hadn't buttoned the second sleeve. It almost slapped him as he lifted his pint. He put the glass down and buttoned the sleeve.

—Younger women, he said. —For younger women.

—No, I said. —Not always.

—Jessica's older than Trish.

—So wha'?

—You're not listenin' to me, Davy. You haven't been listenin'.

—An' you're bein' a pain in the arse, Joe.

—You're soundin' like Trish now.

—Fuck off, I said. —I've been listenin' to every fuckin' word. You walked out on your wife an' kids an' you're calling it a philosophy.

The barman was looking at us. He stayed where he was but he stared at us. I didn't stare back.

—Are we bein' loud? Joe asked.

—Don't know, I said. —I didn't think we were.

—Fuckin' prick, said Joe. —The head on him. Wha' time is it?

—Half-eight, I said.

It was good, saying that – 'half-eight'. It always made more sense than 'eight-thirty'.

—What're we doin'? he said.

—Don't know.

—I don't know why I'm doin' up my fuckin' sleeves, he said. —Habit. Are we havin' another one?

—I suppose so.

—Or a short, maybe – instead.

—No.

—No, you're right. Madness. Whose round is it?

—Don't know. I don't –. Actually, I don't want a drink. I've had enough.

—One more, he said. —It's my twist. An' I need to finish this.

—Finish wha'?

—You were there at the beginnin', he said.

—I wasn't, I said.

—You were, he said. —In George's. Back then.

—No, I said. —I wasn't. You're makin' this up. You're on your own.

—What d'you mean I'm makin' it up?

—Just that, I said. —You are.

—What d'you mean, though? he said.

—Well, look, I said. —Wha' you say you remember an' what I know I remember don't tally.

I felt like I'd slammed a door on my own hand.

—You know you remember?

—Yep.

—You fuckin' *know* you remember? Are we havin' tha' pint?

—Go on – yeah.

—I'll pour the fuckin' thing over you, he said.

—Excuse me?

I was in his way. He lifted himself off the stool and leaned over the counter, so the barman would get a clear view of him.

—Two pints, please.

I watched the barman nod.

—Thank you.

Joe sat back down.

—Fuckin' Noddy, he said. —Did you see him?

I knew what he was doing. He'd become Joe again – the man I used to know – so he could have another go at me. The new version was lurking there behind him.

—Right, he said. —What d'you remember?

—It's what I don't remember, I said.

—What's tha'?

—I don't remember you gettin' off with her.

He closed his eyes, and opened them.

—Okay, he said. —I did.

—Okay.

He looked at me. My eyes slid.

—Okay, he said. —Look. Let's agree on somethin'. I've a suggestion. Davy?

—Yeah, I said. —Go on.

—Okay. I'll accept you don't remember an' you can accept you don't remember, an' tha' way we'll both accept that it happened –

—What happened?

—For fuck sake, he said. —I remember her better than you do. That's reasonable, isn't it?

—Okay.

—It's human, isn't it? he said. —We remember things differently. I've siblings –.

—Yeah.

—An' we never agree on anythin' tha' happened more than thirty years ago – or even last month. An' we grew up in the same house. It's only a matter o' time, we'll be arguing about who our parents were. We won't be able to agree on even tha'. So –.

The barman delivered the pints.

—Two good ones, he said.

—Good man, I said.

I took money from my pocket and found him a tenner.

—Thanks very much.

He went and left us alone. I saw him put the change into a poor box at the taps.

—So, said Joe.

—Was it even my round? I asked.

—I'm not sure, said Joe. —It might be.

—I don't even want it.

—Same here, he said. —But it has to be done. Are we not men?

—We are Devo.

—Fuckin' sure, he said. —So, anyway. I remember what I remember an' you don't remember what I remember. Because you weren't fuckin' there. On tha' particular occasion. But wha' I'm suggestin' is, we bypass that an' continue.

—Okay, I said. —Right.

I'd listen and leave. I knew the man I was listening to and in a minute I wouldn't. It didn't matter. I'd have to be going.

—I'll keep on track, he said. —No distractions. She spoke to me –

—When're we talkin' about?

—Wha'?

—When did she speak to you? I said. —Recently or –?

—Recently, he said. —Yeah, no – I mean last year. When I started meetin' her again.

—Okay, I said. —Sorry – go on.

—I felt it immediately. Like I said. That I'd known her all the time.

—Okay.

—That the first time was actually the five hundredth or whatever the number would be. Before tha' – this is true, I'll admit this. It was the gap in the years an' the fact that I hadn't thought about her – although that's not strictly true either. I often thought about her. But it was the sudden arrival of – I don't know – the possibility. The novelty. I'm not sure if it was sex, Davy. The reality o' tha'. I don't know if I'd have gone tha' far. It was more the fantasy. The thinkin' about it, the anticipation. An' there must be a scent. A fuckin' vibe – energy or somethin'. Because Trish an' meself –. We won't go there again.

—No.

—Grand. So. I go an' I meet her. You know already. An' I feel it. We're already together.

Again, I wanted to hit him. Again, I wanted to go. But I wanted the story; I wanted to hear much more.

—Was it deflatin'? I asked him.

—How d'you mean? he said.

—Well, I said. —You were half hopin' for some sort o' sexual liaison. Sorry – that's crap. But you know what I mean. You said novelty there. An' you said well-preserved earlier.

—Was tha' not you?

—No. You.

—Okay.

—Maybe both of us.

—Right – go on.

—Tha' was wha' was on your mind, I said. —A fling with a woman tha' used to be the girl of your dreams. But then you sit down with her an' it's like the two o' you are in your slippers an' dressin' gowns an' there's nothin' goin' on at all.

—It wasn't like tha'.

—Was it deflatin'?

—No.

—No?

—It was different.

—Okay. And unexpected?

—Very.

—An' deflatin'.

—Fuck off.

—It must've been, I said. —For fuck sake. Or maybe it was a relief, was it?

—Well, there you go, he said. —Tha' might be nearer the truth.

—Is it?

—Jesus, Davy, when did you join the fuckin' FBI?

—Was it a relief? Go on.

—It might've been.

—You could still go home an' ride Trish.

—What's your fuckin' problem? he said. —Hang on, but, I know what it is. I forgot there for a bit. You fancied her as well.

—Trish?

—Stop bein' such a spa, Davy, he said. —Jessica.

—Whose name I didn't know until a few hours ago. It's a long time since anyone called me a spa.

—Well, you are a fuckin' spa.

—You can't say that any more.

—I know.

158

—It was a relief – you said.

—*You* did.

—You agreed with me.

—Okay, he said. —It was. A bit. I'm not sure. Because it stopped bein' abou' tha'. Abou' me meetin' up with a woman I hardly knew. The effort involved.

He surprised me now.

—Did anythin' like this ever happen to you?

—No.

—Really?

—No. You asked already.

—Did I?

—I think so, yeah.

—Okay, he said. —Seriously, though, Davy – there was never another woman?

—Not really, no.

—Not even a deflatin' one?

I didn't answer. It wasn't really a question. Joe lifted his pint. He knocked back a good bit, two swallows, three. He put the glass back down on the beermat.

—But anyway, he said. —Somethin' happened to me.

There was a Saturday, one of the last Saturdays, maybe the last. She was there, with her friends and the cello case. She was sitting under the window when we came in. I walked straight into Joe's back. He'd seen her first. But I'd recovered in time to see her look our way and smile.

And smile.

—Hi, guys, she said.

Guy wasn't the word it is now. Every waitress and lounge girl will address a group of two or more men as guys, no matter their age, the lounge girl and the

159

men. But not back then. We weren't guys; there were no guys. We were young lads, boys, men. But only men in American films were guys.

But we were guys now too, apparently. Although speechless guys – we were in a silent film.

I eventually managed a word.

—Hi.

It was me who said it, not Joe. I was the first guy to speak to her. I know that. I knew it then, and I thought I knew its significance. I was the first to respond, so she must have been talking to me.

We kept on going. I followed Joe, down to our end of the bar.

I was the one who had spoken. Mine was the only voice. I knew it then, at that exact time, and it thrilled me.

It seems pathetic. But it's not – not as I understand the word. We were children when we were together. I was a functioning adult most of the time – all week. But something happened when we were together; joy rushed in and drowned us. Before I met Faye, I experienced happiness only when I was with Joe. I think that's true. Happiness that could be trusted. Happiness that, somehow, I could measure, feel; it was a thing in my chest. When I was with Joe.

I liked being a boy. I loved being a boy. The rush of it, the rib-breaking ache of it. I'm not sure that I'd ever been one before. I couldn't be happy at home. I can't feel it now; I can't construct it. Because it wasn't there. I remember once, when I was twelve or thirteen, watching *Coronation Street* and one of the characters – I can't remember which; a woman – she said to another woman, 'You'll have to fend for yourself.' I knew exactly what she meant.

160

I said Hi to the girl I know was called Jessica. And I knew: it might be the end of happiness. And it might be the start of something new. A different kind of happiness. An adventure. A night. A life.

And I ran.

I took a look at her. She wasn't looking our way. She was listening to one of her friends. She was devoting herself to whatever her friend – another woman; I've no other memory of her – was saying. I could hear words but I couldn't catch meaning; I didn't try to. She wasn't waiting for us. I was disappointed, and relieved. I was safe.

I was shy but I wasn't crippled. I'd stepped up to women and slept with them hours later. I'd met looks and I'd managed to hold them when I'd wanted to, when I'd thought I had to. When I'd trusted my judgement, when I knew – when I thought I knew – I was reading the look correctly. I was surprised if a woman smiled at me, but never shocked. I was shy, but not of women.

I don't know about Joe. I don't know why he didn't say anything to Jessica that time, why I was allowed to be our spokesman. We'd had a few pints on our journey across town to George's. We'd been running, pretending to rush, to get out of the rain. He'd hit the door first. I'd had to negotiate a puddle, hop over the thing – I don't remember. He got there first and was inside before me. He saw her first. But I spoke.

Why devote the space to this? It was the only time I spoke to her. And I was the one who spoke.

—So tell us, said Faye once, after we were married. —What do you find desirable in a woman?

—Words, I said.

I didn't hesitate. I didn't think. I felt I'd had the answer ready, just waiting for the question.

Faye pretended to unblock an ear with one of her little fingers.

—Excuse me? she said. —What?

—Words, I said.

She was pregnant, six or seven months. We were sitting in our new house. I was just in, from my new job. There was no food. The smell of fresh paint would always be the smell of our happiness.

Faye thumped my arm.

—You'd prefer to ride a dictionary than a woman, she said. —Is that what you're telling me now, David?

—I'd prefer to ride a woman who could say I'd prefer to ride a dictionary, I said.

—A big mouth?

—A clever dick.

—She'd have to be a dickess, so she would.

—A clever dickess, then.

—Am I one?

—Yeah.

—Well, I'm lost for fuckin' words, she said.

We were in England. Away from Gorey and her house. Away from Dublin. Away from the ghost of her dead mother and from the ghost of my living father. We were fresh paint. There'd been nothing here – no one here – before us.

—I'm not sure that I approve, said my father.

He'd never said anything like that to me before. It was a few weeks after he'd met Faye. I'd just told him we were getting married.

I was ready for the fight. I knew – I know it now:
I'd been expecting it. It was just the two of us in the
kitchen – his kitchen. It wasn't my home. It wasn't my
country. I wanted to be pushed out. And so did Faye.
We both wanted the shove.

—Approve of what? I said.

He hadn't been looking at me.

He looked now.

—I'm sure she's a nice girl, he said.

—She is, I said.

—I don't doubt you, he said.

—You do doubt me.

He picked up the kettle. I wanted to dash across and
grab it from him. I wanted to open the back door and
fuck the thing out into the garden.

—I haven't been a very good father, he said.

He'd raised his voice, almost to a shout, so he'd be
heard over the roar of the water rushing into the
kettle.

—I wouldn't say that, I told him.

He'd turned off the tap.

—I would, he said.

He was putting a match to the gas. He was an old
man at the cooker. His thin hair was standing, lit by
the sun coming through the window beside him. I
couldn't see his face but, the way he stood, he was
reminding himself, trying to remember why he was
standing there. I wanted to hold him.

I heard the gas. I watched him waiting, not trusting
the flame. He didn't want to turn, to face me. He was
looking for something else he needed to do. All this
was seconds, not minutes.

He turned.

—I mightn't have the right, he said. —But I'll say it anyway. I think you should be careful.

—Careful?

—Yes.

—Fuckin' careful?

—David.

—Sorry. Careful, though? What d'you mean?

—She's very young.

—So?

He shrugged. He smiled.

—Right, he said. —Before you say it. Yes, your mother was younger than me.

—Six years.

—Yes.

He wasn't smiling now.

—She's wild, he said. —Your lassie.

—Faye.

—She was half naked.

—We'd been upstairs.

—I don't want to interfere, he said. —I can see why you –. She was attractive.

—She still is.

—You were introducing her to me and she wore – what was it? – one of your jumpers. I could see her *hair*. For God's sake, David. I'm your father and she was displaying herself. Here! And you, son – you let her. In case you hadn't noticed, David, we're not the bloody Borgias.

The kettle was starting to hiss.

—And it's not that, he said. —If you want to bring a girl upstairs – even though you don't actually live here, let me remind you. But I have no problem with that. I bloody envy you. One-night stands – whatever you call them. They're none of my business and good

164

luck to you. She's a lovely-looking lassie. But I can see, you're serious.

He looked at the kettle, and the steam that was taking over the room.

—Aren't you? he said.

He grabbed a tea towel and lifted the kettle off the hob.

—Is she pregnant? he said.

He'd always been a gentle man. Too gentle, I often thought – gentleness as a type of absence. But he'd never been brutal, or crude.

Faye *was* pregnant.

—No, I said. —She isn't.

If I could relive that evening, I'd do several things differently and I'd say different things.

I'd tell him she was pregnant.

I'd say nothing and walk out of the house.

I'd go home to the flat I'd started sharing with Faye but I wouldn't tell her what my father had said.

I'd go home and tell Faye *all* that he'd said.

I'd stay with my father and ask him why he'd asked if Faye was pregnant, instead of saying Good man or I'm delighted. I'd try to know him. I'd ask him why, so long after my mother had died, he'd finally lashed out. I'd ask him why he was pushing me away.

Faye laughed when I told her.

—Why did you tell him at all? she said.

—I don't know. I just wanted to.

—Without me there?

—I thought he'd be happy.

—That fella? she said. —He doesn't want to be happy. And come here.

She put her arms around me. Faye's a tall woman, as tall as I am, and she looked straight into my eyes.

Faye did that: she was able to hold a gaze – she always won the staring matches.

—Your daddy's misery is none of your business, she said. —And you'll be getting plenty of misery from me. Does it give you the horn?

—Yes, it does.

My father looked at me.

—I wouldn't mind if she was, he said. —Pregnant.

—She isn't, I said.

—Grand, he said. —It must be love, so, is it?

He turned, and took two mugs from the shelf beside the cooker.

—Your mother would be very happy, he said.

—Would she?

—She'd have loved Faye.

I don't know why I didn't tell Faye that my mother would have loved her. I didn't feel it, I didn't know it. But he'd said it to be kind and I never told Faye. I left it out, deleted it, told her half of what had happened. She'd have loved Faye. Maybe that was why he didn't – couldn't – love her. She was too like my mother. But I don't know that either.

We make up our own stories.

—We'll have the baby in England, said Faye that night. —Will we?

—Yeah.

We'd been going, anyway. Faye talked about distance – from Gorey, from family, from expectations and inspections. I'd never thought about leaving. Until Faye said she wanted to wake up some day in air that wasn't Irish. Then I'd wanted to pack.

—Sure, fuck him, she said. —He'll have to come over to see his grandson or his granddaughter, so he will.

She was holding me.

—He'll have to spend a few shillings and vomit on the boat, she said.

—He's never been mean, I said.

—Not with the money, maybe, she said. —But he's tight with the kindness.

She kissed my shoulder.

—So, he can fuck off with himself, she said. —We both deserve better.

I've often wondered if we'd have gone, if I'd told Faye the full story. We'd have left but perhaps not as quickly. We had Faye's money, from the sales of the shop and the house; we didn't have to charge. And she'd made it clear.

—I don't want to be settling in Dublin.

—Okay.

—I don't like Dublin. Does that shock you, David?

—No.

—You're a liar.

—I'm not.

—D'you know what Dublin's problem is?

—What?

—It's only the capital of Ireland, she said. —And that's fuckin' nothing to be stuck up about.

We were going. The real question is, why I never told Faye all that my father had said, why I'd lied to her, why I'd worked myself up to believing what I'd told and hadn't told her. I wanted to be like her, I sometimes think. I wanted to feel isolated, and homeless; I wanted to match her.

We were riding for children, from the start. That feeling was there: we were changing our lives, making something new. We were always going to leave. But I still don't know why I hurt my father, hurt Faye, hurt

167

my children. None of the answers answer the question. There'll never be an answer.

Five years ago – about five years ago – we were sitting beside each other, half watching something on the television. The ads came on and there was one in particular, warning the viewer of the perils of unprotected sex. Immediately, I felt it – I was in our flat in Dublin, with Faye, in bed. Doing something dangerous and wonderful, together. Making up our lives – our life.

I turned to look at Faye, and she'd already turned to me. We said nothing and we kissed, and adjusted our older selves on the couch to face each other.

—Unprotected sex, Faye.

I held her face.

—It was the making of us, so it was.

She held mine.

—So, yeah, said Joe. —Somethin' happened.

—Okay, I said. —Wha'?

—Well, he said. —I still don't know how to say it.

—Did she cast a spell on you or somethin'?

He pushed himself back from the counter. He exhaled loudly – he almost whistled.

—No.

—You hesitated.

—No, he said. —No, she didn't. That'd be fuckin' daft.

—But you hesitated.

—Fuck off, he said. —Look –. There's a film, a kids' thing Holly used to love. I can't remember the name of it. But there's a wall an' when the characters go over it, they're enterin' into a different world – different rules, different everythin'. *Stardust* – that's wha' it was called. D'you know it?

—No, I said. —Don't think so. I mean, I might've seen it – I don't know.

—It's not the film, he said. —It's good, by the way. Holly loved it. But it's not the plot that I mean. The main chap has to cross the wall, into the realm o' the fairies or somethin', I think it's called – I can't remember. Carrie from *Homeland*'s in it, now that I think of it. She's a kid in it – it's goin' back a good bit. D'you watch *Homeland*?

—It's brilliant.

—Yeah, he said. —Although I haven't seen the last couple o' series.

—The new one's great, I said. —Bang up to date. The Russians interferin' with the elections and everythin'. Claire Danes.

—Yeah, he said. —But look, there was no wall or anythin' dramatic like tha'. But I did feel like I'd stepped into another world. Just a bit. I don't want to exaggerate it.

—Sorry, I said. —Is this magic we're talkin' about, or wha'? Hypnosis?

—No, he said. —No. It's psychological, maybe. I don't know. But somethin', anyway. Somethin' definitely happened. In my head – so to speak. D'you know anything abou' tha' stuff?

—Psychology?

—Yeah, he said. —How the brain works an' tha'.

—No, I said.

I didn't want to let us stray. I didn't want to talk about myself.

—I had to have a brain scan, he said.

—Did you?

169

—Yeah, yeah. An MRI.

—Because o' this?

—Wha'?

—Because you met your woman?

—No. No – fuck off. Two years ago, or so. Before me an' Jessica. Yeah, two years ago.

—Why?

—Did I never tell you?

—No, I said. —You didn't.

—Did I not? You sure?

—Yeah, I said.

But I wasn't. I wasn't sure at all. I'd had an MRI of my own, a year before. Mine was more recent than his. I hadn't told Joe. And I didn't want to hear him telling me about his. I could already feel him leaking into me.

—What's wrong? said Faye. —David?

Her voice was different, distant. I was standing at the kitchen door. I was looking out at the sky. I'd decided to stand up. I'd felt like I was waking, suddenly conscious, when I'd moved, stood. And I'd felt that way – waking up, waking repeatedly – as I'd moved to the back door.

Faye must have seen me. She must have been watching me.

—What's wrong? Dave?

I turned to her – I woke.

—Hi.

—Are you okay?

—I've been asleep – have I?

—No.

—No?

I walked past her to the chair I'd been sitting in. The chair I always sat in. My chair – when there was no one else in it. I sat – the chair was under me.

—What's wrong with your back?

—Nothing.

I looked at her. She sat beside me – she pulled a chair from under the table. She was staring at me.

—What's going on?

—I keep waking up, I said.

I was looking around me, up, around.

—Are you stoned or something? she asked.

—No.

It wasn't a ridiculous question. Nothing was ridiculous.

I looked at her, straight at her – woke up. She looked worried.

—What did you eat?

It was Saturday, early afternoon.

—Breakfast, I said. —I think.

—What?

—Toast.

—Did you go anywhere?

—No.

I stood – woke up. There was a rush – I had to sit down. I held the arms of the chair. I sat, woke up.

—I keep waking, I told her.

—You look stoned, she said. —You look doped.

—It's really slow, I said.

—What is?

—It. Every –.

I stood.

I'd forgotten words.

—Jesus, David –.

—Air, I said. —Fresh air.

—D'you want to go for a walk?

I woke up.

—Yeah.

We brought the dog. I bent to put the lead on him – I woke. Faye's hand was there, on mine. I was on my hands and knees. She took the lead from me. She grabbed the dog's collar.

—Dave?

I stood, straightened – woke.

—For fuck sake, David, stop messing.

I smiled. I turned. I smiled at her.

—I'm fine.

—You're not, she said. —Are you having a stroke or something? David?

I walked down the hall. I found my jacket at the end of the stairs. I put it on. Woke. The dog was under me, at my feet. I opened the front door. Faye was beside me. We were out – I closed the door. Woke. I walked between the cars. Faye's car. And mine. The trees were there. And other cars. I looked at Faye. I looked at my feet. At the path. Woke.

—David?

I stopped. I turned – turned – turned.

—Yes, Faye?

—We need a bag. Harry's shit. Did you bring some?

My hand was already in my pocket. I took out my hand. It was holding three or four orange nappy bags.

—Yes.

I opened a bag. Licked a finger, to separate the plastic sides. Put my hand into the bag. Woke. Opened my fingers. Looked at the ground. Saw the shit. Bent down – got down. Woke. I picked up the shit. Three half hard, dark brown lumps. I closed my hand around them. Heat through the orange plastic. Stood up. Woke up.

Looked at the bag. I turned it inside-out. Shit in. Fingers out. I tied the bag.

I saw Faye.

We walked. Under the trees. I heard – I could hear something. Wind. In a tight space. Wind screaming. In the distance – and near. Faye held the dog's lead. That was the noise – the wind noise. The retractable lead. Nylon screamed, in – out, in – rubbing against the plastic handle. A car passed. I heard no noise, no engine.

I stopped. I woke.

—This is taking for ever, I said.

—What is?

I woke up.

—We've been walking for hours.

—Come on, she said. —Come on. I'm getting you to the hospital.

I looked. At the next-door neighbour's gate. I looked at Faye.

—Okay.

—You're worried too, she said.

I wasn't.

I walked.

—Stay here, said Faye.

—Where?

—Here, she said.

She took one of my hands. She put it on the roof of her car.

—Here, she said. —I'll just get the key and bring Harry in. I wish the fuckin' kids were still here.

—Do you?

—For once, I do. Stay there.

I stood beside her car. My hand was on the roof when she got back. I watched her double-lock the front door. I woke. I watched her looking into her bag. I watched her shake it. I watched her take out her phone and drop it back into the bag. The car door – my door, the passenger door – was open. I felt Faye's hand on top of my head.

—In.

She pushed slightly – she made me bend. I watched as I lifted my feet into the car. I looked at them. She closed the door. She didn't slam it. Her door was open. I could see her waist. She leaned in. She held out her bag.

—Hold this for me.

I looked at the bag.

—Jesus Christ, David.

She leaned in further. She dropped the bag on my lap. I held it. She was beside me.

—Can you see properly?

—Yes.

—The tree there – the branches. They're clear, are they?

—Yes.

She started the car.

—Is there any point asking you to phone ahead?

I looked at the bag.

—No, she said. —I didn't think so.

The car moved.

—Put your belt on, she said.

I looked – I felt the belt. I'd already done it.

—Are we going to the hospital?

—That's right, we're going to the hospital.

I woke.

My phone was in my hand. I looked at it. I was supposed to do something.

—You're scaring me, Dave.

—Sorry.

—Are you, though?

—Head injury, said Joe.

—What happened?

—I stood up in the attic.

—You're jokin'.

—I fuckin' amn't, he said. —I nearly broke a cross-beam with me head. I was lucky, though, as well because I landed righ' beside the hatch, you know. If I'd fallen through that –. Cos I was unconscious, ou' for the fuckin' count.

He loved this story.

—I was only startin' to stand up, he said. —An' a mouse ran across me hand. I thought it was a rat. I just shot up – bang. Ou' – gone. Nothin'. Trish heard the thump an' she was ou' the back, sunnin' herself. She was callin' me for ages. But I hadn't a clue. I was knocked ou'. Were you ever unconscious, Davy?

—Not like tha', no, I said. —Literally knocked out. No.

—It's amazin', really, how it can happen.

—Must be.

—When you think about it, he said. —We're so fuckin' frail. I only woke up properly in the Mater. But, apparently, I was conscious when they got me down from the attic.

—Who did that?

—The ambulance lads. I don't remember them – nothin' ever came back. One o' them was a woman. So Holly said. She found me – Holly. That's the legend. She came out of her room when she heard Trish shoutin'. She saw the ladder on the landing an' she climbed up an' saw me. Saved me life.

—Was it tha' bad?

—I'd a fractured skull, Davy – for fuck sake.

—Lads –.

It was the barman. He was looking at us – staring at us.

—Sorry, I said.

—Were we loud? Joe asked me.

—You were, I said. —You must've been.

—Fuck'm, he said, quietly. —There's no way we were tha' loud. It's a fuckin' pub, for fuck sake.

—Did you need a plate or anythin'? I asked him.

—No, he said. —No. Luckily. So, but –. Good ol' Holly.

—It must've been a bit shatterin' for her as well, I said.

I was thinking of Róisín. I was missing her. We skyped, but neither of us liked it. It's like we're in a shit film, she'd said once, months before. You don't look like you. You look, like, stupid.

—She clung to me for months after it, said Joe. —It was –. I don't know, Davy. I *do* know. It was great.

—I can imagine.

—She was terrified I'd die, he said. —Afraid I was goin' to drop dead. I was out o' work for a month, you know.

—Jesus.

—Yeah. An' I never told you?

—No.

—Weird, he said. —Cos I'll tell you now, I told everyone else. But, there – anyway. I had my daughter back, my little girl. You know what I mean, I'd say.

—I know exactly what you mean.

—She stopped bein' a teenager an' became human again. Yeah. So. Tha' was it for a while. An' then I went an' fuckin' blew it.

He sighed again, almost whistled.

—Did I? he said.

I told the neurologist.

—I keep waking up.

—Do you like a drink?

I didn't understand. He looked too young to be asking the question.

—He's not an alcoholic, said Faye.

—Was he drinking?

—Today?

—Yes.

—No, he wasn't.

—Is that true? he asked me.

I looked at him.

—I was reading a book, I said.

—And last night? he said. —A party? Drinks after work?

—Are you Irish? I asked him.

—Yes, I am, he said.

—Me too.

—Yes.

I woke.

—It happened there, I told him.

—You felt you woke up again?

—Yes.

—And last night? he said.

—He was at home, said Faye. —With me. But you're Irish, so you'll know we're more than likely lying when it comes to the drinking.

—Were you?

—A bottle between us, she said. —And it wasn't empty when we turned off the television.

I was standing beside the bed.

—Put one foot in front of the other, said the neurologist. —Toe to heel.

I looked at my feet.

—Take a step now, please. Back foot to the front.

—The drink-driving test, said Faye.

—Similar.

I looked at the foot at the front.

—Take a step.

—I can't.

—Try.

He grabbed me as I fell. He helped me sit on the bed. I looked at his hands. I woke.

—Again.

—Thank you, he said. —That's helpful.

—It's like a dotted line, I said. —Instead of a straight line. Dot to dot.

—Yes.

There was paper in front of me, below my eyes – a writing pad. And a pen – a biro.

—Draw a clock, please.

I held the biro. I looked at the paper.

—It doesn't have to be perfect.

I heard Faye.

—Go on, David.

The doctor – the neurologist – was young, much younger than a specialist should have been.

I drew a circle. It wasn't good.

—Can I draw it again?

—It's fine.

—It's not like a clock.

I woke up.

—I'm interested in the numbers, said the doctor. —The hours.

—He knows his hours, don't you, David? He's very advanced.

I looked at Faye – I looked for Faye. She was behind me, against the window. I couldn't see her – I couldn't turn. I looked at the paper, at the circle that wasn't a circle. I put the pen at the top of the circle. I didn't know what to do.

I woke.

—Again, I said.

—Fine, he said. —The hours – do you know them?

—I think so, I told him.

I brought the biro down a bit, to the right, and wrote a 1. I had it now; I knew what to do. 2, 3, 4, 5, 6, 7, 8, 9, 10, 11.

It took hours – it seemed to be taking hours. I looked at my hand holding the biro.

I stopped. I was back at the top of the circle. I didn't know what came next.

—David?

I woke.

I didn't know the number.

He took the writing pad.

—Thank you, he said. —Stand up.

—Me?

—Yes.

I couldn't. I couldn't make myself do it. I kept waking up. He helped me stand. He didn't have to pull. I stood. I couldn't see the floor – I couldn't look at it. I watched him wrap the black rubber around my arm. I saw the rubber expand, I felt it tighten.

—I'm going to take your blood pressure, he said. —Both standing and sitting.

I felt the rubber loosen.

—It's very low, he said.

—Okay.

—Very low. Sit now, please.

—Sorry?

—Sit down. On the bed.

I felt his hand on my arm.

—Yes, he said as I lowered myself onto the bed.

—I don't care, I told him.

—I'm sorry?

—I don't care.

I felt the rubber tighten, and loosen. I didn't look at it.

—Low again, he said.

—How low? Faye asked.

—Very.

He was looking into one of my eyes. I didn't blink.

—Who's the President of Ireland?

—We're in Britain, I said.

I could see him smile.

—Good man, Dave, said Faye. —Put him back in his box.

—Nevertheless, he said. —Who is he?

—I keep waking up, I said.

—And who is the President of Ireland?

I knew. I knew but I didn't know. I knew I'd known. But nothing would come. It was like the clock – the number at the top. I didn't know what I knew.

I waited for Faye to fill the silence. To rescue me.

She didn't.

I didn't care.

I woke up.

—Michael D. Higgins.

—She'll come round, I told Joe.

—D'you think?

—Ah, she will.

—When, though?

—I don't know, I said. —But she will.

—Just have to be patient, I suppose, he said.

—Yeah, that's it.

—It's hard, though.

—Yeah.

—Fuckin' hard.

—Must be.

—Where were we?

—Wha'?

—I was tellin' you, he said.

—You were climbin' over the magic wall, I said. —Go on.

—It wasn't a fuckin' wall.

—You used the analogy.

—Yeah, I did. But it wasn't a wall.

—I know –. Just –. Does the knock on your head have anythin' to do with this?

—Wha'?

—It's a genuine question, I said.

—Okay, he said. —But it wasn't a knock on my head. I fractured me fuckin' skull.

—Okay.

—Fuckin' fractured, Davy.

—Lads.

It was the barman again.

—Sorry, said Joe.

He looked at me, and smiled.

—We might get ourselves barred here, he said.

—I'd kind o' like that, I said.

—It'd do us good. Gettin' barred.

—Probably, yeah, I said. —Definitely.

We'd never been barred from a pub. We were reliving something else that hadn't happened.

—But the wall, he said.

—Yeah?

—I thought I could cross an' recross it, he said. — Although I only thought o' the wall – tha' film – a few minutes ago. But d'you know what I mean?

—Wha'? I said. —Like, keep two households on the go?

—No –

—A gap in the hedge?

—Would you ever fuck off, Davy.

—Why're you sayin' tha'?

—Right, lads – finish up. Come on.

The barman had come out from behind the counter. He was quickly standing between us, against us. He held the stools, as if he might pull them from under us.

—Are you barrin' us? said Joe.

—If that's what yis want to call it, said the barman. —I don't know yis, so just finish up and hop it – come on.

—Thanks very much, said Joe.

He looked at me.

—There you go, Davy. We're barred.

I listened.

—This one will last five minutes, said the voice. —Do you understand?

—Yes.

I was in the sausage, the scanner. I was lying down, tight against the walls of the bed – or whatever it was. The base, the shelf. My head was trapped. I couldn't move.

182

I didn't care.

I woke.

—I will be counting down from three, said the voice.
—Do you hear me?

—Yes.

They were scanning my brain. Looking for clots.

—Three –, two –.

I knew: the noise was distressing – it should have
been distressing, it could have been distressing.

I woke.

This might be the last time. I thought that, exactly
that. Every time I woke. This might be the last time. I
didn't care if I died. If I didn't. I didn't care.

—Can I go to the toilet first? said Joe.

The barman didn't answer. He was a sheepdog and
he'd herded the two of us through both sets of narrow
doors, and out. He didn't touch us, he didn't say another
word. He went straight back into the pub. I tried to
feel amused but I couldn't quite catch it.

—Should've thought o' tha', said Joe. —Men our
age. Always go to the jacks before you get yourself
thrown out of a pub.

—It's a bit of a let-down, I said. —I expected more.

—We could smash a window, said Joe. —Do a
legger.

I was going home – not home – to my father's house.
I'd have a shower, sleep, go back to the hospice. I was
done. Joe's story was inside, still at the bar. It hadn't
come out with us. I was going to shake myself away,
make the decision. I didn't care. I wanted to sleep. I
didn't want to be struggling or stupid in the morning.
I wanted to sit with my father.

Joe was looking across the road, at the trees and the promenade.

—We'll have a piss over there, he said. —Behind the pumpin' station.

He walked across the parking spaces outside the pub, onto the road. There was no traffic – I couldn't see or hear anything. I followed him.

—I'm goin' now, Joe, I told him.

—We'll go into town, he said.

—No.

—Fuckin' yeah, Davy. Don't desert me now.

He crossed and I followed him. We went in behind the strange structure.

—What is this?

—A pumpin' station, said Joe. —It's won awards.

He pissed against its side.

—Shite or water? I asked.

—Don't know, to be honest, he said.

He groaned – he made himself groan.

—If you can piss like this – a steady stream, like. At our age. You're grand. Your prostate's fine.

—Did Jessica tell you tha'?

—Fuck off, he said. —Have a piss there an' we'll grab a taxi.

—I'm goin' home.

—No, you're not.

—I am.

—No, he said. —Davy. I have to tell you.

—You've spent all night havin' to tell me, I said. —I still haven't a clue wha' happened. Except you fell over a wall.

—Come on an' stop bein' a cunt.

I unbuttoned my fly. The wind in the trees – the branches were alive, creaking.

—Remember we used to come down here?

—No, I said.

—We did.

—We didn't.

—Well, I did.

—Grand.

—Hurry up, for fuck sake. Four or five taxis have gone past while you've been unravellin' your langer.

I knew as I stood there, feet apart, staring at the pumping-station wall: I'd go with him. We were going to go to George's. I wasn't tired and I wasn't being dragged. It was my decision. I wanted it.

We stood at the side of the road, opposite the pub.

—No fuckin' taxis, he said.

I didn't let myself apologise.

—It's not too hot now.

—No, he said. —It's grand. The way it should be. Here's one now, look it.

A car – a taxi – was coming towards us. Joe lifted his arm.

—Here we go.

It slowed. I could see the driver, an African, looking at us. He stopped.

—Grand, said Joe. —We're elected.

He opened the back door and got in. He kept moving across the seat, and I followed him into the car. I waited for him to say something over-friendly, faintly sardonic to the driver. But he didn't. He told him we wanted to go to South William Street or as near as he could get us, and he thanked him. He put on his seat belt and sat back, head back, as far as he could make it go. His eyes were shut for a second, two.

—There was nothin' tellin' me I couldn't – I don't know. Balance it.

185

He spoke softly, just to me.

—I could be fair to both, he said. —Jess and Trish. Jess.

That was new. It caught me on the hop. I didn't know who he was referring to at first. She'd been Jessica all night. There was no radio on in the car. I looked out the side window. We were passing the old Clontarf Baths. The building seemed to have been converted into a restaurant; there were lights on, and two lines of parked cars outside. I said nothing about it.

—I sound like a slug, he said.

I took my eyes from the window, to look at him. He was looking at me.

—Don't I?

—I don't know, I told him. —I don't know wha' to say.

—I know, he said. —Yeah. But I think it's true. I wasn't actin' the maggot, though, Davy. Or just actin' the maggot. At all. I wasn't. She needed me.

—Which?

—Jess.

—What d'you mean she needed you?

—I knew it. When I met her. She –. I just – I don't know. She needed me.

—You haven't told me about it.

—No, you're right, he said. —I haven't.

We were through Fairview, passing the fire station, where we'd been chased when we were walking home from the Ramones film. I didn't remind him.

—Look, I said. —You've suggested it – you said it. You might have a son.

—Okay –

—And you've told me you're livin' with Jessica an' that you're –. Estranged?

—It'll do.

186

—You're estranged from your family.

—Yeah.

—But you've told me nothin' else – not really.

—I know.

—So –

—I love her, Davy.

—Jessica?

—Yes.

—What about Trish?

—It's different.

—For fuck sake.

—It is.

—I said it earlier, Joe. You sound like every middle-aged man who's ever fallen for a younger woman. Except in your case the younger woman isn't any younger. She might even be older than us, is she?

—A year.

—You're infatuated.

—Ah, fuck off.

—Listen, I said. —I talk to one of you, some man just like you, every time I go for a few drinks after work. Which is a big reason why I never go.

—What about you?

—Wha'?

—Have you ever been fuckin' infatuated?

—We're not talkin' about me.

—Go on.

—Listen, I said.

We were still speaking softly, but hissing. I could see the driver's face in the rear-view. He was keeping an eye on us. We were drunk men. We were probably trying not to be, pulling ourselves back. But I was drunk and so was Joe. We were drunk men and we were right behind the driver.

187

—No offence, I said to Joe. —Honestly – no offence. But middle-aged men an' the rediscovery of their spunk eyes.

I saw Joe smile.

—It's boring, I said. —It's really fuckin' borin'.

—I know, he said. —I agree with you.

—I'm here, I said. —I wanted to go home, back to my da's. I've had enough. But I'm here. Because you said you wanted to tell me about it.

—Okay.

—Because I was there when you met her.

—We're buddies.

—I don't know you, I said.

We were over Matt Talbot Bridge, turning right on to the quays.

—I can't believe they named a bridge after Matt Talbot, I said.

—Wha'?

—He was a fuckin' nut, I said. —With his penance an' chains an' feedin' his dinner to his fuckin' cat.

—Now you're startin' to do it.

—Wha'?

—Avoidin' the subject, said Joe. —Evadin', avoidin'. Whatever the fuck. Like tax.

—It's just, I said. —When we were young, when we were goin' to George's, they were namin' the bridges after religious fanatics. And now –. The new one back there, with the Luas tracks on it.

—The Rosie Hackett.

—Who was she?

—A union leader, he said. —I think.

—She was a member of the Irish Citizen Army, said the driver.

—Was she? Thank you.

—She was a very great lady.

—She must've been.

—So, there, I said. —It's a different place.

—Not really, said Joe. —You don't live here.

—Well, it must be, I said. —In some respects. Because you thought you could live with two different women at the same time.

—Okay –

—You thought tha' was possible.

—That's the thing, though, he said. —I didn't think. Think – as in think. It wasn't logical.

—Is he your son? I asked.

—It doesn't matter, he said. —What I'm tryin' to tell you. It doesn't matter.

—It's a shite story then, I said.

—It kind of is.

He took out his phone and looked at the clock.

—We'll have one in the Palace.

It was exhaustion. I hadn't had a stroke; there were no blood clots. Everything was fine.

I was exhausted.

—How? I asked him, the neurologist.

I don't know if I ever knew his name.

—Only you can answer that one, he said.

I woke.

—It's still the same, I told him.

—The dots.

—Instead of a straight line.

—It's a good image, he said. —I might use it with my students.

—You have students?

—Yes.

—Jesus, we're getting old, Dave, said Faye.

She was behind me. Her hand had been on my back, my shoulder, but not now. The neurologist smiled.

—I'm sorry.

—So you should be, she said.

I woke.

—So, said the neurologist. —I go back to my original question.

He was looking at me – down at me. I was sitting in a wheelchair. Just back from the third scan. I thought I could walk now. But they wouldn't let me.

—Are you a drinking man?

—No, he isn't, said Faye.

—Are you? he said.

—No, I said. —Not really.

—Listen, said Faye. —If you asked me, I'd say yes. If this was an Irish conversation we were having. But David – no. He likes his bottle of IPA but he looks at it as much as he drinks it. One or two a week, just. And the odd glass of wine. He used to drink a bit but not now.

—Alright, said the neurologist.

—You think I'm lying.

—No.

—Exaggerating.

—No.

—You do so, said Faye. —Look at him, Dave, he's blushing.

He smiled – he grinned. He grinned over me, at Faye. He grinned at me.

—We'll keep you for a few days, he said. —If that's okay. Is that okay?

—Yes.

—We need to build up the fluids, he said. —You're very dehydrated. Dangerously so. We'll get you into the bed, so we can get you hooked up.

He took his phone from a jacket pocket. He looked at it. He lifted his other hand and tapped.

—I want you to look at this, he said.

His phone was a mirror.

—Is that an app?

—Yes. Look, please.

He was showing me my eyes. My eyes – the irises – are brown. Everything else was red. A consistent, even red. As if I'd coloured in the whites with a marker. I blinked. The red eyes in front of me blinked. I believed what I saw. And I didn't care.

I woke.

I saw him put his phone in his pocket. I saw him adjust his jacket. The weight of the phone had made it slide off one shoulder.

—It's not my business, he said. —But it is. You need to think about why you're here. Why you might be exhausted. *Are* exhausted. Do you understand?

—Yes.

—Perhaps you could talk about that, he said.

He was at the door.

—I'll see you again tomorrow, he said. —No, sorry. On Monday. I'll see you on Monday.

—What day is today?

—Saturday, he said. —My day off.

—Did you come in for me?

—It's the job, he said.

He was gone. I was alone.

—He's such a little fella, said Faye.

I wasn't alone. I couldn't see Faye. She was behind me.

—A little fella playing doctors, she said. —So fuckin'
young – Jesus. I'd say the nurses love him.

I woke. I was alone.

—They can pick him up and put him on their knees.

Faye was in the room. The ward. I heard her feet,
her heels.

—They can give him a bath and wash his botty.

She put her hands on my face and pulled it – me
– to her.

—It's nice to hear you laughing, she said.

I wasn't aware that I'd been laughing. I hadn't felt
it. I didn't feel it.

She let go of me.

—I like your clicks, Faye, I said.

—Jesus, David.

She walked up and down, in front of me, in the space
between the wheelchair and the door.

—Here's some more clicks for you, so.

She says it to me. When she looks at me, when she
makes me look at her. You like my clicks, so you do.
You like my clicks, apparently. When we look at each
other. When she makes me laugh.

The driver took us up D'Olier Street, around past the
Bank of Ireland and down the piece of Westmoreland
Street, to the corner of Fleet Street. I paid him and
looked at the change before I identified a two-euro coin
and gave it back to him, my hand between the two
front seats.

—There you go.

—Thank you, sir.

—Goodnight.

—God bless you, sir. And your friend. You are good people.

—Thanks.

—I hope you are happy.

—Seeyeh.

Joe was looking down Fleet Street.

—Fuckin' Temple Bar, he said.

—We're not goin' down there, I said.

—I know.

—We're too old.

—We've too much taste.

—We're snobs.

There was a crowd outside the Palace, smoking, chatting, laughing. But it wasn't too bad, too packed, inside. There was a free stool not too far from the door. The driver's words had pleased me. He'd seen something in us that I hadn't felt. Something in me, something about us, our past, our present. It wasn't just drink. It wasn't just anger.

Joe took the stool.

—Whose round is it?

—I haven't a clue.

—Okay.

He ordered two pints from a passing barman. He looked around, and at me.

—Good pub, he said.

—Yeah.

—Remember the jacks, back in the day?

—No.

—Ah, you do. Down the stairs, into the Black Hole of Calcutta. The light never worked, you just hoped you were pissin' in the right direction.

—They were all like tha'.

—That's true, he said. —We've come a long way. So, yeah –.

I thought he was going to say something. I thought he'd get going on what he'd wanted to say in the taxi, what he claimed he'd been trying to say all night. But he didn't. He took out some coins and made a neat pile of two-euros, six of them, on the counter.

—They're heavy fuckin' things to be luggin' around, he said. —If you've too many o' them.

I didn't respond. It was up to him.

—It's only a matter o' time before there'll be no cash at all, he said. —It'll all be cards. Would you miss it?

—Cash?

—Yeah.

—I like a bit o' cash in me pocket.

—Same here, he said.

The barman had arrived with the pints.

—Good man; thank you.

He picked up the coins and put them into the barman's hand.

—There you go.

I watched the pints settle as if it was the first time I'd seen it happen, the tan darkening to black and the arrival of the collar. I couldn't help myself.

—It's a fuckin' miracle, really, isn't it?

He knew what I was talking about.

—It is, he agreed.

It wasn't the first time he'd heard it. It had been one of our lines, since we'd heard some oul' lad say it, probably where I was standing now.

Joe picked up his pint and placed it a few inches closer to him. I did the same – I leaned across him and put my glass on top of a wet bar mat.

—I don't think I want this one, I said.

I meant it.

—I'm fuckin' full o' drink, I said – another phrase we'd got from an old man when we were young men, an old man who had probably been younger than we were now.

—We'll take it slowly, he said.

It was up to him. He could use the time we'd left or we could fill it with drivel; we'd hug and never see each other again.

He took the top off his pint.

He put it back down. I really didn't want my one. I held it but I didn't pick it up.

—It's a strange one, Davy, he said.

—Is it?

—I'm a different man, he said.

—Are you?

—You're bein' aggressive.

—Am I?

—You fuckin' are, yeah. An' there's no need.

—I'm not.

—I don't really blame you, he said. —It's all fuckin' weird, I suppose.

—I'm not bein' aggressive.

—Okay.

—You said you're a different man.

—That's right, he said. —Well, we all are. You are.

—Ah, fuck off.

—No, we are, he said. —We're older, we change. We do. But, like, now. I feel like I used to – I think I do. Because I'm with you.

He smiled.

—It's good.

He picked up his drink.

—Come here – cheers.

I picked up mine. We tapped our glasses.

—It's good, he said again.

He wanted me to agree.

—An' tha' makes me think how strange it's been, he said. —How strange it must seem.

—I don't know, I said. —You still haven't really told me anythin'. But yeah, it's a bit fuckin' weird.

—I understand.

—So, educate me, I said. —The only thing you've really mentioned is the wall.

—The wall.

—The wall in the film.

—I know which wall, he said. —Maybe the wall wasn't a good one. A metaphor or whatever. But it probably was. But anyway, that's it.

—What's it?

—Well, I don't know, Davy, he said. —I keep tryin' to think o' the words. Words to do it justice. On paper, like – I'm guilty. I can see tha'. I left me wife an' family for another woman.

—Spunk eyes, I said.

He smiled, he shrugged.

The smile was gone.

—We haven't had sex, he said.

—So you said.

—Did I?

—I think you did.

—Okay.

—Have you not, though?

—No.

—With Jessica?

—Yeah – no. With Jessica. Who else?

—It was just for clarity, I said. —The question.

—Okay, he said. —But yeah. Jess. Just so you know.

—It's none o' my business, I told him.

—Just so you know, he said again. —So, in fact. It's not a case o' me walkin' out on my family – for the gee.

I laughed – it burst from me. I hadn't heard the word in years. It wasn't one of Faye's words.

—Sorry, I said. —I know it's serious. But the gee –

—Drink talkin', he said. —But I hope that's clear, Davy. I didn't do what I've done for – like, a cliché. Okay?

—Right, I said. —Okay. Understood.

—We haven't had sex, he said.

The pub was full but there was no one looking at him.

—I don't care, I told him.

—An' I don't either, he said. —That's my point. It hasn't happened. An' I don't care. An' you mightn't care either but I bet you think it's weird.

—The whole thing's weird.

—The sex, I mean.

—No, then, I said. —Not really.

—Unusual then – a bit.

—Probably, I said. —Yeah. Definitely.

—Interestin'?

—Yeah. I think – yeah.

—Good.

—Why is that important? I asked him. —Why would you care if it's interestin'?

—Well, it has to be somethin', he said. —Jesus, man – I mean.

—What?

—I've – wha'? – erased more than half me life. In a way. An' not even for the sex.

—You haven't erased anythin', I said. —Are you tellin' me you've murdered Trish an' your children?

197

—No, he said. —No. No.

He looked away, at the window and doors, the snug in the corner, the bottles on the shelves in front of us, and back.

—No, he said. —But I've murdered somethin'. Not literally, but I've done somethin' fuckin' dramatic an' maybe wrong. I love my kids, Davy.

—I don't doubt it.

—No, I know you don't. I'm talkin' to myself, really. But it's as if they didn't exist.

—Didn't?

—Don't exist, he said. —No –. Didn't. They exist. But –.

He looked at me. His eyes were wet.

—They didn't matter, he said.

—An' she isn't even a femme fatale.

—No, he said. —No, that's right. Anyway, that's all bollix, the femme fatale business. Blamin' the woman.

—Spunk eyes.

—There you go, he said. —Exactly. My spunk, my eyes. I'll take full responsibility for them.

—You're bein' very noble, Joe.

—Fuck off, he said. —It's true. Those fellas you were mentionin'. The ones tha' go after the younger women. They're responsible for their own decisions. They're not bein' led down a fuckin' path by their mickeys.

—Joe, I said. —This is really borin'.

—Talkin' about women is fuckin' borin'?

—Don't start now, I said. —Be honest. You're not talkin' about women.

—Fuck off, Davy.

—You're still tryin' to avoid talkin' about the one particular woman.

—That's not true, he said. —I did start. I'm startin'
– I am.

—Stop it, I said. —I'll tell you what it is – I'll tell
you. You sound like you've been caught sayin' the wrong
thing by – say, Trish or Jessica. An' now you're tryin'
to talk your way out of it, or you're tryin' to make them
forget wha' you're afraid they might've heard.

—That's a load o' bollix.

—No, it isn't, I said. —An' come here.

I felt so happy saying that – an' come here – so
exultant and free, I almost cried. I could feel it too;
and I understood him – just a bit. I was slipping back,
to a different man. A man I might have been once – I
wasn't sure.

—I'm not interested, I said.

—Not interested?

—No.

—You've been fuckin' plaguin' me all night –

—No, I said. —I fuckin' have not. You've been wantin'
the opportunity to tell me about your adventures an'
I've been willin' to listen.

This wasn't how we'd been. Joe had always been the
one who drove us. I could see him thinking, trying to
catch up and trip me.

—I'm still willin' to listen, I said. —But spare me
the fuckin' all men bad, all women good shite.

I picked up my pint. I could feel my arm shake
slightly, my wrist ached, but the weight of the glass and
its contents steadied me.

—Okay, he said.

I put the glass to my lips. The cold on the bottom
lip felt good; it felt right. I filled my mouth. It was
okay; I'd be able for it. I put the glass back on the
counter; I leaned across him to do it.

—You're right, he said. —There are some slappers out there. Lurin' poor lads onto the rocks.

I didn't respond.

—But, he said. —Anyway. This time –. It wasn't about sex.

—You said it was.

—When?

—At the start, you did.

—Ah, Jesus, Davy, just fuck off, would yeh. Stop bein' so fuckin' pedantic. I love tha' word, by the way.

—Same here.

—A brainy oul' lad's word. Anyway. Yes, when I saw her –

—Jessica.

—Yes, Jessica. For fuck sake. When I saw her –

—In the school.

—Yeah. There was a part o' me thinkin', I definitely would.

—That's reassurin'.

—Oh, good. Great. I'm glad. So, yeah, I admit. We were outside the maths room but I was thinkin' honours biology.

—That's still reassurin'.

—Part o' me was, anyway, he said.

—Part of you?

—Don't be fuckin' crude. I thought she looked great. She *did* look great. Really – fuckin' lovely now. But when I actually met her, all tha' stopped.

—Literally?

—Literally.

—But you went home an' you shagged Trish.

—That's true as well, he said. —But you're a bit of a cunt for bringin' it up.

He looked around again, and back at me.

—I'm makin' it up as I go along, Davy, he said.

—I know.

—I don't mean I'm lyin'.

—I know.

—I'm tryin' to make sense of it.

—So, keep tryin', I said.

—I am, he said. —I fuckin' am. The drink is funny, though, isn't it? You see things clearly but then you can't get at the words to express them properly.

—Or somethin'.

—Or somethin', yeah. But anyway. Here goes – again. I met Jess an' I was hopin' – half hopin' – there'd be a thing. That I'd finally, after nearly a fuckin' lifetime, get to go to bed with the woman of my dreams. Our dreams.

—Your dreams.

—Yours as well – fuck off now. Admit it.

—It's your story, I said.

—Yeah, but –.

—Go on.

—You fancied her too, he said. —But okay. So – yeah. It was there – yeah. The excitement. But more than, way more than excitement. To finally, Jesus –.

He quickly looked around again at the other men and women close to us.

—To ride her. Just be with her. She's lovely, Davy. To feel her under my hands. An' her hands on me.

—Honours biology.

—At least a B+.

—But –

—No, stop, he said. —We're bein' salacious again. I don't like it. We'll leave it at tha'.

—But.

—Wha'?

—I wasn't going to say anythin' salacious, I said.

—Wha'?

—This would've been your first time. With Jessica.

—Yeah.

—But come here, I said. —You said –. Earlier, you said it. Tha' you think you might be the father of her son.

—I did, yeah.

He didn't look cornered, or caught.

—An' you said it didn't matter.

—Yeah.

—Well, I said. —Fuckin' hell, Joe. How does tha' work, for fuck sake?

—Davy, he said. —Give me a fuckin' chance.

—Are you his father or aren't you?

He stood up off his stool, although he didn't quite stand. He lifted both shoulders and extended his arms. Like a half hearted Jesus on a cross built for a smaller man. He sat down again.

—What does tha' mean, Joe? I asked him.

—It means –.

He lifted his shoulders again.

—It means I know an' – I suppose – I don't, he said. —It means there might not be an answer. Or a satisfactory answer.

—Jesus –

—I know, he said. —An' it's the problem with drinkin' like we are. The stories should be gettin' dirtier or whatever. But this one isn't, an' it isn't going to.

—That's not the point.

—I know, he said. —But it kind of is.

—I'm lost, I said.

—Well, he said. —I'm tempted to say the same thing, Davy, an' I nearly would. But I won't.

—Even though you say – what is it? – you might or you might not be the father of a middle-aged man?

—Yep.

He didn't hesitate, or grimace, or smile. Or shrug.

—I think I might go now, Joe, I said.

—Ah, no.

—I'm too drunk to listen.

—Ah, go on to fuck, Davy. It's the only way to listen.

—Bollocks.

—Spoken like a true Englishman.

—Fuck off.

—Look, he said. —Look it. You can't go. Be a pal. Give me a chance.

—What chance? I said. —Wha' fuckin' chance? Wha' d'you even want, for fuck sake?

He'd spoken as if it had been his turn to unburden himself and I was being selfish. He'd endured my late-midlife, early-elderly confessions and now it was his go.

And maybe I was selfish. I hadn't told him about my spell in hospital, the scare that hadn't scared me until months later when I started crying. I'd never mentioned it, yet I resented his lack of curiosity. I needed him to be a bad man, somehow. I had to be the good man. There couldn't be two of us.

—The thing is, he said. —I don't think it matters.

—Wha' doesn't?

—Whether I'm his father or not. His biological father.

—You've never fuckin' met him.

—Doesn't matter.

—You never had sex with her.

—Well, he said. —There now.

—Ah, Jesus, I said. —Wha'?

He gave me the shrug again.

203

—Did I say never, Davy – actually?

—Did you?

—Does it matter?

—I'm definitely goin', I said.

But I picked up my pint and drank from it. The stout went down without a protest. I felt stupidly pleased; I was holding my drink.

—I love her, Davy, he said.

—So wha'?

—It goes a long way.

—Wha' the fuck does tha' mean?

—I want her to be happy, he said. —It's all I want.

—So fuckin' wha'?

—Literally, he said. —Literally. It's all I want. It's not an easy one when you're a bit pissed, is it?

—Wha'?

—Literally. Sayin' literally.

—You keep sayin' somethin' serious, I said. —Or it seems to be serious. An' then you say somethin' frivolous like tha'. To distract us.

—Yeah.

—Why?

—Because I hear meself, he said. —An' I can't fuckin' believe it.

—Because I have to say, Joe, it's very fuckin' irritatin'.

I wanted to go but I was leaning in, almost resting against his shoulder.

—When I met her, he said.

—Jessica.

—Yeah. When I met her. When I met her. I don't know. I felt happy.

—Fuckin' happy?

—Not delighted. Or giddy. Or aroused, or any o'
tha'. Just happy. I'll tell you – I'll tell you what it was
like. You're pushin' me off the stool, Davy.

—Sorry.

—D'you want it – d'you want to sit down?

—No, I said. —No. I'm grand.

—Okay.

—You were sayin'.

—Was I?

—What it felt like when you met Jessica.

—Yes, yeah – brilliant. Yeah. So. We were cleanin'
out the house, me an' the sisters, when me ma died.

—How long ago is that?

—Does it matter?

—No.

—Four years. Five. Five years ago. We were puttin'
the house on the market. Strange fuckin' experience,
by the way. Emptyin' a house like tha'. Because they'd
lived in it all their lives together, my ma an' me da.

—Same as mine.

—Yeah, of course.

—Well, my father did – does.

—Yeah, yeah, he said. —So anyway, I thought it was
horrible, just a horrible fuckin' experience. Throwin'
all their stuff ou'. It made me feel really shite – guilty,
I think. Their lives, you know – into a skip. Or down
to the Vincent de Paul. An' my sisters felt the same
way. The cryin' – Jesus. Everythin' we picked up. An'
the laughing. We can't throw this ou', there's no way
we can throw that ou'. But it had to be done. But the
things we found tha' we didn't even know were in the
house.

—Wha'?

—Nothin' dodgy. Calm down. We didn't find an Armalite or a vibrator –

—Ah, Jesus.

We were laughing.

—Nothin' like tha'. At all. But stuff tha' should've been thrown out years before. Things we'd had when we were kids tha' we'd have forgotten even existed.

—Toys?

—No.

—We've kept the kids' first shoes.

—No. Same here – but no. Trish put them somewhere. But not tha'. Or teeth. Did you keep your kids' baby teeth?

—Some.

—Same here, he said. —After the tooth fairy came down the chimney. No – that's fuckin' Santy. But anyway. Like, we made the decision to save the shoes an' the teeth. Me an' Trish. But this was different. Or, half different. Maybe she decided – I'm guessin' it was my mother. I can't see me da givin' much of a shite. But she decided she'd keep the school reports. But she only kept one.

—Whose?

—Not mine. But we found one letter from the Gaeltacht. One. An' we'd all have gone there at some time – all of us. But she only kept one o' the letters. An' I'm nearly certain I'd have written letters to her when I was there.

—So it wasn't yours.

—No. But then. It was Orla found it. My Holy Communion prayer book.

—Jesus.

—Well, yeah. Exactly. It was in this little – this small suitcase. At the back o' the wardrobe. Like a suitcase a teenager would've had when my ma was a teenager. With a clasp, you know – the lock.

—Yeah.

—It wasn't cardboard like those old suitcases, the ones people emigrated with. It was – I suppose – plastic. Vinyl or somethin'. Lacquer – I don't know. Cream coloured. An' I think Orla was worried openin' it. She was afraid there'd be clothes in it – that our ma might've planned on runnin' away at some time, or somethin'.

—An' what was in it?

—The prayer book – I told you.

—Besides tha'.

—Letters, he said. —Sent to her when she was a kid. Most o' them were from a cousin or somethin' in New York. An' two from a boy called Colm. An' a few photographs. A couple o' bits of ribbon. An ol' record – a 78, believe it or not. Called 'The Old Refrain'. It was stuff she brought with her into the house – into the marriage. Her life before she got married.

—But your prayer book too.

—There you go, he said. —It was slipped into a little side pocket.

—Only yours?

—Only mine. It was the only thing in the case tha' came from after she married my father. An' tha' got the girls' backs up a bit. They were callin' me the white-headed boy. But then Sheila admitted she couldn't remember if she'd had a prayer book. She said she'd almost definitely have had one but she couldn't actually remember it. An' the others were the same. They couldn't remember their own prayer books. But there's the thing.

—Neither could you.

207

—Exactly. I'd no recollection of it. Even when I was holdin' it in me hands. It's a lovely little thing, by the way. The print is nearly faded off the cover but you can still make it out. Souvenir of First Holy Communion. An' a cross, of course. An' inside it has – on the first page. It has my name an' address, an' the date.

—What was it?

—The 29th of June. 1965.

—Christ.

—Yeah.

—That's brilliant.

—Yeah.

—An' the best thing – come here. The thing tha' really fuckin' floored me. It's my father's handwriting.

—Brilliant.

—Ah, man.

—That must've been incredible.

—Well –.

He took off his glasses and gave his eyes a quick rub.

—Look at me, he said. —Fuckin' eejit.

He put the glasses back on.

—But yeah, he said. —You can imagine, Davy. An' you know me an' religion. I hate the fuckin' Church, everythin' about it. But this thing – the little book. Jesus –. This is true now. It was the first thing I packed when I was leavin'.

—Leavin' wha'?

—Trish an' tha'.

—Yeah – sorry. Gotcha.

—The first thing, he said. —It's mad, I know. Given wha' was goin' on, like.

—I can kind of understand it.

—But it made me – I don't know. Happy. So, like – so full of happiness. Even though I'd never missed it or even knew about it. She probably put it away the same day, the day of the Communion. We'll never know why she put it into the little suitcase – why in there. But, anyway. There you go. I just felt so happy. So complete. Complete – yeah.

—Yeah.

—An' that's exactly how I felt when I met Jess. When I was with her again.

He looked happy now too. He'd got there; he'd explained it all to me. He thought he had.

—A complete surprise, he said. —Out o' nowhere. But it still made sense.

I was officially exhausted. And I didn't know why. Nothing had clicked, no one good cause had made itself known. Work, money, sex, kids, grief, marriage – a line of not-reallys. I was a fraud. I believed that.

I'd woken up the morning after I'd been admitted. I knew exactly where I was and why I was there. I was exhausted; I'd been told that the day before. Time had been broken into unjoined moments. But not now. I sat up in the bed; I did it carefully. I knew I had to, because my blood pressure was low – interestingly low, the neurologist, whose name I never knew, had said. I wasn't linked to the drip-stand beside the bed. I would be again, later; the IV valve was taped to my wrist. There was a heart monitor sitting on my chest. It looked like an old-fashioned smartphone, some early prototype, wrapped in thick plastic. It hung around my neck; I had to bring it with me. I sat on the side of the bed. I waited some time. Then I stood.

Wake, know, sit, stand – it was a line, linked moments and knowledge. I stood slowly, one hand still resting on the bed. I stood straight. My head didn't spin. I looked at my feet; I looked down. There were slippers beside my feet. They weren't mine. I didn't own slippers. But they made sense. Faye had bought them in a shop, downstairs. The yellow pyjamas I was wearing now, the slippers, the bottle of Lucozade, *The Girl on the Train* – she'd brought them back up to me before she'd gone home. I was interested in my feet. If I could use them. If I could walk. I lifted the right foot and placed it in front of the left; I'd be stepping away from the bed. I'd be stepping out of something – and I wasn't sure I wanted to. I liked exhaustion. I liked not knowing, caring, not living the measured life.

I took the step. I took the other. I walked to the window. Around the bed. I opened the curtain. I looked out for the first time. At a wall. I smiled – I felt myself do it. A wall – no windows. And a patch of sky the same colour as the wall, just as badly painted. I liked it – I'd tell Faye.

I'd tell Faye.

I was able to eat breakfast; I was hungry. I was told to stay on the bed. I was dehydrated. But I was fine. Fine, but I didn't care. It was what I wanted: I wanted not to care. I looked at the window, at the wall to the side of the window. I waited for, I pressed for the differences – the colours, glass, sky – to stop. I tried to go back to broken time. I wanted it back. I didn't know what I didn't want to face. I didn't know and it didn't matter. I tried to gaze my way back, hypnotise myself. Escape. Unhappiness. Redundancy. They'd been gone. I tried to get back there.

210

Faye was in the room. But I saw her come in – she wasn't just there. I heard her open the door, I saw her. I saw her look at me – smile.

—How are we this morning?

I saw her look at the clear bag suspended from the drip-stand; I was being fed again. I saw her frown – I saw her decide to.

—Is it doing the trick, is it?

She held the collar of the pajamas.

—Yellow's your colour, David.

She had a shopping bag with her. I wanted to see what was in it. I wanted to watch her empty it, comment on each item, place each on the table in front of me. I wanted to look at her do things. I saw: I understood. She wanted this too. She wanted me to watch her. She wanted me to follow her. She wanted to feel my eyes. She wanted to lift me out of death.

—I'm feeling better, I told her.

Regret immediately drenched me; I'd been fooled, found out. I wanted to go back. This might be the last time. I wanted to go back behind there.

But I wanted Faye. I wanted to be with Faye. To look at Faye. I wanted to feel her. She placed an Innocent smoothie, mango and passion fruit, on the table in front of me.

—That'll put hairs where you want them, she said.
—And not the grey lads, either.

She stepped past the table and leaned down, right to my face, my eyes. She kissed my lips.

—I want you better, she said.

She examined both of my eyes.

—They're not as red. Only pink. Pink's your colour, Dave.

—Yellow and pink, I said. —My colours.

—Oh, God, I'm getting the lady horn.

I laughed – it burst out of me.

—That's music to my ears, she said. —Are you back?

—I am.

—Great.

—I think so.

—No thinks, she said. —No fuckin' thinks. You're back or you're not back.

—I'm back.

I said it, but I hated saying it. I hated believing it. Exhaustion was safe and I wanted it back. I shut my eyes but I couldn't keep them shut.

We made it to a party one night. We hung on, we followed. We got into the back of a car. A Mini, I think. We'd no idea where we were going. The two other lads in the car booed as we passed a set of big gates, then clapped, and laughed.

—What's that about? I asked the girl beside me, the Emmylou girl. She was on a lap, to my left.

—Blackrock College, she said.

—Did they not like it?

—They fucking loved it, she said. —They never fucking left it.

—I can't remember the name o' the school I went to, I told her.

—My kind of guy.

The car stopped. I got out, followed others, made sure I was with Joe, went through a gap in a wall. A path under trees. A lantern. But no door.

—How do we get in?

There was an open window. There were people inside. There was music. There was a door around a corner. And the mother.

—Oh, fuck.

A formidable mother. A mother like nothing we'd encountered before. There were steps up to her – this must have been the front of the house. We were never going to get past her. She was gorgeous. Too full of sex to be a mother but definitely the mother, the owner of the huge house right behind her.

Joe got up on the first step.

—Two more 'Rock boys for you, he said.

—Oh, dear God, she said, and raised her colossal eyes to the porch above her stiff hair, and smiled, and moved aside just enough for us to pass and smell her, and rub against her, as we went.

—Fuckin' hell.

—This is a bit fuckin' different.

A house from American television. A flow of people up the stairs, and down. The people coming down held bottles of Heineken. We went up, joined the queue, to a bath full of ice and bottles, and a child with a bottle opener sitting on a shower seat beside the bath. Joe pulled up a sleeve and took two bottles from the bath. The Heineken labels were floating on the water. One of them stuck to the hair on his arm. He pulled it off and threw it back in the bath.

—What's the occasion? he asked the child.

A boy.

The boy stared up at us.

—Why don't you know? he asked.

—I'm testing you, said Joe. —And I asked first.

—Jess is engaged to Gavin.

—Correct, said Joe.

We left the child and went back downstairs. We stood in a full room and shifted to let the traffic pass, and looked at the people who had always known one another – the couples, the friends, the gorgeous tribe.

—Where is she? said Joe.

She was why we were here. Somehow. Our girl – our woman. *Hi.* She'd dragged us here. I looked around. I looked at every chair, along the walls, through both doorways. Where was she? She'd left George's with the rest of them, with us. She'd been outside. We'd seen her get into one of the cars; she'd dragged her cello in with her. We'd heard her laugh. Not *your* lap?! Be good now! The Mini we'd pushed ourselves into was just a bit further down, near the corner of Fade Street. We were all going to the party. She was here, somewhere.

I didn't care. I feel it now, I felt it then. The impossible dream – but I wasn't dreaming. Joe, though – I don't know. I'd been infatuated before; I knew what it was like. The spunk eyes, and the wish to protect the girl from spunk eyes, my own eyes. To be engulfed, protected, changed. To disappear into a woman. To be killed, born. To feel the woman right against you. I don't know about Joe. He was in love with a woman he didn't know. But I don't know. I was looking half heartedly for the Emmylou girl. I wanted to smile at her. See what happened.

—We'll try the kitchen, said Joe. —This is shite.

We battled our way out to the hall – the house kept filling – and found the kitchen, a home in itself. There was a fireplace, a huge black metal oven, a silver fridge. The place was packed. And she was there. She was sitting on a chair, the only person in the room sitting. It took a while to realise that the thing she seemed to

214

be leaning on was the cello. Had she played, was she about to play? She moved to the side, bent down – she disappeared. And reappeared – she'd been getting her bow from the case on the floor. She was going to play. I looked at Joe, at the side of his face. I saw his sneer. Not there for long. He killed it, wiped it from his face. It was how we always reacted to things we didn't know – art, food, the world: we sneered. And that was what Joe did when he saw that she was about to play the cello. At first.

She threw her head back, and brought her hair with her. But it almost immediately fell back in front of her face as she sawed at the strings and, gradually, her movement produced notes and a sound that began to flow and rise. It was probably Bach – I don't know.

I saw the Emmylou girl. She was at the door, looking – like everyone else – at the cello. I left Joe and went across to her. She was by herself. I stood beside her.

—Hi.

She looked.

—Oh. Hi.

We both looked at the woman playing the cello.

—She's not very good, said Emmylou.

—No, I agreed.

I looked across at Joe, to make sure he hadn't heard me. He was gazing – I think that is an accurate word – gazing at her, at her bow hand, at her, hidden behind her hair. It was the look of a man who fancied the woman he was looking at. That was it. He was waiting to see her face again.

I'm making this up. I saw Joe's face that night, almost forty years ago. But I'm lying. I don't know what his expression was like. I didn't care. The woman beside me was holding my hand. I'd made my hand touch hers and she'd taken two, three of my fingers and held them, then opened her full hand to mine. I think her name was Alice – I'm not sure. I slept in her bedroom that night and met her mother the following morning. I remember that but not the girl, the woman, herself – not really.

I didn't stay. Alice started to turn, away from the music. She pressed my hand and I went with her.

We didn't know the cellist's name was Jess. When we watched her play, when I was watching Joe. We didn't know she was engaged, and that she was playing Bach at her own engagement party.

I look again – I try to remember – to see if I can spot Gavin, the fiancé. I have no idea who Gavin was. I can't see him standing beside her, over her. I can't see him leaning against the fridge, staring around, making sure that no one interrupts the performance. I can't see him in George's, with his arm around her shoulder. I don't think I ever did see him. I'm not certain that the child with the bottle opener said Jess and Gavin. I slept with a girl that night and I think her name was Alice, but I'm not sure.

The woman we'd been staring at and thinking of for months was called Jess – I know that now. We were in her house. And I remember, Alice didn't like her. I remember, it had helped me to like Alice, to reach for her hand. I'd done that when I'd heard – she'd let me hear – her irritated sigh. I liked her then, I'd liked her before then. But not enough to remember her name. I'm calling her Alice because it seems fairer – nicer – than calling her the Emmylou girl.

I know that the woman was called Jess. She was the boy in the bathroom's sister and she was engaged. But – before we went into the house and upstairs to the beer – we didn't know her name. We hadn't heard it, we hadn't asked it. That – what we didn't know – is true. Downstairs, in the kitchen, we didn't know we were looking at the fiancée. That must be true. We didn't know she was Jess.

I look again at Joe before I leave with Alice.

I can see it: he's smitten. I decide this.

Joe had gone downstairs, to the Black Hole of Calcutta. I'd been down already. It was well lit, almost beautiful, probably protected; it was like descending into the nineteenth century. I sat on the stool while he was gone. The place was filling and it was the easiest way to protect it. And I was tired. Wired and tired – and drunk. I checked my phone. I was dreading the call and wanting the call.

He'd had another go at explaining to me – and to himself, I thought – how he had felt. Finding Jess, finding what she meant to him, had been like finding something that he'd lost and would have given up on if – in this case – the growing sense of despair, and terror, hadn't made that impossible.

—This is somethin' that happened, I said. —What you're talkin' about now. This is somethin' that happened?

—Yeah.

—It did?

—Yeah, he said. —Yeah.

—Wha'?

—My weddin' ring.

—You lost your weddin' ring?

—Yeah.

—What happened?

217

—Another fuckin' cliché, said Joe. —The Christmas party.

—You took your weddin' ring off.

—Don't ask me why.

—Why?

—Well, there you go, he said. —It makes no sense. The woman knew I was married. So it was – ah, it was stupid. An' nothin' happened, like. Nothin' was ever goin' to happen. But I took it off anyway. In the jacks. Put it in me jacket pocket.

—Where were you?

—Some fuckin' place I'd never heard of. The younger ones always lead the way. So anyway, I'm chattin' to her. I think I might even have been talkin' about the kids, for fuck sake. But somethin' – the drink. Or the fact tha' she *is* a very good-lookin' woman, an' dead-on. I take the fuckin' ring off when I go out to the jacks. Like I'm announcin' somethin' to myself. Givin' myself permission. Connin' meself, I suppose. Totally illogical. Totally fuckin' stupid. An' like I said, I wasn't particularly frisky or anythin'.

—You didn't say that.

—Well, I'm fuckin' sayin' it now. But anyway, I come back from the toilet an' there's someone else sittin' where I'd been, an' I'm glad. I really am. A few more drinks. Mad things – cocktails, you know. Buckets o' fuckin' gin an' vegetables. An' I slide out, I've had enough. Into a taxi an' home.

He remembered the ring in the morning. He was lying in bed. He'd moved to the side that Trish had just vacated, into her warmth, when he remembered. His jacket was downstairs, draped carefully over a chair in the kitchen. He was nearly sure that that was where he'd left it. He was always very tidy and methodical

218

when he was drunk. The jacket was down in the kitchen and the ring was in the pocket and Trish would go through the pockets and find the ring, and she'd know exactly why it wasn't on the third finger of his left hand. She'd know immediately, without having to think it through. There was nothing to think through. He'd taken off the ring because he'd wanted to unmarry himself for the half hour it would have taken him to get into some young one's knickers, and he'd forgotten to remarry himself on the way home because he'd been so drunk – the smell off his breath, off his skin, was proof enough of that.

He sat up in the bed, too scared for a hangover. He was hoping he'd see the jacket on the floor, although he knew he wouldn't. His suit trousers were draped over the back of the chair beside the window, with his shirt and the tie. His shoes were side by side, parked under the chair. His underpants were on him.

—Me heart, Davy, he said. —I'm not jokin' yeh. The poundin' tha' should've been in me head – it had emigrated to my fuckin' heart.

Had he had sex with the woman the night before? He knew he hadn't – he was positive he hadn't. But he was sniffing himself and checking his crotch. Even though he knew nothing had happened. And he hated himself because nothing had happened and he was thanking Christ that nothing had happened. He couldn't think of anything to tell Trish, to explain the ring. She was down there now – he was sure of it – holding the jacket up in one hand, slipping the other hand into the first of its pockets.

Joe had forgotten about Jess or he was trying to make sure that I forgot about Jess. But it didn't matter. It was him at his best, his own hero and villain, genius

219

and eejit, bringing himself to big life in a story. The boy and the man I think I'd wanted to be.

—D'you have form? I asked him.

—Wha'?

—Well, why would Trish have been goin' through your pockets?

—Oh, he said. —That's just Trish. She's a pain in the arse – no. No, sorry – that's not fair. But you know the way I'm tellin' you a story? Now, like. Here.

—Yeah.

—Well, she'd've been tellin' hers, he said. —If tha' makes sense. In her head – livin' the story as she went around the kitchen. Searchin' the pockets – that's what they're there for, kind o' thing.

—A pair of fuckin' drama queens.

—Fuck off, but yeah.

He wanted to go downstairs to the kitchen but he was afraid to. There was a chance she hadn't searched the pockets, and wasn't going to. But she might have been waiting at the foot of the stairs with the ring sitting on the palm of her hand. Or in the kitchen, waiting, pretending there wasn't a fight and a separation on the way. He couldn't think of anything to tell her if she'd found the ring. But he got out of bed and put on his dressing gown. He lifted the shirt and trousers off the chair, to make sure that what he knew was true: the jacket was downstairs. He checked the trouser pockets – and no ring. He thought of a story on the landing. He'd tell her he'd got the ring caught in a towel, one of those small white towels that they stack beside the sinks in hotel toilets. The Clarence – he'd say they'd been in the Clarence; they'd all gone there after the food. They'd been to the Clarence before, him and Trish, so she'd know exactly what he was talking about.

He'd had to take the ring off to free it from the towel because it had become snagged, somehow – he didn't know how; he'd been drunk. And he'd forgotten to put it back on. He must have slipped it into the pocket so he could wash his hands.

Trish was there, in the kitchen. She was making a list, opening and shutting the fridge and the presses. It was a couple of days before Christmas. He'd forgotten all about Christmas. It was why he'd been out with the office gang.

—The dead arose, she said.

Her back was to him. She was looking in the freezer above the fridge. The jacket was where he knew he'd left it. He lifted it off the chair, exactly as he'd pictured Trish doing. He put his free hand into the pocket he'd slipped the ring into the night before. Trish was still rooting through the freezer. The pocket was empty; the ring wasn't in there.

—No fuckin' ring, Davy, he said. —An' I knew I'd put it in there. I fuckin' knew.

Trish had turned.

—What are you lookin' for? she asked.

—Nothin', he said.

—You're not smokin' again, are you? she said.

I'd forgotten: Joe used to smoke. In fact, it was un-usual that he hadn't mentioned it tonight because he often had a smoke – just the one, or two – when we were out together.

—No, he told Trish. —My wallet.

He was delighted – relieved. She hadn't been search-ing the pockets. She'd have known there wasn't a packet of Silk Cut and matches or a lighter in the pockets if she'd already been through them. But Trish loved her drama. She might have been leading him to the trap.

He still had to be careful, and the hangover was kicking in. He was dying. He checked the other pocket as Trish pointed to the black wallet – an anniversary present, from Trish – on the kitchen table.

—There it is, look.

The ring wasn't there. It wasn't in the only other pocket it could have been in. There was just one inside pocket and he would never have put the ring into that one. He was reliving the moment, the night before, soaping the finger, sliding it off, putting it in the pocket – the outside pocket, right side. Trish was looking at him. She'd shown him the wallet on the table and he was now putting his hand into the inside pocket, searching for something he no longer needed to search for.

—Joe, she said.

—What?

—Your wallet's on the table.

—Yeah.

The inside pocket was empty. He was hoping his face was too. But he thought he was going to vomit.

—There's Coke in the fridge, said Trish. —D'you want some? You look like you need the bubbles.

He put the jacket back on the chair. He lifted the shoulders, to make sure it sat well. And saw the wedding ring. On his finger.

—Ah, Jesus, I said.

—I swear to God. On my fuckin' finger.

—That's brilliant.

I laughed. I leaned against him. I put my forehead to the side of his head, for a second. I lifted my head.

—Jesus, Joe, I said. —You're a terrible fuckin' messer.

I knew we'd be having another pint.

—My fuckin' heart, Davy, he said. —An' she asks if I want a fuckin' Coke. An' there was me thinkin' she was goin' to murder me – stab me – or wallop me with somethin' out o' the fuckin' freezer. A leg of lamb or somethin'. The fuckin' turkey.

He kept looking at the ring; he couldn't help it. He kept expecting it to be gone. He couldn't believe that nothing was going to happen. He was almost disappointed.

—I loved fightin' Trish, he said. —I have to say tha'.

—Joe, I said.

—Wha'?

—Why're you tellin' me this?

—Wha' d'you mean?

—You told me this – the story, like. It's brilliant, by the way. But you said it would – I don't know – illustrate how you felt when you met Jess again. And now you're tellin' me you liked the fights with Trish.

—Well, it's true.

—What is?

—The fights.

He looked around; he'd just heard himself. He looked back at me.

—Rows, I meant. Arguments.

—I know wha' you mean.

—Trish, he said. —She's like an opera singer when she's arguing. She's fuckin' amazin'.

—Yeah, I said.

I'd met Trish only a couple of times but I remembered her tearing the face off me once and I'd felt tiny, torn apart and lucky to have been the focus of such attention. She'd held my arm when she'd finished with me. She'd run her hand up and down it, elbow to shoulder, shoulder to elbow. She'd patted it. We were all drunk in a back garden. Any friend of Joe's is a friend of mine, she'd said. I have your back, remember that. I came away feeling lucky and lonely.

—You still haven't told me, I said.

—I miss Trish, he said. —There's a part o' me tha' misses Trish. I have to say.

—You still haven't told me.

—Fuck off, Davy, for fuck sake. I'm gettin' there – I've lost track. It made sense when I started. Yeah, that's it – it was tha' feelin' of elation when I saw the ring. I thought I was fucked, then there it was. But that's goin' off track again. But it was the feelin'. Like a miracle but, actually, it was easily explained. I must've remembered the ring was in me pocket, probably in the taxi on the way home, an' I'd put it back on. Simple as. So, yeah. I found Jess.

—An' it felt miraculous.

—It kind of did, he said. —But a slower burn, if you're with me. Gradual. Like, I can't quite believe this but it's happenin'. At the school an' then when she texted me, I was thinkin' – I suppose – here we go. But then the first couple o' meetin's. An' it settled into this other feelin' – tha' there'd been no reunion, it'd been like this all along.

Joe was back from the toilet. I stood, and he got past me and sat. He brought his pint closer to him with his right hand. I looked at the left.

—You still have your ring on, I said.

—Wha'?

He caught up with what I'd said and he held up the hand.

—Yeah, he said. —An' you spotted it as well. You're a bit of an oul' one, aren't you, Davy?

—Fuck off.

—Well, Jesus, he said. —I can't think o' one other man
– not one – who'd've noticed or given a shite. No offence.

—Only because you were talkin' about it, I said.

—You're grand, he said. —I'm only slaggin' yeh. But,
yeah. I still have it. Trish flung hers at me.

—Did it hurt?

—She missed.

He grinned.

—It broke the glass on a photograph of her mother.
Knocked the fuckin' thing off the wall.

—Brilliant.

—Well, it was. An' she started laughin' before I did.
She's great, Trish.

He tapped the ring with a fingernail.

—Anyway, we're not divorced, he said.

—Hedgin' your bets.

—No, he said. —Fuck off. No. What's done's done.
I've no regrets.

—Is that true?

—It is, I think, yeah. It's true enough. But tha' sayin'
– no regrets, like. It's a bit callous. Is it?

—It could be, I said. —An' it's definitely unrealistic.

—Exactly, he said. —How could you not have regrets?
Some, at least. Everyone has a few regrets.

—Yeah.

—So, then, yeah, he said. —I do have regrets. Fuckin'
big ones. The whole family thing. I miss them – fuck
me. I don't even have to admit tha' – you'd be the
same, I know.

—Yup.

—It'll iron itself out in time, he said. —Whatever
tha' fuckin' means. So I'm bein' told. Every time I open
me fuckin' mouth. But it's true. It has to be. You don't

go from bein' a good dad to an evil one, just like tha'.
Or a husband. They'll calm down.

—Probably, yeah, I said.

—Eventually.

—Yeah.

—Fuck it, he said.

—What about you?

—What about me?

—Will you calm down?

—I am fuckin' calm, he said.

—Grand.

—Calm as – whatever.

He watched me – he was looking at my hand as I took my pint off the counter. He bent slightly and grabbed my other one, the left. I let him do it, so we both looked at the palm and fingers.

—Come here, you, he said. —Where's your own fuckin' ring?

He let go of the hand.

—I don't have one, I told him.

—No?

—I've never had one.

—How come?

—Well, I said. —It wasn't unusual back then, remember. For the groom not to have one. I'd've been happy enough but Faye wasn't havin' it.

—How come?

—She used to find weddin' rings on the table at home, when she was a kid. After her father died.

—Jesus, he said.

—Yep.

—But did men have weddin' rings back then?

—I know what you mean, I said. —But some must've. Cos Faye found them.

—An' her ma was a bike?

—A tandem, I said.

I felt disloyal, and cruel. But there was no real point in trying to explain Faye's mother to Joe. It was too complicated; the drink was drowning the words.

—But it doesn't make sense, he said.

—What doesn't?

—These lads takin' their weddin' rings off. Before they went up with her mother.

—Faye used to hide them.

—The rings?

—Yeah.

—Brilliant.

—Her mother paid her to do it, I told him. —After she did it the first few times.

—That's mad, said Joe. —Kind o' not funny, really. Did Faye think it was funny?

—No.

—She took the money, but.

—She saved it.

Faye was all set to go, before her mother died. She just had to pull herself away from the conviction that she was needed; and the fear that she wasn't. She'd made it to Dublin once, when she was sixteen. Her mother guessed she'd be at her aunt's flat, her father's sister, Mary; and she phoned. Come home, pet. I'm dying.

—The whole ring thing, though, said Joe. —Two women, Davy. Tha' was me for a bit. I sound like a fucker.

—A bit, yeah.

—I know. But I'd like to think I'm not. The fuckin' Mormons an' their polygamy, there's no way it'd work out fairly. For the women – sure it wouldn't?

—No.

—Now there was a religion designed by a man.

—They all were.

—Wha'?

—Religions.

—True, he said. —It's all bollix. I'm feelin' these pints now.

—Behind the head.

—Exactly, he said. —I'm out o' practice. Still, though. Great to see you, man.

He held out his glass. He wanted me to tap mine against his.

—Good to see you too, I said.

We tapped.

I wanted to go now. I wanted to get back before the call. I wanted to sit with my father. Just sit. I wanted to tell him I loved him. I wanted to say it out loud.

—But men have managed it, said Joe. —The two households thing.

—Jesus, Joe –

—I know, he said. —But look it. Tha' was me – in a way, it was me, how I was livin'. For months.

—It must be fuckin' exhaustin'.

—No, he said.

—It must be, I said. —It has to be.

—No, I swear, he said. —I see why you'd think it. But it wasn't.

—It wasn't two households, was it, though – really? Two houses, the works.

—No, he said. —An' – I don't know. Dividin' the time – a night in one place, a night in the other place. Tha' must be a killer. Never mind the economics. Keepin' track o' the lies – fuckin' hell. But look, I wasn't messin'. D'you know what I mean, Davy? I wasn't actin' the prick.

—Well, you must've been.

—No.

—To an extent, I said. —You must've been. Did you tell Trish wha' you were up to?

—No.

—There, I said. —So, you withheld the information –

—Are you fuckin' jokin' me? Trish?

—What I'm suggestin' is, just because you didn't think you were messin' around, that doesn't mean you weren't.

—Lower the voice a bit.

—Was I shoutin'?

—A bit.

I looked to the sides – I saw no one looking away. The barmen were busy. We were okay.

—Did you stay away from home? I asked him.

—The house?

—Yeah.

—Yeah, he said. —A couple o' times. Before –

—Trish found out.

—I told Trish – but yeah.

—How many?

—Wha'?

—Nights.

—Four. For a night, just. You know – a single night. Each time.

Now I lowered my voice; I wasn't sure why.

—But you said you didn't have sex with Jess, I said.

—No, he said. —But –

—Wha'?

—You'll have to get past tha' – the sex. If you're goin' to understand wha' I've been tryin' to say.

—Give me a fuckin' break, Joe.

—Fuck off now, Davy – you give *me* a fuckin' break. I'm not a slug an' I'm not fuckin' stupid either. I knew it couldn't last an' that I'd have to tell Trish. An' I knew what would happen. An' it did. Boy, did it – fuckin' hell. Although even tha' got complicated. But there was a spell – that's what I'm sayin'. There was a spell when it felt perfectly, nearly perfectly fuckin' normal to be livin' the way I was.

He grabbed his pint. I thought for a second that he'd pour it over my head, or his own. But all he did was drink from it.

—What's this? Faye said.

—What's what?

It was two years or so after we'd moved to England. We were still a bit lost and Faye was pregnant again. She was holding a piece of paper, a receipt.

—What the fuck is this supposed to be, David? she said.

She slapped my nose with the paper and stepped back before I could grab it.

—Stop it, Faye, I said.

—Stop what? Stop what, exactly?

—It's not funny, I said. —Stop it.

She looked at the receipt. She brought it up to her eyes, although it was another twenty-five years before she'd start wearing reading glasses.

—Bombay Indian Restaurant, she read.

She stepped up to me again, and slapped me with the receipt. Harder this time; her knuckles brushed the side of my nose.

—Lay off, Faye – please.

—Who is it? she said. —Do I know her?

She was looking at the receipt again.

—Two starters, two mains.

—I hope you're enjoying yourself, I said.

—I am.

—It's boring, Faye.

—What's boring, David? Indian food or adultery?

I laughed.

—What's so funny?

—You are, Faye, I told her. —You're brilliant.

She looked at the receipt. She'd been upstairs, putting Cathal, our eldest, to bed.

—It was in your pocket, so it was.

—No, it wasn't.

—Maybe it's mine, so.

—Maybe it is, I said.

—Who did I meet, I wonder? she said. —Are you interested?

—No.

—Don't worry, though, Dave, she said. —I'd never let any man's tongue near my fanny after he's had a vindaloo.

—Wise move, I said. —It was us, by the way.

—What was?

—You were the woman, I told her. —We ate in that place a couple of weeks ago. We had Cathal with us.

—A likely story.

—You said it yourself, I said. —You'd be the only pregnant woman in England who liked spicy food.

There were times when I knew she was messing and times when she frightened me, when I thought I was sharing the house with a woman I didn't know or like. Her unpredictability became a threat. I thought sometimes that she didn't trust herself, she didn't trust what

231

we were; she was testing herself, rehearsing her mother's madness. It was nasty, brief, sporadic and strategic. She never performed in front of the kids. She let them grow up and when they left, she let them stay gone. They never got the phone calls, Come home, pet, I'm dying.

—Guess what, Dave? she said the day we came home after driving Róisín to college in London.

—What?

—We can do what we want, she said.

—That's true.

—The first time in fuckin' for ever, she said. —We can starve the dog if we like.

—Do we want to do that?

—It can go onto the agenda, she said. —Is what I'm saying. We can do anything we want. Does that appeal to you, David?

It didn't.

I'd no children; I'd nothing. I'd nothing to do and nothing I wanted to do, other than lie down and wait – I didn't know for what. A revelation or a disease – both made equal sense.

She put her arms around me and she cried; she drenched my shoulder.

—They're ungrateful little cunts, she said.

—Are you talking about our children, Faye?

—I am.

—We could watch telly, I said.

—My God, she said. —There's a thought. Telly.

I kissed the top of her head. I knew what she was going to say.

—Never fuckin' kiss me there, David.

I was finally getting to know her.

★   ★   ★

I watched Joe. He'd stopped talking. He'd stopped needing to talk. He was looking around again, as if we'd just arrived.

—This place hasn't changed, he said.

He pointed at a line of old photographs.

—The dead writers are still dead, he said.

—That's reassurin'.

—It kind of is, he said. —I go with it.

—Sorry?

—I go with it, he said. —I'm tryin' to think of a way to describe it.

—Describe wha'?

—I don't know, he said. —That's part o' the problem. The whole thing. What's happened – since I met Jess.

—You go with it?

—Yeah – I think so.

—With the flow, d'you mean? I asked him. —You go with the flow?

—No, he said. —No. Definitely not tha'. Tha' sounds like I'm bein' led by the flute or somethin'. An' I'm not. At all – fuckin' at all.

—Okay.

—I'll tell you what it is, he said.

But he didn't – not immediately. He was looking at the bottles on the high shelves, and at the pictures. He didn't look drunk now. The wetness had gone from around his eyes. He looked older – older than he'd looked a few minutes before. And turning – when he was turning his head – he seemed stiffer; his body had to go with him. The back of his head, down around the neck, looked fleshy.

I waited.

I wanted to leave again. Suddenly. I didn't like my position here, the listener, the tape recorder. I wanted to call Faye. I wanted to see my father.

He put his hand on his glass again.

—It's a thing abou' gettin' older, he said. —At least, I suppose it is. So many memories, you know. It becomes harder to separate wha' happened from wha' might've happened an' wha' didn't happen but kind o' seemed to.

He was looking at me.

—Is it? he asked.

—Is memory reliable? I said. —Is that wha' you mean?

—I think so, yeah.

—Jesus, Joe.

—I know.

—For fuck sake.

—I know, he said. —I remember once. Listen –.

He lifted his glass. He drank. He took the glass from his mouth and held it to his chest.

—Not tha' long ago, he said. —Only – Jesus – only a bit more than a year ago. We'd a do in our house. Aaron's graduation, it would've been.

The name, Aaron, meant nothing but I knew he was one of Joe's kids.

—College graduation? I asked.

—No, no, he said. —He's not the eldest. That's Sam. No, just school. End o' sixth year, you know. A big deal these days – fuckin' hell. Anyway, my sisters were there, an' Trish's sister, Grace. An' the husbands. You know, yourself. The gang. We were ou' the back, in the garden. We've a pond out there now, an' a deck. A barbecue as well, one o' the big lads. Like a fuckin' helicopter under the cover, if you're lookin' ou' the window at it durin' the winter.

—We've one o' them too, I said.

—There you go, he said. —Half the gardens in fuckin'
Ireland have them.

—Does Jess?

—No, he said. —No. D'you know wha', though? I'm
not sure. I haven't been ou' in her back garden.

—Really?

He seemed to be thinking about it, going back over
the months.

—Yeah, he said.

—You live there.

—I know, he said. —It's – wha'? – a bit odd, I suppose. But I don't know. I just haven't gone ou' there.
The wheelies are all out in the front, so –.

—You've looked out the kitchen window, surely.

—I have, he said. —Yeah. An' I haven't seen a barbecue. But anyway, where was I?

—Your back garden.

—That's righ', he said. —Thanks. We were all ou'
there, sittin' around in a big circle, like, an' Trish starts
tellin' a story, somethin' tha' happened when the kids
were smaller, a few years before – another couple o'
years back. There's a school at the end of our road,
d'you remember?

—No, I said.

I'd never been to his house.

—Ah, you do.

—I don't.

—Well, there is, he said. —On the corner. A girls'
school – the national, you know. An' if you're tryin' to
get out, off the road, when all the parents are droppin'
their kids off in the mornin' just before nine, you haven't
a hope. It's jammed. It's a pain in the arse. So, anyway,
Trish was tellin' everyone abou' this one time. The car

– our car, like – was stuck behind a jeep. The woman drivin' the jeep had parked it nearly in the middle o' the road an' she was out of it, gettin' her kids ou' from the back. An' Trish was tellin' them all how I rolled down the window an' called out to her, Excuse me? Exactly like I did do it – I'll never forget it. So, the woman – a big girl, by the way, with a baseball cap. She takes her head out o' the back of the jeep an' turns. The way Trish was tellin' it, it was fuckin' brilliant. An' we were all in stitches – all ages, you know. Kids an' oldies, all laughin'. So anyway, I ask her – your woman with the baseball cap. I say, Would you mind movin' your car, we're just tryin' to get out? An' your woman just says, Fuck off.

—No.

—Yeah, said Joe. —That's all. Fuck off. Straight at me. An' Trish's face, Davy, when she was sayin' it. It was the funniest fuckin' thing. Trish wasn't wearin' a cap when she was tellin' it but, the way she was holdin' her head, you'd've sworn she was. It was fuckin' hilarious. But.

—But what?

—She wasn't there.

—What d'you mean?

—She wasn't in the car – Trish wasn't. I was drivin' an' Holly was beside me. Just me an' Holly. I was droppin' her off to a football summer camp before I went on to work. She's a great footballer, Holly. All sports, really. But it was June, like, so Holly was done with school but the girls' school, the primary, was still open till the end o' the month. That's why she was with me. But the point is, Trish wasn't there. She didn't witness the woman's performance. I told her later.

—Okay.

—You don't think it matters?

—I don't know, I said. —But not really – I don't think so. We all do it, don't we? Embellish stories, add to them. Especially in this country.

—No, I know wha' you mean, he said. —As far as tha' goes, yeah, I'm with you. She hears it from me, she hears me tellin' it fuck knows how many times. So, she makes it her own.

—Yeah.

—Yeah, he said. —It's understandable. It's natural. An' she's a brilliant storyteller – a raconteur. Brilliant. You should see men lookin' at Trish when she's in full flow. Jesus – d'you remember?

—Yeah, I said.

I was lying: I didn't remember watching Trish telling a story. But I'd seen Faye, and men watching her as she spoke, loving her, resenting her, leaning in to take over, sitting back open-mouthed.

—So, I'm happy to hand it over, said Joe. —She's the entertainer. I just happen to be the one who endured the wrath – the fuckin' contempt of Missis Baseball Cap. It doesn't matter. We're joint owners o' the house – still are, by the way. An' we'd a joint account, so we might as well share the stories. I don't know – our fuckin' autobiographies. An' she's better at it.

—Same with me, I said. —Me an' Faye.

—There you go, he said. —An' it's a good thing. We don't feel threatened or undermined.

—No.

—An' they glow, he said.

—Yeah.

—Don't they?

—Yeah.

—So, he said. —It's grand. It's more than grand. But.

—The fact remains.

—The fact fuckin' remains. She wasn't in the fuckin' car.

—But, I said. —So wha'?

—So wha'? he said. —Nothin' – nothin', really. But this is my point, I think. If Trish an' myself hadn't – if we were still together, we wouldn't be havin' this particular conversation, you an' me. Because I'd've let her into the car. I'd've remembered her bein' there beside me, with Holly in the back – eventually. That's wha' would've happened.

—That's possible.

—That's definite, he said. —That's wha' would've happened. I've no doubt about it at all. It's wha' was already happenin', the more I heard her tell the story. I wanted her to be in the car. An' I'd've eventually remembered it tha' way. I'd've seen her beside me in the passenger seat, maybe even me in the passenger seat an' her drivin'. I'd've genuinely remembered it. But then we split up.

—An' she's not in the car any more.

—She's not in the fuckin' car. Are we having another?

—Go on, I said.

I was trying to recall a case of my own, some event that Faye had made her own. But I couldn't remember the last time we'd been in company, when I'd have heard and watched her tell a story. For years now, I've been her only audience. And I'd been hiding from her.

It's my fault.

—Two more, please, Joe said to a barman, the same one, I thought, who'd served us the last time.

The barman raised a hand.

—Two, he said, and kept going to the taps.

Joe took out his phone and looked at the clock.

—Loads o' time, he said.

He put the phone back into his pocket. I checked my own, took it out. I held it beside my leg and looked down. I slipped it back into the pocket.

—I asked Holly, he said.

—Wha'?

—I asked her – Holly. I asked her wha' she thought o' Trish sayin' tha' she was in the car with us.

—When was this?

—Well, when she was still talkin' to me, anyway, he said. —It would've been before meself an' Trish split up. Before she threw me ou'.

—Is tha' what happened?

—Not really, no, he said. —It wasn't really like tha'. I threw myself out. Truth be told – whatever tha' fuckin' means. No, we were arguin' alright, but I was still at home. But Holly would've heard us, I suppose. Definitely. Shite –. But anyway, Holly said she'd been in the car.

—Trish.

—Yeah. She said Trish was there with us. An' I'll tell you. I found tha' very hurtful.

—Why? I asked.

—Well, these things, he said. —Memories. They're precious, aren't they? I used to think tha', anyway. Special. There was me an' there was Holly beside me, an' your woman with the cap tellin' me to fuck off an' we were laughin', the two of us, once we were off the road an' your woman couldn't see us. Just me an' Holly.

—You didn't have it out with her, no?

—Who?

—The woman.

—Are you jokin' me? he said. —Never – Davy. Seriously. Never disagree with a woman who's wearin' a
baseball cap. If you remember nothin' else tonight,
remember tha', for fuck sake. But Holly. It was like she
was erasin' me. From her memory. It hurt.

—Did she say you weren't there?

—No, he said. —No, she didn't. It's just, she inserted
her mother. She was takin' sides.

—Jesus, Joe, I said. —Do you really think tha'?

—I do, yeah – I think I do. An' look, I don't blame
her. She's heard Trish tell the story as often as I have.
An' then there's me – she's furious with me. That's
what I mean about her erasin' me. I'm bein' punished.
Here's the pints. Whose twist is it?

—It might be me.

—It might be me as well, said Joe. —It was never a
question back in the day, was it? We'd've known. Part
o' the muscle memory or somethin'.

He was searching his pocket for notes. So was I, and
I got there before him. I pulled another twenty from
my wallet and held it out, across Joe, to the barman.
He took it and turned to the till.

—I'll get the next two rounds, said Joe.

He watched the barman put the change on the
counter.

—If I fuckin' remember, he said.

He watched me gather the change, the fiver and
coins, and slide it into my pocket.

—So, yeah, he said. —Memory.

—Okay, I said. —What about it?

—Did you ever tell a lie so often you ended up
believin' it?

—Probably, I said.

—Probably me hole. You did.

—Okay.

—So often it becomes a memory, he said. —Some porky you told to get you out of a corner becomes an event tha' you can remember. You cross a line or somethin'. D'you think that's feasible? I'm not so sure.

—No, I said. —Same here – I think.

I was getting drunk for the second or third time that night. I was feeling young. I was feeling thin and tall. I was feeling less than careful.

—But how would you know? I asked.

—Wha'?

—Well, if a lie becomes somethin' you remember, you have to forget it's a lie. Surely. Don't you?

—Good point.

—I mean, I said. —I remember lyin' so convincingly, I almost believed it. But I still knew it was a fuckin' lie. I didn't really believe –. I was impressed, tha' was it.

—When was this?

—Are you askin' me if I've only told a lie once in me life?

—No, he said. —No. Just a – for example. I seem to be doin' all the talkin'. Am I?

—Yeah.

—Fuck off, he said. —Go on.

—Well, I said.

I couldn't think of anything.

—Why are we talkin' abou' this? I asked. —Memories an' stuff – wha' started it?

—Good question, said Joe. —I was – I think I was, anyway. I was tryin' to explain –

I remembered something.

—I've got one, I said.

—Good man, he said.

—I told Faye I had a stalker.

—Fuck off.

He laughed, and so did I.

—Brilliant, he said. —That's fuckin' mad. What happened?

—Well, I said. —It's ages ago. Before the word stalker was even a thing.

—Before you went to England?

—No, I said. —No. Not tha' long ago. I've been livin' in England longer than I haven't been, remember. If tha' makes sense.

—It does.

—Does it?

—Yeah, he said. —You're in England more than thirty years.

—Yeah, I said. —Exactly.

—Fuckin' hell.

—Yeah, I said. —It's hard to believe sometimes. Especially tonight. Somehow. It feels like I've never been away.

He picked up his old glass.

—Good to see you, man, he said.

I picked up my glass and we tapped them again.

—Fuckin' great, isn't it?

—Yeah.

—Fuckin' great, he said. —Move back, Davy – you have to.

—No.

—Go on, he said. —Come home.

—Can't.

—Why not? What's stoppin' you?

—Faye wouldn't have it.

—Fuck her.

★   ★   ★

Faye was watching a film. She'd heard the key in the door. She thought she'd heard a car – the taxi moving away from the front of the house. All the sounds were expected – the car, the key, the front door being carefully opened. Then the unexpected. A rhythm that wasn't mine. Strange feet in the hall.

—David?

I remember my hand on the wall. Beside the light switch.

—Dave?

She found me looking at my feet.

—What's wrong?

I lifted my foot, the one that I'd just realised lacked a shoe. I felt the sock – the sole. It wasn't wet. Was it raining outside, was it wet out there? I didn't know.

—What's wrong with your foot?

I let go of the foot. I let go of the wall. I looked again. The shoe still wasn't there. I looked at Faye.

—God, the state of you, she said. —Come on – come in. Where's your bloody shoe gone? Shut the door there, for God's sake. The dog will fuckin' escape again.

I couldn't speak. I couldn't remember getting home. I couldn't remember being in a taxi; I couldn't remember paying for a taxi. I couldn't remember opening the door. I couldn't turn to close it. Faye did that; she went past me. I heard the rush – the door across the mat, the slight thump and the click. Faye was gentle. She was smiling as she put her arm around me, under my own arm, and escorted me to the couch and let me drop. I lay there, facing the television. There was sound, a gunfight, music, then no sound. The dog was looking at me. Whatever dog it was back then. Front paws up on the couch, right in front of my face.

Faye sat on the floor.

—Are you going to be sick, are you?

I tried to shake my head. I lifted it, I got up on my elbow. I moved my head, right, left.

—Saying no would've been easier, Dave, said Faye.

—No, I said. —No, Faye.

—You remember my name – lovely.

I closed my eyes. But it wasn't nice there. I opened them again.

—Where's your shoe?

—Somewhere.

—Grand.

Something about the way she spoke, about the way I heard it. She thought I was a child. I was lying on my side, my hands were under my cheek. I'd lost one of my shoes. I was a child. My mother was beside me, looking after me.

I didn't like it. I didn't want a mother.

—There's a woman in work, I told her.

—Is there?

I sat up. I felt like I'd slept. I was ready.

—What about her? said Faye.

—What?

—This woman you're dying to tell me about.

—She won't leave me alone, Faye.

—Did she take your shoe?

—No, I said. —I don't think so. I don't know. She's gorgeous, Faye.

—I'm sure she is.

I wanted Faye to slap me. I wanted her to rage. To stand over me and beat me. I wanted to feel her over me, on me.

She was sitting on the couch now. She was holding one of my feet.

—And she's taken your shoe hostage, has she?

I was lying down again.

—You're Cinderella, David, she said.

—What?

—That's who you are, said Faye. —You left the shoe behind when you ran away at midnight. And – sure, look. It isn't even midnight. It's hardly even dark. She'll be going from door to door now, getting all the men to try on your shoe.

—She's gorgeous.

—I bet she is. And she'll be ringing the bell any minute, will she?

I was crying.

—I'd never do it, Faye.

—More fool, you, *Daithí*.

—I'd never do it.

—I know, she said. —I know you wouldn't.

Her face was close to mine. I opened my eyes. She was still there, further away. I closed my eyes. I opened them. She was gone.

—Faye?

—Go to sleep, David.

There was something on me. Faye had put a duvet over me. The television was off, the light was off.

—Faye?

—Go to sleep, for fuck sake.

—Where are you?

—Near, she said.

—Where?

—Go to sleep.

—I don't want to.

—You do.

—I don't.

—Please yourself, so.

—I don't want to.

—You're a pest, so you are. Go to sleep. Don't get up and fuckin' wander. Let the kids stay asleep.

—She was gorgeous, Faye.

—Sure, I know, she said.

She was beside me again. Looking down.

—Make sure you stay on your side, she said. —The basin's beside you there. In case you want it.

She was gone.

—I want to hold you, Faye.

I couldn't get up. I wanted to, but I couldn't. I had to sleep – I had to roll away from this. I needed to shut my eyes. I needed this to end. I needed to start. Start again. Find her. Look at her. Hold her.

—Why did you say tha'? I asked him.

—Wha'?

—Fuck her, I said.

—I didn't mean it like tha', said Joe. —Fuck her. I didn't say tha'.

He smiled.

—More fuck'r, he said. —That's what I said. An' not aggressively. Or dismissively – none o' tha'.

It was like he was ready; he'd planned his response.

—Wha' makes you think you can fuckin' say tha'? I asked.

—Okay, he said. —Look, I shouldn't've said it but – fuck it – I didn't say wha' you're sayin' I said. But I do apologise.

—It's always the fuckin' same.

—Jesus, he said. —Here we go.

—Fuck you, Joe.

—Drink up, Davy, he said. —Before we get fucked ou'.

This was more like it. This was what I hadn't been remembering.

—Just fuck you, I said. —You can't fuckin' say tha'.

—I'm sorry.

—It's like – for fuck sake. It's like you expect me to make a decision – not a decision either. Just fuckin' obey you, just like tha'.

—Where's this comin' from?

—From deep down an' far away.

—What's tha' fuckin' mean?

—Fuck you.

I was going to do what I wanted to do. I was going to go. I'd had enough.

—Seeyeh, Joe.

—I'm sorry, he said. —I didn't mean anythin'. I was bein' flippant – stupid. Sorry.

I was going.

—I don't even want you to come home to Dublin, he said. —Not really. I was just enjoyin' meself an' I thought you were too. So – yeah. Sorry.

—You can't fuckin' say tha'.

—I didn't mean anythin'.

—You can't fuckin' say tha', I said again. —I'm still married, you know. I understand the fuckin' rules.

—Ah, now, he said. —For fuck sake.

He laughed and I still didn't want to hit him. But I wasn't going yet – the need had gone from my legs. I wanted to want to hit him. I wanted to feel myself deciding not to. To forgive him because he needed me to.

—You're a desperate fuckin' bitch, Davy, he said. —I understand the rules. For fuck sake.

—It's always been the same, I said. —But it's not. Not now.

247

—What're you on abou'?

—I always had to drop everythin', I said.

—That's just bollix.

—It isn't, I said. —An' you fuckin' know it isn't.

—An' I'll ask you again, he said. —Where's this comin' from?

—Fuckin' always.

—Wha'?

—But I'll fuckin' tell you, it's different now.

—I'm sure it is, he said. —What is?

—I don't even live in this poxy country.

—Thank fuck.

—You don't even know Faye.

—I know I don't an' I'm sorry for tha', he said. —I am. I didn't mean to – to – hurt your feelin's. Or insult you. Or her – Faye. I really am sorry.

—You even insisted that I fancied Jessica, I said. —Before we even knew who she was. Which we never fuckin' did, by the way, I don't care what you're sayin'.

—Fuckin' hell.

—Just because you fell for her, I had to as well. I broke it off with tha' one – Mags.

—Mags?

—Yeah.

—Mags? he said. —Are we inventin' people now? Fuckin' Mags?

—Yeah – Mags.

—Who's Mags?

—I think her name was Mags.

—You think?

—Yeah.

—Who was she?

—I went with her, I said.

—The love o' your life an' you can't remember her.

—I didn't say she was the love o' me life, I said.
—An' I do remember her. Quite well. I'm just not sure
of her name. It was years ago.

—I'd hope so, he said. —Because, let's face it, you're
married an' you understand the rules.

—Ah, fuck off.

—I'm only quotin' you, he said. —Who's Mags?

—Back, just after I left college, I said. —She had a
flat on Leeson Street.

—You broke it off with a bird with a flat?

He was winning again. He was taking my anger and
clarity from me. And I was letting him do it. Just as
I'd done years before. I was trotting along behind him.
Letting myself be his sidekick.

I drank from my pint. It was warm – it protested; it
didn't want to be drunk. I swallowed.

—I'm goin' to the jacks, I said.

—Good man.

I hadn't been sitting but I felt like I'd just stood up.
I was dizzy. I didn't stagger – I don't think I did. The
spots stayed away from in front of my eyes. But I could
feel myself deciding to take the steps I needed to take
to get to the door down to the toilet. I was remembering
the hospital, trying to put one foot forward, failing.

I watched the steps down, I held the rail. It was good
to be away. Away from him, away from warm drink. I
wanted to go now, to piss – urgently. I unzipped my
fly while I was still on the stairs. I let go of the rail. I
was fine.

I pissed. It was fine. It was normal – strong. I hated
this getting old, the surprises. The quick indignities.
It was supposed to be a slowing down, but it wasn't; it
was a series of shocks. I'd been told that my hearing
wasn't great in one ear. I'd been told that I had low

249

blood pressure, high cholesterol. I'd been told that I had a blocked artery, coronary artery disease. I'd been told that I had a cataract on my left eye – a small one, a growing one. All in less than two years. From man to old man. Dying man. Careful man. Self-pitying, pathetic man. I'd been told not to drink and I was getting hammered – I was already hammered. I was my young self, drunk, sober, drunk, sober several times in a day. I was drunk. I was drunk and angry, drunk and happy. Drunk and lost. Drunk and just drunk. I was missing something.

I checked my phone. I'd missed nothing.

I washed my hands. It was cold here – it was nice. I was still alone. I went to the wall opposite the sink. I kept my eyes on the door upstairs and I put my face, my left cheek, against the wall, the white tiles. I felt the cold go through me. Down me. I was steadier, sturdier. I went back to the stairs. I remembered what he'd said, I remembered what I'd said. I wanted to keep going. To keep going at him. I had to keep the anger. He had to know and I had to get it right.

I was steadier, lighter. I was ready to beat him.

I checked my phone again; I took it out. I'd done it already – I remembered that.

—You said you had a stalker, he said when I got back.

—No, I didn't.

—You did.

—I told Faye I had a stalker, I said. —That's what I said. But you weren't listenin'.

—Ah, Davy.

—No, no – sorry, I said. —But I need to get this straight. You'd no right to say wha' you said abou' Faye there. It was just crude an' you were tryin' to make me

250

go against her, even though you might not be conscious o' that. An' her name was definitely Mags.

He looked at me. That was it – he looked at me. He didn't try to interrupt or contradict. He didn't smile this time, he didn't shake his head. He let me talk.

—There was a gig, I said. —In the Magnet. I'm nearly certain it was the Magnet. The Atrix – the band. I was goin' to bring Mags an' you said I couldn't. You said it was disloyal, I could meet her on Saturday night or any other night o' the week, but not Friday. Disloyal to fuckin' you, by the way. Friday night was our night. An' I remember thinkin' tha' that was a load of bollix, but I didn't say it. An' I didn't go an' meet her like I'd said I would, an' I only had her work phone number an' it was too late to phone her. I was supposed to be meetin' her outside Trinity, I think it was – at the gates. An' I didn't go. An' I really liked her.

—No, you didn't, he said now.

—I did, I said. —But I didn't know that until after.

—Jesus, Davy.

—It was always the same, I said. —I'm not blamin' you. I was always the sap.

I ignored the remains of my old pint and went for the new one. It smelt fine, it smelt good. The glass was cold in my hand. I drank. I put the glass to my cheek.

—We always did wha' you wanted, I said.

—Not true.

—True, I said. —I trailed along behind you. Until.

—Are we havin' another?

—Go on.

The barman didn't hesitate. We hadn't crossed a line. I wanted to stay there for ever. I wanted to go back down to the toilet and stay down there. I wanted to stay with Joe. I wanted to kill Joe.

251

—An' I didn't fancy Jessica, I told him.

—You did.

—Only the same way I'd fancy any woman, I said. —I fancied her, was infatuated or whatever, because you insisted on it. If you fell for her, the world had to fuckin' stop. But – me? Sorry, she was nothin' special. Tha' sounds wrong – sorry. But I wasn't fussed.

—Tha' was the fuckin' problem, Davy, he said. —You were never fussed.

—Wha'?

—The stalker, he said. —Go on.

—Wha' d'you mean, I'm not fuckin' fussed?

—Tell me abou' your stalker, he said. —And then I'll tell you if I'm right.

—I told you already, I said. —There wasn't a fuckin' stalker.

—But you told Faye there was.

—Yeah.

—Why?

—The buzz, I suppose.

He laughed.

—I'm changin' me mind, he said.

—Thanks very much, I said. —Tha' word, but. The phrase – the buzz. I feel so fuckin' old sayin' it. It just seems wrong. Like – there's nothin' worse than a fifty-year-old woman pretendin' she's twenty. An' I'm assumin' it works for men as well – that any self-respectin' woman would gag if she heard me sayin' the buzz.

—Does Faye try to be twenty, by the way?

—Leave Faye alone, I said. —An', no, she doesn't. But I'm bettin' Trish fuckin' does.

—More, thirty, he said. —No – forty. No, Trish is great. An' forty, like – I don't even know what it means. An' who said it was okay to have a go at Trish?

—Sorry.

—Fuck you.

—We're quits.

—Jesus.

—We're quits.

—Okay.

—I've no idea wha' bein' forty used to involve, I said.

—Same here, said Joe. —But a kid, bein' a kid – I remember tha', no bother. An' the twenties.

—Yep, I said. —Like yesterday.

—And now – the way we are now.

—Yeah.

—I could talk all fuckin' night abou' tha', he said. —But the years in between?

—We might as well never've fuckin' lived them, I said.

—It does feel tha' way sometimes, he said. —Maybe we were just too busy. The stalker – go on.

He didn't care about the stalker. He was trying to get me back. He was letting me talk. He was asking me to forgive him. I already had.

—It was just a work thing, I told him. —Like the one you were talkin' about. A Friday.

—Dress As You Like Day.

—I'd say it was before all tha', I said. —The whole dress as you like thing. How long has tha' shite been on the go?

—Oh, fuck. Ten years? Twenty? I don't know. I'd know if it'd started when we were in our twenties. I'd remember the fuckin' day.

—Exactly, I said. —But anyway, the kids were still small – I remember tha' much. It was just down to the pub after work. The English are funny – more formal tha' way. But now an' again someone would just say

253

let's go for a pint an' it would happen. I'd have phoned Faye, to tell her.

—An' no problem?

—No – no, I said. —None. Never. But, anyway, it was just one o' those ones. That's why I was so hammered by the time I got home. I don't think I even had a packet o' crisps all nigh'. I don't do it any more.

—Eat crisps?

—No, I said. —Fuck crisps. I don't do the drinks thing after work any more.

—Same here.

I could tell, my time with the mic was running out.

—I'm the oldest person in the place, I said. —By a distance. An' I feel it if I'm with them.

—I know wha' you mean.

—An' it's not the drink, I said. —This – tonight, like. I haven't drunk like this in – Jesus. Years. But it's the company, the others. I haven't a clue wha' they're talkin' about.

—Same here, he said.

—The words, I said. —The language. I end up wonderin' is it English. An' I'm living in fuckin' England, by the way. But anyway, this was years ago. Down to the boozer with a gang.

—English pubs are shite.

—Not all o' them. But, yeah. This one was okay.

—Wha' d'you drink over there?

—I drink bitter.

—Ah, Jesus. Fuckin' bitter?

—It's an acquired taste, I said. —An' I've acquired it. When in Rome.

—Drink piss.

—I like it, I said. —Anyway –.

I hung there for a while – over a bowl of words and sentences. I could pick one up – woman – and see where, how far I could carry it. I could make up a life to match his. Have an affair. Launch one here, see what I could do with it.

—It was one o' those days, I said. —When you're so tired, so – I don't know – wired as well, you can feel the first pint nibblin' away at you immediately, you know. I was drunk before I was drunk, if tha' makes sense.

—Been there.

—Half an hour later my head was hangin' over the table – I was bollixed. I remember gettin' into a taxi an' it was still daylight – it was the summer, like. An' I got back out of it before it started movin'. I just thought the kids would still be up when I got home an' I wasn't havin' tha', the state I was in. I didn't want them seein' me. So I was staggerin' around the town. Tryin' to walk straight, you know. An' failing fuckin' miserably.

—Where is it again?

—Wantage, I said. —It's in Oxfordshire.

—Strange name.

—Yeah, at first – a bit. A lot o' the place names sound strange, when you're away from the towns tha' have football teams.

—Scunthorpe.

—Macclesfield.

—Hartlepool.

—Halifax, I said. —So, yeah, it's all a bit confusin', even though it's only over the water. But you get used to the names. East Challow, East Lockinge, Stanford in the Vale. It's just English an' that's where we are, so fair enough. An' they haven't a fuckin' clue abou' the place names over here.

—The ones that'd bother comin' over.

—Ah, lay off, I said. —But, anyway, I couldn't remember wha' pub I'd come out of.

—Did yis always go to the same one?

—Yeah, we did, I said. —The Lord Alfred's Head. But I couldn't remember it. I was so drunk, it was like I'd taken tha' date rape drug – what's it called?

—Rohypnol – is it?

—Sounds right, I said. —I was wiped.

—Come here, though, said Joe. —Did someone slip somethin' into your drink?

—I never thought o' tha', I said. —Christ –. There's a fuckin' thought, though. After all these years. But no. I don't think so. An' I found the pub – I figured out where I was. An' I went back in. But I didn't go over to the gang again. I didn't sit down. I went back out an' got into another taxi. But all I remember then is being in the hall, at home, an' one of me shoes was missin'.

—Rohypnol – I'm telling you.

—No. No – but maybe you're right. Why would someone from work do tha'?

—Your stalker.

—But there wasn't a stalker.

—Maybe there was, he said. —Tryin' to get into your boxers.

—She wouldn't've needed to drug me.

—Maybe she did, though, said Joe. —The happily married man. She'd've had to drug your smugness.

—Fuck off, I said. —But, anyway, I had nothin' to tell Faye, so I told her about the stalker, the woman who wouldn't leave me alone.

256

—Out o' nowhere, said Joe.

—Not quite, I said.

—Oh, oh.

—But basically, yeah, I said. —I made her up.

—How did she take it – Faye?

—She was all set to get me into the car an' back to the pub, to point her out an' confront her.

—Brilliant, he said.

—She was hoppin', I said. —Fuckin' furious.

—Fuckin' sure she was. An' there actually was a woman, was there?

—Not really.

—Go on, yeh fucker.

—It was nothin'.

The feeling, the rush of happiness, of achievement, surprised me. I was worth listening to.

—But you see, said Joe. —There's the thing. Faye would've known there was somethin'. She'd've sensed it. She'd've felt threatened.

—There was no need for her to feel threatened, I said.

—You're missin' the point, Davy. You're missin' the fuckin' point. She'd've been feelin' elated, up to the fuckin' challenge. Like Trish.

—You split up with Trish.

—Yeah – but.

—Wha'? Trish can't've been all tha' fuckin' elated, Joe. She threw you out.

—Oh, she was, he said. —She really was. A fight on her hands – she was fuckin' delighted.

—A fight for you?

—For herself.

—Jesus, Joe.

—Wha'?

—You sound – you sound like such a cunt sayin' tha'.

—Wha'?

—Tha' you were doin' Trish a favour by havin' it off with Jessica. Sorry – I don't mean to be crude there. But for fuck sake.

—I'm not sayin' tha'.

—You kind of are.

—Maybe I am, he said. —But it's not as simple as tha'.

I could think of nothing I wanted to say. I didn't want to make up the woman now, or Faye's reaction to her. I didn't trust myself. I didn't trust Joe. He'd examine every word; he'd catch me out. I didn't want to hear his male-infidelity-was-good-for-women theory, and he didn't either. He'd gone silent too. He was looking at his pint. He picked it up. He drank. He put it down. I put my hand around my glass. It still felt cold; I'd be able for it. I picked it up.

—Where were we? said Joe.

—Don't know.

—Tha' stuff there, he said. —Abou' Trish comin' alive an' tha'. I wish I hadn't said it.

—Okay.

—I didn't really mean it, he said.

—Grand.

—Was there a woman?

—No, I said. —There was – no. It's not worth mentionin'.

—Did she get in the car?

—Faye?

—Yeah.

—No, I said. —No, she didn't. I fell asleep.

—You didn't even get a ride out of it.

—Joe.
—Sorry.
—Okay.
—Drink talkin'.
—Yeah.

The air outside was good. The day's heat was gone. I examined my walk, my feet – I was fine. I was surprised, pleased. Joe was beside me at first but the numbers coming at us on the path around to College Green made walking together tricky. There was no talking. I led the way. That surprised me too.

He was beside me again.

—Dublin is unbelievable, he said. —The fuckin' crowds.

—Yeah.

—It's never quiet, he said. —We could drink all night if we'd a mind to.

—There's a fuckin' thought.

We walked side by side, and separately when there wasn't room, beside the new tram tracks, to the bottom of Grafton Street. I wondered if I was fitter than him, if that was why I was in the lead; I could walk faster than Joe. I didn't think so. He wasn't overweight; his breathing wasn't laboured. I half expected him to trip me.

We were on Grafton Street now.

—I need to get cash, he said.

—I've cash, I told him.

—I want some of me own, bud, he said.

We were at the AIB, beside Weir's jewellers. My father had bought me a watch in there, when I started secondary school. I remembered him giving it to me the night before the big day. It was in a box, not wrapped.

—I quite liked school, he'd said.

—Thanks.

—The Brothers weren't the worst.

—Okay.

—Your mother would be proud, he said.

—Thanks.

—Very proud.

Joe had joined one of the queues at the cash dispensers. There were two homeless men – young lads, wrapped up for a much colder night – sitting against the wall, on the ground beside the machines. There was a couple – man and woman – putting down a flattened cardboard box in a shop porch across the street. They were young, my children's age. I'd noticed it before, the last time I'd been in Dublin. But I'd forgotten. Every shopfront seemed to have a lone man or couple.

I looked at Joe. He was at one of the machines, his face close to the screen. He was holding his glasses over his head with one hand as he tapped in his PIN with the other. He looked at the homeless lad beside him; he'd put his glasses back on. I saw him put a hand in his pocket. He bent down slightly and dropped a coin into the lad's paper cup, then straightened and took his cash and card. The lad sitting on the ground said something, and Joe laughed and said something back. The money and card went into the breast pocket of his shirt, before he turned and saw me. He was buttoning the pocket as he came up to me.

—All set, he said.

—Wha' did your man say to you?

—He offered to mind my card for me.

—Brilliant.

—Off we go.

And, again, I was leading. My shoulders, my muscles, seemed to protest; they were pulling me back. But I pushed through the stiffness. I didn't turn, in case I'd see he'd gone and left me alone. I expected to hear him laughing.

We were at the corner of Wicklow Street.

—We could go this way, he said.

I kept going straight.

—Fine, he said.

He'd increased his pace and he came up beside me again.

—I'll go with the flow, he said.

—You said that earlier.

—I was remindin' meself, he said.

—Abou' Jessica, I said. —Yourself an' Jessica.

—Yeah, he said. —A pint in the International would've been nice.

—We're goin' to George's.

—True, he said. —But en route. Wha' was it we used to call them?

—Pit stops.

—That's right, he said. —The pubs between the pubs.

—It's more piss stops these days, I said.

—That's clever.

—Jesus though, Joe, the homeless people.

—I know.

—It's desperate.

I'd been looking at another couple in a doorway. They were both lying down, under an open sleeping bag and a damp-looking blanket. The man – the boy – was leaning on an elbow. She looked even younger; she was lying back, her head on a backpack. He was holding a thick paperback and they were both reading it. Further up the street there was a trestle table, flasks, Tupperware full of sandwiches. Like the remains of a street party – until we got up to it, and passed. There was laughter, there was friendship, I thought. But the faces – caved in, haunted, frightened, and – somehow, some of them – childlike.

—It's desperate, I said again, quieter.

I loved the sound of the word, and the feel of the word, coming from me. I was still a Dubliner and I liked being a Dubliner, despite the homeless men and women – because of the homeless men and women, the wit of the kid back at the bank. It made no sense – it made drunken sense. I felt hopelessly angry, stupidly proud, close to crying. I felt at home. But I wouldn't be coming home. Dublin wasn't my home.

We were on Chatham Street now. I saw the bronze arms holding up the lights on either side of the door.

—Neary's, I said.

—Pit stop.

—Piss stop.

—George's is only a minute away.

—My bladder doesn't do minutes.

We were going where I decided we were going.

Pubs, the world of men. There were women too. But the world – the pub – was made by men, put there for men. There were no women serving, no lounge girls, very few women sitting on the stools along the counters. Dark wood, old mirrors, smoke-drenched walls and ceilings. And photographs of men. Jockeys, footballers, men drinking, writers – all men – rebels, boxers. The women were guests. The men were at home. There was a day, I parked myself on a stool and, although I'd never sat on it before, I knew it was mine. All of the stools were mine. That particular stool was in George's but it was the stool we found in every pub in Dublin. I'd discovered my life. The shy man's heaven. A string of pubs, connected by streets and lanes, the streets in plain sight but secret. Poolbeg Street, Sackville Place, Fleet Street, Essex Street, Dame Lane, Wicklow Street, Exchequer Street, South William Street, Chatham Street, Chatham Row, Duke Street, South Anne Street, Duke Lane, George's Street, Fade Street, Drury Street, Stephen's Street, Coppinger Row, Johnson's Court, South King Street. The streets were sometimes crowded, sometimes deserted, but only we knew why they were there, their real, hidden purpose. They got us to Mulligan's, Bowe's, the Sackville Lounge, the International, the Stag's Head, the Dame Tavern, the Long Hall, the Dawson Lounge, Neary's, Rice's, Sheehan's, the Hogan Stand, Grogan's, Kehoe's, the Duke, the Palace, George's. The one big pub, the Dublin pub, the light, the smoke, the other men. We were men, with other men. The voices. The man at the bar of Sheehan's telling other men – and telling us – how he'd escaped from John of Gods, where he'd been sent by his sons to dry out. His eyes watered, his hand shook as he reached for his glass, but his voice told us what lay ahead and what we already had. So this chap stands up and he says, My name's Jim and I am an alcoholic, and another chap gets up and he says, My name's Fergus and I'm an alcoholic as well, and then the chap sitting beside me, he gets up and he says, My name's Paddy and I'm an alcoholic, so then it seems to be my turn, they're all looking at me, so I stand up and I say, My name's Tommy and I'm going over the fuckin' wall the minute it gets dark enough. The laughter, the love, defiance. Nothing about him scared us. The voice in Mulligan's, the deep voice that shook the glasses on the nearer tables, although it was never loud. Today's Cunt was what we called him. He'd see us come in; he was always there. Today's cunt is Charlie Haughey, or Today's cunt is Leonid Brezhnev. He never repeated a name. Haughey. Brezhnev. Reagan. Johnny Logan. Thatcher. Mr T. Garret FitzGerald. Garry Birtles. Pat Spillane. Today's cunts are Def Leppard. He worked in the *Evening Press*, one of the barmen told us, but he was there whenever we walked in. There was the man with the suit and ponytail who read the *New Statesman*. He sat for hours at the bar. He stood, he left. He ordered his gin and tonic without opening his mouth. He paid for it, he took his change. He never spoke a word. The world of men. Where they – where we – could be who we wanted to be, who and what we were going to be. Today's cunt is the Reverend Ian Paisley. The men stepped out of a world, into their real world. The secret one. The sacred one. The one that only men knew. Today's cunt is Billy Ocean. Everything outside was an act, an endurance. Inside the pub – that was where life was. Nothing mattered, and that was all that mattered. We entered it. I thought we'd stay there.

—You made it, said Joe.

—Just about, I said.

—Never pass a jacks, he said. —Advice for the agein' man. Never waste an erection, never trust a fart, never pass a jacks.

I started to laugh, and so did he.

—The fart one's great, I said.

264

—Isn't it? Ever do it?

—Shit meself?

—Yeah.

—No.

—Same here, he said. —A few close calls, but.

—Close calls don't count.

—That's probably true, he said. —We didn't come in here much, did we? Back in the day.

—Ah, we did.

—It was a pit stop, though, wasn't it?

—Yeah, I said. —I don't think we ever stayed here. For the night, I mean.

—No, he said. —Good pub, though.

—Yeah.

—They're all fuckin' good. There's still plenty o' good pubs in Dublin.

He'd ordered the pints while I was in the Gents. I'd checked my phone but I'd missed no calls or messages. And that was worrying me now; I wasn't sure why.

The place wasn't full. There were empty stools. But we stood. He picked up his pint and brought it to his face, his eyes. He looked at it over his glasses. Then he looked at me.

—Come here, he said. —It's really good to see you, man.

I picked up my pint. It felt good in my hand. We tapped our glasses. We were careful doing it.

—Good to see you too, I said.

—Really fuckin' good, he said. —I'm glad we came into town.

—Yeah.

I looked around.

—It hasn't changed much, I said. —Has it?

—Don't think so, he said. —It's much the same.

—That's good.

—It is.

—We're the oldest people here, I said.

—An' it isn't tha' long ago we'd've been the youngest.

—It feels tha' way, sometimes.

—It fuckin' does, he said. —Fuckin' *tempus fugit*. Look at your woman over there, though. Jesus, the legs. No – sorry. She's half our age – fuckin' less. Jesus, though – fuck it. She's amazin'.

I shrugged. I'd looked at her, the woman – the girl. She was lovely. They were all lovely.

—No harm, I said.

—No, he agreed. —An' I suppose –. I think, anyway. Here's my theory. If we didn't notice things like tha' – the girl there. If it didn't make us sit up, if it didn't give us tha' little bit o' joy. It'd be time to bow out, wouldn't it? Am I righ'?

—No, you're right.

—The one-way flight to Switzerland.

—Yep.

—One last wank an' then the electric chair, or whatever they use over there.

—I think it might be more humane than the chair.

—I read a book about electric chairs once.

—Did you?

—I did, yeah, he said. —I can't remember much about it. But I did – I read it. Very interestin', it was.

—Informative.

—Fuckin' very, he said. —An' great pictures.

—Ah, no.

—Yeah, he said. —Nothin' gory now. Just photographs of empty chairs, mostly. In the different prisons, like – the different states of America. They were like art. They *were* art.

—The chairs?

—The photographs. The chairs too, but. They're spectacular an' – the straps.

—I used to think wha' made them really frightenin' – and fascinatin' as well – was tha' they were nearly like ordinary chairs.

—That's righ' – you're right.

—Big armchairs tha' were designed by a chap who could only design kitchen chairs.

—That's it, he said. —Brilliant. Anyway, I don't think I'd mind goin' ou' tha' way. An electric chair made in Switzerland would be high-end, by the way. Well worth the fare.

—You don't have to go all the way to Switzerland to get yourself electrocuted.

—Tha' might be missin' the point, though.

—The trip is part o' the – the process, is it?

—I think so, yeah. The journey. A day shoppin' in Zurich, then the chair.

We were glowing – I was sure we were glowing. We were fresh again, young again, hilarious. In the world of men – even though there were more women in the place than men. And that, somehow, made it even more a world of men. We were the men at the bar.

He drank. He swallowed.

—Good pint.

—Good pint.

—Good pub.

—Very good pub.

—Good to be here.

—Yeah.

—I haven't forgotten.

267

—Wha'?

—I was tellin' you somethin'.

—About Jessica, I said.

—Abou' me an' Jess, that's righ'.

—You go with the flow.

—That's right, he said. —It sounds flippant, like I don't care – I couldn't give much of a shite. But that's not what I mean.

—That's not what I thought, I told him.

I was liking him. I was remembering him. I was happy here. I tasted my pint. It tasted good – it felt good.

—I love her, Davy, said Joe. —Simple as tha'.

—Okay, I said. —Good.

—Simple as.

—Okay.

—Trish says that a lot.

—Wha'?

—Simple as.

—Okay.

—A dam burst, he said.

—I don't get you.

—Just tha', he said. —I saw her –

—Trish?

—Jess, he said. —Fuck off. No –. No – shit –

—You're fine, I said. —I understand. You're not dismissin' Trish.

—No.

—Go on, I said. —You were sayin' abou' Jess. G'wan.

—I've forgotten wha' –

—The dam burst.

—I saw her, he said. —That's right. In the school. An' the dam burst. The thirty-five years or whatever. Thirty-seven. The missin' years.

—Missin'?

—Kind o', yeah, he said. —I'm not denyin' I'd a life – a good fuckin' life, by the way. I'm not sayin' tha' for a minute. My kids – fuck me, I'd die for them an' that's not the drink talkin' now.

—No, I know, I said.

I wanted to agree with him, I wanted to follow him. I wanted to get this finished.

—An' Trish, he said. —We had a good life. I love Trish – I really do. If she walked in here now, I think I'd start cryin'. I love her. So, like, I haven't been sleep-walkin' around the last four decades. Or – what's the other one? Livin' a lie. I haven't been livin' a lie. I'd never fuckin' claim tha'.

He was looking at me and listening to himself, to what he was saying. I was his mirror.

—I know tha', I said.

—If I could work it, he said. —If we could arrange it –. An' actually, I'm sure we eventually will. It'll be grand. I think it will. But I hate not seein' the kids. I hate, like – tha' they've turned against me. An' I don't blame Trish for that either, by the way.

—No.

—But –. Anyway.

—Goin' with the flow, I reminded him.

—Well, he said. —I wish I'd never said tha'. To be honest with you.

—I think it was me said it.

—Was it?

—I think so, yeah.

—Well, it sounds terrible, he said. —Not wha' I meant at all. What I feel.

—You said, the dam.

269

—The dam, he said. —That's right. The fuckin' dam. Good. This is what I mean. What I mean is – bear with me, Davy.

—I'm here.

—Good man. So. When I met Jess, it wasn't –. The dam didn't burst, exactly. It was more, the water level rose. Like a lock in a canal. A lock more than a dam. The lock gate opened an' the water level rose. Everythin' filled in, if tha' makes sense. The lock – like. It's the years between seein' Jess in George's back then an' seein' her again. It was empty –

—Empty?

—Not empty – fuck it. This isn't perfect, what I'm tryin' to say. Not empty. Why did you interrupt me?

—I didn't interrupt you.

—Ah, you fuckin' did.

—Lads.

It was a barman, a tall young lad with a white shirt and a dickie bow.

—Sorry, I said.

—Keep it down, he said.

—Yeah, sorry, said Joe. —We've had a few, you know.

—No problem.

—We're harmless, said Joe.

—I can see that.

We were twice his age and we probably reminded him of his father, or his grandfather. He moved away from us.

I waited a few seconds.

—Sorry, I said.

—Okay, said Joe.

—I didn't interrupt you, I said. —I didn't. I was just lookin' for clarification.

—Clarification?

—Yes, Joe. You know what it means. You said the lock was empty.

—Fuck the lock – fuck the fuckin' lock.

He was keeping his voice down. He was smiling.

—This is hopeless, he said.

He looked for his pint on the counter, then saw that it was in his hand.

—For fuck sake.

He laughed.

—Jesus, he said. —How did tha' happen?

—Wha'?

—How did I not know it was in me fuckin' hand? We're not tha' drunk. Are we?

—I'm grand.

I held up my pint.

—Mine's here, look it.

—Good man.

—The empty lock, I said.

—God, you're such a bitch, said Joe.

—Well, you dug the fuckin' thing, I said.

—I read a book about tha' once as well, he said. —Russian prisoners diggin' a canal. Political prisoners. Durin' Stalin's time, before the war. A huge fuckin' thing tha' turned ou' to be useless. Thousands o' men were buried under it. Fuckin' thousands o' them.

—The empty lock.

—It wasn't empty, he said. —It was just full o' the wrong liquid. No – fuck. Let's just abandon the canal. This isn't makin' me happy.

He wasn't joking. The glee, the messing, the drunk intelligence – they were gone. He looked tired. He even yawned.

—Sorry, he said. —Sorry.

271

He turned his pint on the counter, an inch, another inch.

—I've changed, he said. —But I keep forgettin'.

—We all change, I said.

—Well, I'm sure that's true. But I hate hearin' it.

—Why?

—It makes it harder to explain the thing, he said. —It's as if it's a thing that happens to every man. We were talkin' about it earlier, weren't we? A midlife thing. Or post-midlife. Or whatever it's called – if it has a fuckin' name. But, look it. I give up.

He looked at the counter. He looked at the floor. I looked at him looking at the counter and at the floor. He looked at the counter and he looked at me.

—She isn't happy, Davy, he said.

I said nothing. I wasn't going to interrupt. I looked at him. He was moving.

It was me. I was the one moving, swaying from foot to foot. Moving to a slowish song I wasn't hearing. I stopped. I put a hand on the counter. Anchored myself.

—No, he said. —I don't think she's ever been wha' you'd call happy. Isn't that terrible?

—Yeah.

—Sad.

—Yeah.

—Never, he said. —Fuckin' awful. It breaks my heart. Serious now – it does. Now –. Before I go on. I have to say this as well. She isn't fuckin' miserable. That's not wha' I mean.

—I know.

—A pain in the arse, I mean. She isn't. She isn't a whinger, Davy.

He was looking at the floor again. He looked back up at me.

—She's, he said. —She's lovely. An' one o' the reasons she's lovely is because she's so unhappy. Davy.

It was like he wanted me to say something. But I knew he didn't. He wanted me to look at him. Straight at him.

—I've never known an unhappy woman before, Davy.

—Trish?

I hadn't meant to say anything. But I loved saying the name. Trish. Its effect – what happened. It was like an electric shock, static electricity, a quick jolt up the arm.

—The happiest woman in Ireland, he said. —Happiest woman ever born – that's my Trish.

He smiled.

—She'd swallow the world, he said. —You know those yokes, Davy?

—Wha' yokes?

—On the water, he said. —The sea.

—I don't know what you mean.

—Ah, you do. The yokes. Noisy fuckin' things. But good crack.

—I don't know.

—You fuckin' do, he said. —You do. I can't think o' the fuckin' name. Jet ski – jet skis. I knew I knew it. D'you know what I'm talkin' abou'?

—Jet skis?

—Exactly.

—Wha' about them?

—Ah, for fuck sake. Wha' I'm saying – what I'm sayin' is. Fuckin' –. Trish is a fuckin' jet ski. That's what I mean. She's fuckin' brilliant.

—Wha'? I said. —You ride her in the water?

He laughed – he burst out laughing. He exploded.

—For fuck sake.

He wiped his eyes. I was laughing too. He put his hand on my shoulder. He staggered, a bit. He kept his hand there, then dropped it, and looked at the counter for his pint.

—Her energy, he said. —That's all I meant.

—Why didn't you just say energy then? I asked.

—Fair enough, he said. —Fair enough. Cunt.

He picked up his glass. It was half full. I was ahead of him.

—Forget jet skis, he said. —Dams, locks, fuckin' jet skis – forget all o' them. Here's one – here's –. Trish is a force o' nature. Is tha' clear enough for you?

—Yeah – grand.

—It passes muster.

—It does.

—Ah, good, he said. —If a force o' nature is a good thing – yeah?

—Yeah.

—Trish is a very good force o' nature, he said. —I'll tell you, man, I've been blessed.

—Okay.

I was wishing I knew Trish.

—Jess, he said. —Jess. Davy?

—Wha'?

—I'm talkin' abou' Jess now, okay?

—Yeah.

—Wha' sort of – wha' kind of a machine is Faye, by the way?

—Wha'?

—Trish is a jet ski, he said. —What's Faye?

—You said we'd forget about jet skis.

—Fuck jet skis. Come on. What machine is Faye? It is Faye – I'm right, yeah?

—Yeah.

It wasn't just the drink. He was being nasty again, when he could concentrate.

—I haven't thought about it, I told him.

—Go on, come on, he said. —She has to be somethin'. A toaster.

—No.

—A fuckin' –. I don't fuckin' know. A hairdryer.

—Forget it, Joe.

—A Dyson yoke.

—Fuckin' forget it, Joe.

He looked at me. He shrugged. He smiled.

—Grand, he said. —Point taken. No machinery.

He looked at his drink. He brought it to his mouth.

—Actin' the maggot, he said.

He drank.

—Sorry, he said. —It was wha' my mother always said. Anyway. You're actin' the maggot, Joseph.

He drank again. He put the glass back on the counter. He parked it. He brought it slightly forward, and back. It almost toppled.

—Yikes – shite. Leave well enough alone. Whatever tha' fuckin' means.

He picked the glass up again.

—The things we say. We don't even know wha' they mean. Jess isn't a force o' nature.

—So, I said. —Jess isn't a jet ski.

He didn't laugh. He shook his head.

—No, he said. —She isn't. You're right. I love her, Davy, d'you know tha'?

—You told me, yeah.

—Yeah, he said. —Yeah – well. I think that's why I love her. I think.

275

—She's different to Trish.

—Yeah. No – yeah. I don't know. I don't think so. It's not either or. Well, it is. Unfortunately.

—Is tha' wha' you want, Joe?

—Wha'?

—A *ménage à trois*?

—A wha'?

—You know what I mean, I said.

—No, he said.

He'd thought about it.

—No, he said. —No, I know wha' you mean. An' no. I don't want one o' them – a menage. An' come here. Not because it wouldn't work.

—It wouldn't.

—God, no. Fuck, no. Never. But it doesn't matter. It never really occurred to me – not the sex thing way, anyway.

He'd lowered his voice. He was looking at me now over his glasses. Then he lifted his head.

—I make her happy, he said.

I took a guess.

—Jess.

He didn't nod or shake his head.

—I don't have to do anythin', Davy, he said. —I don't really know how to explain it – sorry. It must be a pain in the arse.

—No.

—Listenin' to this shite. It must be.

—No.

—Go on to fuck.

—Okay, I said. —It is.

—Is it?

—No, I said. —I'm messin' with you. It isn't.

—I appreciate tha', he said. —Good to see you, man. Where's my fuckin' pint? Here – look it.

He put his hand around his glass, then – as if bracing himself – lifted it.

—I'm reluctant, he said.

He examined the word. He looked as it passed his eyes.

He was happy with it.

—I'm reluctant to say this, he said. —I'm nearly reluctant. But I'll say it an' we'll see where it gets us.

He looked at his pint. He drank from it.

—It's like livin' in a fairy tale, he said.

—Yeah, I said. —You mentioned the film – earlier.

—Did I?

—Tha' one –

—Wha' one? *Stardust*. It must've been *Stardust*.

—Yeah, I said. —You mentioned *Stardust*.

—No, he said. —No, I mean I did. But I don't mean I'm livin' in the story of tha' one. In the plot – I don't mean tha'.

—Okay.

—I mean, he said. —Like – I'm reluctant to say it. I said tha'. Cos it's mad. But there you go.

—I don't understand.

—Join the fuckin' club, Davy.

He finished his pint. He put the glass down, then picked it up and put it at the far edge of the counter, as far away as he could put it.

—The demon drink, he said. —That's a phrase I can understand. No problem understandin' tha' one. I don't drink much, by the way. That's why I'm hammered. Are we hammered, Davy?

—We are.

—Grand, he said. —I am, anyway. I have magical powers.

He looked at me.

—I do, he said. —Magical powers.

He held up his hands, wriggled his fingers.

—Not the spooky kind, he said. —I can't –. Fuckin' –. Bend spoons an' tha'. I can't bend spoons, Davy. I'm not Uri what's his name. Geller.

—That's a relief.

—There was a fuckin' chancer.

—Yeah.

—Spoons, me bollix.

He picked up his empty glass.

—What I mean, he said. —Wha' it is. The fairy-tale thing. It's like this. I can make her happy. An' by the way. I think I'm the first person to be able to do tha'. So – come here. Just let me concentrate for a bit. I'll sober up. Then I can explain it properly. Once an' for all. Once an' for fuckin' all. An' forget abou' magical powers by the way – that's not wha' I mean.

—Are you happy, David?

Faye had looked up from her plate. I didn't know what to say. It was a trap. It wasn't.

—Yes, I said.

—Good, she said. —So am I.

—Are you?

—Yes, she said. —I think I am. But.

—What?

—What does it mean? Happy.

—I don't know.

—I'm not giddy, like, she said. —I'm content. Are you?

—Yeah.

—Are you?

—Yes.

—Good, she said.

It was terrifying.

—That's all I want, she said.

—Same here, I said.

—What?

—I want you to be happy.

—Well, she said. —We seem to be quite efficient at it, so. Making one another happy. Aren't we great?

She smiled.

—How's the beef? I asked her.

—Oh, I'm very happy with it, thanks, David, she said. —Very happy. It's a lovely piece of beef. Fair play to you.

—It's not too pink?

—God, no. It could never be too pink. As the man said. You seem nervous.

—No.

—Tense.

—No.

—Are you happy enough, yourself? With the beef.

—I am, yes, I said. —I think I timed it well.

—I think you did too. It's all I want.

—Beef?

She smiled.

—You, she said. —You to be happy. Do you believe me?

—Yes.

—Do you?

—Yes.

—Good.

★　★　★

He was staring at his glass again. He looked up.

—All I have to do is listen, he said.

—To wha'?

—Jess, he said. —She –. Everythin' I say must sound mad. How long've we been drinkin'?

—Hours.

—Hours, he said. —We ate earlier, didn't we?

—Yeah.

—Tha' seems like days ago.

He was right. I couldn't remember what I'd eaten.

—So anyway, he said. —I've been tryin' to get to the point all night. Find the words that'll make sense. An' that's it – after all tha'. I listen.

He was changing again. His eyes had cleared. He'd said he was going to sober up, and that seemed to be happening. I looked at him and remembered what he'd said about having magical powers.

—So, he said. —Listen. I go home.

—New home?

—New home, he said. —Yeah. Yeah – I think I can call it tha'. It feels like home. I suppose.

—Where is it?

—Clontarf, he said. —Not far from where we were earlier.

—Right.

—Dollymount, more.

—Okay.

—So, yeah. I go home. An' it's like I've always been there. I said that earlier as well – or somethin' like it. An' it's not necessarily because I think I've always been there. But she does.

He seemed happy, relieved; he'd said what he'd wanted to say.

—I don't get you, I said. —Sorry.

—Wha' don't you get?

—She thinks you've been livin' with her for years?

—Not exactly, he said. —But yeah. That's it.

—Is that okay?

—Wha'?

—Are you alright with it?

—With wha'?

—Tha' she thinks you've been livin' with her since the early '80s.

—It's not fuckin' exact, he said. —I told you. Not literal. But she feels it. So – so do I.

—You're made for each other – somethin' like tha'?

—That'll do, he said. —Tha' covers it, I think. Like I said. I listen. An' I don't think I ever did tha' before. I don't think I had to. Trish didn't give a fuck if I was listenin' or not.

—Tha' sounds unfair.

—You're right, he said. —I regret sayin' it. Kind of. Not really, though. Fuck it, Davy, I'm in love. I run home, just to see her.

I remembered that. I remembered charging for the train, the bus, to get to Faye's house, our flat, wherever I was going to see her. She was often there ahead of me and I'd loved that too, watching her as she saw me arrive, the smile – the glee, the reined-back excitement – that it provoked. There was once, we'd just moved to England, and I charged in the door. She was watching *Neighbours*.

—I was lying back in the bed in my lingerie, she said. —But then I got up when you weren't coming home.

—What lingerie?

—Well, I'll tell you, David, I hid it. And it's going to stay hidden, so it is.

281

I could still imagine that charge, a man of my age, of Joe's age, racing to see a woman, to be seen by a woman. A sixty-year-old man's charge, but the excitement and the honesty could still be there. It didn't have to be a different woman; I wanted to run to Faye. I wanted to look at Faye and find her looking at me. Without the questions or the concern, or embarrassment.

I could feel it on my skin, in my legs; I wasn't drunk, again. We were stranded on some island of sobriety. We had a few minutes to talk. I had a few minutes to listen; the tide would be coming in again. Any minute.

—What's it like? I asked him.

—Like?

Aggression took over – I could see it – but he pulled it back.

—The house, d'you mean?

—Not really, I said. —But yeah.

—Well, it's nothin' like ours, he said. —Jesus, listen to me – ours. I mean –

—I know what you mean.

—It's in bits, he said. —I'm tellin' you. Trish would go fuckin' spare if she ever saw it. You left me for this? But it's cosy.

—Fuckin' cosy?

—Wrong word, he said.

He grinned.

—Comfortable, he said. —An' anyway, it's not the house tha' matters. The décor. I never gave a toss about tha' shite, anyway. It's her, Davy. I'm in a different world, man. I'm livin' in a life I never actually lived.

—Sounds mad, Joe.

—Fuck off, it's not. Well, it is. A bit, just. But I've been given a second chance.

—Joe –

—More to the point, he said. —Give me a minute here. More to the point. She's been given a second chance. That's what it is, Davy. I'll tell you a thing she said to me early on an' it nearly killed me. I shouldn't be tellin' you this but wha' harm, you're my buddy. An' you know her.

—I don't.

—You did. Back in the day. I hate tha' sayin' or whatever it is. Is it day or days?

—Day.

—Yeah, well. Only cunts say it.

He grinned.

—In our youth, he said. —You knew her in our youth. An' you fancied her as well.

—I didn't.

—You fuckin' did so.

—Wha' did she say?

—Will we have another pint here? he asked.

—Go on, yeah, I said. —We'll never get to George's.

—'Course we will.

He called the barman.

—Excuse me –. Yeah, two more, please. Thanks.

—Wha' did she say? I asked him again.

—Well, I could tell you. Word for word, like. But without the context, it'll sound dreadful. But come here, you're sound as a pound, I know tha'. But –

—Tell me an' then work backwards.

—Why're you so keen to know?

—I'm not, I lied. —But a minute ago you were all set to tell me.

—'I wish I hadn't lived.'

—She said tha'?

—Yeah.

—Jesus, Joe.

—Yeah.

—Jesus – on your second date?

—Fuck off now. But yeah. It was the saddest fuckin' thing, Davy, I'm not jokin' you.

He looked at me. I looked at him. And we laughed. I held his right arm, he held my left. And we laughed.

—It's not funny.

—I know.

—It wasn't funny.

—I know.

—It isn't.

We laughed. He took off his glasses and wiped his eyes, and put them back on and took them off again.

—The fuckin' things are steamin', he said. —The heat off me face.

—She said tha'? I said.

—Yeah.

—What age is she? Fifteen?

—It wasn't funny.

—Okay.

—It really wasn't funny. I swear to God. Don't look at me, for fuck sake, I'll start laughin' again. I don't want to.

That got us going again.

—Laughin' like tha', I said. —It makes me want to piss, sometimes it does. Is it the same with you?

—No, he said. —I don't laugh much, but.

—I'm not fuckin' surprised.

We laughed again.

—Enough, he said. —Enough.

We were wiping our eyes. Mine were sore, too big, both dry and saturated.

—She's a bit of a clown, Joe, I said. —Is she? She must be.

He was putting his glasses back on.

—Wha' did you fuckin' say?

—Come on, I said. —I didn't ask to be born.

—That's not wha' she said.

—Near enough.

—Fuck off, Davy. Fuck you.

—Wha'? I said. —We were laughin' a minute ago.

—It wasn't insultin' a minute ago.

—Only because she isn't here.

—Fuck off.

I didn't want this to happen.

—Explain it then, I said.

—Fuck off.

—I'm listenin'. Go on.

I could hear myself, and I didn't sound as I felt – how I wanted to feel. I sounded like my forehead was leaning into his; I was pushing him, goading him. I was rushing past myself, out of my own control.

—Sorry, I said.

It didn't matter. I didn't care about truth. I didn't want the fight.

—Fuck you, he said. —Listen.

—Wha'?

—Trish spoke to Faye once.

—When was this?

—Back in the fuckin' day, he said. —They had a good oul' chat, Trish said. So listen, pal, don't be callin' Jess a fuckin' clown.

—Ah, fuck off, Joe.

—A right fuckin' nut job, Trish said.

—Fuck off.

—You fuck off.

—Fuck off.

★   ★   ★

I looked at my eyes in the toilet mirror. They weren't too red. They fitted in the face; they weren't too bad. They belonged.

I'd say sorry again. I'd go back in and say sorry. I'd finish my pint and leave. He'd tell me to fuck off and I'd go. He'd tell me to fuck off and I'd let him have it; I'd rip his fantasy apart. I'd smash my glass across his head. I'd go back in and he'd be gone. I'd go in and he'd be waiting; he'd tell me something that would knock me to the floor, that would make me hit another man for the first time in my life, that would shut me down, destroy me.

I knew the man I was looking at in the mirror. I was okay, I'd be fine.

I'd apologise. And I'd go. We'd go on to George's, and then I'd go. We'd meet again, we'd keep in touch. He'd let me know he'd gone back to Trish. He'd let me know he'd never really left her. He'd send me a photo of Holly's graduation. I wouldn't apologise. I'd stand there with him and pick up my pint. It was up to him; we could move on, or we wouldn't. He could start a row, continue the row. I didn't care. He could fuck off – I didn't care.

I felt the phone in my pocket. I took it out and looked.

—I have to go, I told him.

—Wha'?

—I've to go, I said. —Sorry.

—What abou' the pints? he said. —We haven't touched them.

—Sorry – I've got to go.

—What's up? he asked.

He could tell I wasn't just deciding to leave; I hadn't come back from the toilet ready to storm out. He could see it was something else.

—Is somethin' wrong?

—My father, I said. —Yeah – my da.

—Is he okay, is he?

I wasn't sure if he heard my answer. I wasn't sure if I spoke the word.

—No.

—Wha'?

—No.

—Ah, Christ, he said. —I'm sorry, Davy. Let's go. Are you goin' home – to his place? I'll come with you.

—No, I said.

—Wha'?

—I'm not goin' home.

I watched Joe lift his fresh pint and take three or four fast gulps from it. The glass was half empty when he took it away from his mouth. I waited.

—Waste not, fuckin' want not, he said.

I wanted him with me.

And I didn't.

He put the glass back on the counter, then placed his hand on his stomach.

—Might regret tha', he said. —I might be climbin' into the bed beside your da. Come on.

I didn't want him to come – I don't think I did – but I got in behind him as he walked quickly to the door. He held it for me and we were out on to Chatham Street.

—Right – where's best for a taxi? he asked himself.

—Stephen's Green.

—South William Street, he said. —There's always a line of empty ones comin' up tha' way.

I followed him across to Chatham Row, to the corner of South William Street.

—Are you sure we don't have time for one in George's?

—No, I said.

—Only jokin', he said. —A pity, though. Here we go, look.

There was a taxi, its roof light lit, almost at us. Joe lifted his hand, and it stopped. He went to the nearest back door, and opened it. He stood back.

—In you go, bud, he said.

—Thanks.

—No bother.

I slid across the seat and he followed me in. He shut the door. And again, properly.

—Howyeh, he said to the driver. —Here, Davy, where're we goin'? Which hospital – Beaumont or the Mater?

—No, I said.

—Your da's house?

—The hospice.

—Jesus, he said. —Jesus, Davy. You never fuckin' said. The Raheny one?

—Yeah.

Joe leaned towards the driver's shoulder.

—Saint Francis Hospice in Raheny, he said. —D'you know it?

—I do, said the driver.

He was our age, maybe ten years younger.

—I do know it, he said. —Unfortunately.

We were moving.

—Brilliant place, though, said the driver.

—Yeah, said Joe. —So I'm told.

—Amazin' people, said the driver.

We were on Johnson Place.

—There's George's now, Davy, said Joe.

We both looked at the corner, and the doors, the porthole windows.

—Are you sure we don't have time for a fast one? said Joe.

I smiled.

—Sorry.

He spoke quietly now.

—Your father's in the fuckin' hospice?

—Yeah.

—How long?

—Two weeks, I said. —Sixteen days.

—Jesus.

The car had turned right; we were on Longford Street. The driver slowed, and stopped. The lights ahead were red.

—Have you been home for two weeks? he asked.

The words came from deep inside me. They were wet.

—Four months.

—Fuckin' hell, Davy.

I heard him breathe.

—In your da's house?

—Yeah.

The driver took us off Aungier Street, down on to South Great George's Street. We were passing another of the old pubs.

—We never made it to the Long Hall, said Joe.

—No.

—Next time, he said.

—Yeah.

—Great pub.

—Yeah.

—Smashin' pub, said the driver. —My da, God rest him, lived in there.

—Is tha' right?

—Oh, yeah, said the driver. —Lived in the place, he did. More than once my mother, God be good to her, sent me down to get him.

—Was he alright with tha'? Joe asked.

—Ah, he was. He just preferred the pub to the house. And he wasn't alone there.

—No.

—A lot o' men would've shared that preference.

—They would, said Joe. —An' still would.

Joe was looking at me.

—Is your belt on there, Davy?

—Yeah.

—Four months.

—Yeah.

—Why didn't you tell me? Even tonight, like – you didn't mention it.

—I didn't want to, I said. —I didn't think I could. To be honest.

—Okay.

—I've been –.

I looked out the window, at College Green and the crowds. I looked at the back of the driver's seat.

—I've been watchin' the man rot, I said. —For four months.

—Ah, Davy.

—Yeah.

—Alone?

I nodded.

—Davy –.

We were over O'Connell Bridge now, coming up to Beresford Place.

—Come here, said Joe. —I meant to tell you. Back there.

He indicated, with his thumb, the world outside the taxi.

—Wha'?

—The Sackville Lounge, he said.

—What about it?

—Gone.

—Shut?

—Yeah.

—Shut down, you mean?

—Yeah.

—For fuck sake, I said. —Tha' makes no sense.

—No.

—I often had a quick one in there, meself, said the driver.

—Sad, isn't it?

—Ah, it is.

—It's not sad, I said. —It's outrageous. It makes no fuckin' sense.

Joe spoke quietly.

—Where's Faye?

—At home.

—Okay, he said. —In England? Just –. Not in your da's house?

—No, I said. —Home, in Wantage.

—Okay.

I heard him adjusting himself, moving in the seat. I felt his hand on my shoulder. He patted it, held it, let go.

—You've been alone in the house.

—Yeah.

—With your father.

—Yeah.

—No help, no?

—No, I said. —There was –. There was a HSE nurse. Twice a week.

—Okay.

—Mondays and Thursdays. Two of them, actually. Job sharin'.

—Okay.

—They were good, I said. —Nice. Especially one o' them.

—Four months, Davy, he said. —Why didn't you fuckin' call me?

—I did.

—Today, he said. —Ten hours ago.

—I know.

We were past the Five Lamps, over the canal bridge, back the way we'd come earlier in the night, and all the nights decades before, walking home, swaying home, staggering, and running away from the hard men.

—I couldn't, I said.

—Okay, he said. —But I don't understand it.

—I don't either, I said. —I just –.

I had to do it alone. Devote myself to the man. Punish myself. Let him see me, make him see me. I'd had to endure it. Alone.

We were on Fairview Strand. We passed Gaffney's.

—Good pub.

—I remember it, yeah.

Joe was struggling to get something from his pocket.

—Here, he said. —Here.

I didn't know what he meant at first. Then I saw the chewing gum, Wrigley's Extra; he was opening the packet – he was trying to.

—I never come out without them, he said. —Or, I used to. I got them in the Spar on the way to the restaurant.

—What restaurant?

—We were in a restaurant.

—That's right.

—We met there.

—That's right, I said. —For fuck sake.

—Sorry, lads, said the driver. —Am I goin' straight up the Howth Road?

—The coast, I said.

—No, said Joe.

—I'll drop you off first, I told Joe. —It's on the way.

—You will in your hole, he said. —I'm comin' with you.

—No.

—Fuckin' yeah, Davy.

He put his open hand on my chest, and took it away.

—Howth Road, he told the driver.

—Grand.

—Wha' was the message, by the way? he said. —I meant to ask you.

—What message?

—From the hospice.

—Oh, I said. —I got a text from the nurse on duty tellin' me to phone her. She'd tried to phone me a couple o' times but I didn't notice.

—Jesus.

—I don't know why not, I said. —The phone was in my pocket all night. On mute, vibrate, like. I'd normally have felt it. But she phoned me when we were talkin'. In Neary's.

—Okay.

—Just before she texted me.

—Okay.

—So, yeah, I said. —I've been lookin' after him for four months and now I nearly miss his –.

I cried. Four months – sixty years – were behind my eyes, pushing.

He patted my shoulder again.

—Have a chewin' gum, go on. You can't go in stinkin' o' the gargle.

—Thanks.

—No bother. Why tonight?

—What?

—Why did you come ou' tonight?

—Oh.

I thought. I tried to think. The days were mush, my life was mush. The hospice weeks were one long day. The days at home were broken years. Broken sleep, broken talk. Sliding thoughts and memories. My father calling out to me at night, through the night, hauling me awake – a voice I didn't know, I'd never heard before.

—One o' the nurses, I said. —She said I should get out for a while. She – well. She persuaded me.

—Nice one. How?

—Keep it clean, Joe.

—Okay – sorry.

—She said she didn't think there'd be anythin' dramatic happenin'. She's really sound – the best o' them. They're all brilliant. Anyway, she said I needed a change o' scenery. I needed to talk to someone who wasn't a health professional or a priest.

—She sounds good.

—I nearly asked her out.

—Did you?

—No, I said. —Not really. But, anyway. I phoned you.

—Well, I'm glad you did, Davy.

We passed Harry Byrne's.

—Not a bad pub, said Joe. —Unless there's fuckin' rugby on.

We passed the Beachcomber.

—Not a bad pub either.

—That would be my local, said the driver.

—Is tha' right?

—If I had a local, he said. —I don't be bothered much these days.

—How come?

—Lost the taste for it.

—How did that happen?

I watched the driver shrug. I saw one shoulder lift above the seat, and drop.

—Ah, sure, he said.

—I'm the same, said Joe. —Except for tonight. An' it wasn't planned. Sure it wasn't, Davy?

—No, I said.

—It just took off, said Joe. —We could stop for one in the Watermill, Davy. On the way.

—No.

—I'm only messin', he said.

He spoke quietly now – I thought he did. Sound was playing tricks – Joe was sitting to my left but I was hearing him from the right, from the window glass. I was hearing music that wasn't in the car. I could hear, and feel, something working its way up through me. Something growing, something liquid.

—Wha' did she say? he asked. —When you phoned the hospice. The nurse.

—She said –. She said there'd been a shift. I think she said a significant shift. In his condition.

—He's on the way out.

—Yeah, I said.

—I always liked him.

—Thanks.

—I did. I should've dropped in to him. Now an' again. I could've.

—Why would you have done that?

—To say hello – I don't know. See how he was. With you being over in England –. Sorry.

We were in Raheny village.

—He was always nice to me, said Joe.

The driver was slowing, to turn left on to Station Road.

—See they've renamed the Manhattan the Manhattan, said Joe.

I looked out.

—Ah, yeah – that's good.

—Isn't it?

—Why?

—Why did they do it – give it back the old name?

—Yeah.

—Don't know, he said. —D'you know? he asked the driver.

—I heard there was some sort of a referendum, he said.

—A referendum?

—In the area, yeah. So I heard.

—On the same day as the abortion referendum? said Joe.

We went over the bridge, over the railway.

—I don't know about tha', said the driver. —It wasn't a legal thing – I don't think. More, door to door. Or online – an opinion thing.

—Remind me, said Joe. —What did they call it before they changed it back? The Bull's Cock?

—The Cock an' Bull.

They laughed.

—I was close, said Joe.

—Not close enough, said the driver. —And it was the Station House before tha'.

—Why did they change it in the first place?

—No idea.

—New owners, I said.

—That's right, said Joe. —Tha' makes sense.

We were nearly there, and we were filling the car – pushing back the dread – with words. I'd have to get out. I'd have to go in. I could see the Hilltop Centre ahead, and the traffic lights. They were green and the road was empty. The driver took us right, on to Belmont – I knew the swerve and potholes by heart – and another quick right, up the hill, and over.

—This is it, said Joe. —Is it?

—Yeah.

The driver stopped at the front door.

—Here we go.

I didn't move.

—Davy?

—Okay.

I opened my door. The driver, in front of me, did the same; he opened his. He was out ahead of me – he hadn't been drinking all night. He put his hand out.

—I'm sorry for your trouble, he said.

He shook my hand. He held it.

—I've been there, he said. —It's dreadful. But I'll be prayin' for you.

—Thank you.

—No, he said. —The best o' luck now.

—What do I owe you? I asked him.

—You don't owe me anythin', he said. —I'm just glad to be able to help.

—Are you sure?

—I am.

—Thank you – thanks very much.

—I'm off, said the driver.

He got back into his car.

—Come on, Davy, said Joe.

The car moved slowly off, around, and back out on to the road.

—Your man didn't charge us, I told Joe.

—Saw tha', said Joe. —He was sound.

—That was a big fare, I said. —It must be – wha'? – twenty euro from town. More.

—There or thereabouts, said Joe. —Twenty-five, maybe. Come on.

—You sure about this, Joe?

—Wha'? he said. —Of course. You'll have to lead the way, though – come on.

There was a breeze. It was cool – it was reasonable – for the first time in weeks.

—Hang on, I said. —The heat in there, wait an' see. Just a sec.

He stood beside me.

I inhaled – exhaled, inhaled.

—Okay, I said.

I pulled open the door, felt myself do it, felt the effort, the decision, momentum. There was nothing holding me back. I nodded to Denis, the security man. He smiled back.

Joe was beside me.

Down the short corridor, through the land of the teddy bears – a couple of couches decked in large stuffed toys – and on to the longer corridor.

—Are there wards? Joe asked.

—They moved him to his own room, I said. —Three days ago – four. Here.

The blinds were down and closed. The 'Family Only' sign hung on the door.

I put one hand on the handle, the other on the door glass, and pushed as I also held it back. I realised, I recognised it: this was something I did – used to do – at home in Wantage, with the front door, to stop it from creaking, to stop myself from falling forward. I could hear Faye. You could always oil it. Or stop drinking. Whichever's handier.

The room was empty.

But it wasn't. My father was there. In the bed. *On* the bed, suspended just above it. He was hardly there. His size was a shock. It had been a shock for months, every time I left and came back.

Joe was behind me, beside me.

—Jesus, Davy, he's so small in the bed.

I nodded.

—Was he small? he asked. —Is he small? He wasn't, was he? I don't –

—No, I said. —The same size as me, about. I mean, everyone shrinks when they're getting older.

—He's tiny.

—Yeah.

—Jesus, Davy.

I could hear his breathing, my father's breathing. The rattle was sharper – both weaker and stronger. The death rattle. The name made sense in the room. It hadn't been like that when I'd left to meet Joe. The sister, the nurse – *my* nurse – Margaret, had told me that he'd days left.

—Short days, she'd said.

—How do you know?

—I've been doing this for years, she said. —Sometimes I feel like an Indian scout. In one of the old westerns. Looking into the sky or putting my ear to the tracks.

—What does short days mean?

—It means you can meet your friend for a meal and a few drinks.

—And he'll still be here.

—He'll be here – yes.

Joe had closed the door and now it opened again, behind us. We were standing at the foot of the bed.

I turned.

It was another sister, a different nurse. The different ranks wore different uniforms, different colours. She was one of the senior ones. They seemed to have more clout than the doctors, who I'd rarely seen. They were older, firmer; I believed what they told me.

—You're here, she said.

—Yes, I said. —I made it.

I hated what I'd just said. I hadn't felt drunk, I'd stopped being drunk. But now I was drunk again, just stupid. It was some sort of a game – touch the bed before your father dies.

—Good, she said. —You hear him.

—Yeah.

—He's nearly there.

She got past us.

—Sorry, said Joe. —I'm in your way.

—You're not.

She went to the top of the bed. She looked down at my father. She looked at the drip – the morphine. The room was dim, almost dark. The candle on the shelf above the radiator was electric. I'd show it to Joe when she left us alone. I'd turn it on and off.

—He's comfortable, she said.

—Thanks.

—He's very comfortable, she said. —We'll turn him again in half an hour.

—Thanks.

I couldn't remember her name. I couldn't read her name tag.

—I'm Joe, by the way, said Joe. —A friend of Davy – David's.

—You're very good to keep him company, she said. —I'm Maeve.

—I was just sayin', said Joe. —He's so small there.

She smiled.

—Like a child or somethin', said Joe.

—Did you have a good night, anyway, lads? she asked.

—Yes, thanks.

—Good, she said. —Good – I'll leave you alone for a little while.

—Will it be tonight, Maeve? I asked.

—Yes, she said. —I think so.

She was at the door.

—I'll just be across the way, she said. —You know where to find me.

—Yes.

She was out, gone. The door was shut.

—She's nice, said Joe.

—Yeah, I said. —They're all great.

—Nice room.

—Yeah, I said. —It is. It's very peaceful.

There was a little garden on the other side of the window.

—We can sit down, I said.

—Grand.

—You go that side, Joe, I said. —Go on.

I sat on the chair to the right, at the top of the bed, near my father's head – his face – on the pillow. Joe placed a chair opposite me.

—Is this okay? he asked.

—Bang on.

—He's –. He's right down to basics. Isn't he?

—Yeah, I said. —You're right. Did you see your father dyin', Joe?

—No, he said. —He just died, like. In the garden. I wasn't there. No one was.

—Was he there long?

—A couple of hours. My mother found him.

—That must've been awful for her.

—She was in the house the whole time, he said. —The doctor told her he'd died immediately – dropped dead. But –.

—The poor woman.

—Yeah.

We looked at my father. We listened to the rattle. His face was already stretched, at the mouth and cheeks, as if he'd already reached out for his last breath.

—You haven't seen anyone die before now, I said.

—No, he said. —Have you?

—No.

—We're both virgins, so.

—Yep, I said. —How long ago was that?

—My da?

—Yeah.

—Fifteen years. Yeah – fifteen.

—Jesus –. Time.

The window behind me was open.

—It's not too bad tonight, I said. —Not too hot.

—It's grand.

—There's a water fountain thing out there, I said.
—But they had to turn it off.
—'Cos o' the water restrictions?
—Yeah.
—Fair enough, I suppose.
—It was a nice sound, though, I said. —At this time
o' night, you know.
—Yeah, he said. —What's the smell, Davy?
—Is there a smell?
—I think so, yeah.
—A bedsore.
—A bedsore?
—A fuckin' bedsore, yeah.
—Christ.
—It's the stuff they use to mask the smell, I said.
—It's in the dressing.
—Grand.
—Zinc, I think they said.
—Really?
—I've lost track, a bit, I said. —The HSE women
tried somethin', different things, to mask it – the smell.
And that got changed in here – the dressing they're
usin'. I don't notice it now, really. The real smell's
horrific.
—Must be.
—Fuckin' horrific, I said. —Embarrassin'.
—How come?
—Just is, I said. —I didn't look after him properly.
—Ah, Davy.
—I had to change the dressing, myself, I said. —The
weekend before he came in here. I couldn't do it prop-
erly. I tried –
—'Course you did.
—So fuckin' inadequate.

—He's very old, Davy.

—I know.

—You're not a nurse – a fuckin' health professional.

—I know.

—Are you alright? he said. —Do you want something to drink?

—There isn't a bar.

—There's a vendin' machine – lay off. We fuckin' passed it.

We laughed quietly.

—Can he hear us?

—They say he can, I said. —Or could. He might be too far gone – I don't know. It's hard to imagine he can hear us. Lookin' at him.

—If they say he can –.

—Maybe – yeah.

—D'you want somethin' to drink? A Coke or whatever.

—Lucozade might be nice.

—Fuckin' hell, he said. —Can I have that in writin'?

—I like the occasional bottle, I said. —I've low blood pressure – sometimes.

—An' it helps, does it?

—Seems to.

—Okay.

—The sugar, I said. —D'you want to hold his hand?

—No – can I?

I stood up and leaned across my father, and lifted the blanket and sheet enough for Joe to see his hand, and take it.

—Is this okay?

—Of course.

—It's warm.

—He's alive.

—Yeah –. Yeah.

—That thing beside you there, I said.

He looked at the lamp – the blue, then green, then blue lamp – on the locker beside the bed.

—That helps with the smell as well, I said.

—Clever.

—They put somethin' in it. Some kind of oil.

—Wha'?

—They told me, I said. —I can't remember.

—You're shite.

—I know, I said.

I looked at Joe looking at my father. I looked at my father.

—They prefer to call them pressure sores, I said.

—Sorry?

—The bedsores, I said. —They call them pressure sores. It's marketin', I think.

—Wha'?

—Men our age – which sounds worse? Bedsore or pressure sore?

—No competition. Bedsore.

—So, just change the fuckin' name, I said. —That's what I mean. They should be ashamed of themselves – the HSE, the fuckin' system. For lettin' the man develop a bedsore like tha' – for lettin' me look after him on my own for that long –.

My mouth was full of water – I didn't know where it had come from. I waited, then swallowed it back.

—So, I said. —Call it a pressure sore an' it's not too bad.

—You're being hard on yourself, Davy.

—When I was doin' it, I said. —Changin' the dressing. I had to get him to stand, hold on to his walker, you know. I was tryin' to clean it without lookin' at it, at his bum and – you know. And he was half conscious, half himself, an' I just wanted it to be finished. I was tryin' not to breathe till I was done. I had all the windows open in the house. It was hot back then, two weeks ago, too. I was tryin' to get the bandage thing to hold an' to get the nappy onto him. And he said –.

I was choking again, my head full. There were tissues behind me on the windowsill. I grabbed a couple and blew my nose.

—Sorry.

—What did he say? said Joe.

—This is no kind of a life.

—He said that?

—Yeah.

—Well –. He was right. Wasn't he?

—Yeah.

—He wasn't blamin' you, Davy.

—Yeah – no. I know that. Just –.

—The end's so fuckin' messy, isn't it?

—Your father, I said. —That's the way to go, isn't it? Gone before you hit the ground.

—You'd still be leavin' a terrible fuckin' mess, though, Davy. Believe me.

—Yeah.

—The shock, the grief, he said. —Dealin' with the siblings. There's another word I hate, by the way. Siblings. Jesus, the tension. You're kind o' lucky you've none.

—Okay.

—You don't sound convinced.

—I wouldn't mind a few now, I said.

—Right, he said. —I think I know how you feel.

—Yeah.

—I'll ask again, he said. —I don't mean to be snotty.

—No – go on.

—Where's Faye?

—At home – I told you.

—Why isn't she here, Davy?

—Ah, well.

I looked at my father. I hadn't stopped looking at my father.

—I didn't want her to be here, I said.

—Why?

—It's somethin' I had to do on my own, I said. — Somethin' like that, anyway. He's my father.

I shrugged.

—Okay, said Joe.

—I don't know, I said. —I might have treated him badly. I might have been unfair. I *was* – unfair.

—Okay.

—Years ago.

—Right – okay.

—I felt, I said. —I thought I should do it – this – on my own.

I was wrong: I knew that now. This time, I'd been unfair to Faye.

—He said thank you, I said. —That time. When I was pullin' up his pyjamas.

—Now – that's fuckin' amazin'.

—It is, a bit.

—It's fuckin' brilliant, said Joe.

He let go of my father's hand. He was wiping his eyes. I leaned across the bed, held out the tissues for him.

—Thanks, he said.

He took one, and another. He took off his glasses and put them on the bed, close to my father's shoulder. He put his hands to his face and kept them there. He moaned, softly. He took down his hands. He looked at the tissues. He turned in his chair and put them on the locker. He looked at my father. He got his glasses from the bed and put them back on.

—Strange night, he said.

—Yeah.

—A good night.

—Tell me about Jess, I said.

—Jesus –.

—Go on.

—I've been tellin' you.

—Go on, I said. —Please.

—Your da might be listenin'.

—Go on, I said. —He liked women. I think. That's what's so fuckin' sad, I think. One of the things.

—He lived alone?

—For so long, yeah.

I'd kept Faye away from him, and Róisín – she'd never really known him. I loved all three and I'd been cruel to all three.

—We all dream o' that a bit, now an' again, said Joe. —Do we? Livin' on our own.

—Probably – yeah. Now an' again.

—So, he said. —Trish –. This is a while back.

—A year.

—Yeah – a bit more. But yeah. She was drivin' me fuckin' mad. That's not fair, but fuck it. She was drivin' me mad. She wanted to move house – an' we're only just finished with the fuckin' mortgage, by the way. Then she wants to knock the whole back o' the house an' put in glass. This is in the same breath as sayin' she wants to move. It seems like that, anyway. An' it's all money. That's not fair either but it is – money. An' I'm fuckin' sixty, Davy.

308

—You're not.

—I nearly am. An' so are you. An' I don't know –. I was thinkin' I'd love just to live in one room, on me own, like. Just deal with myself. An' I met Jess. An' it was like all that fuckin' pressure – everythin'. Gone.

The rhythm changed, shifted. My father's breathing – it quickened. There was a new click in it now, like something had loosened, broken away.

—Will I get the nurse?

—Hang on.

I watched my father. His face – the mask – didn't change. The breaths, the gaps between them, were definitely quicker. Then, as if he'd stopped snoring or had turned in the bed, the click sound stopped. He was grabbing air in little gasps but the rhythm was steady again.

—Will I get her?

—No, I said. —She'll be in in a bit anyway. He sounds alright again.

—Does he?

—I think so.

I sat back. I couldn't help yawning.

—What about your Lucozade? said Joe.

—He'll die if one of us stands up an' leaves the room.

—You don't believe that.

—I kind o' do, I said. —I went out for a pint with you an' look where we ended up.

—Fair enough.

—But no, I said. —Not really. I don't believe it. But then – I've hardly been out of this place since he came in. It's horrible, walkin' out. Walkin' away from him.

—Includin' tonight.

—Yeah, I said. —Go on, though.

—Jess?

—Yes, please.

—Right, he said. —Jesus. I feel like I'm doin' a job interview now.

—Chief executive adulterer.

—Fuck off.

—The job's yours. Go on – you met her.

—Yeah, he said. —And everything. Lifted. After I realised tha' we wouldn't be shaggin' in the back of the car or anythin' like tha'. And tha' now – it was a relief, really. But. Anyway. We'd be chattin' away and I realised – it occurred to me, gradually. But there *was* a moment, a for fuck sake moment. One o' those – when it occurred to me. I loved listenin' to her, Davy. Her voice. Just that.

I nodded. I knew exactly what he meant.

—Just that, he said again. —But then as well, I realised when I was listenin'. She'd be talkin' abou' somethin' that had happened years before but she wasn't just tellin' me. She was remindin' me.

—Of what?

—There you go, he said. —She was assuming –. What it was. She was includin' me. The things she was talkin' about – the houses, the places, family. The children. I was there too, as far as she was concerned.

—Did you say anythin'?

—No, he said. —No, I didn't. Because.

—What?

—I'm thinkin' – sorry. I'm tryin' to express it. How's your da gettin' on, d'you think?

—It's even again – is it? The breathin'.

—Not even, no. He's breathin' like he has a tiny chest. A bird's chest – lungs.

—But it's regular.

—It is, he said. —Fairly regular, yeah.

—Go on.

—Fine, he said. —Okay. I don't feel like I've been drinkin' all night. Do you?

—No, I said. —I don't. Not now.

—What's that, d'you think? The shock?

—Maybe.

—It sobers you up or somethin', he said.

—Adrenaline.

—D'you think?

—I don't know, I said. —It wouldn't surprise me.

—Nothin' would surprise me any more, Davy, he said. —Fuckin' nothin'. So – right. You asked me if I said anythin' to Jess. About me not actually bein' around in the things she was talkin' about. And I didn't. I didn't say anythin'. Because – this sounds mad. But I don't care. She seemed – she *was* happier when I was there with her.

—In the stories.

—Yeah, he said. —An' so was I.

—Happy?

—Yeah, he said. —I think so, yeah. I went along with it, you know.

—With the flow.

—That's it. I went with the flow. Her flow – so to speak. I let it happen.

—You indulged her.

—No, he said. —No.

—Sorry.

—No – you're grand.

—Give us an example, I said. —A story.

—Well –.

—Nothin' private, if you don't want.

—No, no, you're grand. I know what you mean. A holiday.

—Where?

—France.

—And you were there?

—Accordin' to her. Yeah, I seemed to be.

—But you weren't.

—No, he said. —But – like. It didn't matter. When I saw the impact it was havin' on her.

—Joe?

—Wha'?

—Is she ill?

—No, he said. —No. She's not. She's – lonely would be part of it. Alone. Unappreciated, under-appreciated, somethin' like that. Unfocused.

—Okay.

—An' sad, he said. —Definitely that. Not sick, though. I don't think. Or if she is – fuck it.

—Okay.

—It doesn't matter. We're all fuckin' mad.

—True.

—Somehow or other. Am I right?

—Probably, I said. —Where in France?

—The Dordogne.

—Was it nice?

—Lovely, he said. —Fuckin' fabulous.

—I didn't mean to belittle her there, I said. —Or you.

—No, no – I know, he said. —The funny thing is, though. I *was* there.

—With Trish?

—No, he said. —Like – actually – I've never been in tha' part of France. But it doesn't matter. I was there with Jess.

—And her kids?

He sat up. He shrugged. He looked at my father.

312

—It doesn't matter, he said.

—Does it not?

—And there are the things I definitely do remember.

—There's a balance?

—No, he said. —But kind of. Remember tha' party? In her house. D'you remember it?

—Yes, I said. —I do. The beer in the bath.

—That's right, he said. —I'd forgotten tha' detail. You remember it better than I do.

—Her little brother guardin' it, I said. —It must have been her brother.

—That's right, he said. —Yeah. A prick, by the way.

—Is he?

—God, yeah. Grew up into a right little cunt. But anyway, she was playin' the cello. In the kitchen.

—Yeah.

—Amazin', he said. —Jesus. Mesmerisin'.

I thought he was waiting for me to agree with him.

—Yeah, I said.

I stared at my father.

—And later, he said. —After she'd finished playin'. I plucked up the courage. I got talkin' to her. Couldn't believe myself. Tha' was the night I got off with her. D'you remember, Davy?

I was looking at my father. I looked at Joe – I made myself look at Joe. He was looking at my father.

—Yeah, I said. —I remember that night.

It was Jess's engagement party, the little brother had told us. She was going to marry a chap called Gavin.

—I remember it well, I said.

I smiled.

—So, like, said Joe. —There are some things I can definitely account for. And others –.

I looked at him again. He was still looking at my father.

—It's one o' the big advantages o' getting' older, he said. —Probably the only fuckin' advantage. If you live long enough, you can add to it, make it up. You can even believe you lived it. Things you make up bleed into things tha' definitely happened. Like describin' an event, an actual occasion. You add to it, you take things out. You forget exact details. I don't think it's dishonest.

—No.

—It's human. I'd say.

—Yeah, I said. —I think you're probably right.

—I think so too.

—So, I said. —You were in that part of France. The Dordogne.

—Yeah.

—With Jess.

—Yeah, he said. —Exactly.

—Exactly?

—Yeah.

—Literally?

He shrugged. He made himself smile.

—I don't know what to say.

—Okay, I said. —Is it not hurtful?

—To Trish?

—Is it not?

—The details aren't, I don't think, he said. —To be honest, I don't know. But.

—What?

—With Jess, he said. —I don't care if it's true or not. I mean, factual.

—Okay.

—I remember some things, not others. Like everyone.

—Okay.

314

—Now I'm kind o' rememberin' things that I shouldn't be able to remember, he said. —It's subtle.

—Is it?

—I think so.

—Okay.

—It's the best thing, though, Davy, he said. —Makin' her happy. It makes me feel – I don't know. Powerful.

—Really?

—I think so, yeah, he said. —And good.

—Okay.

We stopped talking for a while. We looked at my father. Joe stood up. He stretched. His hands went to the ceiling, his shirt came out of his jeans.

—I'll go get those Lucozades, he said. —Did we pass a toilet on our way in?

—Yeah, I said. —Go back past the teddy bears.

—Gotcha.

He took change from his pocket and looked at it on his palm.

—I think I've enough, he said.

—You sure?

—I've loads here. Back in a bit.

—Grand.

I looked at him as he opened the door. He looked back as he left and smiled. He shut the door, slowly.

I looked at my father. I got up and leaned in, close to his face. The skin was blue, and tight against his skull. It was like his hair had vanished. It was there but faded, diminished; strands of it danced in the breeze coming in from the open window behind me. I put my hand on his head. I listened. To his breathing. I'd been falling asleep every night on the bench below the window; falling asleep, fitfully and unwillingly, to a different rhythm. This was feebler, but more urgent.

—Alright, Dad?

This is no kind of a life. It was the one occasion, the only time he'd conceded that he wasn't well and that he was never going to be well. I'd spent the months pretending I was just visiting. I'd put him to bed. I'd helped him sit on the side of the bed. I'd given him his last pill of the day, a sleeping tablet. Then I'd helped him lie back and lifted his feet and legs and straightened him, centred him, in the bed. Every movement had hurt him, no matter how slow. I'd covered him with the duvet. I'd lifted the rail so he wouldn't roll out. I'd leaned over the rail and kissed his forehead. I'd slowly closed the door. It was a hospital bed and it was downstairs, in the front room. The kitchen light was on, down the hall. I'd close the door until he'd tell me to stop. He had the three inches of light he wanted. He'd become afraid of the dark, afraid he wouldn't be coming back out of it.

We didn't speak about it. We didn't speak about him, me, the two of us, Faye. I fed him his pills, anxious – afraid – that I was giving him the wrong ones, too many of the right ones, unwilling, unable, to trust my own competence. I was poisoning the man. I was killing the man.

We chatted but we didn't talk. He told me about the time he met my mother. It was a story I'd heard before.

—I was drunk, I'm afraid.

—You?

—Yes.

—You were never drunk.

—I used to be young, David.

It was at a dance, a tennis club hop, and she told him to go away and come back the following Saturday.

—Do you believe in an afterlife, Dad?

He didn't answer. He told me he'd love a boiled egg. He ate the first spoonful and none of the soldiers.

I heard the door. I looked, and saw Joe slip back in. He shut the door.

—Here you go.

He held out a bottle, over the bed. It looked like a torch, or a stunted sword.

—Thanks, Joe, I said.

I stood, stretched, and sat back down.

—I never asked you, said Joe. —What is it?

—What d'you mean?

—Your father, he said.

—Oh, I said. —The cancer, d'you mean?

—Yeah. Which one is it?

—A selection of them, Joe, I said. —He's fuckin' riddled.

—Ah, no.

—Yep.

—Ah, God love him. What started it – which was the first? Do you know?

—I was told, I said. —I have it all written down. But.

My head was filling again.

—I'm fuckin' hopeless.

—Stop.

I opened the bottle, twisted the lid and listened to the short hiss. I drank carefully. I was afraid the stuff would rush out at me, or I wouldn't be able to swallow it. But it was good, it was cold.

—It was his GP phoned me, I said. —He was surprised I hadn't been in touch. That Dad hadn't told me.

—He didn't tell you?

—No. He didn't. But I should've known – I did fuckin' know. The last time I came over to see him. He

317

could hardly walk. I found him leanin' against the radiator. I rang the bell, you know – the front door. I always did it. Before I put my key in the door and went in. So he wouldn't be surprised to find someone else in the house. And – Jesus. There he was. In the hall. Holdin' onto the radiator. Fuck knows how long he'd been there. He said he'd been comin' to answer the door but I don't think he was. I had to help him back to the kitchen. Fuck –.

—What?

—And I went home.

—What d'you mean?

—I stayed a night and went home. He told me he was fine, just a bit stiff. And I decided to believe him. He didn't get up to see me out to the door. I decided it wasn't important. Significant. My father's manners, Joe – d'you remember?

—Always very polite.

—Yes.

—Gentle.

—Yeah.

—He always spoke to me like I was an adult.

—Yes, I said. —And he'd have brought you to the door when you were leavin' – I don't know if you remember that. If he'd known you were goin', I mean.

—I know.

—Not that he was tryin' to get rid of you.

—No, I know.

—But anyway, he didn't stand up when I was leavin' for the airport and I decided that it didn't really matter.

—You're bein' hard on yourself, Davy.

—I shouldn't have left.

—You have a family.

—I should have kept at him – to tell me what was wrong.

Joe opened his Lucozade. He lifted it to his mouth. I heard him gulp.

—It's fuckin' sweet, this stuff.

—It works.

—Whatever that means.

—I'm exhausted, Joe.

—You must be.

—Fuckin' exhausted.

—It's nearly over, he said.

We were both looking at my father, both listening to him.

—Yeah, I said. —I'm not sure.

—You don't think he's goin' to go tonight?

—No, I said. —I mean, I do. But –. It doesn't mean I'll sleep or feel better or – I don't know – clearer. When I wake up. I'm so fuckin' tired.

—You have to be.

—I don't phone Faye. I hardly ever phone her. I can't think of the words – things to say. I dread it – the decisions. How to say things. It's not just the sleep. Fuckin' hell, Joe, he'd wake me up half an hour after takin' the fuckin' sleepin' pill. I was wonderin' if he was hiding them under his tongue – like Jack Nicholson.

—In *One Flew Over the Cuckoo's Nest*.

—Yeah, I said. —He could hardly talk but he was able to shout – like, screech. He still wakes me, even though he's been like this for four days now – asleep. Unconscious. I still hear him.

—That'll stop.

—Then I won't hear him at all.

I sat up straight. I wiped my eyes.

319

—Sorry, I said.

—You're grand.

—Self-pity.

—For fuck sake, Davy. Your father's dyin' in front of you. Take it easy.

We both heard the door. We turned, to see who it was.

Maeve seemed to fill the door and frame. There was a younger nurse behind her; she was pushing a trolley. Maeve smiled as she moved to the top of the bed. Joe had to stand, make room. He shifted his chair – the legs squealed on the floor.

—Sorry.

I laughed – two short barks; they burst out through the water. Joe laughed back. It was a school moment and I was sixteen, for a second. For a great, floating second.

—He's very comfortable, said Maeve.

—Thanks.

—He's exactly the way you'd want him, she said.

—I'm not sure about that, Maeve, I said.

Joe laughed again. So did Maeve. So did the other nurse.

—You know what I mean, said Maeve.

—I do.

—We'll turn him now, she said. —You can wait in the room beyond. We'll only be a few minutes.

I felt like I hadn't walked in months.

—How long? I asked her at the door.

—It'll be soon, she said.

—Okay. Thanks.

We stood outside.

—Let's get some air, said Joe.

—No, I said. —We'd better not. They'll need to know where we are.

—Right, yeah – okay. How long are we here, by the way?

I took out my phone and looked at the clock.

—Less than an hour, I said.

—Jesus, said Joe. —I feel like I live here.

—I do live here, I said.

—That'll stop.

—Yeah.

—What's the food like?

—Not bad, I said. —It's alright. An' there's a café across the way, at the Hilltop. They do a good soup an' sandwich.

—Tha' right?

—And the coffee's very good.

—That's good, he said. —To have it near.

—Yeah.

We needed my father. We needed him there before we'd start talking properly again. It already seemed like a long time since we'd been in the room. We stood outside while they turned him in the bed, gently, professionally; we waited while they cleaned him. There were voices, further up the corridor and around a corner – up where my father had been until he'd stopped waking up. People talked quietly, someone laughed.

The door opened. The younger nurse wheeled out the trolley; she smiled at us. Maeve had stayed in the room. Joe got to the door before me but he stopped, and stepped back.

—After you, he said.

He was eager too.

I walked in.

It was different – my father was different. He was facing the window now, the same shape, reversed, like the negative of a photograph. But his face was different. His mouth was open wider, in a silent howl. I couldn't hear his breath.

—Is he alive?

—Yes, she said. —But he's nearly there.

—Okay. Thanks.

—It'll be soon.

—Thank you.

She left. She shut the door. I sat in the same chair. He was facing me now. The mouth, the howl: he wouldn't accept it was happening. I leaned in, put my hand on his head. I took it away and searched for his hand, just under the sheet. It was dry, and tiny. Not cold.

—Alright, Dad? I said, again.

The mouth – the pain. The end.

—I can't hear him, said Joe; he whispered. —Can you?

—No, I said. —I'm not sure.

I stood and put my head, my ear, closer to my father.

—I can, I said. —I think.

I sat again. I had to – I felt dizzy. I stayed still, shut my eyes. Took in breath, let it go. He'd die while my eyes were closed. I opened them. The mouth was there, staring at me.

—I wish –.

—What? said Joe.

—I wish I'd spent more time with him.

—You're with him now.

—When he was well.

—You're with him now, Davy. He knows you're here.

—He does in his hole, Joe.

—You've been with him for the last four months, he said. —He knew that.

322

—Okay.

—Stop beatin' yourself up.

—Okay.

I looked at the mouth.

—He liked you, I said. —Did I tell you that already?

—I liked him too, said Joe.

My head was full again, a rush of water and Lucozade. I gasped, I coughed. I pushed it back. I sat up,
pushed my back against the back of the chair.

—Where did you sleep? Joe asked.

I pointed at the bench.

—There.

—Every night – since he came in here?

—Yes.

—No wonder you're fuckin' exhausted.

—It's not too bad.

—If you insist.

—I do.

—You're a better man than I am, so.

I was looking at my father.

—I'm glad you're here, Joe, I said.

—So am I, he said. —I'm glad too.

—I'm glad.

—Grand, said Joe. —We're all fuckin' glad.

There was a gasp, a hiss. An explosion we hardly
heard.

—Was that it?

—Think so.

—I'll get Maeve.

I didn't notice her arriving. My father hadn't changed.
His hand wasn't cold. She put fingers to his neck, his
pulse. I watched her.

—Yes, she said.

—He's gone.

323

—Yes.

—He's dead.

—Yes, she said. —He's gone. I'll leave you with him for a little while.

—Thank you.

Joe was standing beside me. He put a hand on my shoulder. I let go of my father's hand. I knew: it would be cold the next time I touched it. I let it go, and stood.

Joe hugged me.

—I'm sorry for your trouble, bud.

—Thanks.

—It's shite.

—It is.

—You did well, Davy.

—Okay.

—You did.

—I'm goin' to phone Faye.

—Good man.

I went to the door.

—No, he said. —Come here. You stay here, I'll wait outside.

—No, I said. —It'll be easier –.

—Okay, he said. —I'll stay.

—You don't mind?

—It's an honour – go on.

Faye must have been awake.

—Hi, Dave.

—Hi.

I couldn't speak. I couldn't say the words. She must have realised, or heard me; I might have moaned.

—Oh, David.

I could speak now.

—He died, Faye.

—I know.

—A minute ago.

—I'm so sorry, she said. —I'm so sorry. I wish I was there.

—Yes.

—Do you want me to come over now? David?

—Yes.

—I'll be there tomorrow.

—Good.

—I love you, David.

—I love you too.

—I do.

—I know. I'm sorry, Faye.

—Stop it.

—Okay, I said.

—The kids, David.

—I'll phone them.

—You sure?

—Yeah, I said. —Thanks.

—I'll be there soon.

—Yes.

—In a couple of hours.

—Yeah.

—He had a good innings, she said. —So he did. Isn't that what they say?

I smiled; I knew I was smiling.

We stood outside the hospice. It was five o'clock, already day. Joe's app told him the taxi was two minutes away, on its way up from Raheny village.

—We could find an early house, he said.

—God, no – fuck.

—Ah, go on, he said. —Molloy's or the Windjammer.

—No way, I said. —I'm bollixed.

—I'm only messin', he said. —You'll have things to do, anyway.

—Yeah.

—The undertaker an' tha'.

—Happy days.

—You're an orphan now, Davy.

—Yeah – yeah. For fuck sake.

—A big orphan.

—Yep.

—What's keepin' this fucker?

—Ask your phone.

He looked down at it. He brought it up to his face.

—One minute, he said. —It says, anyway.

—Grand, I said. —There's no mad hurry.

—What about –? he said. —Do you want to come an' meet Jess?

—No, I said. —No. Thanks.

—The early breakfast, no?

—No, I said. —Thanks.

—You'd like her.

—I know.

I didn't want to see her. She'd be too real and too human. I'd leave them be, her and Joe, with the things that had happened and the things that hadn't happened.

—Another time, he said.

—Definitely.

—Here he is now, look.

We watched the taxi come up over the hill, down, and towards us.

—Pity it's not our man, said Joe. —The lad who brought us here.

—He was sound, I said.
—He was, said Joe. —Sound.
We watched the taxi slow, and stop.
—You'll soon be home, Davy, said Joe.
—Yeah, I said. —I will.

Acknowledgements

My thanks to Lucy Luck, Dan Franklin, Nick Skidmore, Daisy Watt, Deirdre Molina and Paul Slovak.

LIVE & WORK in...

CANADA

Withdrawn
From Stock

Visit our How To website at **www.howto.co.uk**

At **www.howto.co.uk** you can engage in conversation with our authors –
all of whom have 'been there and done that' in their specialist fields. You
can get access to special offers and additional content but most
importantly you will be able to engage with, and become a part of, a wide
and growing community of people just like yourself.

At **www.howto.co.uk** you'll be able to talk and share tips with people
who have similar interests and are facing similar challenges in their lives.
People who, just like you, have the desire to change their lives for the
better – be it through moving to a new country, starting a new business,
growing their own vegetables, or writing a novel.

At **www.howto.co.uk** you'll find the support and encouragement you
need to help make your aspirations a reality.

You can go direct to **www.live-and-work-in-canada.co.uk** which is part
of the main How To site.

How To Books strives to present authentic, inspiring,
practical information in their books. Now, when you buy a
title from **How To Books,** you get even more than just
words on a page.

LIVE & WORK in...

CANADA

Comprehensive,
up-to-date,
practical
information about
everyday life

BENJAMIN A. KRANC
& KARINA ROMAN

howtobooks

Published by How To Books Ltd,
Spring Hill House, Spring Hill Road,
Begbroke, Oxford OX5 1RX, United Kingdom.
Tel: (01865) 375794. Fax: (01865) 379162.
info@howtobooks.co.uk
www.howtobooks.co.uk

First edition 2000
Second edition 2002
Reprinted 2003
Reprinted 2004
Reprinted 2005
Third edition 2008
Fourth edition 2009

British Library Cataloguing in Publication Data
A catalogue record for this book is available from the British Library

ISBN: 978 1 84528 338 4

Cover design by Baseline Arts Ltd, Oxford
Produced for How To Books by Deer Park Productions, Tavistock
Typeset by PDQ Typesetting, Newcastle-under-Lyme, Staffs.
Printed and bound by Cromwell Press Group, Trowbridge, Wiltshire

NOTE: The material contained in this book is set out in good faith for general guidance and no liability
can be accepted for loss or expense incurred as a result of relying in particular circumstances on
statements made in the book. The laws and regulations are complex and liable to change, and readers
should check the current position with the relevant authorities before making personal arrangements.

Contents

Preface   ix

1   Deciding to come to Canada   1
    Defining your goals   2
    Keeping expectations realistic   2
    Joining your family   4
    Making preparations   4
    Sticking to your decision   6

2   Learning a bit about Canada   9
    The history   9
    Identifying the population   17
    Understanding the government   18
    The legal and judicial systems   19
    Looking at geography and climate   20
    The economy   24
    Attitudes   26

3   Immigration to Canada   29
    Understanding policy and politics   29
    Illegal immigration   30
    Knowing the general requirements   31
    Temporary visa issues   32
    Obtaining permanent residence   39
    Family-based immigration   44
    Business immigration   47
    Fees   48
    Qualifying for citizenship   48
    Being removed from Canada   49
    Summing up   49

4   Understanding health and social security   51
    Number-counting   52
    Public versus private   53
    Knowing where to go   54
    Controlling disease   56
    Eligibility and the health card   56
    Looking at the details   57
    Social security   58

5	**Taxation**	**63**
	Income tax	63
	Goods and services tax	65
	Provincial sales tax/harmonised sales tax	66
	Property taxes	66
	Corporate taxes	67
	Other taxes	67
	Seeing where it all goes	67
	Tipping	68

6	**Finding a place to live**	**71**
	Assessing household characteristics	72
	Renting	72
	Owning	75
	Discrimination	78
	Government-subsidised housing	79
	Obtaining telephone, television and the Internet	79
	Considering safety	81
	Obtaining household goods	81

7	**Getting a job**	**85**
	Applying for a Social Insurance Number	86
	Having the right qualifications	86
	Location, location, location	87
	Looking for a job	90
	Doing it yourself	96
	Looking at custom and practice	97
	Foreign workers	99

8	**Going to school**	**105**
	Funding/jurisdiction	105
	Outlining levels of instruction	106
	Categorising types of schools	109
	Examining facilities	110
	Enrolling	111
	School breaks	111
	Going on to higher education	112
	Foreign students	120

9	**Driving in Canada**	**127**
	Province to province	127
	Knowing the rules of the road	129
	Drivers' licences	131
	Owning a car	132
	Insuring and registering	134

Joining motor associations 134
Gasoline 135
Using other transport 135

10 Having fun **139**
Enjoying sports and recreation 139
Outdoor recreation 143
Exploring the arts 146
Using the media 151
Nightlife 154
Taking holidays 154
Visiting famous sites 154
Speaking the language 155
Keeping in touch 156

Glossary 159

Further reading 163

Useful addresses 167

Index 177

THIS MAP IS NOT TO SCALE

ATLANTIC
OCEAN

NEWFOUNDLAND & LABRADOR

St John's

PRINCE EDWARD ISLAND

Charlottetown

Halifax
NOVA SCOTIA

NEW BRUNSWICK

Montreal

Fredericton

Quebec City

Lake Ontario

QUEBEC

Ottawa

Lake Erie

Iqaluit

Lake
Huron

Toronto

Hudson Bay

Lake Superior

ONTARIO

Lake Michigan

MANITOBA

Yellowknife

NUNAVUT

NORTH-
WEST
TERRITORIES

SASKAT-
CHEWAN

Winnipeg

ARCTIC
OCEAN

Whitehorse

Edmonton

ALBERTA

Regina

YUKON
TERRITORY

BRITISH
COLUMBIA

Calgary

UNITED STATES
OF AMERICA

Vancouver

PACIFIC
OCEAN

Victoria

viii

Preface

Welcome to the fourth edition of *Live and Work in Canada*. Canada is a very diverse, exciting and liveable country, something we're sure you'll agree with when you come yourself.

Whether your stay in Canada is to be permanent, as a temporary worker, as a student or as a holidaymaker, there is some fact and fiction to sort through before venturing to this huge nation. We hope that this book helps you to do so.

This edition has been fully updated to reflect the latest changes in how to get into Canada and enjoy living here. In addition to the ten chapters of information on what you need to know before coming to Canada, there is a useful address section at the back of the book. It is by no means an exhaustive list, but it should provide some good contacts to start with. Throughout the book and in the useful addresses section, we've included many more website addresses and email contacts than ever before.

Phone numbers in the book are listed with the city code in brackets followed by the phone number. Canada's international code is 1. All monetary sums are quoted in Canadian dollars, unless otherwise specified.

Much of the quantitative data in this book, the numbers that is, come from Statistics Canada, an agency of the federal government. Statistics Canada recently completed its 2006 Census of the people of Canada. However, the agency releases the collected data to the public, on such things like population, religion and immigration slowly over the course of a number of years. We have used the latest data, when available, but in some cases we've had to rely on older statistics.

You may have heard alluring things about Canada from Canadians abroad who are missing home or from people from your own country who have visited Canada. Undoubtedly, you would have heard a bit about Canucks (an informal name for Canadians): that they don't mind the cold and are fairly laid-back. But relaxed as they may be about some things, they can get riled, becoming fervent about politics, especially when it comes to protecting their prized health-care and education systems, as well as the environment.

A century ago Sir Wilfred Laurier, Canada's eighth prime minister, said, 'The 20th century belongs to Canada'. In many respects, he was right. At the end of the last century Canada was rated number one out of 174 countries on the United Nations human development index, which takes into account life-expectancy, education and standard of living. It was the sixth consecutive year for Canada at the top of the list. However, in the last few years, Canada has fallen in the ratings to as low as sixth place before rebounding to third place at the end of 2008, trailing Iceland and Norway – a reminder that there's always room for improvement. Nevertheless, the 21st century promises to be as exciting as the last for Canada – something you will hopefully discover for yourself.

The adventure of going to a new country, for a short while or for the long term, can be a bit daunting. Just remember that under those bulky winter parkas, Canadians are a warm-hearted bunch.

We hope you have a terrific time in Canada and come to enjoy the country as much as we do. Best of luck.

We would like to acknowledge the help and support of many friends and family throughout the researching and writing of this book. Thanks also to all the front-line people in the various departments of the Canadian government for being so obliging with their assistance and advice.

Karina Roman and Benjamin Kranc
Toronto

To my children, Saffire and Austin – BK

To Kevin, for making me smile and keeping me sane – and to Sophie for showing me what life is really about – KR

1

Deciding to Come to Canada

So you want to come to Canada, eh? First of all, contrary to widespread belief, we don't say 'eh' all the time. In fact, there are a few untruths out there about the country, one of which is that it's a cinch to get in. It's important to dispel the myth that Canada's doors are wide open to whoever wishes to enter, so that you can ensure you're one of those who does get in. Ninety per cent of skilled worker applicants are successful, but this is partly due to a preliminary self-assessment they are encouraged to do, resulting in many deciding not to apply. But, if you have the skills and the profile that Canada is looking for, you could be off to a new life in a vast and beautiful country. This book will help you to achieve your goals.

DEFINING YOUR GOALS

■ Perhaps you want to come to a country less restricted and/or more stable than your own.

■ Maybe you have family here whom you'd like to join, or you simply fancy a lifestyle change. You may feel Canada offers a higher standard of living than your own country.

■ Are there employment opportunities in your field that don't exist in your country? Is there a business you'd like to start that you think would prosper better in a competitive and growing economy like that of Canada?

■ Perhaps you prefer to first sample life in Canada through a working holiday programme or a limited-time working permit.

■ Do you want to take a particular course of study at a Canadian university or college? Or are you just coming over on a short-term student exchange?

■ Maybe you just want to backpack around the country or visit friends and relatives for longer than a few weeks.

KEEPING EXPECTATIONS REALISTIC

When you have determined your motives in wanting to come to Canada, it's important to identify the realities of what lies ahead. It's wonderful to have great expectations, but it's imperative that you become well-informed on certain aspects of Canadian life. There is plenty of opportunity, but no country is perfect.

Addressing myths and truths

Health care is free

What's that about there being no such thing as a free lunch? It's true in Canada that when you visit your family doctor you don't pay any money to the doctor directly. But the health care system is funded by the taxes Canadian residents pay. Canadian health care spending is estimated to have reached almost 172 billion dollars in 2008. or $5,170 per person.

Multiculturalism has eliminated racism

Canada's **Multiculturalism Act** is indicative of a progressive society. Immigrants are 50 per cent more likely to be self-employed than other Canadians are and immigration is expected to account for 100 per cent of all labour force growth by 2011. In addition, they don't use public services and social assistance as much. Despite these statistics there are people who believe that immigrants drain the welfare and social systems. Yet paradoxically, immigrants are sometimes accused of stealing jobs from long-time Canadians. Canada is known for egalitarian values and for being a 'cultural mosaic' rather than a 'melting pot', but that does not mean that racism is non-existent. However, in most cases Canadians know that Canada needs more people to continue to grow (the birth rate has been in decline for several years) and to prosper.

High-level skills lead to a high-level job

For the most part this is true. And the higher the level of skill and expertise you have, the better your chances of getting into Canada. For example, engineering, financial, science and health professionals score high points on skilled worker immigration applications. Unfortunately, however, immigration does not take into account whether your certification or accreditation stands up in Canada. You could face years of further study in Canada – at your own expense – to be recognised in the profession you were in in your homeland. This challenge will be dealt with in the chapter on getting a job.

Seeing the up side

On the other hand, you may have heard a few discouraging things about Canada that are far from the truth, such as myths about bears in the streets, everyone living in igloos and it being cold all the time. In the following chapters you will learn more about Canada and, in turn, learn that the above is false. For example, there is ready access to natural spaces where, yes, there are bears, but in the majority of cities the most aggressive wildlife you would encounter would be racoons ravaging garbage cans. Housing in Canada comes in all shapes and sizes and igloos exist only in the far north. In fact, with 90 per cent of Canada's population living 160 km from the US border, most Canadians enjoy warm summers in addition to the cold winters – and in some parts of Canada, like the West Coast, the winters are actually quite mild.

JOINING YOUR FAMILY

One major attraction of moving to Canada may be that you have friends or family who have moved there already. Your relatives can help with advice and assistance in your application process. In fact, having immediate family in Canada can offer one avenue to immigrate here; the chapter on immigration deals with this option. The adjustment to life in a new country can also be a great deal easier with the help of friends and relatives.

MAKING PREPARATIONS

Different preparations are involved depending on whether you are immigrating to Canada or coming on a student visa, a working permit or just as a visitor. For the purposes of this section, the following points mostly pertain to immigration.

Getting help

There are many people who do their own visa preparations when it comes to immigrating. Most buy a book like this one to get the information they need. Immigration Canada's website and local consular offices also have detailed information on how to apply. But some people, especially those who feel they have complicated cases, might choose to hire an immigration lawyer or an immigration consultant. Both cost money, of course. Immigration lawyers are lawyers with a speciality in immigration and are regulated by their provincial law society. They will guide you through the process and try to minimise any legal quagmires that may arise. Immigration consultants are often less expensive than a lawyer and will guide you though the process, but they are not legal experts. It's also very important to note that immigration consultants are regulated by and must be in good standing with the Canadian Society of Immigration Consultants (CSIC).

Restrictions

Pets

It would be difficult to leave a beloved pet behind, but there are some conditions to be met in order to bring your animals with you. First of all, Canada is a signatory to international agreements banning the importation of exotic and endangered species. That means there are some animals you are entirely barred from bringing in.

But for those animals you can import, the conditions you must meet will depend on what type of animal you are bringing in and what country you come from, because some countries are certified rabies-free and some are not. Also, at the time of publication, birds from certain countries were banned from import because of fears of avian influenza (bird flu).

You will have to prove your animals are pets and that you don't plan to sell them. Depending on the animal and how old it is, there might be quarantine or vaccination requirements. For some animals, you'll need to get a permit to bring it in, which requires an application and a fee. Assistance dogs (seeing-eye, hearing-ear) are exempt from permit requirements if they accompany the person who needs the assistance.

Your pet will also be subject to an inspection when you come to Canada. You should also be aware that if you are coming to Canada temporarily, your pet may be required to be quarantined on your return to your home country, sometimes for long periods of time.

To find out what is specifically required for your pet, you can contact the Canadian Food Inspection Agency (CFIA) (see Useful Addresses). Their website (www. inspection.gc.ca) also has a wealth of information. CFIA also regulates the importation of plants.

Drugs

It's wise not to bring any drugs, except prescription drugs, into Canada. Even marijuana and hashish are considered narcotics and being caught with them carries a prison sentence. Can you think of a worse way to start your new life in Canada? You are allowed to bring in up to a three-month supply of prescription drugs as long as you can prove they were prescribed by a licensed physician and dispensed by a pharmacy.

Firearms

Canada has tight gun control laws. The federal law governing firearms is the **Firearms Act**. Individual provinces may have additional requirements, particularly regarding hunting. You must be 18 years of age or older to bring in firearms.

There are three classes of firearms: non-restricted (such as rifles and shotguns for hunting); restricted (for specific purposes such as target shooting, not allowed for hunting or self-protection); and prohibited. Prohibited firearms include automatic firearms and some semi-automatic ones, many handguns (depending on barrel length and calibre) and replica guns. They cannot be brought into Canada.

You must have a valid firearms licence and a Canadian registration certificate for each firearm. If you are coming just for a visit, you can declare your firearms through a non-resident firearm declaration (this must be signed by a customs officer at the border and is good for 60 days and the fee is $25) or apply for a five-year Possession and Acquisition Licence (PAL) and register your firearms in Canada. The latter option requires proof you have passed the required safety courses and costs $60 to $80 depending on the firearms.

If you are moving to Canada for an extended period of time or permanently, the PAL option plus registration is required. For more information, contact the Canada Firearms Centre (see Useful Addresses).

Health

Canada, of course, aims to prevent diseases from being imported into the country. You will need certain vaccinations for diseases. If you are immigrating you will have already been screened for diseases such as yellow fever and tuberculosis during your mandatory medical. If you are a visitor, a student or coming on a work permit, you may also require a medical depending on what country you are coming from or what occupation you may be undertaking while in Canada (such as working with children). Check with your Canadian Embassy or consulate.

STICKING TO YOUR DECISION

Once you start making serious preparations to come to Canada – especially if it's to settle for good – you may begin to have doubts. It is a courageous act to leave a life you know for one that is unknown. You may be worrying about cultural differences, homesickness or you may be afraid that your bravery will lead you to failure. This is perfectly natural. Just remain clear about your motives, informed about your choices and prepared for what will greet you. And know that even if you don't have family or friends awaiting you, you are not alone. There are agencies and organisations in many Canadian communities that are set up to help immigrants and new visitors.

Settlement

The host programme

This helps you get settled in your community. It is a free service that introduces you to a Canadian who helps you learn about how things are done in Canada. For example this person will help you with the following:

■ grocery shopping

■ registering your children for school

■ how to use local transport

■ how to arrange television, phone and other utility services.

To join the host programme, contact a local immigrant service agency (see Useful Addresses). There is also the Language Instruction for Newcomers (LINC) programme and the Immigration Settlement and Adaptation Program (ISAP).

Adjusting to culture shock

Canada is like most industrialised countries, so if you're from the Western world you may not find it all that different. The greatest adjustment will probably be getting used to the climate and the vast spaces. Make sure the clothing you bring is appropriate for the season, but don't overdo it. You don't need three featherdown jackets all at once in the wintertime, but a warm jacket, gloves, a hat and boots are necessary. If you bring clothing you can layer, your wardrobe will be at its most versatile for any season.

Canada's biggest cities are so multicultural that anyone of any race or religion is bound to find a community they can feel comfortable in. Smaller towns, however, are less diverse and the adjustment might be more dramatic. But smaller centres can also be less isolating because everyone knows everyone. A recent Statistics Canada study found immigrants did better, sooner, in terms of income levels and language skills in smaller cities compared to those who settled in big centres.

Other than that, the differences are bound to be little ones only you would notice: office etiquette, slang words, hours of operation for businesses and shops etc. You'll soon settle right in.

Before you leave

If you're coming to live in Canada as a permanent resident, don't sell your house or give up your job until your papers have come through. You have about a year to get to Canada once you receive your visa. Regardless of whether you're coming as an immigrant, temporary worker, student or visitor, do not make any life-altering decisions based on your travels, until you are certain you are going and have your visa or work permit in your hand.

When you do come, don't pack your official documents in your suitcase, but carry them with you. This includes your passport; visa/immigration papers for you and anyone else you are travelling with; birth certificate; baptismal certificates; marriage certificates; adoption, separation or divorce papers; school records, diplomas and degrees; trade or professional certificates; immunisation, vaccination, dental and other health records; driver's licence and any accident record from your insurance company; car registration (if you are importing your car); employer reference letters.

Also, bring with you two copies of a detailed list of all personal or household items you are bringing with you or that will follow you later. Last but certainly not least, make sure you have sufficient funds for short-term living expenses.

And off you go!

2

Learning a Bit About Canada

Canada doesn't often make the foreign pages
of newspapers around the world. Many
outsiders think of it as a snowy country, full of
quiet, laid-back people — rather a quiet and
boring nation, in fact. That just goes to show
how little they know. If you're thinking of
coming to Canada, here are the basics.

THE HISTORY

Europeans arrived in the 1400s but they weren't the first to set sights on this vast
land. The earliest known site occupied by people is the Bluefish Caves of the Yukon.
In 1000 AD the Vikings from Iceland and Greenland reached the Labrador coast
and Newfoundland, but they didn't stay.

It was the North American Indians who greeted the Europeans. As far back as
30,000 BC, the people arrived in North America from Asia by crossing the Bering
Strait. These aboriginal people developed distinct languages, customs and religious
beliefs. They depended on the land and developed specialised skills to deal with the
climate and geography. The Inuit came after the North American Indians (they are
not related to them, however) and settled predominantly in the Arctic.

First contacts

French beginnings

In the early 1500s the Spanish, French, British and Italians were all vying to get to North America. The French explorers and missionaries got to Canada first. Jacques Cartier landed at the gulf of the St Lawrence waterway and this led to the founding of New France. It is thought that Canada got its name from Cartier who noticed the Huron and Iroquois inhabitants referring to the land as 'Kanata' which means, 'cluster of dwellings' or 'small community'.

The French had discovered a land rich in natural resources and one of their main activities was fur trading with the native peoples – that is, until the natives realised they were not properly profiting from the trades. The French and natives fought throughout the 1600s because of this and because of the French development of aboriginal land.

Britain steps in

France wasn't all that interested in its new colony even though another of its men, Samuel de Champlain, settled Quebec City and Montreal by 1642. The Hudson's Bay Company was founded in 1670, primarily as a fur trading enterprise (it is Canada's oldest business enterprise, existing today as a major department store chain). The English moved into the Hudson Bay area and by the early 1700s had taken over most of Nova Scotia and Newfoundland. Canada is known as a peacemaking country, but its roots are, like most nations', rooted in war. In 1745 all hell broke loose with the British capture of Fortress Louisbourg from the French. England officially declared war on France in 1756, starting in Europe what is known as the Seven Years' War. Part of that war was played out in Canada.

France v. Britain

The French seemed the stronger nation for four years, but the tide changed in one of Canada's most famous battles. Both the French and English generals died in the battle, but it was the British who defeated the French in 1759 in Quebec on the Plains of Abraham. In 1763 France handed Canada over to Britain in the Treaty of Paris. However, most of Canada's population was French. The conclusion of the Treaty of Paris gave rise to concerns over losing their rights and heritage. In response to these fears, Britain passed the Quebec Act in 1774 which granted religious (Roman Catholic) and linguistic freedom to the French.

But what's history without a little revolution and rebellion? The American Revolution saw Britain's 13 colonies in the south fight for independence from Britain from 1775 to 1783. This led to the migration north to Canada of about 50,000 'Loyalists', so called because of their loyalty to Britain, balancing the number of French and British in Canada. In 1791 Lower Canada (Quebec) and Upper Canada (Ontario) were formed.

Birth of a country

The War of 1812 is often thought to have brought about the beginnings of Canada's national identity. The Americans invaded Canada believing it would be an easy victory. The British, native peoples and French banded together and, although outnumbered, stood their ground. Many battles were won and lost by both sides, but it was their first defence of their country against an invader that saw the people of 'British North America' choose their way of life over that of the republicans to the south. Many heroes and war legends were created. Perhaps one of the least known is that in August 1814, the British captured and burned Washington, including the White House (which in those days wasn't so white and had to be painted white to cover the damage). The war ended in a draw in December 1814 with the Treaty of Ghent.

It wasn't long until the people of Upper and Lower Canada started itching for their own independence. In 1837, rebellions occurred in both colonies, which prompted Britain to join them under a common legislature. Soon afterwards they were granted responsible government and their first taste of political autonomy. More autonomy was on the way with the achievement of Confederation. In 1867 the Dominion of Canada was created under the **British North America Act** (BNA Act) passed by the British government. Sir John A. Macdonald became the first Prime Minister of the Dominion that included Ontario, Quebec, Nova Scotia and New Brunswick. Within the next six years Manitoba, British Columbia and Prince Edward Island were admitted into the Dominion.

The building of the railway

If you come to Canada with children, they will undoubtedly learn in school about the building of the **Canadian Pacific Railway** (CPR). Many scandals erupted during that time, but when it was completed in 1885, the CPR was the longest railway in the world and its construction within five years was considered a great engineering feat. It was built to connect the country from east to west and to encourage settlement.

This was met with resistance from the native peoples who were already settled on that land. The aboriginals lost their fight and large numbers of European immigrants came on promises of free land in the west. Between 1881 and 1891, 680,000 people immigrated to Canada and many of them are responsible for the emergence of large-scale grain farming. The South African War, also known as the Boer War, from 1899 to 1902, marked Canada's first official dispatch of troops to an overseas war. In 1904–5 Alberta and Saskatchewan entered Confederation, leaving only Newfoundland on its own.

Modern history

The 1900s saw rapid change due to the industrial revolution: Canada was a significant participant in both World Wars, notably at Vimy Ridge in WW1 and Dieppe and Normandy in WW2, as well as in the air and at sea. English-French tensions continued and the labour movement became organised with the creation of the unions. Canada developed social security programmes such as unemployment insurance, welfare and eventually 'Medicare'. The Canadian Broadcasting Corporation (CBC) was formed and natural resource industries became an integral part of the Canadian economy. Women got the vote, Newfoundland joined the Confederation in 1949 and more than 26,000 Canadians served in the Korean War between 1950 and 1953. In 1965 the Maple Leaf flag was adopted as Canada's national flag.

In 1967 Canada turned 100 years old and celebrated with Expo festivities in Montreal. In the 1970s there was major upheaval in Quebec when the separatist movement took on a violent nature, but in 1980 a referendum showed the majority of Quebecois were against independence. Also in that year, Canada officially adopted *O Canada!* as its national anthem, although the original French version dates from 1880. Speaking of national symbols, the beaver is Canada's national animal.

The last three decades

The 1980s were characterised by constitutional issues. Canada's constitution (the **BNA Act**) was an act of the British Parliament and, as an independent country, Canada wanted to 'bring home' the constitution. In 1982, parts of the BNA Act were changed and it became a Canadian act: **The Constitution Act**. Included in it is the **Canadian Charter of Rights and Freedoms**. Quebec is the only province that did not sign the new constitution and two subsequent attempts to bring it in, the Meech Lake Accord and the Charlottetown Accord, failed. In 1995 another Quebec referendum on independence took place and the 'no' side (against independence) won by a very narrow margin.

In the late 1990s, Canada played an important role in trying to bring stability to two areas experiencing serious conflict, namely Kosovo and East Timor.

The terrorist attacks on 11 September 2001 affected the United States directly and most profoundly, but Canada has been impacted as well, not only on the day of the attacks, when Canada accepted hundreds of air passengers not allowed to land in United States, but also since then in terms of Canada's domestic security policy and foreign policy.

Canada's military mission to Afghanistan began shortly after the attacks. At the time of writing, 127 Canadian soldiers and one diplomat have been killed since the beginning of the mission. Sadly, by the time you read this the tally will probably be higher. It is currently Canada's largest foreign military deployment. There are also missions in the Balkans, the Caribbean, the Middle East and Africa, but Canada declined joining the US in Iraq in 2003.

Other major events in the new millennium include the SARS crisis in Toronto and Vancouver and the hydro-electric blackout in Ontario in the summer of 2003. Also, after much controversy, debate and a Supreme Court decision, parliament made gay marriage legal in 2005. In 2006, Canadians elected the first Conservative government in more than a decade, albeit a minority government. The Conservatives were re-elected, again with a minority parliament, in the fall of 2008, meaning an election could happen again at any time. In the last couple of years, the government has made a number of official apologies to particular groups. In 2006, it apologised and paid compensation to the Chinese for the racist Chinese immigration act of 1923. In 2008, it made a historic apology in the House of Commons to the country's aboriginal people for the abuses of the residential school system they were forced into decades ago.

Inventions and discoveries – in Canada, by Canadians or both

- acrylics
- air-conditioned vehicle
- aircraft de-icer
- antigravity suit

- dental mirror
- electric light bulb (Henry Woodward sold the patent to Thomas Edison)
- five-pin bowling
- ginger ale
- lacrosse
- heart pacemaker
- walkie-talkie
- snowshoes
- birch-bark canoe
- winter parka
- mukluks
- kayak
- electron microscope
- canadarm (used on space shuttles)
- pablum (baby cereal)
- instant mashed potatoes
- MacIntosh Apple
- the chocolate bar
- the paint roller
- the telephone (Alexander Graham Bell)
- the wireless photograph transmitter
- the friction match
- the chainsaw
- the snowmobile
- rotating snowplough
- kerosene
- standard time
- the push-up bra
- clothes zipper
- insulin
- battery-less radio
- IMAX technology
- Greenpeace (founded in Vancouver)
- green, plastic garbage bag
- Trivial Pursuit
- ice hockey
- basketball.

Source: Lonely Planet Canada, 1997 and *Made in Canada*

Celebrating identity and diversity

Canada's reputation as a peacekeeping nation has grown through its involvement as a member of the United Nations. It is also a member of the Commonwealth, la Francophonie, the Group of Eight (G8) industrialised nations, the North Atlantic Treaty Organisation (NATO), the North American Aerospace Defence Agreement (NORAD) and the Organisation of American States (OAS).

Canada is a diverse and tolerant nation. Canada as it is known today would not exist if it weren't for immigration, both past and present (see Figure 1). In 2007 more than 236,000 people immigrated to Canada. In fact, the 2006 Census showed that the proportion of foreign-born people in Canada reached its highest level in 75 years and among Western countries is second only to Australia. The faces of those who come have changed over the years. During the settlement of the prairies, the immigrants were mainly from Eastern Europe. Leading up to 1961, 25 per cent of immigrants had come from the United Kingdom. Now, a majority of immigrants come from eastern, south-east and southern Asia, although immigration from the UK and the US has begun to increase recently. In the federal government's 2009 Immigration Plan, the goal is to admit between 240,000 and 265,000 people as permanent residents to Canada. That does not include other immigration classes such as people applying for temporary work permits or people coming as refugees.

Languages

More than 60 languages are spoken by more than 70 ethnic groups across the country. Multiculturalism became an official government policy in 1971. In 1988, the Government of Canada passed the **Canadian Multiculturalism Act** stating that every citizen, regardless of origin, has an equal chance to participate in all aspects of the country's collective life.

One of Canada's distinguishing qualities is that it is a bilingual country: English and French. When you come to Canada you will discover that even the boxes of cereal tell you the nutritional content in both languages. But, although the country as a whole is officially bilingual, the only province that is officially bilingual is New Brunswick. Quebec sees itself as French-only and the other provinces carry out their business in English. Recently, the city of Moncton, which is in New Brunswick, made itself the first officially bilingual city in Canada. Ottawa, the nation's capital, is not officially bilingual but is considered functionally bilingual.

Composition of Canada
Top ten ethnic origins

Ethnicity cited	Number of people
Canadian	10 million
English	6.6 million
French	4.9 million
Scottish	4.7 million
Irish	4.4 million
German	3.2 million
Italian	1.4 million
Chinese	1.3 million
North American Indian	1.3 million
Ukranian	1.2 million

Source: Statistics Canada, 2006 Census

Immigration (Permanent Residents) in 2007
Top ten source countries

	Number	%
Total	123,143	52.01
China	27,014	11.41
India	26,054	11.00
Philippines	19,064	8.05
United States	10,450	4.41
Pakistan	9,547	4.03
United Kingdom	8,128	3.43
Iran	6,663	2.81
Korea	5,864	2.48
France	5,526	2.33
Colombia	4,833	2.04

Source: Citizenship and Immigration Canada

Fig. 1. Canada's immigration statistics.

Another distinguishing mark is that the last thing a Canadian wants to be mistaken for is an American. Canadian culture, attitudes and politics are very different from those of its southern neighbour and Canadians are proud of it.

Religion

Religious freedom is a cornerstone of democracy; many different religions exist and grow within Canada. A large proportion of Canadians are Christian: Catholics and Protestants. Other major religions include Judaism, Islam, Hinduism, Sikhism and Buddhism. However, there's a discrepancy between affiliation and attendance. More than 80 per cent of Canadians say they belong to a religion but only 34 per cent say they attend religious service. And in 2001, about 16 per cent of Canadians said that they had no religious affiliation – up from about 12 per cent in 1981.

IDENTIFYING THE POPULATION

There are a mere 33,504,680 'Canucks'. Ontario and Quebec are the most populous provinces, with Toronto and Montreal the largest cities. Montreal followed Toronto's lead recently, becoming what is known as an amalgamated city. Amalgamation sees many of the city's suburbs join onto the city proper to become one giant mega-city. Ottawa and other Ontario cities have also been forced to amalgamate. Amalgamation has been controversial with residents quite opposed, but with the provincial governments going ahead with it anyway, claiming it will reduce costs (it hasn't). But, amalgamation has meant the new Toronto can now claim to be one of the largest cities in North America, with a population of 5.5 million.

Province/Territory	Population	Capital City
Newfoundland and Labrador	505,469	St. John's
Prince Edward Island	135,851	Charlottetown
Nova Scotia	913,462	Halifax
New Brunswick	729,997	Fredericton
Quebec	7,546,131	Quebec City
Ontario	12,160,282	Toronto
Manitoba	1,148,401	Winnipeg
Saskatchewan	968,157	Regina
Alberta	3,290,350	Edmonton
British Columbia	4,113,487	Victoria
Yukon	30,372	Whitehorse
Northwest Territories	41,464	Yellowknife
Nunavut	29,474	Iqaluit

Source: Statistics Canada, 2006 Census

UNDERSTANDING THE GOVERNMENT

Canada is a constitutional monarchy. Queen Elizabeth II is Canada's official head of state. The **Governor General** is her representative in Canada, although in many ways the Governor General's role is largely symbolic. Officially, the Governor General is appointed by the Queen on the advice of the Prime Minister. In Canada, powers and responsibilities are divided between the federal government and the provincial and territorial governments. If a bill is defeated in either a provincial legislature or in the House of Commons, the government in power is usually forced to call an election, as the defeat represents non-confidence.

Three tiers of government

Federal government

The **federal government** is based in Ottawa, chosen to be the capital of Canada as a compromise between Toronto and Montreal and because Kingston was too close to the US (and the war of 1812 was still pretty fresh in the Queen's memory). Parliament has an elected **House of Commons** and an appointed **Senate**. The House of Commons is the national legislature that approves all legislation. The Senate is the Upper House that gives a 'sober second thought' to legislation. The final stamp of approval on a bill comes from 'royal assent' given by the Governor General, although a Governor General has never refused a bill, which is why the role is seen as symbolic.

There are several political parties; the one that wins the most seats (out of 308) in an election forms the federal government. The leader of that party becomes the Prime Minister who chooses the Cabinet from the Members of Parliament (MPs) in that party. Each Cabinet Minister has a particular portfolio to oversee. The party that gets the second most seats forms the Official Opposition and its leader becomes the Leader of the Opposition. Canadian citizens can vote at 18. The governing party's term is a maximum of five years. But the Prime Minister can, and often does, call an election before that time.

However, parliament has passed legislation that will see a fixed election date every four years, unless there is a minority government (when the opposition parties still have the power to bring down the government). That would mean an upcoming election date of October 2012, unless the current minority government falls before then.

Several provinces and one territory have changed to having fixed election dates including British Columbia, Ontario, PEI, Newfoundland and Labrador and the Northwest Territories. Others are considering it as well.

The federal government is responsible for such matters as defence, criminal law, banking and foreign relations.

Provincial/territorial government

The provinces each have their own governments with certain responsibilities. The provincial legislatures do not have a Senate. For legislation to become law, the provincial assembly and the **Lieutenant Governor** (the Queen's provincial representative) must approve it, just as the Governor General does with federal legislation. Parliament delegates powers to the territories; the territories are not sovereign units but they have elected assemblies run very much like those of the provinces.

The provinces are responsible for health, education, property and civil justice. They pay for those responsibilities through provincial taxes (which the provincial government has the right to raise or lower) and transfer payments from the federal government. Some provinces, unfortunately known as 'have not' provinces, receive equalisation payments from the federal government. That money is generated from the so-called 'have' provinces.

Local government

Municipal governments run things most immediate in people's lives: schools, local transport, police, etc. They are elected regularly but do not have constitutional powers. The higher governments, usually the provincial level, delegate to them their responsibilities. This set-up has led to many conflicts between city governments and the provincial and federal governments. The provinces have downloaded responsibilities like social housing onto the cities. But city governments do not have the same revenue-generating capabilities as the provinces and can raise only property taxes and user fees. At the same time, more and more people are moving into the cities and city governments are finding it hard to cope. There has been much talk about creating a 'new deal for cities' but nothing has happened yet.

THE LEGAL AND JUDICIAL SYSTEMS

Canada's legal system is based both on English common law and the French civil code. In nine out of ten provinces the laws are determined by legal precedents, not by written statutes. In Quebec, however, civil law applies which is based on a written code that contains general principles and rules.

Canada has several levels of courts both at the provincial and federal levels. Each province has its own court of appeal and there is also a court of appeal for the federal level. The judiciary is independent; judges are appointed by the provincial and federal governments but are not beholden to government agendas in any way. **The Supreme Court of Canada** is the highest court in the country. It has the final decision on any matter pertaining to law in Canada, including interpreting constitutional questions. There are nine Supreme Court justices, three of whom must be from the province of Quebec.

The RCMP, or the **Royal Canadian Mounted Police**, is Canada's national police force. The RCMP is headed by a commissioner, but the Solicitor General (a cabinet minister in the federal government) oversees the organisation. One hundred years ago, it started as a small rural force. Now it comprises 17,000 peace officers and about 6,000 civilian employees. Widely recognised by the world as red-coated, broad-hatted officers on horseback, Mounties are responsible for the following:

■ acting as the municipal force in about 200 cities and towns;

■ providing provincial police services in all provinces and territories other than Ontario and Quebec, which have their own provincial forces;

■ enforcing 140 laws and statutes dealing with serious crimes;

■ representing Canada as a member of the International Criminal Police Organisation (INTERPOL);

■ enforcing national security (although in 1984 the Canadian Security Intelligence Service, CSIS, took over the RCMP's intelligence-gathering responsibilities).

Many municipalities, especially the large urban centres, have their own police forces. Overall in 2006, there was one police officer for every 520 Canadians. The number of police officers in Canada has been on a slight rise over the last few years, mostly due to an increase in the number of RCMP officers.

LOOKING AT GEOGRAPHY AND CLIMATE

Okay, so you know Canada is big, but many people really can't grasp just how large it is until they visit. Canada has a landmass of 9,970,610 km^2 making it the second-largest country in the world after Russia. Yet because it has a population of only about 32 million, it has one of the smallest population densities in the world: three persons per square kilometre.

Until 1 April 1999, Canada was made up of ten **provinces** and two **territories**, but on that day the map was changed when the Northwest Territories was divided in two to create a third territory: Nunavut. Eighty-five per cent of Nunavut's population is Inuit. Nunavut means 'our land' in Inuktitut, the Inuit language. This had been a long-time dream for the Inuit of the NWT. The new Nunavut government oversees land of about two million square kilometres.

The border between Canada and the United States is 8,892 km and it has coastlines on the Atlantic, Pacific and Arctic Oceans. That means it has the longest coastline of any country. The Arctic islands come within 800 km of the North Pole.

The landscapes and climates in Canada are remarkably varied. No, it isn't all snow and ice, but because a great deal of Canada is in a harsh northern climate, 90 per cent of the population live within a few hundred kilometres of the US border.

Canada has one-seventh of the world's fresh water made up from the Great Lakes and the infinite number of large and small rivers and lakes throughout the country. It has almost everything: flat plains, high mountain peaks, green valleys, beaches, cliffs, etc.

Canadian regions

Canada has seven distinct geographic regions:

- The **Pacific Coast** has a temperate climate. There you find rain forests and the oldest trees in Canada: 1,300-year-old western red cedars and 90m high Douglas firs.

- The **Cordillera** stretches from British Columbia to just east of the Alberta border. The Rocky Mountains, the Coast Mountains and the Elias Mountains are the main attractions. Canada's highest point, mount Logan (6,050m) is in part of the Elias range in the Yukon.

- The **Prairies** are known for their endless wheat fields and for having very few trees. Some of the largest concentrations of dinosaur fossils in the world have been found in this dry region that is also famous for its petroleum production.

- The **Canadian Shield** wraps around the Hudson Bay. It is a rocky region that reaches as far east as Labrador, south to Lake Ontario and northwest to the Arctic Ocean. Its granite rock is 3.5 billion years old; this region has been the stage for most of Canada's mining. But it is also home to boreal forest of spruce, fir, tamarack and pine.

- The **Great Lakes** – St Lawrence Lowlands contain Canada's two largest cities, Montreal and Toronto. It is prime growing land for fruits and vegetables and even the odd vineyard. This is also one of the most photographed regions in the autumn time when all the leaves change colour.

- The **Atlantic Provinces-Appalachian** region contains the four smallest Canadian provinces (the Maritime Provinces). It is also prime agricultural land and gets quite a bit of precipitation.

- The **Arctic** is north of the tree line. It has nearly continuous daylight during its short summer as well as some fairly warm temperatures that help the flowers bloom on the tundra. But the winters are long, cold and at their depth, very dark indeed.

Canadian climate

Canada is a country of extremes. Some cities can see lows of $-30°$ in the winter and yet highs of $+30°$ in the summertime. The West Coast can be mild but gets a lot of rain. The prairies are dry in the summer but cold and snowy in the winter. Central Canada sees a bit of variety. Toronto's winters are not nearly as harsh as those of Ottawa, Montreal or Quebec City – you could see temperatures as low as $-50°$ in Quebec City – but both Toronto and Montreal have quite hot and humid summers. The east usually isn't very hot in the summer but can be snowy and cold in the winter.

You should know that technically spring is March, April and May, summer is June to August, autumn/fall is September to November and winter is December to February. However, practically speaking it doesn't always work out that way. And more and more, the norms are not really the norms. As in much of the world, Canada is seeing its weather go topsy-turvy. In the past several years, parts of the country have suffered extreme drought, while other parts were flooded. There have been record heatwaves in the summers and record snowfalls in the winters. Whether you blame it on climate change or not, the weather isn't always predictable. Still, the chart in Figure 2 will help make sense of it all. Remember, however, that the following are averages and on any given day, temperatures can be much lower or much higher (for example: the coldest day on record in Iqaluit is $-46°$, the warmest $+24.4°$).

**Average coldest and warmest temperatures
(in degrees Celsius) in capital and major cities**

City	Average lowest temp/month	Average highest temp/month
St John's	-8.7/February	20.2/July
Charlottetown	-12.2/January	23.1/July
Halifax	-10.6/February	23.4/July
Fredericton	-15.4/January	25.6/July
Quebec City	-17.3/January	24.9/July
Montreal	-14.9/January	26.2/July
Ottawa	-15.5/January	26.4/July
Toronto	-7.9/January	26.5/July
Winnipeg	-23.6/January	26.1/July
Regina	-22.1/January	26.3/July
Edmonton	-17 /January	23.0/July
Calgary	-15.7/January	23.2/July
Vancouver	0.1/January	21.7/August
Victoria	0.3/January	21.8/July
Whitehorse	-23.2/January	20.3/July
Yellowknife	-32.2/January	20.8/July
Iqaluit	-31.0/February	11.6/July

Fig. 2. Canada's climate.

It might help to compare the temperatures in Figure 2 with those in other capitals. London, England, for example, has an average low of 5° in January and February and an average high of 23° in July. Paris, France sees its low in January at 4° and its high at 24° in July.

When you hear of excessively cold temperatures in Canadian cities, it's usually due to something called the **wind-chill factor**. The wind-chill makes the actual temperature feel much colder. You'll hear the weather people saying that it's −10° but feels like −25° with the wind-chill. At times like those, you'll also hear warnings about how long skin can go unprotected before frostbite kicks in. This is something to take very seriously. They don't make featherdown and waterproof jackets for nothing.

On the hottest days the weather forecasters will tell you that 'with the **humidex** it's 30°. This reading takes into account the humidity level, which in cities like Toronto and Montreal can make a big difference. That's when you're grateful for air conditioning.

In both summer and winter on very sunny days, forecasters will warn you of the UV index. High levels from seven upwards means skin will sunburn quickly.

THE ECONOMY

Over the last few years, Canada's economy has often outperformed those of the other G8 countries, which include France, Germany, Japan, Italy, USA, Russia and the UK. But at the time of writing, the world was in the midst of a global financial crisis, to which Canada was not immune. While Canada has no magic elixir to avoid a recession (especially when its major trading partner, the United States, spirals into one), it is not suffering as much as either the US or the UK. Canada's sound (and risk-averse) banking system is not in trouble and while the economy shrinks, it is not as dramatic a contraction as in other nations. Still, jobs are being lost, especially in the manufacturing, automobile, forestry and media sectors. And even the booming oil-driven economy of Alberta has slowed, which is affecting the number of temporary workers being sought by companies there.

After several years of unprecedented growth, Canada's economy is projected to shrink by 3 per cent in 2009. Compared to other countries suffering the global recession, that's not too bad. And the Bank of Canada projects that the economy will grow in 2010 by 2.5 per cent and by a healthy 4.7 per cent in 2011. The Bank of Canada has been known to err on the optimistic side, however. The central bank continues to aim to keep inflation at 2 per cent. Through the recession, it will probably dip lower than that, but the bank hopes to get back on target by the end of 2011.

Not unlike other industrialised countries, such as the US and the UK, Canada's interest rates are at an all-time historic low. At the time of writing the key interest rate, upon which commercial banks set their lending rates, was 0.25 per cent.

Unemployment had been declining since 1994 (the end of the last recession) when it was 10.4 per cent. The national unemployment rate sank as low as 6.1 per cent not too long ago, but it has surged to 8 per cent at the time of writing. Not every sector is suffering and, in fact, some are doing very well. But the unemployment rate is one statistic to take into account when considering your employment prospects when coming to Canada (see more about finding a job in Chapter 7).

Canada's biggest trading partner is the United States which accounts for more than 85 per cent of exports. Canada has been working on beefing up its trade with other countries, namely China as well as key countries in Europe and South America. But it is still highly dependent on trade with the US, which is why trading feuds make headlines in Canada. Natural resources are a large part of Canada's exports, but Canada is also a leader in aerospace engineering.

Assessing living expenses

The cost of living in Canada is not unreasonably high but, because of higher taxes, which pay for social services, consumer goods are not as cheap as in the US or Mexico, though they are quite a bit cheaper than in the UK or France. One commodity that has a big affect on the cost of living is gasoline. Regular unleaded gasoline in the early part of 2009 averaged 88.4 cents per litre. That's a far cry from record high prices in mid 2008 of $1.37 a litre. However, gas prices vary across the country. For example, gas is more expensive further north and in Quebec. (For housing, automobile and education costs, see the appropriate chapters.)

The Canadian dollar continues to trade poorly against the British pound, but has recently soared against the US dollar. It trades poorly against the Euro, but well against the Australian dollar. Currently the exchange rate is approximately $1.80 = £1, and $1.23 = $1 US, and $1.62 = 1 euro.

In 2008, each Canadian household spent, on average, $48,770 on goods and services, with 20 per cent on personal income taxes, 19 per cent on shelter and 11 per cent on food, 14 per cent on transportation and 36 per cent on other things. Those other things include recreation, personal insurance and pension contributions, household operations, clothing, gifts, entertainment and contributions to charity. The lowest income households spent a much greater proportion of income on shelter and a much smaller proportion on personal income taxes.

In 2006, more than 68 per cent of Canadians owned their own homes, the highest rate of home ownership on record in the country. Ninety-nine per cent of homes have telephone service. The long-distance market is very competitive, with overseas rates as low as 5¢ per minute to the UK, 5¢ to the US and within Canada and 7¢ to Hong Kong. In fact, most markets in Canada are very competitive which keeps prices low.

Banking

The federal government regulates all banks and most trust companies. Banks are also members of the Canadian Deposit Insurance Corporation (CDIC), so most of your deposits are insured up to $100,000. To open an account you will need proper identification, such as one or more of the following: a bank card from a reputable financial institution, a credit card, passport and a Canadian driver's licence.

Not having a job or a minimum deposit should not prevent you from opening an account, although the bank might do a credit check to determine such things as your daily withdrawal limit with a bank card or whether to hold deposited cheques until they clear.

When opening an account, you will have to sign an account agreement that outlines the rules of the accounts, what kind of account you are opening (chequeing, savings etc.), account number, interest to be paid on the account, service charges etc.

If a problem arises with your bank that cannot be resolved directly with them (a serious attempt must be made), you can contact the Canadian Banking Ombudsman (see Useful Addresses).

The national debt

One of Canada's continuing challenges, however, is its national debt. Currently it stands at $458 billion. Over the past several years, the federal government had been chipping away at the total debt thanks to repeated budget surpluses. But due to the current economic conditions, the government is projecting budget deficits for the next few years and, therefore, will be adding again to the country's debt. At the time of writing, the estimated national debt in 2011 will be $522 billion. Increased debt means, of course, more money going to interest payments, taking away from funds that could go towards social programmes or lowering taxes.

ATTITUDES

It is difficult to generalise about a nation's attitudes. Generally, however, Canadians are concerned about the environment, enjoy the outdoors and take human rights very seriously. They understand the importance of democracy and the value of their right to vote. However, voter apathy is on the rise. In the 2006 federal election only 64.7 per cent of Canadians cast their ballots, and in 2008 only 58.8 per cent did, which was the lowest voter turnout in Canadian history. In the 1980s, voter turnout averaged 73 per cent.

Canadians work hard, but consider their jobs just one part of life. Family time, sports, recreation and the arts are important too. Which is why there is much grumbling about lack of vacation time in Canada compared with other countries, especially Europe. On average, a Canadian will get two weeks off a year, in addition to special holiday days, like Christmas and Canada Day.

Canadians believe in equality, as outlined in the **Charter of Rights and Freedoms.** Women have made great gains in equality in the work place – but inequalities still exist. Similarly, people of different racial groups and physical capabilities are protected from discrimination under law, but that is not to say that discrimination doesn't exist. All in all, Canada is a pleasant country that is accepting and easy-going. It is not difficult to adapt to life here; most people enjoy visiting, living and working in Canada.

3

Immigration to Canada

The political, economic, and legal climates in Canada are constantly shifting when it comes to immigration, both temporary and permanent.

UNDERSTANDING POLICY AND POLITICS

As in many parts of the world, there is a movement towards restricting access to Canada for immigrants, but there are also countervailing economic and social realities. Indeed, Canadian immigration law was altered on 28 June 2002 (and further since) generally making the rules more restrictive. By contrast, certain programmes regarding temporary entry have been made less restrictive – for instance for computer professionals – recognising the realities of the economic demand in this sector. As such, though we hope to provide accurate, up-to-date information about Canadian immigration law and policy, you must investigate matters pertaining to your own case with the appropriate government office or professional at the time that you seek immigration, permanent or temporary. Further, Canadian immigration law covers volumes and volumes, which obviously cannot be condensed into just one chapter, so discussion, though as thorough as possible, is obviously limited.

There are a few important principles of which you should be aware, for an understanding of our immigration policies and philosophies. An understanding of these will often lead to a better understanding of the underlying law and regulations, and therefore the guidelines which will affect you.

Guiding principles

There are a number of principles set out in Canada's Immigration Act. Canada's immigration laws are designed to promote, for example:

- cultural and social enrichment;
- trade and commerce through temporary entry of visitors;
- Canada's international humanitarian obligations;
- a strong and viable economy;
- maintenance of Canadian society's health, safety and security.

These basic principles are then moulded to fit specific issues. With regard to entry for **temporary workers**, the philosophy is 'net benefit to Canada'; that is to say, does an applicant provide Canada with some benefit to justify the hiring of a foreign worker? Contrast this with the philosophy pursuant to the previous law which was 'Canadians first'. As will be discussed below, this leads to various procedures required to satisfy immigration officials before a foreign worker will be entitled to enter and work in Canada, and also an elaborate system of exceptions which must be considered.

With regard to **permanent residence**, the guiding principles go on to shape the criteria employed for selection of immigrants. Indeed, recognising demographics, commerce, and other issues, Canada promotes immigration, though in recent times there sometimes appears to be a harsher attitude among those making the selection decisions. Canada's Federal Court is full of cases of rejected immigration applicants and there appears to be no let-up in sight.

With this in mind, let us explore some of the issues in Canadian immigration.

ILLEGAL IMMIGRATION

Before looking at the general issues involved in getting into, or staying in, Canada, it is important to realise that violation of Canadian immigration law could have severe consequences. We will discuss below the various programmes and policies affecting immigration to Canada which will allow people to come to, and remain in, Canada. Certainly, however, in the last few years, there has been a rise in illegal immigration to Canada, and the authorities are taking an increasingly harsh stance against people caught in this position. If you attempt to enter Canada without the appropriate legal authorisation and documentation, you will meet a stern turn-around from Canadian immigration authorities, whether before you board the plane or after you land, whenever the problem is detected. Canadian immigration authorities are now conducting checks of persons at airports abroad before people can even board the plane.

Similarly, someone already in Canada who breaches Canadian immigration or criminal law will face possible deportation. Meeting the requirements of Canadian immigration is no laughing matter, and the consequences of failing to obey the rules could lead to deportation and the inability to return to Canada ever again.

KNOWING THE GENERAL REQUIREMENTS

If you are seeking to enter Canada, you should ensure that all proper requirements are met. These may include:

- Obtaining a visa before arriving, for certain nationalities. The list changes from time to time – see Figure 3 for the current list. A Canadian Visa Post should be consulted if there is any question.

- Ensuring that there is no criminal bar to entry – a criminal record could lead to denial of entry to Canada for permanent or temporary purposes.

- Ensuring that there is no medical inadmissibility issue – the existence of an ailment which could jeopardise Canadian health and safety, or be a burden on our health system, could lead to inadmissibility.

- Further, specific requirements may be needed in particular instances, such as a work permit for those seeking to work in Canada.

We give you here the basic idea about the legal issues involved in the process. Once you feel that you may qualify under one of the areas discussed, you will have to deal with the procedures involved. You will need to:

- obtain the appropriate forms – note that since November 2008, all skilled worker permanent residence applications are sent to a central processing centre in Sydney, Nova Scotia. From there, files are screened and sent to the geographically appropriate visa post for further processing. Basic information is submitted to Sydney, but further documentation is submitted only upon request by the local visa post;

- look at the practical issues involved in submitting an application;

- ascertain the proper documentation which will be required from a Canadian Visa Post, to be ready when the time comes.

Canada divides the type of people entering the country into two basic groups – **temporary** and **permanent** – both of which are discussed on pages 32–43.

TEMPORARY VISA ISSUES

Temporary entry can be broken down further into three branches:

- **temporary residents (formerly 'visitors')**
- **students**
- **foreign workers.**

There are exceptional circumstances which can give rise to entry on other grounds (through, for instance, a **Temporary Resident Permit** where someone may not otherwise be admissible), but these are the basic categories. It should be noted that even for those people for whom the student or worker categories seem applicable, the issues relating to temporary residents discussed below relate as well and should be considered.

Temporary residents/'visitors'

Visitors are temporary residents who come to Canada neither to study nor work. Visiting can of course have various purposes, from the simplest form of someone who is just a tourist, to those coming for a business visit. Anyone who is not a student or worker will be put into this broad category.

Technically, anyone seeking to come to Canada as a visitor must obtain a **temporary resident visa** at a Canadian Visa Post (Embassy, Consulate or High Commission dealing with immigration matters) before entering Canada. Nationals of certain countries, including the United Kingdom, have been exempted from this requirement (see Figure 3 for list of countries requiring visas). However, this does not mean that British citizens, as just one example of a visa-exempt country, are immune to the enforcement of Canadian immigration law. Indeed, anyone appearing at a Canadian port of entry (anywhere where one enters Canada, either at an airport, sea port, or land crossing) must justify his or her entitlement to enter Canada, and may be questioned as to the reason for seeking entry.

Denying entry

Canadian immigration officials have the right to deny entry whenever they feel that it would be in violation of Canadian immigration law; for instance, in a case where there is concern that the person may be inadmissible due to a criminal problem, or if there is concern that the person would not leave at the end of the visitation period (often granted for six months initially). Without reviewing all grounds for

Afghanistan
Albania
Algeria
Angola
Argentina
Armenia
Azerbaijan
Bahrain
Bangladesh
Belarus
Belize
Benin
Bhutan
Bolivia
Bosnia-Herzegovina
Brazil
Bulgaria
Burkina-Faso
Burundi
Cambodia
Cameroon
Cape Verde
Central African
  Republic
Chad
Chile
China
Colombia
Comoros
Congo, Democratic
  Republic
Congo, People's
  Republic
Costa Rica
Cuba
Czech Republic
Djibouti
Dominica
Dominican Republic
East Timor
Ecuador
Egypt
El Salvador
Equatorial Guinea
Eritrea
Ethiopia
Fiji
Gabon
Gambia
Georgia
Ghana
Grenada
Guatemala

Guinea
Guinea-Bissau
Guyana
Haiti
Honduras
Hungary
India
Indonesia
Iran
Iraq
Israel (only Israeli
  citizens holding
  valid Israeli 'Travel
  Document in lieu of
  National Passport')
Ivory Coast
Jamaica
Jordan
Kazakhstan
Kenya
Kirabati
Korea, North
Kuwait
Kyrgyzstan
Laos
Latvia
Lebanon
Lesotho
Liberia
Libya
Lithuania (e-passport
  holders only)
Macao S.A.R.
Macedonia
Madagascar
Malawi
Malaysia
Maldives
Mali
Marshall Islands
Mauritania
Mauritius
Mexico
Micronesia
Moldova
Mongolia
Montenegro
Morocco
Mozambique
Myanmar (Burma)
Naura
Nepal
Nicaragua

Niger
Nigeria
Oman
Pakistan
Palau
Palestinian Authority
Panama
Paraguay
Peru
Philippines
Poland (e-passport
  holders only)
Qatar
Romania
Russia
Rwanda
Sao Tomé e Principe
Saudi Arabia
Senegal
Serbia
Seychelles, The
Sierra Leone
Slovak Republic
Somalia
South Africa
Sri Lanka
Sudan
Surinam
Syria
Taiwan
Tajikistan
Tanzania
Thailand
Togo
Tonga
Trinidad and Tobago
Tunisia
Turkey
Turkmenistan
Tuvalu
Uganda
Ukraine
United Arab Emirates
Uruguay
Uzbekistan
Vanuatu
Venezuela
Vietnam
Yemen
Zambia
Zimbabwe

Fig. 3. Countries whose citizens need visas.

33

inadmissibility (which are numerous), persons seeking to enter Canada should be aware that certain issues are foremost in the minds of Canadian immigration officers when determining whether to allow entry of a foreign national. A criminal history, as noted above, is an important reason for entry being denied, and virtually any prior criminal history will be caught in the dragnet of Canadian legislation. Medical grounds can also lead to refusal of admission to Canada, based on a threat to the Canadian public or a possible burden on the Canadian health system.

Obtaining a visa does not stop an immigration officer from denying entry. It does, however, allow the person concerned to 'pre-screen' any contentious issues, and give some later flexibility.

Students

In addition to the issues discussed above, those wishing to study in Canada must meet some further requirements, and must generally obtain the visa for studying before arriving in Canada. First, a student must have an acceptance to a Canadian educational institution. Certain institutions will not qualify, and it will be necessary to check with a Canadian Visa Post or immigration professional before making application.

As a student, you will also have to demonstrate your ability to support yourself while in Canada – perhaps with a sum of some $10,000 to $15,000 or more – and the intention to return when studies are concluded. It is again important to note that a student visa is temporary and applicants must convince an officer that it is not their intention to remain in Canada permanently. That being said, it is possible to extend student visas after arriving in Canada, as the educational programme proceeds from year to year or other time frame, or if there is a change of institution. Eventually, however, the visa will end.

Students in some cases will also be entitled to a non-renewable one-year or two-year work permit at the conclusion of their programme to work in their field of study.

See also the discussion in Chapter 8 about some of the exchange programmes and other student-specific programmes for coming to Canada.

Foreign workers

This is perhaps the most asked about, and misunderstood, aspect of Canadian immigration. People often say if they can't get permanent residence, they will just come to work temporarily. Unfortunately, it's not that easy. A **temporary work permit** is not a substitute for permanent residence, or a lesser form of permanent residence. It is sometimes more difficult to get a temporary work permit than permanent residence. See also Chapter 7 for information about working in Canada.

The usual process

Subject to exemptions discussed later (which should be tried first when possible), the general procedure to obtain a work permit is as follows.

Canada's policy, as indicated, is 'net benefit to Canada'. A foreigner can work in Canada only when this is justified, and may include issues as to whether there is no Canadian to fill a position. Therefore the process begins with the employer.

According to the legislation which took effect 28 June 2002, an employer must establish a number of factors to an officer of Service Canada (operating on behalf of Human Resources and Skills Development Canada) before a '**positive labour market opinion**' (also referred to as a Confirmation or LMO) can be provided, which is the precursor to a work permit application. The Service Canada officer will consider factors including:

- whether the work is likely to result in direct job creation or job retention for Canadians (Canadians includes citizens and permanent residents);

- whether the work is likely to result in the creation or transfer of skills and knowledge for the benefit of Canadians;

- whether the work is likely to fill a labour shortage;

- whether the wages and working conditions offered are sufficient to attract and retain Canadians;

- whether the employer has made or has agreed to make reasonable efforts to hire or train Canadians;

- whether the employment of the foreign national is likely to adversely affect settlement of a labour dispute.

Once Service Canada provides a positive Labour Market Opinion, a foreign worker may then proceed to apply for a work permit at the appropriate Canadian Visa Post (or in some cases, port of entry). The worker will need to substantiate that his or her credentials meet the requirements of the job in question. Obviously, as well, a temporary work permit is indeed temporary, generally issued for an initial period of one year, and renewable thereafter – if the reason for the renewal can be substantiated.

Based on the structure of the programme, the reality is that the less sophisticated a job or an applicant's credentials, the less likely that Confirmation and/or work permit will be granted, since it is less likely that there are no Canadians to fill the position.

Typically, the occupations permitted are considered NOC 0, A, or B. Though somewhat beyond the scope of this book, NOC is the National Occupational Classification. All occupations are placed on a grid and '0' level are management positions; A and B are high level – usually requiring a university degree – occupations (more information about NOC and the categorisation of occupations can be found at http://www23.hrdc-drhc.gc.ca/2001/e/generic/matrix.pdf). Service Canada, however, does now offer a 'low skilled worker program' (NOC C and D) which will allow employers to seek a Confirmation for low-skilled workers if the employees meet certain recruitment and working condition requirements. There are a number of conditions to be met in this regard, and perhaps most notably, a sustained attempt to look for persons for the position.

Service Canada offers, from time to time, 'enhanced' programs that may benefit employers (and hence employees). For instance, there exists at the time of publication of this edition, an expedited labour market opinion process for British Columbia and Alberta. Through this process, an employer can essentially register that they are often in need of certain occupations, on a prescribed list, and when they have a need in that field, they can submit a simplified application which will be processed in just a matter of days. Though this process does not change the legal requirement of an LMO, it does change the procedure to allow faster processing for companies who have established a need (further information can be found at http://www.hrsdc.gc.ca/eng/workplaceskills/foreign_workers/elmopp/elmo.shtml).

Information on Service Canada programmes generally can be found at http://www.hrsdc.gc.ca/en/workplaceskills/foreign_workers/index.shtml with further branches for specific programmes and requirements.

The exemptions

As noted earlier, sometimes there are exceptions to the rules of when a Labour Market Opinion, or even a work permit itself, will be required.

With regard to categories of persons not requiring work permits, these are listed in the regulations to the Canadian Immigration and Refugee Protection Act. Some examples are: foreign journalists, certain clergy, certain athletes participating in events in Canada, diplomats, certain performing artists, foreign crew members and certain members of foreign armed forces. Business visitors may also enter for a limited time, as may employees of a corporation with a foreign component who are in Canada to consult with other members of the organisation.

■ Proper counselling as to whether your occupation is available for work permit exemption should be sought when applicable, due to changing procedures, requirements and definitions.

With regard to those exempt from the need for a Labour Market Opinion, sometimes some creativity will be required. There are provisions, for instance, in Canadian law to argue that someone shouldn't need to go through the Service Canada process where they are creating or maintaining jobs in Canada ('significant benefit') – so where the XYZ company in Toronto needs a specialist to repair its new high-tech machine for employees to get back to work, the Visa Post can be approached directly and the argument made. Similarly, someone with specialised knowledge or management capacity can obtain a working permit without a Labour Market Opinion as an intra-company transferee. At this time there are also programmes which specifically eliminate the need for individual Labour Market Opinions in certain occupations – most notably computer professionals. In this case, where a person meets certain job descriptions set out by the Canadian government in the computer field, a simple job offer will do the trick to allow for a work permit, as Service Canada has issued a 'Blanket Confirmation' for these people. Again, care should be taken in determining if the Blanket Confirmation applies, since the job definitions applicable are limited, as is the time frame for the existence of the programme.

There are numerous other times where the need for a Labour Market Opinion can be avoided, and these should obviously be explored wherever possible. Other examples may include people carrying out certain research, and intra-company transferees.

International agreements

Certain international treaties and instruments now also lead to more lenient processing of temporary work permits in some cases.

For instance, Canada is now a party to the following international agreements:

■ GATS – the General Agreement on Trade in Services (a cousin to the more famous GATT), to which both Canada and the UK are signatories.

■ NAFTA – the North American Free Trade Agreement, to which Canada, the United States and Mexico are signatories.

■ CCFTA – the Canada-Chile Free Trade Agreement, to which Canada and Chile are signatories.

Though each of these is different, there are some common elements to the immigration provisions in the documents. Each agreement provides for nationals of signatory states to enter the territory of the other for the purpose of working, and in particular in certain categories including intra-corporate transferees, business visitors and professionals.

General agreement allowances

As noted, certain types of workers generally fall under these agreements and there are some similar characteristics. Appropriate legal advice should be sought about the specific requirements of any one agreement and the application of the agreement to your situation.

■ An **intra-corporate transferee** is someone who has an executive or managerial level position in an organisation, or who has specialised knowledge in the organisation and is being transferred to a related company in Canada. Note that the rules regarding required length of previous service in the company, job specifications, relationship of foreign and Canadian companies and other matters vary from situation to situation, and specific advice must be sought when use of one of these agreements is being considered.

■ A **business visitor** is someone coming to Canada to conduct business affairs on behalf of a foreign entity in a signatory state, where that person will not directly enter the work force. Indeed, no work permit may actually be required – just a record of the reason for entry. Generally, the person may be marketing services or establishing a commercial entity.

■ A **professional** is someone coming to Canada to work in his profession; each agreement has a list of accredited professions from the other signatory countries who may work in Canada, if invited by a Canadian company to do so, but who must meet the eligibility to work in that profession in Canada (such as licensing issues). Examples of some professions, under NAFTA, for instance, are: accountant, graphic designer, urban planner, librarian, lawyer, veterinarian, geologist, physicist. Reference must be made to the specific agreement for your particular case.

Special programmes

Canada also implements, from time to time, certain special programmes to allow foreign workers to come to Canada. For instance, there is a programme which allows farm workers from Mexico and certain Caribbean countries to enter Canada during agricultural harvest periods. There are exchange programmes in some high-tech fields. There is also at this time the IT Workers Programme as previously noted, which allows easier entry for computer programmers in certain specific programming fields to enter with a Blanket Labour Market Opinion (see 'the usual process' above).

Contact your nearest Canadian Visa Post or a legal representative to see if there is a specific programme in place for your field at this time.

Extension of status

Once in Canada, it is your obligation to extend your visa prior to its expiry – usually about one month pre-expiry. At that time, it is necessary to justify the need for your extension of the visitor, study or work permit. Failure to extend the visa may result in removal proceedings, as legal status has expired. Applications for extension are made through the Canada Immigration Centre in Vegreville, Alberta, and applications can be obtained by calling a local Canada immigration telephone number, found in the blue pages of most Canadian telephone books, or through www.cic.gc.ca the Canadian Government Immigration website.

OBTAINING PERMANENT RESIDENCE

For many hundreds of thousands, if not millions of people around the world, Canadian **permanent residence status** is a dream. Proper pre-assessment and guidance can make that dream become a reality. This aspect of Canadian immigration law is susceptible to change, and proposals are currently in place to change the criteria affecting selection. The information provided here is up to date at the time of writing.

Skilled worker immigration

The most common method of obtaining Canadian permanent residence is through what is often referred to as the 'skilled worker system'. Under law enacted 28 June 2002, the following factors are considered in this category:

- **Age**: maximum points are 10 if aged 21–49, with 2 points deducted for each year above or below.

- **Education**: maximum points are 25 with 5 points for secondary education which could lead to higher education, 15 points for most trade school or community college credentials, 20 points for a university degree, and 25 points for a Master's Degree or higher (there are further breakdowns, but these are the most common categories).

- **Arranged employment**: 10 points if Service Canada approves a job offer, or in some cases, if you are currently working in Canada. (This is different from a labour market opinion discussed above.)

- **First official language**: generally this will be English for readers of this book. 16 points maximum 'with high proficiency' in reading, writing, listening and speaking.

- **Second official language**: generally this will be French, for which a maximum of 8 points is available. (Note: depending on levels of fluency, English and French can be reversed.)

- **Experience**: maximum 21 for 4 years or more in a field listing in categories Ø, A or B of the National Occupation Classification (NOC). (For more information, see page 36.) Though somewhat beyond the scope of this book, NOC is the National Occupational Classification; all occupations are placed on a grid and '0' level are management positions; A and B are high level – usually occupations requiring a university degree (more information about NOC and the categorisation of occupations can be found at http://www23.hrdc-drhc.gc.ca/2001/e/generic/matrix.pdf).

- **Adaptability**: this factor is composed of five sub-elements (note that the maximum available is 10 points):

5 points are available for previous study in Canada

5 points are available for previous work in Canada

5 points are available for having a close relative in Canada

up to 5 points (of the spouse 5 points) are available for the educational credential of the spouse of the principal applicant

▪ 5 (additional) points for having arranged employment.

A total of 67 points must be achieved, subject to the further discretion of the immigration officer to grant visas to those with fewer than 67 points, or refuse visas to those with more than 67 points.

However, in addition to the foregoing, ministerial instructions added a further requirement in that an applicant must (a) have arranged employment, (b) be a foreign national living legally in Canada for one year as a temporary foreign worker or an international student, or (c) have an occupation on the list below.

NOC	Occupation
0111	Financial Managers
0213	Computer and Information Systems Managers
0311	Managers in Health Care
0631	Restaurant and Food Service Managers
0632	Accommodation Service Managers
0711	Construction Managers
1111	Financial Auditors and Accountants
2113	Geologists, Geochemists and Geophysicists
2143	Mining Engineers
2144	Geological Engineers
2145	Petroleum Engineers
3111	Specialist Physicians
3112	General Practitioners and Family Physicians
3141	Audiologists and Speech Language Pathologists
3143	Occupational Therapists
3142	Physiotherapists
3151	Head Nurses and Supervisors
3152	Registered Nurses
3215	Medical Radiation Technologists
3233	Licensed Practical Nurses
4121	University Professors

4131	College and Other Vocational Instructors
6241	Chefs
6242	Cooks
7213	Contractors and Supervisors, Pipefitting Trades
7215	Contractors and Supervisors, Carpentry Trades
7217	Contractors and Supervisors, Heavy Construction Equipment Crews
7241	Electricians (Except Industrial and Power System)
7242	Industrial Electricians
7251	Plumbers
7252	Steamfitters, Pipefitters and Sprinkler System Installers
7265	Welders and Related Machine Operators
7312	Heavy-Duty Equipment Mechanics
7371	Crane Operators
7372	Drillers and Blasters – Surface Mining, Quarrying and Construction
8221	Supervisors, Mining and Quarrying
8222	Supervisors, Oil and Gas Drilling and Service
9212	Supervisors, Petroleum, Gas and Chemical Processing and Utilities

Furthermore, you must provide evidence of 'settlement funds' – sufficient funds to show that you and any dependants can take care of yourselves for the first few months after arrival in Canada. It is expected that, on average, a family will take six months to settle in, and in particular to find employment and begin active life in Canada.

A quick summary chart to work out your own score is given in Figure 4. Note that this is a simple, general form only, as is the information above. You must contact a Canadian Visa Post or appropriate legal adviser for up-to-date information about the issues in an application for permanent residence (and also find a substantial amount of information at www.cic.gc.ca).

Effective November 2008, all applications are submitted to a central processing centre in Sydney, Nova Scotia, and from there, after review, redirected to the geographically appropriate visa post for further processing.

Canadian Experience Class

In 2008, Canada Immigration introduced the Canadian Experience Class. For the first time, it is now possible, effectively, to 'convert' temporary work status in Canada to permanent residence. After two years of work in Canada in an NOC Ø,

Factor	Maximum Score	Your Score
Age:	10	
Education:	25	
Arranged employment:	10	
Experience:	21	
First official language:	16	
Second official language:	8	
Adaptability		
Previous study in Canada: 5		
Previous work in Canada: 5		
Relative in Canada: 5		
Spouse's education: 5		
Arranged employment bonus: 5		
Maximum	10	
Total	___	___

Fig. 4. Permanent residence assessment chart.

A, or B occupation (or after two years of study, and one year of work), in valid status, one can apply for permanent residence, without the need to qualify on the skilled worker system. Though there are still issues of English proficiency, there is no need to establish all the elements of a skilled worker as set out above – simply that one has been engaged in Canada on a work permit for the appropriate period. This is a boon for people who come to work in Canada, to allow them to trade up to permanent residence relatively easily.

Provincial immigration programmes

In recent years, immigrating to Canada based on provincial nomination has come into its own. Each province now has a programme, and though each province's programme is unique, they are invariably faster than the 'ordinary' federal system. As the name implies, one must first be nominated by a province to get the benefits of their programme, and there are restrictions in terms of qualifications, the need for a job offer, quotas by province, etc., that must be considered. It should also be noted that nomination by a province usually brings with it the ability to secure a work permit rapidly, so one can be up and running in Canada while their permanent residence application is pending.

Quebec

The most notable of the programmes is Quebec's (though this programme is a selection programme and differs from the others, which are nominee programmes). This is particularly appealing for French-speaking applicants, and the province of Quebec has its own selection criteria. Many investors have also found that the investments available in Quebec provide favourable conditions, and the Quebec investor programme has certainly been one of the more popular programmes. Persons seeking to utilise this system should obtain appropriate counsel and information.

Other programmes

Besides Quebec, and as noted, each province now has its own nominee programme. The details of each programme can be found at each province's website, listed in the 'internet contacts' section, at the end of this book. Full elaboration on each programme is beyond the scope of this book, but a quick summary of each of the programmes, and comparisons, can be found at Figure 5. Information on each province's programme can be found at the relevant provincial government website which is has a format www.gov.xx.ca, where xx is the two-character abbreviation for the province.

FAMILY-BASED IMMIGRATION

In addition to providing assistance in a Skilled Worker application as discussed above, a relative in Canada can help get you to Canada in other ways. While the points provided by a relative in Canada in a Skilled Worker application do not place any obligation on the Canadian resident relative, the situations on page 47 do place an onus on that relative.

Sponsorship

Certain family members in Canada can sponsor you. The Canadian relative must be at least 18 years of age and you must be related to them as one of the following:

- father
- mother
- grandfather
- grandmother

Program type available					
Non-business based					
	AB	BC	MN	NFLD	PEI
Employer-driven (application submitted by employer)	Y	Y	Y	N	N
Applicant-driven 'skilled worker'	N	N	Y	Y (job offer required)	Y
International students	N	Y	Y	N	N
Family-based	N	N	Y	N	N
Shortage list-based	Y	Y	Y (see strategic recruitment)	N	N
Others	Low skilled workers	N	Community sponsored; strategic recruitment	N	Connections
Business based					
PNP business program	N	Y	Y	Y	Y
Business case or plan required	N	Y (business skills nominees)	Y	N	Y
Investment (CAD)	N/A	$800,000	$150,000	$200,000	$200,000
Net worth	N	$2M	$250,000	$450,000 (of which $350,000 liquid)	$400,000
Exploratory visit Other requirements	N	Recommended $^1/_3$ equity in BC business; five new jobs; active management	Y	Y Five years' experience; investment in strategic sector	Y
Prior ownership, business and/or management expertise/ education	N	Y	Y	Y (for senior management)	Y/N
Deposits: refundable and non-refundable	N	N	$75,000	$25,000	$100,000
Alternate business programs	N	Regional business outside major centres; $600,000 net worth, $300,000 investment	Farming business	N	'Partner' ($150,000 investment active role)

Reproduced with the permission of Canada Law Book.

Fig. 5. Provincial Nominee Program Comparison Chart.

Program type available					
Non-business based					
	SK	NB	ON	YK	NS
Employer-driven (application submitted by employer)	N	N	Y	Y	N
Applicant-driven 'skilled worker'	Y (job offer required)	Y (job offer required)	N	Y (job offer required – in specific occupations)	Y (job offer required)
International students	Y	N	Y	N	Y
Family-based	Y	N	N	N	Y
Shortage list-based	N	N	Y	Y (combined with offer above)	
Others	Truckers; health professionals	N	N	N	Community identified
Business based					
PNP business program	Y	Y		Y	Y (criteria being reconsidered)
Business case or plan required	Y	Y		Y	
Investment (CAD)	$150,000	Variable	$10M	$150,000	
Net worth	$250,000	Variable	N/A	$250,000	
Exploratory visit Other requirements	Y	Y Language, active management	N/A Create 25 jobs; allows five nominations	Y Language, primary industries preferred	
Prior ownership, business and/or management expertise/ education	Y	Y	N/A	Y	
Deposits: refundable and non-refundable	$75,000	N	N/A	N	
Alternate business programs	Farmers		N	Self-employed professionals	

Fig. 5. continued.

- dependent son or daughter (generally under 22, or still in school and financially dependent on the parents)
- spouse, or common-law partner or conjugal partner
- brother, sister, nephew, niece or grandchild who is orphaned, under 19 and unmarried
- adoptive child (meeting certain conditions) (this is now expanded to include guardianships in some cases).

Where a Canadian resident has no relatives in Canada whatsoever, he or she could sponsor you, if you are a more distant relative, even if you are not on the above list.

The Canadian resident will also have to meet certain income requirements. The sponsor must show an income based on the total family size, which includes his or her family members in Canada and you and your accompanying dependants. As always this information can change, and should be checked with a Canadian Visa Post at the time you wish to apply, as well as at an inland Canada Immigration office where your relative will need to make a preliminary application.

The required income starts at $20,584 for one person, and further amounts must be included for each additional person to reach the total income required for a sponsorship. So a Canadian family of four sponsoring a mother would need to show income for five people $43,913, at this time. The information above is just a guideline.

BUSINESS IMMIGRATION

There are three categories of business immigration:

- investor
- entrepreneur
- self-employed.

Investor

An investor is a business person with a net worth of at least $800,000 and who will invest in Canada in a prescribed investment of $400,000. The investment is passive, and is to be repaid, without interest, after five years. In most cases a lump sum (generally in the region of $120,000 to $130,000) can be paid at the outset, without any return, (essentially financing the investment) but sometimes this is actually more cost-effective.

Entrepreneur

An entrepreneur is someone with business experience who intends to be active in a business in Canada, and will have to employ, within three years of arrival, at least one Canadian citizen or permanent resident, essentially start or contribute to a business, and be actively involved in management. You will have to show business experience, and you will need $300,000 net worth to succeed. You will also need to meet the qualifications set out in Figure 4, though the threshold will be different.

Self-employed

A self-employed person is still a business person, but need not employ others. The difference between a self-employed candidate and an entrepreneur is that the self-employed person must show ability to run a business which has some cultural or athletic aspect; for instance a musician, an artist, or some other culturally contributing person.

FEES

Some processing fees relating to Canadian immigration at this time are (in Canadian dollars):

Application for Permanent Residence	
Adult:	550
Child (up to and including age 21):	150
Right of Landing Fee (per adult, refundable only if refused landing):	490
Business Application (additional per family):	500
Employment Work Permit:	150

QUALIFYING FOR CITIZENSHIP

This is an area which is set to change in Canadian law. Currently a permanent resident must show three years of residence in the last four, to qualify for Canadian citizenship. Though at this time physical presence is sometimes not required in order to justify 'residence' for citizenship purposes, it is thought that this will soon be changed to require actual physical presence in order to calculate the appropriate time period in Canada. There is also a test of knowledge of basic Canadian issues such as history, politics and language.

BEING REMOVED FROM CANADA

Once you're in Canada, the game is not over. You can still be removed if you violate Canadian immigration law. As noted in some of the sections above, there are various issues which can lead to denial of entry into Canada – those same issues, plus new matters, can also lead to removal once you're here, even if you are a permanent resident.

As with the issues discussed above, criminality is a major concern. Anyone in Canada who is not a citizen and commits a criminal offence is subject to deportation. Permanent residents can sometimes plead to stay on humanitarian grounds (e.g. it was a small matter, an isolated occurrence, I have no family back home, etc.) but the authorities are harsher every day in such cases. In temporary visa situations, overstay is grounds for removal, as is violation of the terms of the stay, such as working while on an ordinary visitor visa.

It is important to be on your best behaviour in order to stay in Canada once here, and to be allowed to return in the future. Deportation, if this is the penalty imposed, is a life-long sentence and can be overcome only with the consent of the Minister of Immigration.

SUMMING UP

The information in this chapter is for general reference only, and not specific legal advice. Each person's case is different and we have tried to give you only a basic understanding of some of the programmes, so that you can see what may be relevant to you. Each programme has much more detail which you can investigate, once you know that you're headed in the right direction. Also, you will certainly need to obtain relevant advice, forms, and guidance to deal with your individual case, which of course will be unique to you. You may wish to begin with a check of www.cic.gc.ca the government's website, previously referenced.

4

Understanding Health and Social Security

The health care system in Canada runs on the principle of universality: every person has free access to basic health care, with a few exceptions. Universal medical coverage was first introduced in Saskatchewan in the early 1960s and the first **Medical Care Act** was legislated in 1968. Doctors bill the public system but they do not work for the government. In fact they are deemed as self-employed and have a great deal of autonomy over how they run their practice (albeit within Canadian guidelines).

There is a lot to be praised about the system, but funding cuts, mismanagement and an ageing population have led to a great deal of upheaval and problems. Most years, polls show that health care is the number one concern for Canadians, although recently the environment and the economy has battled health care for that top spot. Several years ago, due to outcries from Canadians and provincial governments, the federal government transferred a lump sum to each province in order to restore health care funding to levels similar to what they were before all the cuts. Since then, provincial governments continue to increase their funding of the system, but with the costs of health care continuing to climb, combined with an ageing population, that money seems only to keep the system from completely falling apart.

Compared with many industrialised nations, Canada's health care system is excellent in its standards of care and accessibility. Canadians, for all their complaining about the 'health care crisis' know this and are grateful for all the system offers. But that is not to dismiss their complaints. This chapter is not out to promote the perfection of the Canadian health care system. It is written to provide you with a realistic view of what to expect. Some of the problems being faced are: long waiting lists for some surgeries, delays in some kinds of cancer treatments, a shortage of family doctors and overcrowded emergency rooms.

Health care falls under provincial jurisdiction but a federal ministry of health ensures that the provinces adhere to the Canada Health Act. Otherwise, provincial and territorial ministries oversee the administration of what is unofficially called **Medicare**.

NUMBER-COUNTING

It is estimated that in 2008, health care spending reached nearly $172 billion, of which 70 per cent was public sector spending. The remainder was spent by the private sector (including out-of-pocket expenses and private insurance). For a number of years, private spending was growing at a faster rate than public spending, but recently it has stabilised to a 70–30 split. Overall, total health care spending in 2008 is estimated at $5,170 per person.

- Most medical expenses are paid for by taxes. Two-thirds of funding comes from general income tax and federal grants through 'block funding' which means the provinces get money based on a per capita basis and can choose to spend it as they like. British Columbia and Alberta do charge premiums, however, and Ontario recently brought in a separate health tax.

- There were 66,992 physicians in Canada in 2009. Of those, 34,403 were family physicians and 32,562 were specialists.

- Male doctors continue to outnumber female doctors, but the number of females is growing and, in fact, growing at a faster pace than the number of men training to be doctors.

- In 2006 there were 270,845 registered nurses (RNs) in Canada.

- The majority of doctors are in Ontario with 24,135 physicians, both GPs and specialists. The territories have the least with 136.

- In 2008, Alberta and Manitoba ranked first and second for the amount of health care spending per person ($5,730 and $5,555, respectively). Health care spending per person was lowest in Quebec ($4,653) and British Columbia ($5,093).

- Life expectancy at birth in Canada is 78.69 for men and 83.91 for women.

PUBLIC VERSUS PRIVATE

Debate rages concerning Canada's health care system and, as some people claim, its increasing Americanisation. Private clinics do exist in Canada and there is the fear that with long waiting lists in the public system, people with money will want to pay for procedures rather than wait, the result being a two-tiered system: one for the rich and one for the poor. With a limited number of specialists in the country, there is also a fear that they'll move to the private clinics and the waiting lists in the public health system will grow longer. But for now, those clinics are funded with public funds and there is officially no queue jumping.

User fees and extra billing by doctors who also bill the province are not allowed under the **Canada Health Act**. When a person covered by the provincial health plan goes to the doctor, that person does not pay a fee for the visit. The doctor will bill the provincial plan. This pertains to medical doctors only. Psychologists and naturopath doctors, for example, are not covered under provincial plans, chiropractic doctors are only partially covered in some provinces, not at all in others. Some services from medical doctors, such as medical examinations for summer camp forms or visits to get a medical note for work or school absences, are also not covered and a small fee will be levied.

Things not covered under Canada's Health Act, therefore, have to be provided for with private funds. Prescription and non-prescription drugs, dental services, certain tests, nursing homes and vision care are examples of expenditures people must cover out of their own pockets via direct fees or private insurance. Some provinces partially cover prescription drugs and, for the most part, the government pays for prescriptions for the elderly and people on social assistance.

Going for additional cover

Private insurance plans for individuals and families can be purchased that include a variety of the above, uncovered services. Some of those benefits include: private or semi-private hospital rooms, chiropractic and massage therapy, travel insurance, speech pathology, naturopaths, psychologists, prosthetic appliances etc. Plans vary, but the amount of benefits included is directly related to the cost of the plan. For an individual person, a very basic medical and dental plan can start at around $70 per month. Family plans work out less per person and start at around $140 per month, but for that price very few benefits are included. It is possible that you would be covered by your employer as many companies offer employee benefit packages that include cover for all those things for you, your spouse and your dependent children. A portion of the cost of insurance is often deducted from your pay cheque and the company chips in the rest. If you work for yourself, however, or if you are a contract worker, you will probably have to purchase your own plan. The cost of the plan can be deducted as a medical expense on your income tax return.

KNOWING WHERE TO GO

Hospitals, doctors, walk-in clinics, community health centres and other health care providers are all available. In some provinces, groups of hospitals have merged in attempts to keep costs down. Every major city has several hospitals, smaller cities will have at least one and rural areas usually have a hospital nearby or a clinic within the community. However, rural areas continue to be underserviced despite government incentives to get doctors to set up practices there.

Doctors

Most Canadians choose one family physician to take care of their basic needs. This ensures that the doctor who treats them is someone who knows their medical history. If their medical problem requires a specialist, their doctor will refer them to one.

To find a doctor you can ask friends, co-workers and family for advice or you can look in the business section of the telephone book. You can also try using the provincial College of Physicians and Surgeons as a resource. The colleges are the regulatory body for doctors in each province and many have a 'find a doctor' service you can access over the phone or even online. Some of the colleges just have a list of doctors whom you can call and see if they are taking new patients. Others actually have a list of doctors in your area who are taking new patients. Doctors limit the number of patients they accept, so you may have to look around a bit to find one who is available. No one is obliged to remain with a doctor if they are dissatisfied. If you find another doctor whom you prefer, you can have your records transferred. You are also entitled to a second opinion from another doctor without changing doctors. This can be done if surgery has been recommended or if a serious condition has been diagnosed.

Patients must make an appointment to visit a doctor. A well-organised doctor's office should be able to fit you in on the day you call if it is a serious problem. It is recommended that everyone in the family gets a yearly check-up.

Hospitals

There are more than 1,000 hospitals in Canada. Most are general hospitals, but a small percentage are convalescent or chronic care hospitals. Ninety-five per cent of hospitals are private, not-for-profit corporations. The administrators who manage them report to hospital boards made up of public trustees. Clinical staff makes the medical decisions, however.

Hospital emergency rooms have been strained under cuts to funding. Some emergency doctors complain that the emergency rooms are overcrowded because people come in with trivial problems, especially as many people are without a family doctor. Both rural and urban areas are experiencing a shortage of family physicians (and specialists) so it's likely both a shortage in funding and non-emergencies have led to the problem of long emergency room waits.

In the case of an emergency, an ambulance would take you to the nearest and least busy hospital emergency room. If you are scheduled to go to the hospital for any reason, you may be slated to go to a hospital at which your family doctor has hospital privileges unless you are going in for a service available at only certain hospitals or for surgery. Where you go for surgery depends on the surgeon involved.

If a life is in danger, there is an emergency telephone number to call; in most cities that number is 911. This will get you ambulance, fire or police services immediately. In other communities you can call the operator by dialling 0. If the doctor determines you did not need the ambulance, you will be required to pay for it. In some provinces, part of the ambulance fee must be paid even if the ambulance was required, although some private insurance plans cover this fee.

Clinics

For visitors, people without a family doctor or for after-hours care, an alternative to hospital emergency rooms is a walk-in clinic. Some are small, staffed by one or two doctors, while others are comprehensive clinics with their own specialists. They are not 24-hour care facilities but the hours are longer than those of a regular doctor's office. If you need more serious care or X-rays, the clinic may send you to a nearby diagnostic centre where they specialise in X-rays, ultrasound and lab work. These are privately run, but if you're covered by provincial health care the tests will be covered. The clinic may also send you to a hospital emergency room.

CONTROLLING DISEASE

Canada's public health laws protect its people in various ways. One of those measures is compulsory vaccination to inoculate against certain diseases. Polio, diphtheria, mumps, measles and chicken pox have been eliminated or reduced because of high public health standards. It is the law that children must be immunised against serious infectious diseases such as diphtheria, polio and tetanus. Children are not allowed to go to school without an immunisation card to prove their vaccinations are up to date. Inoculations can be arranged through a doctor or public health clinic.

In 2006, Health Canada approved the vaccine to protect girls from the human papilloma virus (HPV), which is responsible for most cases of cervical cancer. Since then, most provinces have developed publicly-funded programmes to inoculate girls in school. Some programmes start as early as grade 5, others are in grade 8. The vaccinations are not mandatory, however.

Some high schools and most universities have included condom machines in the student washrooms. This is a measure to try to control sexually transmitted diseases.

ELIGIBILITY AND THE HEALTH CARD

Provincial health insurance plans cover essential medical services for all Canadian citizens and permanent residents. Visitors must have travel health insurance. Visitors in Canada on a working permit may be covered by a provincial plan, but this depends on the province, the job and the length of contract. In Quebec, for example, workers from France with contracts for more than three months are eligible for coverage for the time of their contracts. Quebec also has agreements with citizens of Sweden, Finland, Norway, Denmark, Portugal and Luxembourg. Quebec does not have an agreement with the United Kingdom. It is important, as a worker, that you check with the province you will be working in as to what their rules are. Moreover, even if you are covered, there may be a waiting period before you are entitled to the coverage. For student coverage, see Chapter 8.

Obtaining a health card

If you are eligible, you must obtain a **health card**. Each province has its own particular requirements. When you arrive you must apply right away for a health card at the province's ministry of health in your city. When you apply you must bring with you your birth certificate, your immigration visa and passport. Some provinces also require documentation showing your name and address and your signature. Every member of your family must get a health card.

In most provinces you will be eligible right away, but in British Columbia, Ontario and New Brunswick there is a three-month waiting period. Temporary workers may face different waiting periods in those and the other provinces. For the time that you as a worker are not covered, you should buy cover through a private insurance plan, such as travel insurance from your home country.

If you move to another province, you may face a waiting period before being eligible for the health plan in that new province, so you should apply right away. In the meantime you will be covered by the plan of the province you just left. If you are simply visiting another province, your card can be used in an emergency.

LOOKING AT THE DETAILS

Medicines

Prescription drugs are strictly controlled in Canada. There are many examples of drugs that are available over the counter in Europe and America that are available only by prescription in Canada. Most drugs for minor maladies such as headaches, colds and sore throats are available in the aisles of the pharmacies. When you need something more serious, your doctor will write a prescription for you which you take to the pharmacist to get filled. Prescription drugs can be quite costly, which is why most people get private insurance, which covers all or part of the drug costs (employer plans do this too). Herbal medicines are available over the counter in both mainstream drug stores and natural/health food stores. Health Canada monitors such products, which are regulated under the Natural Health Products Regulations.

Dental services

Unfortunately, dental services are not covered under provincial health plans. You can get cover through your company's benefit package (if available) or through a private insurance plan that also covers prescription drugs. If not, you can pay as you go. It is recommended that people, including children, get a check-up and cleaning twice a year and X-rays every few years (to identify cavities and structural problems). A cleaning and check-up can cost from $60 to $95. Filling cavities can cost hundreds of dollars, which is why it is cheaper to have regular check-ups and catch problems before they become serious. Teeth, their health and their appearance, are a high priority for Canadians. It is very common for teenagers to undergo orthodontic work to straighten teeth and bites. Orthodontic work is very expensive, however.

Pregnancy

Most women choose to have their babies in a hospital, but home births with a midwife are gaining popularity. Pregnancy is taken seriously in Canada and the standard of care is excellent. In addition to a family doctor monitoring a pregnant patient, the prospective mother will likely solicit the services of an obstetrician/gynaecologist, even if the pregnancy appears to be normal. Hospitals and clinics offer childbirth and child care courses.

Abortion is a very controversial subject in Canada, as it is elsewhere in the world. Demonstrations and serious violence have shown that. Regardless, you should know that abortion is not illegal in Canada, although it is not available at all health care facilities.

Accountability

Provincial colleges of physicians and surgeons regulate doctors and handle complaints about doctors. But, there are also complaints about the colleges for being inefficient and protective of doctors. Despite this, the colleges remain the only real mechanism for accountability, although a new and controversial website (www.ratemds.com) has sprung up allowing patients to write online about their experiences with a doctor. Otherwise the only other option is through legal means, in terms of malpractice lawsuits, which are also cumbersome and fairly expensive.

SOCIAL SECURITY

Old age pensions, family allowance, unemployment insurance and welfare are just some of the programmes in Canada's extensive social security network. Specific circumstances must be met in order to qualify for each type of government assistance, such as having worked a required amount of time leading up to the benefit. Other benefits require that you have paid into them to be eligible to receive them. A person may qualify for more than one programme, but each must be applied for separately. To qualify for any of the benefits a **Social Insurance Number** is required. See Chapter 7 for more information on how to get a **SIN**.

Old Age Security

An **Old Age Security** (**OAS**) pension is for people over the age of 65. A Canadian citizen or permanent resident who has lived in Canada for 40 years after the age of 18 is eligible for a full OAS pension. Seniors who have lived in Canada for less than 40 years may receive a reduced pension. Permanent residents from some countries may be able to get old age security from their original country.

Pensioners with little or no other income may be eligible for the **Guaranteed Income Supplement** (**GIS**). If between 60 and 64, the spouse of a low income or deceased pensioner may qualify for the **Spouse's Allowance** (**SPA**). GIS and SPA are available to pensioners who can prove they are in need of the money. Pensioners have to apply for these two benefits, which don't kick in automatically even if your income tax return indicates you are below a certain income. In other words, the government won't tell you if you're eligible. It's up to you to find out.

Canada and Quebec pension plans

To qualify for these, people must have contributed to the plan during their working years. Usually an amount is automatically deducted from one's pay cheque. Eligibility is extended to Canadian citizens, permanent residents, visitors and holders of a Minister's Permit who have been in Canada for one year and whose income during that year was subject to Canadian income tax and CPP/QPP deductions. Monthly payments begin at 65 years of age (a reduced pension is available at age 60) and the amount paid depends on the amount contributed. Spouses of deceased pensioners are entitled to survivors' pensions.

Included in these plans are disability pensions – both for short-term and long-term disability. As well there are benefits for dependent children of disabled parents and death benefits for children whose parent(s) have died.

Child tax benefits

The **Canada Child Tax Benefit** (CCTB) is made in monthly payments to parents or guardians on behalf of a child under the age of 18. The amount varies according to family income, number of children and their ages. To qualify, you must be the parent or guardian of the child who lives with you. You or your spouse must be either a Canadian citizen, permanent resident, visitor or holder of a Minister's Permit who has lived in Canada for at least 18 consecutive months before applying for the benefit.

The CCTB may include the **National Child Benefit Supplement** (for low-income families) and the **Child Disability Benefit**. Several provinces and the territories have supplemental child tax credit programmes as well.

The federal government recently introduced the **Universal Child Care Benefit** (UCCB). It is for children under six years of age and is paid in monthly instalments of $100 per child. You must apply for it; the benefit is not automatic.

Employment Insurance

The government has recently renamed unemployment insurance, **Employment Insurance**. This has brought on a smidgen of ridicule, as some believe this was to soften the negative connotations of the word 'unemployment'. Most people still refer to it as 'unemployment insurance' in conversation. Regardless of what you call it, this is how it works. Payments to Employment Insurance (EI) are made through deductions from a person's pay cheque. To qualify, a person has to have worked for a minimum amount of time (required amount of time depends on where you live and the unemployment rate in that region) and has to have lost his or her job through no fault of their own. For example if the reason for unemployment is the birth or adoption of a child, enrolment in a national training programme, work sharing or job training, a person may be eligible. As well, if a person is laid off from a job through company restructuring or due to bankruptcy, a person will usually qualify. After a certain period of time, if a person has not been able to find a job, EI benefits cease and the person must apply for Social Assistance.

Employment Insurance also covers maternity leave. Maternity benefits are payable to the mother for a maximum of 15 weeks (although she can take 17 weeks off) as long as she worked for 600 hours in the last year. There is also parental leave for up to 35 weeks. A mother can add that to her maternity leave, share it with the father, or the father can take all 35 weeks. Parental leave is also available to adoptive parents. Some employers 'top up' your income for a number of weeks, but don't count on it. In most cases, employers are obliged to keep your job for you when you return, regardless of whether you take the 17 weeks or a full year off. Quebec has its own maternity and paternal leave programme that is, in some ways, more generous than the federal programme.

Social Assistance

Often called 'welfare', this benefit is solely for people in need who are not eligible for other benefits. Payments are to help pay for necessities such as food, shelter, clothing, prescription drugs and other health services. Local offices of the provincial or municipal departments of social services usually oversee and administer Social Assistance. The size of payment varies from region to region, as do eligibility rules. In some cases there is the ability to join programmes to train for available work.

Workers' Compensation

If you get injured at work you may qualify for financial benefits and medical and rehabilitative services. You must prove your injury was work-related and offer medical reports for assessment. The decision regarding your eligibility rests with the provincial workers' compensation board offices. In Ontario that board is named the Workplace Safety and Insurance Board, rather than the Workers' Compensation Board as in other provinces.

Applying for social security programmes

Except for workers' compensation and child tax benefits, benefits are applied for through Service Canada. There are branches in all cities. You will need a birth or baptismal certificate, passport and a Canada Immigration visa. For the child tax benefit you need to apply to Canada Revenue Agency. Again, an immigration visa needs to be provided as does proof of birth for each child.

5

Taxation

No one likes to pay taxes and Canadians are no exception. However, taxes are the necessary evil needed to pay for providing a social security net. Someone has to pay for all the government programmes people need and enjoy. Even though Canadians recognise the need for taxes, it is a sore spot for many who feel the tax system takes too much out of the pockets of hard-working individuals. You'll find promises of tax cuts usually surface during any election. Because of that, the information in this chapter is a rough guide only. Taxation rates, laws and rules change all the time — even accountants have a hard time keeping up.

INCOME TAX

Personal income tax is the portion of money people pay out of their earnings – from working, from investments, or from renting their property out to others – to the government. It was first employed in 1917 to help pay the war debt. It was meant to be a temporary measure until the debt was paid off, but it has never been discontinued and it now accounts for a large portion of government revenue.

Canada's income tax system is 'progressive' in that it requires people who make more money to pay a larger percentage of their income in tax. Tax is paid on an individual's taxable income, which is that person's income after deductions, such as valid medical expenses, moving expenses, charitable donations, tuition, **Registered Retirement Saving Plan** (RRSP) contributions, etc.

An RRSP is a retirement plan that you register with the federal government. Many people do so through a private investment firm or financial institution, often investing in mutual funds, stocks, and money markets. For some people the amount they squirrel away in an RRSP will be their entire pension; for others it is in addition to a pension being built through their employer. Each year you have a limit of what you can contribute to your RRSP based on your income, and those contributions are tax deductible, thereby reducing your income tax.

Any income you earn in the RRSP is usually exempt from tax for the time the funds remain in the plan. You pay the tax when you cash it in or make withdrawals (usually upon retirement). The thinking is that when you retire, your income will be less and therefore your tax bracket lower so that you end up paying less tax overall.

Federal Taxation Rates

Taxable income	Rate
$40,726 or less*	15%
$40,726.01 - $81,452	22%
$81,452.01 - $126,264	26%
$126,264.01 or more	29%

In 2009, Canadians could claim a basic amount of $10,320 before being taxed.

This is how it works: you are taxed 15 per cent on the first $40,726 or less that you earn; then any amount above that but less than $81,452, you are taxed 22 per cent; then any amount above that but less than $126,264 you are taxed 26 per cent, and so on.

In addition to these basic rates there is a federal surtax, provincial taxes (which vary from province to province, but, except in Quebec, are calculated by the same federal

Tax On Income – or TONI – method; in Quebec it's calculated as a percentage of the federal tax payable) and provincial surtaxes. The combined effect of this can see the people in the top bracket paying more than half of their income to the government. If you run your own business or are a contract worker, you set up your own payment plan with the government. This usually means making quarterly payments to the Canada Revenue Agency.

During the year, your employer will automatically deduct income tax from your pay cheque by an amount corresponding to your tax bracket. Even so, every year you must file a tax return claiming your income and deductions. When you start work with an employer you will fill out a form that will determine how much tax is taken off your pay cheque. That form, the T1, can indicate that although you earn X amount per year, less tax should be taken off because you will have deductions like tuition, RRSP contributions or a dependant (such as a child or ill parent). At the same time, you could also indicate that more tax should be taken off than would normally be for your annual income. This would be done in the case where you know you have other sources of income that will add to your taxable income.

Depending on whether you have overpaid or underpaid through payroll deductions, the result of your tax return will mean either you are entitled to a refund of what you overpaid or you owe a balance to the government.

Foreign income, income you earn through business, overseas investments, etc., is not exempt.

GOODS AND SERVICES TAX

The **Goods and Services Tax (GST)** was implemented on 1 January 1991. It is a general sales tax that applies to the sale of most goods and services. It was brought in to replace existing 'hidden' manufacturing taxes. The GST is 5 per cent, lowered in the past couple years from 7 per cent. It is charged at the time of purchase. Its proposal and eventual implementation raised a huge political debate and although subsequent governments promised to remove it, they found they could not afford to because, like income tax, it has become an important source of revenue.

If a person's income is deemed low enough, he or she may be eligible for a GST credit, something a person applies for on his or her income tax return. If you are just visiting Canada as a tourist, you can apply for a GST refund for purchases over $50.

PROVINCIAL SALES TAX/HARMONISED SALES TAX

All the provinces, but Alberta, have a sales or retail tax that you pay on goods you purchase, in addition to the GST. The three territories also do not have a sales tax. Some provinces charge the PST separately from the GST, others combine the taxes into one, called a harmonised sales tax, or HST. Quebec and Prince Edward Island are the only two provinces which charge the PST on top of the GST. Rates vary from province to province, as do which goods are exempted from the sales tax (see Figure 6). In many provinces, certain goods and services such as liquor, hotel accommodation and cars are subject to a different sales tax rate (often higher) from the main one.

Province	GST/HST	PST	Combined rate
British Columbia	5% GST	7%	12%
Alberta	5% GST	0%	5%
Saskatchewan	5% GST	5%	10%
Manitoba	5% GST	7%	12%
Ontario	5% GST	8%	13%*
Quebec	5% GST	7.5%	12.88%**
Newfoundland and Labrador	13% HST	n/a	13%
Nova Scotia	13% HST	n/a	13%
New Brunswick	13% HST	n/a	13%
Prince Edward Island	5% GST	10%	15.5%**
Yukon Territory	5% GST	0%	5%
Northwest Territories	5% GST	0%	5%

*Ontario is aiming to move to a Harmonised Sales Tax in 2010.
**In Quebec and Prince Edward Island, the GST is included in the provincial sales base.*

Fig. 6. Provincial sales tax rates.

PROPERTY TAXES

Property taxes are municipalities' principal income other than user fees (water, transit etc.), fines, permit fees, investment income and transfer payments from the province. These taxes are based on the value of land and buildings that you own (e.g. your house, business building etc.). In major cities, the rates can translate into a couple of thousand dollars a year and upwards on a house. The money goes to such essential services as snow removal, garbage removal, public transport etc. It is an annual tax.

CORPORATE TAXES

Corporations pay a corporate income tax on the income they earn. The federal government is lowering those taxes, as it is with personal income taxes, over the next few years. Currently the general corporate income tax rate is 19 per cent. In the last federal budget the government pledged to reduce the general corporate income tax rate to 15 per cent by 2012. Small businesses (those making less than $500,000) are charged 11 per cent. The provinces also charge a corporate tax and the combination of their rates and the federal tax can average out to about 30 per cent, depending on the province.

Those rates may be further reduced through incentive provisions and tax breaks that encourage businesses to stay in Canada.

One problem for Canada has been that it has higher corporate taxation rates than the United States and Mexico with whom Canada has a free trade agreement. One of the reasons for the government's goal of lowering corporate taxes is that over the years, some industries have moved south where the tax and labour costs are lower, which has meant some Canadian job losses.

OTHER TAXES

- **Tariffs or duties**: taxes on the value of goods entering or leaving Canada. They are used to protect Canadian industry from foreign competition.

- **Excise taxes**: sales taxes that are imposed on the sale of a specific item.

- **Luxury tax**: an excise tax on a good considered to be a luxury.

- **Capital Gains tax**: tax that arises when you profit from the sale of an asset (i.e. stocks). Some investments, such as your principal residence, are exempt.

SEEING WHERE IT ALL GOES

Taxes pay for social programmes, public works, education (all levels), health care and more. Unfortunately, because of the large debt Canada has accrued, Canadians' tax dollars also go to paying the interest payments on that debt rather than going directly to fund programmes.

The federal government collects federal income tax and also collects the provincial income tax on behalf of the provinces through an agreement it has with the provinces. The provincial governments' revenues come from such taxes as well as from transfer payments for the federal government. This is partly due to the fact that the provinces have some of the costliest responsibilities: health and education. And, as mentioned before, the federal government also doles out equalisation payments to the less prosperous provinces.

Most municipalities receive some sort of transfer payment from their respective provincial governments or operate programmes on a cost-sharing basis with the province. This is because municipalities have limited sources of revenue, which is a constant source of friction between the cities and the other levels of government, especially when the federal government continues to pull in billions of dollars in surpluses due to gas taxes and employment insurance premiums. For several years, the cities got little in return; there had been minimal help for cities to deal with roads, public transportation and housing. But in the last few years, the federal government has begun to dedicate funds to those kinds of needs. They've done that through giving a portion of the gas tax back to municipalities and through special targeted infrastructure programmes. Some provinces have followed suit.

TIPPING

This is not really a tax, but you should know that tipping is customary in Canada. It is predominantly supposed to reward good service, but people often feel compelled to tip because they think it's expected. If you do tip, 15 per cent (before tax) is the usual amount for such service providers as waitresses, bartenders, taxi drivers, hairdressers and chambermaids (hotels). The choice is yours, of course, but keep in mind that jobs like waitressing and bartending make lower wages because it is expected that people in those positions will make it up in tips.

6

Finding a Place to Live

Finding a place you can call home will probably be one of the most important decisions that you make when coming to Canada. Whether you're coming to work for a short period of time or to live permanently, the place you trudge 'home' to every night will make a big difference to how you adjust to your new life. However, most newcomers do not start out in a palace and should not worry if they are not all that keen on their first apartment. In fact, moving might be the first very Canadian thing they do. One out of every two Canadians moves every three years. In 2008, the average household spent $12,990 on shelter.

There are numerous factors to take into account when choosing the place you want to call home. Renting or owning, location and cost will probably be the most important factors.

ASSESSING HOUSEHOLD CHARACTERISTICS

In 2006 the average number of people in a household was 2.5. Because Canada has some fairly bitter winters, most houses and apartments have insulated walls, double glazing and central heating. Most homes are heated by a hot air furnace or electric heating. The principal heating fuels are piped gas and electricity, and the majority of households cook with electricity. According to the latest figures, almost 27 per cent of households have more than one refrigerator (73 per cent have just one), 82 per cent of households have a washing machine, almost the same percentage have a clothes dryer, 59 per cent of households have a dishwasher, 48 per cent have an air conditioner, 93.5 per cent have a microwave oven, 40 per cent have three or more telephones and 71 per cent have a cellular telephone.

RENTING

Renting an apartment, house or part of a house is how most people start out. The typical apartment is a self-contained unit in a multi-floor building, but many houses have been converted into rental units so a tenant may rent the first or second floor of a house, each floor being its own self-contained unit. These are usually called 'flats'. You can also rent an entire house or a room in a house (the latter is called 'shared accommodation'). It's hard to say when is the best time to look for accommodation, because it depends on the city. In university towns, a large number of students will be looking for leases that start in the autumn, so it's best to avoid that time. In major cities, spring, summer and autumn are all good times to look. Good bargains can be found in the winter, but it's not fun to move in that season and there's less to choose from. When looking for a lease, start a month or two before you want to begin renting, as listings don't usually come up more than a month or two in advance. Be aware that while in some cities vacancy rates have risen a bit (as people choose to buy instead of rent), in other cities the market is still tipped in the landlord's/owner's favour, with rates barely above 1 per cent.

Choosing the type of dwelling

One of the cheapest options is to rent a room in a shared house. Many students and single people do this when they are starting out. Bachelor apartments consist of one main room with a kitchen, sleeping area and a separate bathroom. They are designed mainly for one person, two at the most. After that there are one-, two- and three-bedroom apartments. Some are even larger than that. Then there are penthouse or loft-types that fall under the category of 'luxury apartments'. Furnished apartments and rooms can also be rented.

Counting the cost

Rental costs vary widely from city to city. Prices tend to be much, much higher in urban areas, especially cities like Vancouver and Toronto. It is very difficult to give general estimates because prices within a city vary as well, with downtown prices being far costlier than outlying neighbourhoods. In big cities you could be looking at several hundred, perhaps a few thousand dollars in rent for an apartment, depending on the size of apartment and the type of neighbourhood. In a smaller city or town, prices are usually less. But it also depends on the local economy and supply and demand, so some small cities are more expensive to live in than you might expect. Each province also has rules on how much a landlord can increase the rent each year for an existing or new tenant. Disputes between tenants and landlords can be taken to the appropriate rental authority or tribunal.

It is important to note that rent paid may or may not include such utilities as heat, electricity, gas and water. Before you agree to a rent, find out what it includes. Cable for television and the cost of a telephone line are usually not included and you will be billed directly by the respective utility companies for those amenities.

The landlord pays the property taxes and takes care of insurance for the building, but the tenant is responsible for insuring individual personal items.

What comes with an apartment?

Every apartment should have its own private entrance (off the street or a common hallway) through a door that can be locked. It should have a kitchen with a sink and tap supplying both cold and hot water, and a bathroom with a sink, toilet and a bath or shower. Appliances such as a stove and refrigerator should also be included. The apartment should be equipped with light and electricity, sewage pipes, telephone lines (you will have to pay for hook-up) and, of course, a heating system. Optional facilities that might make a place more enticing are laundry and parking facilities.

The landlord is responsible for maintenance of the unit. If things like an appliance that came with the apartment, a door or a roof are broken, you can call the landlord to arrange to get a repair person in to fix it. Unless you are responsible for the breakage, the landlord also absorbs the cost.

Taking steps to find an apartment

The best places to look are in the classified advertisements in local newspapers or online. Your friends, co-workers and family may hear something by word-of-mouth that may be a lead to a place not listed. In the bigger cities some people even hire real estate agents to find rental units, but doing so is by no means necessary. The other method is to drive around prospective neighbourhoods and look for signs saying 'for rent' or 'for lease'.

It is wise to be selective and to look at a few places before deciding. The risk, in competitive markets like Vancouver, Calgary, Toronto and Ottawa, is that in the meantime someone else gets the apartment. In fact, for some types of markets you're likely to have to fill out an application to be compared with other would-be renters. When you go to see the apartment, make sure you look neat and clean and be at your friendliest. Making a good impression in person can go a long way to furthering your paper application. Find out when the landlord plans to make a decision and if you don't get a call by then, check back. Some landlords don't want tenants with pets or tenants who smoke. In some provinces it's against the law to refuse a person an apartment based on that. But it's hard to prove that you lost out on an apartment because you had a pet or you're a smoker.

Factors you should consider when deciding on a place are nearby public transport (especially if you do not have a car), conveniently located shops, parking and schools. If these things are in order and you like the size, price range (find out how much utilities cost the last tenant) and neighbourhood, you are probably making a good decision.

Following the right procedure

It is proper procedure to telephone to make an appointment to see an apartment. If you decide you want it and the landlord accepts you as a tenant, you will probably be asked for the first and last month's rent as a deposit except in Quebec where they're not allowed to ask for last month's rent. Whenever you move on, that last month's rent will be applied to your last month, saving you the cheque at that time. In some provinces, the landlord must also pay you a certain percentage interest on that last month's rent deposit.

The next step is for you and the landlord to sign a rental agreement or lease. Most landlords will ask you to sign for a year's lease. But month-to-month and other rental periods are allowed. Make sure you make note of any damage at the start and point it out to the landlord so as to not be blamed for it yourself.

In most cases, the landlord will do a credit check to ensure that you have enough money to pay rent and that you have a good credit rating.

Renting other properties

Renting a house is a similar process to renting an apartment, you just end up with more space and appliances.

To rent a condo apartment you will most likely need to enlist the help of a real estate agent. Rent is paid to the owners of the condo not to the building's management.

Renting an apartment in a co-op building means you are also responsible for some task in the maintenance or running of the building.

OWNING

Owning a house or condominium is a big deal. It is a huge responsibility, both financially and practically. Like a renter, a buyer should take into account many factors when looking to purchase property. But unlike a renter who can move easily, factors like location and condition of the property are extremely important. After all, you will probably be in that house for a long time.

Buying a house

The best time to look is spring and early summer. The real estate markets for houses vary greatly from city to city. The bigger the city, generally, the more expensive the real estate. Figure 7 lists average house prices west to east.

In 2008, the average price of a house, nationally, nudged above $300,000 for the first time, largely driven by the boom in Alberta and Saskatchewan. However, since then, because of the global financial crisis, prices have fallen in most cities, although there are still some hot markets where demand exceeds supply. At the time of writing, the national average house price was $288,641.

How to buy a house

Again, the best sources for information will be classified ads (whether online or in

City	Province	Average price ($)
Victoria	British Columbia	441,380
Vancouver	British Columbia	530,763
Yellowknife	Northwest Territories	305,764
Edmonton	Alberta	309,032
Calgary	Alberta	372,114
Regina	Saskatchewan	246,268
Saskatoon	Saskatchewan	266,720
Winnipeg	Manitoba	211,408
Hamilton	Ontario	263,120
Toronto	Ontario	362,050
Ottawa	Ontario	287,911
Montreal	Quebec	254,502
Quebec City	Quebec	199,350
Fredericton	New Brunswick	161,087
Saint John	New Brunswick	158,731
Halifax	Nova Scotia	229,548
St. John's	Newfoundland and Labrador	205,040*

Based on March 2009 figures from the Canadian Real Estate Association.
*April 2009

Fig. 7. Average house prices.

newspapers), real estate agencies, friends and neighbours. See Useful Addresses for a list of newspapers in which you can search the classifieds on their websites.

In an attempt to avoid fees and commissions some people try to do private sales, but the majority of buying and selling is done through real estate agencies. Most buyers obtain pre-approval for a mortgage first (see mortgages section below) so that sellers and real estate agents know the buyer is serious and know how much the buyer has to spend.

A real estate agent will show you several houses based on what you have stated to be your price range, desired type of neighbourhood and taste in architecture. Once you decide on a house, you normally make a legal written offer (this includes the deposit) on the condition that the house passes an official inspection of its condition and structure. Usually you will negotiate (in writing) with the seller to get the best price you can and once the seller accepts an offer it becomes an agreement to purchase.

Mortgages

Unless you have money to burn, you will probably need to set up a mortgage with a bank or trust company. First, you will have to pay a deposit that is ordinarily 20 per cent (or more if you want to reduce your monthly payments) of the total price. The rest of the purchase is paid in monthly payments, including interest (interest rates are set by lenders based on the Bank of Canada rate, but they are negotiable). You may qualify for a smaller down-payment of as little as 5 per cent, but you will have to take out mortgage insurance, which will add to what you are already paying each month.

There are three mortgage loan insurers in Canada. The Canada Mortgage and Housing Corporation is the largest and is 100 per cent backed by the federal government. The two others are private corporations: Genworth Financial and AIG.

The federal government also has a programme for first-time home buyers whereby they can withdraw up to $20,000 from their RRSP (Registered Retirement Savings Plan) towards the cost of building or buying a home. That amount gets paid back into the RRSP, interest free, but has to be repaid within 15 years. Any balance remaining is deemed income and taxable in the 16th year. However, if you are new to Canada you won't be likely to have an RRSP yet. At the same time, you might not plan to buy for a few years (and rent in the meantime); you could take that time to start investing in an RRSP so that when you are ready to buy you have that option to borrow from it.

Mortgages come with either a fixed interest rate for a term of one to five years or a variable rate, which fluctuates over time. Usually, the shorter the term agreed upon, the lower the interest rate, but the higher the risk that interest rates could be higher when you negotiate your next term. Many buyers look for clauses that allow them at certain times to put more money towards the principal and therefore pay off their mortgage sooner. On average, most buyers pay for their homes over 15 to 25 years, but 35-year mortgages are available. With the latter, however, you end up paying more interest over the long term. Right now, interest rates are at historic low levels to encourage home purchases and other kinds of borrowing in an effort to stimulate the economy.

What you own

If you hold a freehold estate, you own both the house and the land that it sits upon and only the government has rights to interfere with the land (it must give notice, of course). Most ownership in Canada is freehold. If you own a leasehold estate you own the house but not the land.

Other costs

Your home will have been assessed for property taxes, which you have to pay every year. Such taxes vary from region to region, from property to property. Larger properties have higher property taxes, as do properties occupying corner lots.

As an owner, you are also responsible for the maintenance of the house and appliances within the house. Whether it is a clogged drain, a leaky pipe or a leaky roof, you have to organise and pay for the repairs. There will also be utility costs, such as hydroelectricity, heat and water.

Buying a condominium

These are individually owned apartments or townhouses (terraced houses) where common areas (gardens, pools, walkways, etc.) are owned together. On top of your mortgage payments and your property taxes, a condominium fee is levied to cover maintenance and repairs by the management of the condominium.

The condominium is usually managed by a condo board made up of people who live in the building or property (i.e. your neighbours). Condo fees can be a few hundred dollars a month or more. Condos are often more affordable than houses, but you often get less square footage for the money you're paying. But there is the convenience of not having to mow the grass or shovel the snow.

DISCRIMINATION

The **Canadian Charter of Rights and Freedoms** protects prospective renters and buyers from discrimination based on a whole host of factors such as gender, race and religion. That means a landlord or seller cannot refuse to rent or sell to you based on such factors. However, this is not to say it does not happen. If you feel you have been unfairly discriminated against you can contact the **Human Rights Commission** in your province.

GOVERNMENT-SUBSIDISED HOUSING

In most cities there is special housing for people with low incomes or special needs. Through the 1990s, governments said they will not 'be in the housing business' and, therefore, the existing stock had not been added to for years. However, recognising there is a lack of affordable housing, the federal government recently initiated a programme with the provinces and cities to build some affordable housing units. The programme has funds of hundreds of millions of dollars, but even that will see some cities get at most only 1,000 new units, when there are thousands of people and families on the waiting lists.

You may know such housing as 'social housing' or 'council housing' in the country from which you came. You may, however, be quite surprised at the differences between such housing in Canada and that in your former country.

Subsidised housing usually comes in the form of apartment buildings, not houses, therefore there is no option to buy. To avoid the creation of ghettos, most subsidised housing was not built all in one area, but was scattered throughout city neighbourhoods. However, that's not to say ghettos don't exist, especially since some buildings are clustered together all in one area. Some buildings have units that are rented at a normal rate for those who can afford it, while other units in the building are rented at rates geared to a tenant's income. There is also special housing for the disabled and the elderly that is income-geared. But as mentioned, demand far outstrips supply and there are some fairly lengthy waiting lists for such housing, some as long as seven or more years.

OBTAINING TELEPHONE, TELEVISION AND THE INTERNET

Getting hooked up

Once you know where you will be living, you need to get in touch with the telephone company and have them hook up the line that probably already exists in your new home. They do not need to come to your place to do this, unless no line exists or you want more telephone sockets or more than one line put in. The local telephone company has a huge assortment of options for phone service, and you can either rent or buy a phone from the company, or you can buy one from an electronics store. The hook-up costs a one-time fee, and the line is paid for monthly and ranges in price from city to city. The monthly fee can cost anything from $20 to $35 with no additional features (such as an internal answering machine, call waiting and call display). It includes all local calls. You can choose a local phone company to be your long distance carrier but you can choose to have one company provide your local service and another to be your long-distance carrier. It pays to shop around.

Television

There are three ways to get a television signal: over-the-air (with an antennae), cable and satellite. Not many people stick with basic over-the-air signals any more, but if you do choose to go that route, be aware that you will need a digital converter box to watch US stations as of 12 June 2009 and Canadian stations as of 31 August 2011. That's because over-the-air stations will be switching to digital from analogue signal on those dates.

If you choose to get cable for your television, there are a few cable companies to choose from. There's usually a one-time hook-up fee (per television set). Basic cable can cost from $17 to $25 per month. Extended cable is available for about $40 a month, which gives you approximately 60 channels. Digital cable is more expensive, but can offer hundreds of channels and special viewing features like movies and television episodes on demand, rather than at a set time.

Satellite television is another digital option and is also more expensive than basic cable, but again offers more channels and features such as personal video recorders (PVRs). They allow the recording of a television programme onto a hard drive. To get satellite television you need to rent or buy a satellite dish from the company (to put on your roof or balcony; some apartment buildings or multi-unit homes don't allow dishes, so check first). Then you pay a monthly fee based on how many and which channels you have selected to receive.

Joining the Internet

Internet service can be acquired through telephone lines or through cable. Telephone companies, cable companies and local Internet service providers (ISPs) offer various packages and, again, it pays to shop around. Telephone companies and ISPs offer both dial-up and high-speed service. Cable companies only offer high-speed service. High speed is clearly much faster than dial-up, but also more expensive, ranging from $35 to $50 per month, which does not include hook-up and set-up costs, although high speed comes with unlimited hours online. Dial-up ranges from $10 to $25 per month, depending on the number of hours you sign up for. In some remote locations, high-speed Internet isn't available and you only have dial-up as an option.

CONSIDERING SAFETY

It is not much good to live in a place you like and yet not feel safe. Your home should have smoke and carbon monoxide detectors. If you rent your abode, the installation of such devices is the responsibility of the landlord. You should also have fire extinguishers placed around the house. Canadian cities are very safe and the crime rate is actually declining, but it is still a good idea to lock doors and windows.

In recent years there have been a number of tragedies where young children have fallen out of windows from the upper levels of a house or a high rise building. Make sure your windows have screens and that those screens are securely fastened, and that there is no easy way for a young child to climb up on furniture near a window. If you have a balcony, make sure you supervise your children if they go on it.

OBTAINING HOUSEHOLD GOODS

Bring or buy?

First consider the electrical compatibility of your country with Canada. Canada operates on 110-V, 60-cycle electric power. Hairdryers and razors often have dual-voltage capability, but appliances like televisions, stereos and microwaves do not. If your country uses a higher voltage, you could buy a transformer for each appliance as well as a plug adapter. But sometimes even that won't solve the problem and the appliance (especially VCRs – in Canada the system used is VHS, not PAL which is used in the UK) is impossible to use. DVD players as well, are not compatible with all DVD discs. In fact the discs and players are coded for a region, of which six exist in the world. Therefore, a disc coded for Region 1 cannot be played in a DVD player coded for Region 3. Canada is Region 1 and shares that coding with the US only. Europe is Region 2. There are DVD players that will initially play all types of discs, but after a few times they will ask you to permanently choose a disc code.

Adapting, transforming and shipping costs may total more than the cost of buying a new appliance in Canada. Figure 8 gives a list of prices of a sampling of Canadian goods, if bought new. There are also stores that sell used consumer goods.

There is a great deal of choice in Canada. There are stores that specialise in bulk or discount prices while others cater only to the top of the market, and there is more selection in major cities than in rural centres. In the north, prices are usually higher.

You're allowed to bring all personal and household effects you have owned, used or had in your possession before getting your immigrant status. You will not have to pay duty or taxes on any of these items, but customs may require receipts to prove when they were acquired. An exception could be your mattresses. To import those, you must have them cleaned and fumigated and get a certificate (to accompany the mattresses) that is signed by the exporter attesting to the fact the mattresses have been cleaned and fumigated. The certificate must also give complete details of how they were cleaned and fumigated and must include a statement that the procedure was actually conducted. It may be simpler to buy new in Canada.

When you go through Canadian customs you must bring a list of goods you have with you and a list of goods you are having shipped over. The list should include the items' serial and model numbers and approximate value. The shipping list will be stamped by customs and there is no time limit for when those goods must be brought in. Business and commercial equipment is subject to duties and taxes and the amount varies widely from item to item. To find out more, you can call your Canadian Embassy or consulate or get in touch with customs in Canada (see Useful Addresses).

Major Appliances

Refrigerator	$900 – $10,000
Washing machine	$450 – $2,000
Tumble dryer	$400 – $1,500
Vacuum cleaner	$150 – $1,500
Oven/stove	$500 – $3,000

Houseware

Microwave oven	$150 – $750
Toaster (two-slice)	$16 – $85
Iron	$40 – $120
Blender	$45 – $170
Food processor	$85 – $220
Toaster oven	$30 – $150
Kettle	$20 – $45
Mixer	$20 – $100
Coffee maker	$30 – $300

Bath and Bedroom

Mattress and boxspring bed (double size)	$300 – $1,800
Towels (one bath towel)	$6 – $60
Sheets (double bed set)	$30 – $100
(single bed set)	$20 – $80
Shower curtain	$10 – $60
Pillow (regular size)	$20 – $250

Electronics

Television (27″)	$450 – $1,000
VCR	$120 – $450
DVD	$200 – $600
Stereo mini system (CD player, radio)	$200 – $1,200
Clock radio	$15 – $200
Cordless phone	$70 – $300
Non-cordless phone	$10 – $150
Computer system	$500 – $6,000

Fig. 8. Sample household goods prices, in Canadian dollars.

7

Getting a Job

Choosing a career path is not an easy decision. You may wish to continue in the occupation you are in now or want to try something new. Finding the right job and working environment can make all the difference to your quality of life. If you are coming on a working holiday visa, you might be less concerned about what job you actually do because your main priority is to sample Canadian life. But if you plan to come as a temporary foreign worker, skilled worker or business investor, the type of work you do is probably a primary concern. You'll want to take into account the current economic conditions, job market and how your credentials will be recognised in Canada. After all, getting good and agreeable work is a big part of making life enjoyable.

APPLYING FOR A SOCIAL INSURANCE NUMBER

No one can legally work in Canada without a **SIN**. It is a unique number that a person is assigned that enables him or her to get a job, pay income tax and receive benefits (Employment Insurance, Social Assistance, etc.). As a newcomer you are likely to receive an application form when you first arrive, but if you do not you can go to any Human Resources and Skills Development Canada (HRSDC) office. Branches are listed in the phone book. To apply you need to show your birth certificate, immigration visa and passport as well as pay a small fee. You can also get applications at Canada Post Offices and at agencies that help immigrants.

Once you are hired your new employer will ask for your **Social Insurance Number**. You are not obliged to give it before then.

HAVING THE RIGHT QUALIFICATIONS

It cannot be stressed enough that before deciding to go to Canada you should ensure that your educational and training qualifications are accepted here if you want to do the job you do now. Just because Citizenship and Immigration Canada only allows certain occupations to apply under the skilled worker class or gives more points for more education and work experience does not mean that you will be able to continue in your chosen field of work once in Canada.

The reason the government is limiting applications to those with certain qualifications is because it believes those are the jobs Canada needs to fill and, therefore, those immigrants would have a better chance of working in their chosen fields. But 'better chance' is the key phrase. Also, the reason more points are awarded to people with more education is that the government feels those people are more inclined to work hard and succeed in whatever they do, even if it isn't what they do in their country of origin. It is a sad truth that many engineers, doctors and other professionals end up in low-paying, low-skill jobs because their degrees are not recognised in Canada. Often, an immigrant is required to undertake many years of equivalency training, at the immigrant's expense. Sometimes what is needed is Canadian experience, which means the immigrant has to undertake some volunteer work in his or her field before being hired in a paid position.

In terms of trade workers like electricians, carpenters and tool and dye makers, qualifications often do stand up as long as the immigrant has enough work experience. You will still have to pass a licensing exam, however. Make sure that you bring to Canada all your original certificates, documents and letters of recommendations.

The first step in finding out whether your credentials will be recognised in Canada is to gather as much information about how your profession works in Canada. It is usually a provincial body or agency that ultimately gives you the go-ahead or not to work in your profession, not a federal one. Also, getting your credentials recognised works differently depending on whether you are from a regulated or non-regulated field of work. And you will need to make sure you have all your papers, certificates, licences, etc. in order (and translated into either English or French if they are in a different language).

The best place to start to understand what's involved is on the Internet The government's new Foreign Credentials Referral Office (FCRO) is a good starting place (www.credentials.gc.ca) as is 'The Working in Canada Tool' (www.working incanada.gc.ca). It's also imperative that you contact the Canadian Information Centre for International Credentials (www.cicic.ca) (see Useful Addresses for its mailing address and phone contact information).

If your job is considered a regulated profession in Canada, you will probably have to deal with a professional association. There is a long list of regulated professions, but to give you some idea, they include doctors, engineers, lawyers, nurses and teachers. Professional associations often have internal evaluation services before granting someone a licence to work in that field, regardless of what evaluation is given by an external credential assessment service.

Impending labour shortages, especially in terms of skilled workers, are forcing changes to the way immigrants' credentials are being evaluated and to government policy in creating opportunities for immigrants. That has included legislation (in Ontario) which forces professional associations to treat immigrants more fairly when assessing credentials and the creation of designated residency places for foreign-trained doctors. But challenges remain.

LOCATION, LOCATION, LOCATION

You might choose a city because you have family or friends there, but if you are free to go wherever you like it is wise to take stock of what different locales do and do not offer.

Unemployment rate

This varies enormously from province to province (see Figure 9). If you have a particular skill needed by a province with high unemployment, the high rate should not deter you from moving there. The national unemployment rate in Canada is 8 per cent as of March 2009.

Minimum wage

Each province and territory has a general minimum wage (see Figure 10) although some have lower minimum wages for workers under 18, for people who do bartending work (and other work that usually involves tips) and for less experienced workers. Students and women make up a greater proportion of minimum wage workers, but that's not to infer that women do not hold senior positions. Minimum wage jobs are highly concentrated in the restaurant and retail industries.

Incentives

Some provincial governments offer incentives for certain types of professionals and workers in order for them to move away from urban areas to areas that need their services. Medical doctors are one example. Some provincial governments will pay doctors more to set up practices in what they call 'underserviced' areas. Some provinces are more in need of tradespeople than others are, depending on the predominant industries there. During the oil boom, Alberta was one of those provinces. And while the recession has dampened the need there and across the country, it is predicted skilled tradespeople will be once again in demand soon.

There are many other types of occupations eligible for incentives and they change from time to time depending on demand.

Other factors

Some regions have inherent challenges or opportunities you may want to consider. For example, during the economic boom in Alberta, an amazing number of jobs were created but growth was so fast that there was a shortage of housing and social services for all the people there. And areas prone to booms are also prone to busts, meaning if you plan to head to an area doing very well economically, make sure that growth is likely to be sustained by the time you get there. In more stable economies, such as the one in Ottawa where the federal government is the principal economic driver, there are other challenges. A job in Ottawa often requires bilingualism

Province	Unemployment rate (March 2009)
Newfoundland and Labrador	14.7%
Prince Edward Island	11.5%
Nova Scotia	8.9%
New Brunswick	9.5%
Quebec	8.3%
Ontario	8.7%
Manitoba	5.1%
Saskatchewan	4.7%
Alberta	5.8%
British Columbia	7.4%

Source: Statistics Canada Labour Force Survey

Fig. 9. Provincial unemployment figures.

Province	Minimum wage/hour
Newfoundland and Labrador	$9.00 ($9.50 Jan 2010; $10.00 July 2010)
Prince Edward Island	$8.40
Nova Scotia	$8.60 ($9.20 April 2010; $9.65 Oct 2010)*
New Brunswick	$8.25
Quebec	$9.00 ($8.00 for those receiving gratuities)
Ontario	$9.50 ($10.25 March 2010)**
Manitoba	$9.00
Saskatchewan	$8.60 ($9.25 May 2010)
Alberta	$8.80
British Columbia	$8.00***
Northwest Territories	$8.25
Yukon	$8.58 (adjusted annually to CPI)****
Nunavut	$10.00

*$8.10 for inexperienced persons.
**$8.25 for liquor servers; $8.90 for students under 18.
***$6.00 for first job/entry-level until 500 hours accumulated.
****Consumer Price Index.

Fig. 10. Provincial minimum wages.

(English and French) and getting a job with the government or a company that does business with the government can involve a very lengthy security clearance process. As well, Canadian citizens are given priority when the federal government hires.

There is sometimes more to consider than your own desires. If you are bringing over a family, you will want to find a location that suits the needs of everyone. You will want to ensure that there are job opportunities for your partner and a good school not too far away. Day care, something you may require for your children if you and your partner both work, is not always easy to find and can be very costly. Quebec subsidises day care in a major way and so it is less expensive in that province than others.

LOOKING FOR A JOB

You should start your search even before you leave your home country, even if it's just to get an idea of what's out there. For example, British newspapers sometimes carry Canadian job advertisements. You can also check relevant trade journals or order specialist publications from Canada. See Useful Addresses for the contact details of such publications in addition to Internet jobsites and other useful contacts for some of the organisations mentioned below.

Human Resources and Skills Development Canada's 'Service Canada' centres, specialise in helping people find jobs. The phone book will tell you where the nearest centre is to you (or go to www.servicecanada.gc.ca). There are general postings on bulletin boards at the centres as well as counsellors who can help you.

Contacting an employment agency or head hunter, either in your home country or in Canada, is another starting point. Almost all Canadian newspapers are on the World Wide Web and you can try searching their classifieds. Be aware, however, that many employers who advertise in papers and through agencies are looking for immediate help.

Many jobs are not advertised at all. Hearing about a job opening through a friend of a friend of a friend is quite common. If you have any contacts already working in Canada, have them keep an ear out for you and an eye on internal postings.

Another tactic is to call companies that are in your specific field of work, even if they're not advertising. This is especially useful for the trades who are always looking for people and often don't bother advertising because if they always advertised when they needed someone, they'd have a permanent ad in the paper. For non-trades professions, most companies have specific human resources departments that can tell you if there are any openings.

It will be much easier to look for a job when you finally reach Canada. There are non-profit organisations existing solely to help newcomers find jobs.

Each province has different programmes run by different not-for-profit organisations. HRSDC offices can point you in the right direction and tell you whether you are eligible for government-sponsored skill training programmes that might help you improve your job prospects.

Once you have ideas of what posts you want to apply for, you need to send in a cover letter and résumé. Remember that companies receive hundreds of applications. It is important that yours stands out.

Writing the cover letter

If you are applying from overseas you should indicate in your cover letter when you expect to get your immigrant status or your work authorisation (see section on working visas later in this chapter and in Chapter 3) if you do not have it already.

The purpose of a cover letter is to highlight aspects of your résumé as well as information about yourself that is not in it (travel, second language, past promotions etc.). Write about specific work experience or training that is directly relevant to the job you are applying for. State why you are interested in the job and what you can bring to it and the organisation. Try to get your personality across a bit as well.

Use good quality paper and envelopes. The letter and address on the envelope should all be typewritten and make sure there are no spelling mistakes. The cover letter is the first thing a potential employer will see. In many cases if it does not stand out or if it is sloppy in any way, the person will toss it and the attached résumé in a 'no' pile right away without even looking at the résumé.

Composing the résumé

Because companies receive so many résumés, they usually do not spend a great deal of time reading them on first glance. For this reason it is best to keep your résumé to two to four pages. There are varying opinions on how best to format a Curriculum Vitae, or 'CV', but general principles do apply. If your strong suit is employment history then put that first, but if your education stands out it should go first instead. Always list the most recent experience first within your work history and education sections.

When you are applying for an assortment of positions at various companies, it does not hurt to create different résumés, each tailored to the job and/or company to which it will be sent. Figure 11 shows a fictional sample résumé. This is a very brief résumé. You may wish yours to be 'fleshier' and to describe your various positions to a greater extent. You can also put a section at the very top, called 'summary of qualifications', which should list five skills you have that are generally related to the job you are applying for. A person with more experience than Jill Doe (see sample résumé) would continue on a second page. A second page could be used to list volunteer work and other work experience or extra curricular activities if you are fresh out of university. You can also add a line listing hobbies or interests. You never know if a fellow hiking enthusiast or gardener is the one screening the résumés!

Explaining gaps

If your résumé contains gaps in employment or education, it is important to explain them in your cover letter. Do so honestly and as positively as possible. Were you actively looking for a job? Undergoing further training? Or maybe you were travelling abroad? In terms of education, if you did not complete your studies, point out what you did achieve (e.g. finished two years of radio and telecommunications studies). If you do not explain holes in your résumé, the person hiring will imagine worse reasons than what really happened.

Nowadays, changing jobs or careers is often looked upon as a positive thing. Employers like to know you have a range of skills. However, if you were at a different job every few months, that would be a problem. If there's a logical reason for you moving about a lot, give it. But if you just did not like the jobs or the employers, steer clear of saying so. Highlight any long-term commitments you did make during that time such as taking part-time studies in the evenings over the course of a few years.

Jill Doe

14 Blackburn Road
Suffolk JW2 46X
England
jdoe@email.com
Tel: 44-1473-290-821
Fax: 44-1473-290-263

JOB OBJECTIVE: Financial services marketing manager.

MARKETING EXPERIENCE

ATK Marketing Inc.   2005 to date
Brand manager

● Responsible for marketing line of CD ROMs.

Nichemarketing Ltd   2000–2005
Marketing representative

● Promoted financial products for mutual fund client.

FINANCIAL INDUSTRY EXPERIENCE

Bowman Mutual Funds   1998–2000
Financial assistant

● Assisted broker in all aspects of financial services.

● Co-ordinated stock and asset research.

EDUCATION

Penticton School of Economics   1991–1995
BA Honours in Economics and Political Science
Dean's List 1987–1990

Lakeside Secondary   1985–1991
General Certificate of Education A Levels in Maths, Statistics,
Economics and English

OTHER SKILLS/DETAILS

● Member of the Financial Planners Association of England.

● Computer skills: word processing, spreadsheets and graphics.

References available on request

Fig. 11. Sample résumé.

Supplying references

You do not need to supply references until asked. Have ready a list of three referees, ones who you know will speak well of you, to fax or send to the company when it requests them. If they ask if they can call your previous employers and there is one you would rather they do not call, weigh the options. If that employer will simply be less than enthusiastic about you, it may not be worth sounding the alarms. But if you know that they will speak badly of you, tell the company that you would prefer that it not call that particular referee. You will probably have to explain why, so be honest but positive. Do not say how much you hate the person or they hate you. Maybe allude to creative differences or that you got along but they were unhappy with you because you left.

Assets

Canadian employers value some assets above all others and it is useful to know what those are:

- Strong grasp of both spoken and written **English.**

- Ability in **more than one language**. For many government jobs French is a must, but any second language is a plus.

- **Experience**. If you have ever worked in Canada before, even if only on a working holiday or temporary work visa, that will be a definite asset.

- **Training**. Canada seeks workers with high credentials. Employers like people with a higher education or people with a great deal of practical training.

- **Computer skills**. There is a special initiative now to entice computer specialists to come and work in Canada. See Chapter 3 for more details.

- **Driver's licence**. As soon as you can when you arrive, start the process of obtaining one from the province in which you're residing (see Chapter 9).

The interview

There are so many interview tips floating about that it is difficult to know where to start. First, research the company. Nothing looks worse than not knowing about your potential employer in the interview. Many factors play into giving a good interview and even if you do everything right, you may still not land the job. But knowing right from wrong is half the battle.

Appearance

Be clean and tidy. This includes your hair, nails and clothes. Men should shave or tidy their beard. Women should not wear a lot of makeup and although it is advisable for both sexes to dress conservatively (a suit) and modestly, it cannot hurt to have some style. In other words, do not go so far that you look dowdy.

Attitude

Be positive and enthusiastic. Be early, never late. Sit a bit forward in the chair; it looks as if you are disinterested if you lean back. In all your nervousness, try not to forget to smile. When you shake the interviewer's hand, make it a firm handshake, even if you are female. In Canada it is not thought unladylike to provide a firm handshake. A limp one conveys weakness.

Answering questions

Be concise but thorough. Avoid both monosyllabic answers or ones that ramble on. If you feel the question is too general or you do not understand it, do not forge ahead aimlessly. Ask for clarification.

Catching you offguard

Interviewers undertake many methods to get at who you are. Some tactics are fairly unorthodox (like suddenly leaving the room and then coming back in). Be prepared and no matter what, stay calm. It is imperative that you sit down a night or two before, come up with a list of potential questions and then practise your answers. But, do not go into the interview with a script in your head, flexibility is key.

At the end

As the interview winds down it usually comes to an end with the interviewer asking if you have anything else to add. Never decline this offer. Perhaps you forgot a point in a previous answer that you think is important. Perhaps a question was never asked that would have addressed something you would like to be known about yourself. However, if the interviewer does not offer this opportunity, do not rush in at the end with additional information, unless it is really important. Instead, ask a question or two about the job or when you will next hear from the company, but don't enquire about salary at this time. If the interviewer actually asks if you have any questions, again never decline. Always have one or two ready otherwise you will look disinterested. Do not forget to say thank you.

After

Send a thank you note to the interviewer or interviewers if there was more than one. Be simple and to the point, but do not delay.

If you have not heard back about the job within the time frame they indicated, call them. If you still do not hear back, call again. There's a fine line between being persistent and being too aggressive, but do not just sit and wait for the phone to ring.

If you didn't get the job, ask politely for feedback about what you could improve upon in terms of credentials or interview performance for the future.

If you're finding the job search isn't going well, some cities have not-for-profit skill development programmes that include practice firms. Those are places where you work for six or more weeks to brush up on both work and office social skills as well as to get advice on improving your résumé and interviewing skills. You can find out more about practice firms at HRSDC offices.

At the end of the Useful Addresses section of this book, there is a list of websites, many of which are job search and employment sites and some are specifically geared to immigrants.

DOING IT YOURSELF

Perhaps you want to start your own business or continue the one you ran in your home country. The laws and regulations pertaining to businesses in Canada are complex and vary from province to province, city to city and business to business. This chapter will simply point out a few general factors to consider.

Most of the recent economic and job growth in Canada has been due to small- and mid-size businesses. Therefore many banks are flogging small-business loans and if you have a good idea, and can sell the idea to the bank, you will get some sort of start-up money. Canadians consistently vote entrepreneurs as one of the most respected professions in Canada; but running your own business means long hours and a great deal more financial risk than if you work for someone else.

Taxes in Canada are quite high and some businesses just cannot survive because of them, and the Canadian market may not respond well to your product. Do not think that just because it was a success in your country it will be so in Canada. Research the Canadian market first.

At the same time, many immigrants have found that Canada's growing multicultural society has offered business opportunities, whether it's opening an ethnic food shop or other service geared to their ethnic community.

Buying a franchise

If you do not want to forge ahead with your own idea or product but still want to be your own boss, there is the option of buying a franchise business. These are often chain stores such as cafés and snack stores of which there are several in a city. You gain the security of a product that has already proved it can sell, but lose some of the autonomy of it being entirely your own business.

Also, because you are purchasing a brand that is already established, these businesses can be quite expensive to buy. But if you have the capital to put up, and you get a good location, franchises can pay off in the long run.

LOOKING AT CUSTOM AND PRACTICE

Unions

Unions are groups of working people who are organised to protect their rights in the workplace. What began as a struggle to be heard has evolved into a powerful movement. In the 19th century the first unions were formed to protect members against financial disaster in times of illness or unemployment. From the start, employers and management vehemently opposed unions.

Today nearly 4.5 million full-time paid workers belong to a union. In 2005, 429,000 workers were involved in 261 work stoppages (strikes or lockouts) that resulted in an estimated 4.1 million work days lost, a huge increase over previous years. However, that was because of the large size of the unions involved in disputes that year. In 2006, work days lost totalled more than 800,000, a record low, although the number of work stoppages was in the same range as before. Compare that with the US, where in 2006 there were only 20 strikes or lockouts, and the UK where there were 145 from September 2005 to September 2006.

Different unions exist for a variety of work. **Craft unions** join together skilled workers in a particular craft or trade. **Industrial unions** are for all workers in a single industry, whatever the skill. Some unions have mandatory membership while others are optional. Union fees are usually deducted from the pay cheque.

Unions are organised into locals that represent union members in a specific workplace or local area. Various unions are grouped together under Labour Councils and each province has a provincial Federation of Labour. Nationally, most unions belong to the Canadian Labour Congress, while others belong to the Canadian Federation of Labour (the building trades unions), the Confederation of Canadian Unions (small group of nationalist unions) and the Confédération des Syndicats Nationaux.

Holidays

It is often a great shock to Europeans when they come to Canada and find out those many weeks of holidays they used to enjoy are no longer. Canada just does not offer such luxuries!

Most full-time permanent jobs offer two weeks off per year to start with, once you've been with the company for a certain period of time – usually six months to a year. As you continue to work at the company, that time is increased so that after three or four years you may get up to four weeks. Except for high-end jobs and professionals who work for themselves (e.g. doctors), it does not go much higher than that. Of course, there is the odd statutory day off or bank holiday, but that hardly totals much more than an additional week. Teachers get the summer off, but they often teach summer school or take professional development courses. Compared with other countries, Canada is in the middle of the pack for the average amount of hours people work.

An increasing trend is for companies to hire contract workers. Some Canadians resent this, as they desire more permanency and security, but others enjoy the flexibility of signing on for a project for a few months and then having some time off before bidding for another project.

Discrimination and harassment

Canadian laws protect people from discrimination when seeking employment and once employed. Women still, on average, earn less than men for equal work. Sexual harassment is strictly forbidden. If you feel that you have been discriminated against or that you are being harassed, contact the Human Rights Commission in your province. If you feel you are being exploited at work, contact Human Resources and Social Development Canada or the Ministry of Labour in your province.

FOREIGN WORKERS

This category pertains to those people who are seeking to come to Canada on a temporary work visa or a working holiday visa. For more detailed information see Chapter 3.

Temporary work visa

It is not an easy process to get a temporary work visa. In most cases you need what's called a positive labour market opinion or confirmation from Human Resources and Skills Development Canada (HRSDC), which essentially requires that you already have a job offer and that it meets certain requirements. If you have a job offer from a Canadian employer, there are steps that the employer must take in order that your work authorisation is approved.

- The employer must give details of the job offer to Human Resources and Skills Development Canada (HRSDC).

- An HRSDC counsellor will verify that the offer meets wage and working condition standards for that occupation. An employer cannot offer you or pay you less than the going rate.

- The counsellor will consider several factors when deciding on the opinion. He or she will look at whether the work will lead to further job creation/retention for Canadians, if the work means skills and knowledge will be passed on to the benefit of Canadians and if the work is likely to fill a labour shortage. The counsellor will also look at whether your employment will negatively affect the settlement of a labour dispute.

- Finally, what might be the stickiest point is whether the employer has made reasonable effort to find or train a Canadian for the job. And in many cases there is a Canadian who *can* do the job. One way to combat this is for the employer to prove your set of skills is unique or so superior that no ordinary Canadian would do. However, it's questionable whether an employer would go to such lengths to hire you if there are Canadians willing and able.

Once the HRSDC approves the job offer, potential employees can then apply for a work permit from the local Canadian Embassy, High Commission or Consulate in their country.

Some jobs are automatically exempt from HRSDC approval and it is a good idea to check with an HRSDC office or with a Canadian embassy or consulate first before going through all the trouble for nothing. There will be a processing fee.

Because it can take a long time to go through this entire process and some industries need certain types of workers faster than this allows for, the government has an expedited labour market opinion (ELMO) pilot project for particular occupations in Alberta and British Columbia. See Chapter 3 for more details.

To get your permit, you will have to establish that you meet the criteria of the job and provide documentation such as educational certificates, employment references and work samples. You will also probably have to get a medical examination at your own expense to assure the Canadian government that you are healthy before entering the country.

If all goes well you will get your permit and be on your way. The permit outlines that you can work at a specific job, for a specific employer and for a specific time.

When you arrive, bring your permit, your passport and any other travel documents you need. It is the employer's responsibility to arrange for your medical cover when you arrive, but make sure it is arranged before you arrive.

If while you are in Canada you discover that your work will take longer or your job changes, you will have to apply to change your permit 30 days in advance of its expiry date.

Residents of the US, Greenland or Saint Pierre and Miquelon can apply for a work permit at a port of entry to Canada, but these special people must still have confirmation of an offer of employment.

Working holiday programmes

Working holiday visas usually involve age restrictions. Some are for university students only while others are employer-specific and work more like a temporary work visa. Canada has different agreements with different countries, which cannot possibly all be listed here. In general, such visas are restricted to 18 to 30-year-olds. Quebec has its own agreements with particular countries, especially Belgium and France.

In some cases a medical examination will be required before a visa will be issued.

Australia

Canada's agreement with Australia is one of its most open ones. The programme is not restricted to students, but is limited to Australians 18 to 30 years old (inclusive). The visa is a two-year, open permit visa. That means you don't have to find an employer before going to Canada in order to get the visa. Australians look for work once they arrive and can work for more than one employer. Other criteria include, but are not limited to: proof of having enough funds to sustain yourself (AUD $4,000), not having a criminal record, and passing a medical examination. Once you get the visa you have a year to enter Canada. In order to get the visa for the full two years, your passport expiry date must be after those two years would be up. It is, therefore, recommended that your passport be good for three years after the date your visa is issued. The fee for this visa is $190.

To apply you must do a brief online application at www.whpcanada.org.au and you will then be sent a full application form.

New Zealand

A similar programme to the Australian one is available for citizens of New Zealand. The fee is $220 and there is a link on the Australian WHP website for the New Zealand programme (NZWHP), or go to http://www.dfait-maeci.gc.ca/asia/whp/ intro-en.asp

Student work abroad schemes

This is how most young people from other countries get to have a working holiday in Canada. Unlike the Australian programme, these programmes require that foreigners are either full-time university students, or have recently graduated.

International Exchange Programs

Also for New Zealanders and Australians, IEP has working holiday programmes in Canada, for both first timers and returning youth. Go to www.iep.co.nz for more information.

British Universities North American Club (BUNAC)

Under this programme, one-year, working holiday visas are available to students from the UK who are taking a year off from university or who have just finished their 'A' levels and hold an unconditional offer to attend university. You must be between 18 and 35 years old. Applicants must show proof they are returning to school or continuing with higher education. BUNAC also has a programme for non-students. Enquire at the Canadian High Commission in London or go to www.bunac.org.uk BUNAC's website.

A similar programme exists for Irish citizens through USIT (www.usitnow.ie). For students in Finland go to www.cimo.fi and Swedish students should apply through the International Employment Office and in Sweden (phone: 46 23 93700).

Other schemes

France, Belgium, Germany, Sweden and Japan all have 'youth mobility' programmes that are like working holiday schemes. They include professional development placements, internships, summer jobs and student practicums. Most of these programmes have yearly quotas, age restrictions and time restrictions. Some kinds of work are also off-limits. If you are a citizen of one of the above-named countries, check with the Canadian Visa Post there (by phone or online) for details (see Useful Addresses).

Live-in Caregiver Program

Caregivers are people who are qualified to care independently for children, elderly or the disabled. There are some requirements you have to meet in order to participate in this programme.

- You must have the equivalent of a Canadian high school education.

- You need to have six months of full-time training or 12 months of full-time paid working experience in the field or occupation that is related to the live-in caregiver job you are looking for. The paid work experience must include six months of continuous employment with one employer. Examples of relevant fields are early childhood education, geriatric care, paediatric nursing and first aid. Your experience must have been gained within the three years prior to your application.

- You must be able to speak, read and understand either English or French.

The work permit is often valid for up to three years and three months. To renew it, the employer must provide a signed contract showing the job as a live-in caregiver is being offered beyond that time.

As a live-in caregiver you will live in your employers' home. If for any reason you wish to change employers, you may do so. You cannot be deported for quitting your job, but you must find a new employer, and you must have applied for and received a new work permit before working for the new employer because the work visa for this programme is employer specific. It's also important to note that you can change jobs only if it is to do another caregiver job. There have been some problems in the past with this programme where employers have told their caregivers they can get a supplementary job doing something else to make more money. This is not true and you can be deported if found to be working as something other than a caregiver, whether in addition to being a caregiver or instead of being a caregiver altogether. There are other conditions and regulations pertaining to this programme. To get more detailed information, contact your nearest Canadian Embassy or consulate. After completing at least two years of employment as a live-in caregiver, you can apply for permanent residence in Canada.

Other programmes

From time to time the government creates working or exchange schemes to address a particular need in the Canadian labour force or a social need. Check with your Canadian Embassy or consulate to see what is currently being offered.

MAXIMUM
30

08:00-17:00
SCHOOL
DAYS

DO NOT PASS

PLAYGROUND
ZONE ENDS

8

Going to School

The education system in Canada varies from province to province because it is not a federal responsibility. But generalities do exist. First, it should be noted that 'public schools' in Canada do not mean the same thing as they do, for example, in the UK. Public schools are those funded by taxes and available free to every child. Private schools are those paid for by the parents of the child. Ninety-five per cent of all children in Canada attend public schools, which are co-educational. Teachers in all provinces must be qualified and licensed.

Generally, the school year runs from September (the day after Labour Day) to the end of June for elementary and secondary schools and from early September to the end of April for universities. There are some exceptions, however. Some public schools in Canada have been experimenting with all-year schooling with shorter holidays spread out during the year and some university programmes, especially some professional courses, run through the summer.

FUNDING/JURISDICTION

Although education is under the jurisdiction of the provinces, funding comes from all levels of government: municipal property taxes, provincial taxes and federal taxes (a portion given to the provinces through transfer payments). The federal government provides funding for post-secondary education and is responsible for the education of aboriginals, armed forces personnel and inmates of federal penal institutions.

Responsibility for the administration of elementary and secondary schools is delegated to local elected school boards or commissions. In some provinces the provincial governments have become more involved but these boards generally set local budgets, hire and negotiate with teachers (who are unionised) and shape school curriculum within provincial guidelines.

It is usually the individual schools that set, conduct and mark their examinations but some provinces are heading back to province-wide exams, much to the chagrin of some students!

In recent years, there has been much conflict between the provincial governments and school boards, especially in Ontario. The issues are complex and it is not possible go into detail here. But basically public school boards say they are underfunded and can't deliver the education they should with the money they're given. The province has put more money into the system, but not as much as was asked for. Part of the problem is while the province holds the purse strings, the board still has the responsibility to negotiate contracts with teachers and staff. The result has been budget deficits and cuts to special education programmes, as well as school closures (the students are merged with another school).

OUTLINING LEVELS OF INSTRUCTION

This really depends on the individual province, but generally primary education starts at the kindergarten level (junior and senior) at the age of 4 or 5 and continues to the end of grade 6, although some schools continue to grade 8. In some provinces there is a junior high level, either grades 7 and 8 or 7, 8 and 9. Secondary education, or high school, goes from grade 9 or 10 to grade 11 or 12, again depending on the province.

Pre-school

Some parents choose to place their children in a school-like setting before it is legally required to do so. For pre-school, children are usually aged 3 and 4 and attend only a half-day of 'class'. It is not a structured setting and the focus is on the basics: the alphabet, numbers, arts and crafts, songs and play. Studies have shown that children's minds are very absorbent in their first five years of life. Pre-school can enhance a child's vocabulary, motor skills and social skills and is a good option as an alternative to regular day-care if parents work.

Kindergarten to grade 6

Junior kindergarten is usually just half a day, but after that children attend for a full day, although for the younger grades a rest time is usually ensured. In elementary school, children have the same teacher for all their subjects with a few exceptions. Special education and French classes are taught by teachers trained particularly for those courses. The curriculum emphasises the basic subjects of reading, writing, maths, geography, history, science, social studies and introductory arts. Small tests and projects are assigned as well as homework. These school years often involve special projects, field trips and dramatic presentations (Christmas pageants, musical recitals, etc.). In some provinces children get the opportunity to learn a musical instrument like the recorder or even play in a small school band in grades 5 and 6. In some provinces enriched or accelerated programmes are available for academically-gifted students, as are special programmes for slower learners and students with disabilities.

Grades 7 and 8

For the purposes of this book, it will be assumed that these two grades are attended at a separate school and are not grouped with grade 9. For those schools that go from grade 6 to 8 or for those schools that include grade 9, the curriculum is not any different. The only difference is how the levels are divided.

A child in grade 7 is about 12 or 13 years of age. At this stage a lot more is expected from the students and subjects are studied in greater detail and depth. Often, each subject has a separate teacher so that students have a 'homeroom' teacher who teaches one subject and then they travel together as a class to other teachers to get instruction in the other subjects. Students do not choose their subjects; the courses are all mandatory. They are instructed in English, French (not all provinces), maths, science, history, geography and physical education. In many schools, mid-year and end-of-year examinations are given in addition to tests, assignments and essays. Enrichment and remedial learning programmes are available as well.

High school

By law, children must attend school from the age of 6 until the age of 15 or 16, depending on the province. Ontario recently brought in legislation making attendance in school mandatory until 18 or graduation, whichever happens first. The new law includes fines for parents who allow their children to drop out before that time, and fines for employers who hire students during school hours when the students should be in school. Also, students who have dropped out of school before they're 18 can have their driver's licence suspended; or cannot obtain a driver's licence if they don't already have one. Most provinces have grades 9 to 12, but Quebec students finish in grade 11 before going into the CEGEP system (more on that later).

High school entails taking compulsory courses and having the option of choosing electives. All schools offer a core curriculum mandated by the province. They differ in what electives they offer. Some schools are very academic-oriented while others offer trade and technical courses.

Usually the courses taken in the last year of high school are the ones that universities and colleges look at when deciding whether or not to admit a student. Most universities look at the mean average grade of these courses when assessing a student's application. In Quebec, after grade 11, students go to a CEGEP, which is like a junior college, before heading to university.

If students have advanced skills in a subject, beyond the grade to which they are automatically designated because of their age, they can be tested and put ahead a year (or more) so that they remain challenged. This does not mean they automatically obtain credits for the courses they skipped, but it does mean they have more room in their timetable for other courses.

At some high schools there is also the option of enrolling in enriched courses that provide advanced-level academia for students who have shown exceptional ability in a particular subject like English or maths. There are also special programmes for students with learning challenges, such as attention deficit disorder, autism, dyslexia, etc. In some schools those students are integrated into the regular classroom with help from additional education assistants and therapists (occupational, speech, etc.) while in other schools, there are separate classes for those students.

CATEGORISING TYPES OF SCHOOLS

Deciding what school to enrol your children in is a personal choice. There is no right or wrong answer to the question of what kind of school is better. There are pros and cons for all the choices and, of course, it comes down to what's convenient for where you live and what you are able to afford.

Public schools

Most students go to public schools. They may be less elite and specialised than private schools but parents who advocate public schools say that they offer just as good a level of education as private schools as long as the student works hard. There is often a broader selection of courses and the same amount of extracurricular activities as at private schools, but in some provinces public schools face funding problems that have resulted in large classes and the downsizing of special programmes. Public schools are co-ed, books do not cost extra and neither do most field trips. Sometimes extra fees are charged for special trips. But schools often undertake fundraising drives to raise money for such trips or projects. Public schools are non-denominational and any religious instruction is usually given in the context of a world religions course.

Private schools

Smaller classes, a focus on academic courses and superior athletic facilities are what private schools offer in comparison to the public school system, but it comes at a price. Not including extras like the cost of uniforms, athletic equipment and books, the yearly price tag ranges from about $10,000 to $20,000 per child. Yet parents of children who go to private school still pay taxes that fund a public system they don't use. Because of that, five Canadian provinces (B.C., Alberta, Saskatchewan, Manitoba and Quebec) give some funding directly to some independent schools.

Of course, most private schools offer scholarships and bursaries. To get in, prospective students must pass an entrance exam in most cases.

Private schools offer longer vacations for students under the premise that the time students do spend in class is more rigorous and demanding than time spent in public schools. Most of the private schools are girls-only or boys-only but there are a few that have become co-ed in the face of financial difficulty. Also included in this category are schools such as those offering the Montessori educational method.

Boarding is available at many private schools for families that want to send their children to a private school quite a distance from their home. Additional fees for this are, of course, applicable, sometimes upwards of $7,000 a year.

Separate schools/alternative schools

Provincial legislation allows for the establishment of separate schools by religious groups. Mostly Roman Catholic, these schools offer a curriculum based on religion, from kindergarten through to secondary level. There are schools of other religious denomination as well. Uniforms are usually required and some schools are segregated by gender while others are mixed.

Both Alberta and Ontario fund Catholic schools as they do public schools. Children do not have to be Catholic to attend. Alberta also funds some Protestant and charter schools on the same basis as they do public schools. (Charter schools are independent schools that have performance-based charters, or contracts, with the province.)

Schools of other denominations are not publicly funded and parents interested in having their children educated separately must pay for it themselves. This has been a source of great controversy.

Alternative schools are those that provide an 'opening learning' environment for students, where they can work at their own pace.

French immersion

There are both French and English language schools throughout Canada, with French schools being most numerous in Quebec. Outside Quebec, French public schools are often referred to as schools with French immersion programmes in which all subjects are taught in French. These schools begin in the early grades, as it is considerably easier for children to learn a new language from an early age. If you want your children to go to one of these schools at a later stage, they will have to be tested to see where their language skills stand.

EXAMINING FACILITIES

Most elementary schools have an indoor gymnasium and an outdoor playground. Secondary school facilities depend on the size of the school, with some having more than one gymnasium and most having a regulation-sized sports field for outdoor sports. Outdoor tracks and swimming pools are common for secondary schools and some even have weight rooms. Due to tight funding the upkeep of such facilities has been a struggle. Private schools in the cities have less expansive grounds than those in the suburbs or those outside the city altogether, but many private schools have extensive playing grounds, even if housed downtown.

ENROLLING

The first step is to arrange a visit with the school. For public school there are restrictions in terms of choice. Normally you need to send your child to the school in your district. By calling your school board you can find out which school that is. If the local school doesn't have a special programme your child may be allowed to go to another school further away that does have it. To enrol you need to bring your child's:

- birth or baptismal certificate
- immigration landing papers
- passport
- medical records (vaccination certificate)
- any previous school records.

The school will decide which grade your child should attend and if they need special lessons in English or French. Many schools offer English or French as second language (ESL or FSL) classes to help students catch up. If you think your children may have been incorrectly placed, talk to their teacher, guidance counsellor or school principal.

If you wish to acquire general information about Canadian schools before arriving in Canada, you may contact the **Canadian School Boards Association** (CSBA) (see Useful Addresses).

SCHOOL BREAKS

In elementary and high schools, students get two months off in the summer (July and August), approximately two weeks at Christmas time and a week in March (called March or Spring Break). Private schools often get longer periods of time off, with a couple of extra weeks in June and an extra week for March Break. People of religions other than Christianity are entitled to take off their holy days as well, such as Ramadan and Rosh Hashanah, although students have to catch up on the work they missed on those days.

In university, students get approximately four months off, from May to the end of August as well as a week in February. This is based on a regular eight-month programme. Students at semestered universities and those in co-op programmes might have school or a work placement in the summer months.

GOING ON TO HIGHER EDUCATION

Every year about 180,000 university degrees and 600,000 college diplomas are granted in Canada. For most Canadians getting a university or college education has become an important step in getting a good job. Canada spends (public and private funds) 5.2 per cent of its GDP on education. Investment in education, as a percentage of the country's GDP has declined over the years in Canada just as other countries have upped their spending. The US is now at 5.6 per cent and the UK at 5.4 per cent. However, in terms of attainment of post-secondary education, Canada has one of the highest levels of any country in the Organisation for Economic Co-Operation and Development (OECD). Forty-seven per cent of 25- to 64-year-olds hold what's known as a tertiary degree.

Universities

Canadian universities have been through some turbulent times of late due to huge cuts in funding coupled with increased enrolment, but tuition is still relatively low in contrast to comparable US schools. Every possible programme is offered somewhere, but most schools fall under specific categories such as medical/doctoral, primarily undergraduate or liberal arts only. Therefore not every programme is offered at all of Canada's 40-plus universities. Most have extensive full-time, part-time and continuing education programmes. As mentioned previously, the academic year lasts from September to mid-May although some programmes run through the summer. Some courses are also offered in the summer if you choose to accelerate your studies or if you unfortunately fail a course.

A general undergraduate degree, if done full-time, usually takes three years, while an honours degree takes four years and often involves doing a thesis or major research project. Masters programmes vary from one to three years and PhD programmes range from four to seven years. Professional degrees like medicine or law usually require an undergraduate degree while other professional degrees like engineering

(PEng) or a Masters of Business (MBA) require a couple of years of working in the relevant field either before or after the degree programme. Basically, graduate studies are more research-based, the admission materials required are more extensive and tuition often much higher.

The study period for a law degree (LL.B) lasts three years after which the student articles with a law firm for one year before taking the bar examinations to become a licensed lawyer. There are graduate degrees in law as well. Lawyers who move to another province must pass the bar exam for that province. Degrees in medicine (MD) take three to four years, then a student interns for one to two years after which they are licensed by the provincial medical boards. However, for speciality medicine (heart surgeons, neurologists, etc.) internships are far longer. Students are paid while interning.

Programmes such as business, engineering and architecture are offered at some universities as a co-op degree, which means part of your study includes working during your course in your relevant field. You study for two or three terms (a few months each) and then work for a term, then study for another couple of terms and work another term. The degree takes longer to obtain (e.g. architecture can take seven years) but in turn you get practical experience, make money to help fund your studies and hopefully get your foot in the door somewhere. Universities try to help students to find their work placements.

Universities range in size from a total enrolment of 800 to 60,000. Some are in a city's downtown while others are in more suburban or rural settings.

Applying

Canadian citizens and landed immigrants essentially go through the same process when applying to Canadian universities. There are application forms and varying fees for each university you apply for. For Ontario universities, because there are so many and because Ontario has the largest population, the limit on how many any one student can apply to is three. In applying to Ontario universities, students must go through a central application centre, the Ontario Universities Application Centre (OUAC) in Guelph, Ontario. OUAC requires students to rank their top three choices of school and programme and to pay one overall fee. For part-time studies, students need to apply directly to the universities.

Tuition

Full-time tuition varies greatly from school to school so it is difficult to put a general figure on it. Suffice to say it's far from free. For a liberal arts programme, undergraduate science degree or business degree a student could be looking at tuition from $2,000 to $14,000 per year. For the 2006–2007 academic year, the average tuition for one year of an undergraduate programme in Canada was $4,724. Since 1990 tuition fees have increased, on average, between 3 and 7 per cent per year. Some professional programmes have been deregulated so that the universities are no longer subject to government tuition caps, meaning tuition for such programmes is much higher. The federal government, through its **Canada Student Loans Program**, assists students who can prove that they do not have sufficient resources to fund their own studies. The provinces have complementary loan programmes but even with both a federal and provincial loan, most students will have to work part-time and in the summer to meet the costs of school and living. However, the way some of the provincial loan programmes are set up, the more you work the less loan money you get. Most loan payments are due in monthly instalments plus interest after six months from graduating, although during that six-month grace period, interest is accruing. However the annual interest you pay on your loans is tax deductible. Also, some loan programmes have a loan forgiveness option in extreme circumstances.

Universities and even some corporations offer scholarships and bursaries based on academic proficiency and/or financial need. Usually a portion of tuition fees, sometimes as much as 60 per cent, is due before you start classes.

Tuition fees for foreign students are higher than for Canadians or permanent residents. See the foreign student section later in the chapter.

Books/supplies

This is where the costs can add up. Depending on the programme, your books can cost upwards of $800 for the year, sometimes much higher. Science students can also assume higher costs due to the need for lab supplies. Calculators, pens, pencils, binders, paper and white-out are the least of your concerns. Although universities have computer labs, they are often packed full and closed at night when you would most likely be doing that last-minute essay. It is usually best to get your own computer equipment, which can cost from $700 upwards depending on what you choose and need.

University life

Life at university is often about more than studying. Self-discovery, meeting people from varied backgrounds and extracurricular involvement are all part of university life. Student journalism, student government, recreational and competitive athletics, debating, Amnesty International and many other organisations are available for students to join. Many universities have clubs or organisations that are specifically geared to a common cultural or ethnic group. There is likely to be an international students office and adviser as well.

University residence/housing

Unless you are going to a university in the city in which you live already, you will probably live in a university residence or in off-campus housing. Even students who could live at home sometimes choose to move out at this time in order to be more independent, but of course doing so is more expensive. The first year of an undergraduate programme is when most students live in residence. Residences come in many shapes and sizes: small, large, new, old, co-ed (floors, not rooms) and single-sex. Some universities have limited residence space and getting a residence room is based on age (preference given to younger students), where the student comes from (local students get less preference) and grades (the higher the better). International students on visas usually have little trouble getting a residence and many large universities have international student housing. Residence rooms are usually single or double with a series of rooms, or entire halls, sharing a bathroom that usually has several sinks and showers. Some residences are in old rambling houses that provide a cosier atmosphere; some are apartment-style where there is no cafeteria and students cook for themselves. There are also residences for mature and married students.

Choosing residence

In terms of economics, residence can either be a good choice or an expensive choice, depending on the city. The price of residence often includes a meal plan and if you prefer to cook, eat out or if you simply do not eat very much, this can be expensive. In a big city where housing can be expensive residence is often a good choice, but in some cities off-campus housing is very cheap and plentiful. It's also important to point out that in many cases, the cost of residence is up front, at the beginning of the academic year, unlike the monthly rent of off-campus housing. Many students forego the economics and, in the first year, choose to live in residence for the social aspect and convenience factors. However, such residences are not only filled with first year students, 'freshmen', but also senior students. Some of these senior students take on a resident advisory role.

Residences naturally have more rules than housing in which you live independently. Quiet hours, drinking rules and who you can bring in as a guest are par for the course. Living off-campus clearly offers more independence, but one perk of residence life, aside from an easy avenue of meeting people, is that you are paying for eight months only. Off-campus housing often entails finding someone to rent your place for the summer, moving out entirely and finding a new place in September or just paying rent for four months that you're not there if you go home for the summer.

It is very difficult to estimate residence costs because they vary so greatly from city to city. You could be looking at anything from $3,500 to $6,500 (including meal plans) per year. That is in addition to tuition, books and supplies.

Choosing off-campus housing

Off-campus housing is usually accommodation in which a few students share a house or an apartment. Universities have housing departments to help students find both residence and off-campus accommodation. In university towns, (towns in which the university is a major fixture) housing is often cheap and student-oriented, but in big cities you are competing with all the other wannabe-renters. For example, what you find for $500 a month in Halifax, you would pay $900 or more a month for in Toronto. Leases are usually for a year but in student-oriented housing subletting (when you rent to someone else if you go home for the summer) is allowed. (See Chapter 6 for more details on how to find rental accommodation.) The chart in Figure 12 may help estimate a year's cost. It does not include medical expenses or plans, the latter being much costlier for foreign students, nor does it include clothing or other optional items. Since entertainment is such an integral part of university life, it is included.

Remember, however, that part of your tuition and rental expenses can be used as deductions from your income tax.

University requirements

To go to a university you must have a high school diploma or equivalent, although

	Non-residence	Residence
Tuition	$1,900–$14,000	$1,900–$14,000
Housing*	$2,800–$8,000	$3,500–$11,000
Books/supplies	$600–$1,600	$600–$1,600
Food	$1,600–$2,500	$600**
Transport***	$800	$600
Entertainment	$600–$1,000	$600–$1,000
TOTAL**	**$8,100-$27,900**	**$7,600-$28,300**

*Based on eight months. Costs are much less if student lives at home with parents.

**There are always food costs in addition to meal plan coverage.

***Based on public transportation including going to and from school and travelling within the city. Does not include trips home.

****These are estimates, a year at university can cost less or more depending on individual needs.

Fig. 12. Estimating a year's university costs.

many universities allow adults over 25 or 30 to enter as mature students, based on their individual abilities and background rather than on previous education.

Although some schools advertise entrance cut-off grades at 65 per cent (for a liberal arts programme; sciences and other programmes are advertised as having much higher cut-offs), it is actually much more competitive than that. In other words, if you apply with a 65 per cent, you're likely not going to get in. Most schools publish an official 70 or 75 per cent cut-off and even then, you really need higher marks than that to get in.

To enter in a September class you should apply by the previous autumn, but some schools do allow January or May starts because they run on a semester basis. Regardless, apply to university a year in advance from when you want to start.

If your first language is not English, or you come from a non-English speaking country, you will probably be required to take the American Test of English as a Foreign Language (TOEFL) or another language test of the university's choice. Generally, French universities determine the level of French skills on an individual basis, which could include both written and oral tests.

Transfers and exchanges

If you have been attending another university in your own country you may be able to have some, or all, of your credits transferred to count towards your degree, but many universities do not recognise foreign credits and it is possible that you will have to start from scratch. Check with the individual university when you are applying.

If you are coming on a formal exchange you are probably in Canada for only a year or so and plan to finish your degree at the university you started at in your home country. In this case it is likely that the exchange programme ensures credit transferability, but it is always best to check first that the credits you earn in Canada will be accepted when you return home.

Passing the course

In terms of passing courses at Canadian universities, again standards vary. Some courses require you to simply earn a grade of 50 per cent or more while others can only be passed with 60 per cent or higher. Even if you pass all the courses, you may still be in trouble if you have not obtained a high enough overall average; but universities also understand about the demands of the first year as well as specific personal problems you may run into in any year. If something happens in your life that is affecting your academic work, it is best to see a counsellor in your university's academic office, or a professor or dean who you feel comfortable talking with.

To be able to get into a master's, doctoral or professional programme (having completed an undergraduate programme), your undergraduate marks must be above average and, except in rare cases, you will be required to sit a standardised exam such as the LSAT (law), the MCAT (medicine), the GMAT (business) and the GRE (graduate school). They are marked on a percentile basis so that you are judged in comparison with those who sit the exam in the same year.

The college system

Colleges have been going through a boom time lately. Promising jobs, they have been able to compete with universities because they offer more specialised and practical training geared to the job market. There are close to 150 community colleges and institutes in Canada, all members of the Association of Canadian Community Colleges (ACCC). You will hear community colleges called by many names:

- colleges of applied arts and technology
- institutes of applied arts and sciences
- community colleges
- technical/vocational colleges
- institutes of technology or technical institutes.

Each institution has its own entrance requirements and methods of assessing candidates. In most cases these institutions offer diplomas, not degrees. In recent years many university graduates have gone on to a college in order to specialise in an area and become more 'hireable'. At the same time, students in colleges sometimes wish to transfer to a university. This is possible but not for all universities or all programmes. Most college programmes cost significantly less than study at university does.

Colleges' main objective is vocational training through hands-on training. Becoming licensed in a trade involves apprentice work, classroom work and the passing of a provincial examination. Some schools run programmes like universities, that is for eight months of the year, while others go straight through the summer for 12 months in order to accelerate a student's ability to get his or her diploma. The range of courses and programmes is immense. Colleges offer everything from radio and television arts to computer programming, hairdressing, computer animation, carpentry and business administration. Most also offer continuing educational courses that run for a few months (at night) and are open to anyone with an interest and the money for the fee (usually a few hundred dollars).

Chiropractic and naturopathic colleges

There are two special types of colleges that should be discussed separately. Chiropractic College, of which there are only two (one English and one French), is in a field of its own. It is very competitive to get in, requiring a university science degree and good marks. It is also much costlier as it is not subsidised by the government. You can get student loans, but $16,000 plus in yearly tuition is still a steep order. It is a four-year programme with the last year-and-a-half running through the summer months. At the end, graduates become doctors of chiropractic medicine, but are not considered medical doctors (MDs). Falling into a similar category is the Canadian College of Naturopathic Medicine in Toronto. Graduates of this four-year programme become doctors of naturopathic medicine. Tuition is in the same price range as for the chiropractic colleges.

Correspondence courses

A growing field is correspondence education. For those who cannot afford to go away to school or who want to do their education on the side while they continue in their job, some universities and colleges offer courses by correspondence. This involves self-instruction with the aid of textbooks and the mailing in, or emailing of written assignments. Of course, the Internet has really boosted this type of 'distance' learning with audio and visual capabilities so students can observe a class or tutorial from home.

Women in higher education

More than 55 per cent of all university students are now women and more women graduate from university than do men. More and more, women are finding that the best way to break through the 'glass ceiling' is to be better educated and accredited than their male counterparts. The same can be seen in college figures where more than 53 per cent of full-time college students and nearly 63 per cent of part-time college students are women. These figures apply to all types of programmes, including formerly male-dominated ones like medicine.

Student safety

Partly because of the increased presence of women at universities, and partly because of the growth of universities both in number of students and size of campus, student safety has become a huge issue at universities and colleges. Large universities often have their own police stations on campus and there are walk-home programmes run by student volunteers for anyone wanting an escort home after dark. Campus pay phones are equipped with special emergency buttons, parking lots are well lit and crisis hotlines have been set up. Campus crime still exists, but these measures have ensured that campuses are as safe as possible.

FOREIGN STUDENTS

A foreign student is not one who has come as a refugee or a landed immigrant. Foreign students are those visiting Canada on a student visa. As a foreign student, you may go to Canada to study as an exchange student or you may go having organised it on your own.

Canadian universities covet foreign students and often boast of the percentage attending their school. This is because foreign students add prestige to a university, and also because they have to pay more tuition. You may want to study abroad because to have a year or more of education at a foreign university that is well recognised by the international community can be an asset when it comes time to look for a job. You may desire a year of study in Canada as a trial run to determine whether Canada is a country you may want to live in permanently. In addition to this chapter, there is more information about student visas in Chapter 3.

Tuition

The downside is that tuition fees for foreign students are much higher because the government does not subsidise education for foreigners. So while a Canadian student pays $4,000 for a year in a liberal arts programme, a foreign student may pay more than double that, sometimes three times as much. This is part of the reason universities covet foreign students. Unfortunately, foreign students are not eligible for provincial or national student loans or bursaries. However, some universities have scholarships especially for international students, and although it varies from university to university, after a year of study international students may be eligible for in-course scholarships which are based on the previous year of study.

Applying to a Canadian university, for the most part, works the same for foreign students as it does for Canadians and permanent residents.

Visas

You do not need a study permit if your studies are in a short-term programme of six months or less. But if you think you might want to extend your studies or do another programme afterwards, it's wise to get the permit before coming to Canada. Then, you can apply to study the new programme from within Canada, rather than having to leave and apply again from abroad. If you are from the USA, Greenland, or Saint Pierre and Miquelon, you can apply at a port of entry when you arrive at the Canadian border.

Getting a student visa involves a certain amount of paperwork hassle, but as long as you satisfy the requirements, you're on your way to studying in Canada. To apply for a **student permit** you need to:

- have a valid passport
- have a letter of acceptance from the educational institution
- have enough money to support yourself (tuition, living expenses and money for

transport home)
■ proof that you will return home at the end of your studies
■ complete an application form
■ pay the $125 fee.

Depending on what country you are from, you may even need to get a visitor's visa in addition to the student permit, as well as a medical examination. Check with the Canadian Embassy or consulate in your country to find out whether this is necessary for you or not.

Before going any further, it's important to note that some courses of study do not require a student visa. Those are:

■ an English or French language course that lasts a maximum of three months

■ non-academic, professional or vocational studies such as:
  – self-improvement, general interest courses such as arts and crafts
  – courses included in tour packages as a secondary activity for tourists
  – day care or nursery school programmes that are not a compulsory part of the elementary school system.

You have to get your student permit before leaving to study in Canada. There are a few exceptions to this rule, but again, the nearest Canadian visa office is where to check for the most up-to-date information. There are also helpful foreign student guides on Immigration and Citizenship Canada website (see Useful Addresses).

The **letter of acceptance** from the educational institution is imperative. The college or university will decide if you meet its academic and language requirements and, therefore, you have to deal directly with the school itself.

If you are planning to study in the province of Quebec, you must apply directly to a Quebec Immigration Service Office to get both your visa and obtain a Certificat d'acceptation du Quebec (Quebec Certificate of Acceptance or CAQ). QIS offices serve citizens of France, Monaco, Austria, Lebanon, Syria, Mexico and Hong Kong. If you are a citizen of any other country, applications are made to the regional office covering the territory in which the educational institution is located, or for the Montreal area, to the 'Direction des services de l'immigration sociale et humanitaire'.

Again, there are exceptions that mean you do not have to apply for a CAQ. For more information and for addresses and phone numbers for all of the above types of offices, check Quebec's immigration website (see Useful Addresses). You can also get information at your local Canadian consular office.

You must not have a criminal record. If you decide to change schools or your course of studies, you will have to reapply to the new educational institution and for another student visa but you can do so from within Canada.

Health insurance

Canada does not cover medical costs of foreign students. In some cases, the educational institution itself will have a health insurance programme for foreign students, with the premium included in their student fees (however it's not cheap, often several hundred dollars). Some of those plans cover dental insurance, some don't. But if the university does have such a plan, it is compulsory to enrol unless you can prove you have cover with another insurer. And in Quebec, with few exceptions, it is compulsory even if you do have cover. University health insurance usually has options for family plans if an international student has a spouse and/or children with them in Canada.

If the province does have cover, universities can often provide additional cover for medication, ambulances and dental work. The provinces that do have some form of health care cover for foreign students are:

- British Columbia: three-month waiting period before you are covered by the B.C. Medical Plan and the B.C. Hospital Insurance Plan. Must have own insurance for that time. Study period must last more than six months. $54/month for a single student.

- Alberta: the Alberta Health Care Insurance Plan covers foreign students on study permits that will last at least 12 months. It's free but foreign students have to apply within 90 days of arrival.

- Saskatchewan: apply and register through the International Student Office. A card will be issued within a month. Optometrists, dentists, medication and ambulances are not covered. No charge for cover. Conditions that apply are arrival in Saskatchewan directly from your country of origin and not having been in another Canadian province for longer than three months.

- Manitoba: covered under the international students health insurance plan (MISHIP). Automatically enrolled with student registration. Annual cost is $456 for a single student, as long as the proposed plan of study is for more than six months. You pay the fee to the university along with tuition. The university then pays the province.

- Quebec: citizens of certain countries (Denmark, Finland, France, Luxembourg, Norway, Portugal, Sweden), students participating in particular scholarship programmes and students who also work in Quebec can apply for Quebec Medicare.

- Nova Scotia: you can apply to enrol in the provincial plan if you are in the province for more than 13 months and are not absent for more than 31 days that whole time. Cover doesn't begin until the first day of your 13th month, so you are responsible for your own insurance for the first 12 months.

In the case of the above provinces, even though they allow cover under their health plans, it is probably a good idea to get travel insurance for when you first arrive to cover the first few days, weeks, or months of your stay.

Exchanges

There are formal exchange programmes orchestrated by non-governmental organisations (NGOs) but the majority of student exchanges are done by the individual institutions. If you know where you would like to study, contact the schools in that province or city and see what exchange programmes they offer. Check with your own university or college to see if it has any special agreements with particular schools in Canada.

Working

Foreign students are now allowed to work while in Canada. First, if the work is an essential and integral part of your study, it is allowed. This does not include accountants, medical interns and medical residents. It is permitted if it is related to an approved research or training programme. International full-time students can work at jobs that are on the campus of the school they attend. Canadian universities and colleges have student centres, athletic centres, bars and restaurants on campus that provide employment opportunities for students. Students can work off-campus for up to 20 hours per week during academic sessions, and full time during scheduled breaks. Students have to apply for a work permit to do so, however, and they have to be enrolled at a participating institution. See www.cic.gc.ca for a list of such institutions. Once you finish your study in Canada, you can get a three-year open work permit.

See Chapters 3 and 7 for more about work permits.

9

Driving in Canada

Driving in Canada can be both a pleasure and a challenge. For people from smaller countries, it can be quite an adjustment to drive in a country that spans six time zones. Canadians won't think twice about driving for hours to a destination for a mere weekend away — or even just for day excursions. With long, open roads and often spectacular scenery, driving in Canada can be a liberating and magnificent feeling. At the same time, city driving can be anything but liberating and remaining patient is not easy for anyone, not just newly-arrived immigrants and visitors. Knowing what to expect can go a long way to making the whole experience a lot easier.

PROVINCE TO PROVINCE

Canada's roads are fairly decent, although the ice and snow in the winter and heat and humidity in the summer can wreak havoc on the roads of some of the most populous cities which is why there are always ongoing roadworks. City roads are fairly wide since most cities were planned for automobiles, not like the more historic cities of

Europe. Cities like Quebec City and parts of Halifax are exceptions to this. Most roads are well marked, although if you don't read French, you may have difficulty in Quebec where French-only signs exist.

City driving

If you come from a big city like London, New York, New Delhi or Sydney, you may find cities like Toronto or Vancouver quite tame, but by Canadian standards traffic in big cities is chaotic and every year it seems to get worse. However, most cities are planned on a grid system, which makes them fairly easy to navigate. At the same time, downtown sections are usually made up of many one-way streets to help with traffic flow, which can see even the best navigators end up going in circles. Roundabouts are, for the most part, novel entities. Since most streets run north, south, east and west, junctions are controlled by traffic lights. Rush hour (from about 7am to 9am, and 4pm to 6pm) is to be dreaded, especially when there are road closures due to perpetual repairs. People can get into bad tempers, but there are relatively few cases of real 'road rage' in Canada. Some cities, such as Toronto, are busy at all hours except the very early morning. Montreal is known for its daring and aggressive drivers.

Rural driving

Some country driving, like that in the Prairies, is flat, straight and very boring, but in other parts roads can wind endlessly. Either way, it's important to pay attention and stay alert. Wildlife, poor visibility and other sleepy drivers can make rural roads treacherous. On gravel roads you need to be aware of dust and flying stones from other cars and trucks. One of the most important things is to try not to drive longer distances than you can manage in a short period of time, especially at night. You may be eager to get somewhere, but many drivers get into trouble when they ignore their increasing drowsiness.

Travelling on highways and freeways

The main routes in and out of the big cities are usually high-speed, multi-lane freeways (also called expressways or highways). In Britain such routes are called motorways and in mainland Europe they are known as autobahns, autoroutes and autostradas. A few of Canada's expressways charge a toll, the incentive to use them being less traffic. Most major arteries are well lit.

Linking towns and cities across Canada are highways that stretch for miles and miles. The recently upgraded ones near cities have three to four lanes on either side, but once you get to more rural areas there is usually only one lane on either side, sometimes with the odd passing section when it expands to two lanes for a short distance.

Canada has about 24,500 km of highways. The **Trans Canada Highway**, which runs from St John's, Newfoundland to Victoria, British Columbia, is a whopping 7,306 km, the longest in the world. Along most main highways are service stations that include one or more restaurants, rest room facilities and a gas (petrol) station. But for driving in more out-of-the-way areas drivers are advised to bring extra gasoline, food, water, warm clothing in winter and a cellular phone. Music tapes or CDs could also be useful for when you are travelling in rural areas where radio station options are limited.

Deer crossing

In some areas, alongside the usual road signs warning of sharp bends or rock avalanches, there are signs alerting drivers to beware of certain wildlife that roams nearby. It's not just to protect the animals; deer, elk and moose can be a real hazard for cars and their drivers. They often get mesmerised by car lights and stand frozen in the path of your car, or can bolt across the road out of nowhere. If you hit one of these large animals, especially a moose, you can be killed. Smaller animals like racoon, squirrels or skunks aren't a danger, but you won't enjoy the smell if you hit them, and it's never nice to think you've killed an animal.

KNOWING THE RULES OF THE ROAD

In contrast to the other Commonwealth countries, Canadians drive on the right-hand side. That means that the lane to the right is the slowest and the one on the left is the passing lane. Seatbelt-wearing is compulsory throughout the country.

Car seats for children are also mandatory. For babies less than 9 kilograms and under one year of age, the car seat must be rear-facing. Forward facing car seats are for children between 9 kilograms and 18 kilograms who are older than a year. Car seats must always be placed in the back seat. If your child is under eight years of age and/or less than 36 kilograms and/or shorter than 145 centimetres, they must use a booster seat.

Some rules vary from province to province and you will need to familiarise yourself with the particular rules of the province you're staying in. For example, on the island of Montreal it is illegal to make a right-hand turn on a red light.

Each province enforces a point system whereby certain driving offences result in the loss of a specified amount of points from a base amount. If a driver has lost a large amount of points, he or she may be called in for an interview or may get his or her licence suspended automatically. When a driver loses all his or her points, the licence is usually taken away for a certain period of time.

Keeping to speed limits

Speeding is a big problem in Canada where impatient drivers take advantage of the wide, open roads. There have been numerous graphic advertising campaigns launched as an attempt to point out the tragic results of speeding. Nevertheless, it continues to happen and there are stiff fines for those who are caught. If you are used to the imperial system, it might take some time to get used to the metric system employed in Canada. Don't make the mistake of interpreting a sign that says '90' to mean 90 mph! The speed limit on highways is usually 100 km/h (60 mph) and in cities and towns it is usually 40–50 km/h (25–30 mph) or less.

Drunk-driving

Drunk-driving, called drink-driving in countries such as Britain and Australia, is a serious offence. The legal blood-alcohol limit is 0.08, or 80 milligrams of alcohol per 100 milligrams of blood. If you're caught with more than that while driving, you have committed a criminal offence that can lead to licence suspension, hefty fines and even jail. Killing someone while driving when drunk is considered a form of murder and carries with it a maximum jail sentence of 14 years. However, it should also be noted, that while it's not a criminal offence, having a blood-alcohol count of more than 0.05 (and less than 0.08) will also be punished with sanctions, such as licence suspension and/or fine.

One method of catching impaired drivers is random breath testing. It is an offence to refuse a breathalyser test. Some provinces have graduated licensing so that in the first year of driving there is a zero tolerance policy – a driver caught with a higher than 0.0 level will end up with a suspended licence for a prescribed period of time. This policy is an attempt to deter younger people from driving under the influence of alcohol since a leading cause of death of teenagers is car accidents.

Making way for pedestrians

Unlike in some countries, where at unmarked crossways pedestrians run hurriedly to get out of a car's way, Canadians take their time crossing a road. It's not because they're trying to provoke you; it's because pedestrians have the right of way – everywhere. So even though jay walking is illegal, if you hit a person who is doing so you're in big trouble. There used to be an advertising campaign aimed at pedestrians that said, 'You're right: Dead right' in an attempt to emphasise that people should not be careless when crossing just because it's a car's duty to stop. As in many countries, in Canada there is special signage to indicate when children, the elderly and the blind might be crossing, so that drivers take extra care. Another thing to note is that when a stationary school bus has its red lights flashing, you must stop regardless of what direction you are driving. The flashing lights mean children are getting on and off.

DRIVERS' LICENCES

Regulations vary from province to province in terms of how long a driver can drive on a valid foreign licence before having to seek a local licence. This time period is usually 90 to 120 days for a new resident. As a tourist, however, this period of grace is usually the full six months, because a tourist visa is temporary. You can also obtain an International Driver's Permit from your home country that is valid for one year.

When it comes time to get a local licence, it varies from province to province in terms of the requirements. Provinces such as Ontario, Quebec and Prince Edward Island have graduated licensing which means there are different levels of licences. A lower level licence is the first stage for a new driver and usually includes restrictions on night driving and/or blood-alcohol limits. Once a driver passes that level, he or she takes the test for the next level and eventually becomes a fully entitled driver. There are fees involved at all testing stages of these licensing programmes.

Some provinces do not require any re-testing and you can make a direct exchange with your foreign licence for a local one, although there may be an age requirement or you might have to have a certain number of years' driving experience. Some provinces require both written and road tests and the amount of provable driving experience you have will determine at what level you begin your testing (i.e. in the graduated licensing programmes). Licences are usually good for three to five years and renewing it only requires a fee and a new photo being taken, not a re-test of the driver road exam. However, if a licence is left to lapse, a new written and road test is required.

Each province has its own ministry of transport that can provide information on that province's requirements and advise you on your own particular situation.

OWNING A CAR

In 2007 there were 20.6 million registered motor vehicles in Canada. The main cities have public transport systems, but many people feel a car is necessary for travelling longer distances, especially if they live in the suburbs or a rural area.

Buy it in Canada or bring your own?

There are stiff restrictions on foreign cars (those made outside either Canada or the US), so you may find it completely impractical or even impossible to import your own. According to the **Motor Vehicle Safety Act and Regulations**, all vehicles imported into Canada must comply with Canadian safety standards. For the most part, foreign cars do not comply and cannot be modified to comply. This is not a case of the driver's side being opposite to those in Canada; that is not an issue. Usually it comes down to something like the seatbelt anchorage point being in the wrong place. Cars older than a *full* 15 years are exempt from this law, as are buses manufactured before 1 January 1971. Cars bought in the United States can often be modified, if necessary, to meet Canadian safety standards unless they have been already altered to fit another country's requirements. Vehicles that have been designed, built, tested and certified to meet either all of Canada's standards or all US standards might be allowed in if they come with a 'statement of compliance' label affixed by the original manufacturer (as long as the car has not been altered since it was made and the manufacturer's certification has been maintained).

Visitors and tourists, however, can bring in a motor vehicle temporarily without complying with the Canadian safety regulations as long as the car is used exclusively by a person who is a visitor or a person passing through Canada to another country. People who are coming to Canada on a work permit or student visa are considered visitors in this regard. You can't, however, sell or dispose of such a vehicle while in Canada.

Even if your car meets the requirements, it must go through customs and is subject to duty, which may be more expensive than you think. Servicing a foreign car can be costly because of the lack of parts. To determine the suitability of your car contact Transport Canada (see Useful Addresses).

Buying new

If you come from a country with a currency that trades strongly against the Canadian dollar, buying in Canada might be a good idea. The recent surge in the Canadian dollar against the American dollar, however, has lured some people to buy in the US and import into Canada. Even with duties and the cost of modifications, some vehicles are still cheaper if bought south of the border.

Prices in Canada range widely depending on the brand and features of the car. Lowest prices for a new car are around $12,000 for something like a small hatchback. Mid-size cars are usually in the $20,000 to $40,000 range. Top-end cars are pricey to buy and to take care of. Right now, the auto industry in North America is in trouble and there are definitely deals to be found. Eco-friendly (smart cars, hybrids and electric cars) and fuel-efficient vehicles are also becoming very popular.

Buying used

Buying a used vehicle is also an option. Auto trading magazines and the classified advertising sections of the newspapers are the best places to search. New car dealers also sell used cars, although the increase in accountability of a dealer usually comes at a higher price. The advantage of a used car is that the major portion of depreciation has already taken place, but you may end up sacrificing having a warranty in the process. It's extremely important that you get a qualified mechanic to check the car to ensure it's not a money pit waiting to happen.

Leasing

Leasing-to-own is one of the most popular options now because many people can't commit to buying a car outright. A deposit of a few thousand dollars is usually required and then a monthly payment is agreed upon, with interest. After a certain period of time you have the option of buying the car by paying the remainder of the price or trading in the car for another, newer car (and getting a new lease). The downside to leasing is if you cannot afford to buy it, or choose not to buy the car, when your option to do so comes up, the deposit and monthly payments are lost money. However, because leasing is so popular, dealership competition means that there are some very cheap leases that make economical sense. And for those who own their own business and use the car mostly for that business, lease payments can be used as an income tax deduction (as a business expense).

Things to take into account

Remember that cars have a shorter life span in Canada because of salt put on the roads in the winter. Rust can develop before you know it. Cars last longer on the mild West Coast. You will probably have to invest in a pair of winter tyres or at least some all-season radials. In the coldest regions you may have to 'plug in' your car overnight to prevent it from freezing up. The device is called a block heater and can be purchased and installed at most repair garages. If you think you will need a car, but not often enough to spend the money to buy one, there are companies that offer car sharing services for a monthly or yearly fee.

Finally, Ontario has a 'drive clean' programme that began in Toronto and Hamilton and has now expanded to south western and eastern Ontario. The programme requires an emission test every two years. If your car fails, you must pay for whatever service repairs are needed to get your emissions to a prescribed limit.

INSURING AND REGISTERING

Insurance is mandatory. As a foreigner (unless you are American) you will be considered an inexperienced driver unless you can prove your driving experience or there is a reciprocal agreement between the province and your country (e.g. Ontario and Japan). Insurance rates are highest for inexperienced drivers, drivers under 25 and in general young male drivers. Rates are also dependent on the age and make of the car, and the city you live in (major metropolitan areas are more expensive than smaller cities). The cost of insurance ranges widely, but generally you're looking at $880 to $2,500 a year.

Registration with the provincial registry of motor vehicles office is also mandatory and includes an annual fee of $53 to more than $255 depending on the province, and the city in which you live.

JOINING MOTOR ASSOCIATIONS

The Canadian Automobile Association (CAA) provides 24-hour emergency roadside assistance for any trouble you may have from locking your keys in the car to a flat tyre or complete breakdown. Many people find the annual membership fee (ranging from $55 for basic services to $120 for premium services) worth the money, especially if they own an older car or drive long distances.

Some car dealers offer their own roadside assistance as part of the sale package.

There is no obligation to buy any such plan or association. If your car breaks down or you lock your keys in the car, you can pay for a tow truck or service person to come and help at that time.

GASOLINE

Also known as petrol in Europe, gasoline (gas – or gaz in Quebec) varies in price across the country. You'll find higher prices in the far north and the east, especially in Quebec. Prices often inexplicably rise before weekends and holidays and you will see this noted in newspapers from time to time. Gasoline is sold by the litre.

Despite heavy competition between gasoline companies, price wars are rare. In fact, at an intersection with two competing stations, the prices are likely to be close if not identical and to rise and fall together. Most stations are self-serve but there are full-serve options as well.

USING OTHER TRANSPORT

As mentioned before, major cities have some form of public transport, such as buses, streetcars (trams), light rail and underground train systems. Montreal and Toronto are the only ones with underground trains, called the Metro in Montreal and the Subway in Toronto. They also have commuter trains serving the suburbs and outer regions. If you live in the city core, you may not need a vehicle; for longer trips there's the option of renting a car.

For long-distance travel Canada has a bus system, such as Greyhound or Voyageur Colonial, that serves major centres as well as some rural ones. A bit more expensive but faster is VIA Rail that connects major centres across Canada. Even pricier is flying, although it's also the most common method of travel for long distance in Canada, since the country is so big.

Canada has one major and several smaller airlines. The industry in Canada has been in turmoil over the last several years. Canada's second major airline, Canadian Airlines went bankrupt and was taken over by Air Canada – now the country's only national airline serving major and minor centres in Canada and the US and major cities worldwide. However, in 2003 Air Canada filed for bankruptcy protection, emerging from that 18 months later. And now in recent months there are rumours the airline is in trouble again.

Canada 3000, formerly Canada's biggest charter airline, went bankrupt after the September 11 terrorist attacks in the US. Since then, domestic discount carrier JetsGo also went under. Can Jet recently downgraded itself from a scheduled airline to a charter airline. And an upstart airline, Zoom, which launched in 2002, collapsed in the summer of 2008 due to skyrocketing fuel costs. Hundreds of passengers were stranded in the UK and in Paris.

One success story is Porter Airlines, which flies between major cities in Ontario, Quebec and the north-eastern US. It's based at the Toronto Island airport and has major plans to expand at the time of writing. And then there's Air Transat, a well-established charter airline specialising in holiday packages.

Domestically, Air Canada's biggest competitor is West Jet, which started in the west but has rapidly expanded to serve many cities in Canada and the US. Of course, there are also small, regional airlines such as Bearskin Airlines and Central Mountain Air. Even with competition, airfares are not as cheap as they are in the UK, Europe or Australia. Beware: a flight from Toronto to Vancouver can cost as much as or more than one from Toronto to the UK.

Not unlike elsewhere in the world, the September 11 attacks led to tighter security at airports and other ports of entry to Canada. To pay for higher security costs at airports, the government instituted a security fee for all passengers that currently sits at $17 for international flights. There is a lower fee for domestic flights between airports that have benefited from investments in security.

And, of course, there are other fees that make flying expensive: fuel surcharges, airport improvement fees, insurance surcharges, etc.

Because Canada has so many bodies of water within its boundaries and on three of its borders, marine travel is by no means obsolete. Because of the islands on the West and East Coasts, ferries and cruises are particularly popular there.

10

Having Fun

After a long winter Canadians like to make the most of their summers by enjoying activities in the great outdoors. With such ready access to nature, Canadians are blessed with a multitude of choices. And even though hibernation in winter is a cosy prospect, six or more months of colder weather is not enough to stop a real Canuck from playing outdoors. Some 4.4 million Canadians, 15 years or older, participate in organised or club sports. Arts and cultural events are alive and well too. When it comes to relaxing and kicking back, Canadians have some unique ways of doing so.

ENJOYING SPORTS AND RECREATION

You don't have to be an Olympic athlete to enjoy sports in Canada. With so much nature right at the doorstep, all you need to do is step outside. There are fun, recreational and competitive leagues for any sport you can think of. Schools have physical education classes as well as sports teams, universities have recreational and competitive teams and many companies have office teams. Canada has had its share of shame with doping scandals, but it has also been a leader in the fight against doping in sport. It is ranked among the top 15 countries as a sporting nation.

Canada has hosted almost every major international sporting competition: the Summer and Winter Olympics, Commonwealth Games, Pan-American Games and World University Games and FIFA Under-20 World Cup.

Ice and snow

When most people think of winter sport in Canada they think of hockey. Although lacrosse is Canada's official national sport, hockey is by far the favourite spectator sport and one that is played recreationally by kids and adults alike. More than 450,000 young people participate in organised hockey leagues and many more play on frozen lakes, outdoor rinks and in the streets.

Hockey is not the only winter sporting activity. There's also ice-skating, speed-skating, figure-skating, tobogganing, ice-climbing, downhill-skiing, cross-country skiing and curling, to name a few.

Spring, summer, autumn

Many people probably don't even think of warm weather when they think of Canada, but if you ask Canadians what some of their favourite sport activities are they will cite swimming, baseball, tennis and track. Granted most outdoor sports can be, and are, accommodated indoors, but when Canadians can play them outside, they will. Some favourites, other than those mentioned already, are: soccer (European football), field hockey, lacrosse, basketball, triathlon, rock climbing, surfing, sailing, cycling, hiking, ultimate frisbee, golf, rugby, football (Canadian style) and horseback riding.

Summer days seem especially and wonderfully long because of daylight savings time. On the second Sunday in March, everyone (except for most of Saskatchewan) sets their clocks forward by one hour. It has the effect of making the daylight stretch well into the evening in the summertime and makes it perfect for outdoor activities. However, in the autumn (from the first Sunday in November), the clocks go back by an hour again.

Participating in amateur and professional sport

Olympics

Every four years Canada sends its best athletes to the Olympics. Canadians have excelled in sports like figure skating and skiing, but you may be surprised to learn that it is a leader in synchronised swimming, rowing and horse show jumping as well. Unfortunately, like in the UK, athletes and their coaches have long complained of underfunding and a lack of support from the government.

Canada has hosted a few Olympics, the most recent being the 1988 Winter Games in Calgary. Vancouver will serve as host for the 2010 Winter Olympics.

Hockey

Canada has six teams in the National Hockey League (NHL): Vancouver, Calgary, Edmonton, Toronto, Ottawa and Montreal. There used to be teams for Winnipeg and Quebec City, but monetary problems drove those teams to move to the United States. In fact, when the Colorado Avalanche, which used to be the Quebec Nordiques, first moved to Colorado, most of the names on the back of the players' jerseys were French.

In coming to Canada, it is important that you understand how entrenched hockey is in the psyche of Canadians. Even those who are not fans feel possessive of it as a Canadian sport. Canadians aren't well known as nationalists, except when it comes to hockey. It has been difficult for Canadians to see teams proliferating in the US as the Canadian teams struggle because of expanding player salaries and a low Canadian dollar. When Canadian hockey hero Wayne Gretzky retired from the sport in April 1999, it was a day of mourning for Canadians, even though he played most of his career for American teams. In fact, the day in 1988 when he was first traded to an American team from the Edmonton Oilers is called 'The day Canada stood still'.

However, Canada's hockey confidence was given a huge boost recently when in the 2002 Winter Olympics in Salt Lake City, both the women's and men's hockey teams won gold against the US teams. Canadians, ignoring cold temperatures, spilled out into the streets of every city across the country in celebration. In 2006, the women's team won gold again at the games in Turin.

Although there are more American teams than Canadian ones, the majority of NHL players are Canadian. The NHL hockey season runs from October to June when it concludes with the playoffs for the Stanley Cup, a trophy symbolising hockey supremacy in North America.

In addition to Olympic competition, international competitions include the World Junior Championships, the World Championships and the Canada Cup.

Basketball

Not many people know it was a Canadian who invented basketball, especially as it remains a sport dominated by Americans through the National Basketball Association (NBA). Canada has only one NBA team, the Toronto Raptors. Its Vancouver team, the Grizzlies, recently moved to Memphis due to financial woes (and poor fan turnout). The Raptors are relatively popular, even if they haven't fared all that well in the standings. The basketball season runs roughly parallel to the hockey season, also culminating in a playoff championship series.

Soccer

While Canadians don't go nearly as mad for soccer as Europeans do, it is gaining popularity, both for women and men. The 2002 FIFA Women's World Cup for under 19-year-olds was held in Edmonton and attracted record crowds, more than 25,000 people at some games. The Canadian team won silver. In the summer of 2007, several Canadian cities hosted the men's FIFA Under-20 World Cup. FIFA considered it one of its most successful tournaments ever with most games selling out.

Canada's women's team fares quite well internationally, but the men's national team rarely qualifies for the high profile FIFA World Cup tournament. That's probably why Canada's best players continue to play in Europe rather than at home. In fact, Canada's most famous soccer export, Owen Hargreaves, plays for England thanks to dual citizenship.

However, soccer is one of the most popular sports for both boys and girls to play recreationally in Canada.

Football

Football in Canada is not what's called football in the rest of the world – that is soccer to Canadians. Football is the game with the oval-shaped dark leather ball being thrown about by individuals sporting massive padded equipment. In Canada the US-style game is played with a few modifications. The Canadian Football League (CFL) began as a league of only Canadian teams, and then managed to expand to include a couple of American ones. But now it's back to an all-Canadian line-up of teams. Canadian teams include Calgary, Edmonton, Regina, Hamilton, Montreal, Vancouver, Toronto and Winnipeg. They play for the Grey Cup at the end of the season.

Baseball

Again, this is an American dominated sport. Canada once had two teams, but now has only one, in Toronto. The Montreal Expos moved and became the Washington Nationals in 2004. The season begins in the spring and ends in October with the World Series championship. The name of the championship is a bit of a misnomer as the series is just North American. In 1992 and 1993 the Toronto Blue Jays won the World Series causing pandemonium in Toronto and even a trickle in the rest of Canada.

OUTDOOR RECREATION

Canada's geography lends itself naturally to 'outdoor rec'. Camping, both in summer and in winter, is a popular activity, especially for family trips. Canoeing is also a national pastime with its Native Indian roots. Even fishing can be done all year round. In the winter people go out on frozen lakes, place a wooden hut on the ice, drill a hole or two in the ice and cast a rod in the water. Such is the ritual of ice fishing. In the summer, fishing is a little bit more accessible. Canada is covered with walking and hiking trails. In fact, in the works is a project to build a continuous trail from one end of the country to the other. It's called the Trans Canada Trail and once completed it will be the longest recreational trail in the world, at almost 21,500 kilometres. It is being built by linking existing trails with new construction. It is projected that the trail will be 'substantially complete' by the autumn of 2010.

When you come to Canada you will hear a lot about 'cottage country'. It is quite popular to go 'up north' or 'to the country' in the summer and even the winter for one's vacation.

There, people either own or rent cottages (also called cabins, camps or lodges in different parts of Canada) that range from rustic accommodation to glamorous getaways. Often small towns that are relatively quiet most of the year come alive in the summer months, although some cottages are winterised and used all year. These towns are usually near a lake and outdoor recreation is centred on water sports like water skiing, boating, jet skiing, swimming and fishing. Hunting in some areas is also popular, and is allowed under certain conditions.

Dangers – or not really

Canada is fairly safe for those who like to spend their time outdoors, but there are things that you should be aware of. In terms of diseases, rabies has not yet been wiped out in Canada, although incidence rates are low and no human has ever died from rabies in Canada. The West Nile virus, a mosquito-borne disease, has crept into Canada from the US, having been found in animals (mostly birds) in every province but Newfoundland and Labrador. In the summer of 2007 there were 2,000 human cases, which was a record year. Twelve people died. But then in 2008 there were only 36 human cases and no deaths. While health officials credit better surveillance, pesticide and public education programmes, they caution that numbers could rebound with little warning.

On a less serious note, in the spring pesky black flies can drive you mad. They are tiny flies that bite, you don't feel it but you do bleed a bit. They also, annoyingly, get caught in your hair. Mosquitoes are probably more annoying because their bite itches and there's nothing worse than when you are camping and nearly asleep and you hear a faint buzzing around your ear. Then you know a mosquito is about to strike.

Aside from the above and from the odd bumble bee or sand gnat, there is not much to worry about regarding stings and bites as Canada has no poisonous spiders or insects. Canada does have the rattlesnake, which is poisonous, in Ontario, Alberta and British Columbia, but bites are rare (they're shy animals) and anti-venom treatment is available.

When people first come to Canada, they seem to worry a lot about bears. It's very unlikely you will see a bear in a major city. Bears usually live in wild areas. But, if you go camping in a National Park or live in the north, near forests or mountains, precautions are necessary. Keeping food sealed and stored away from where you sleep (tent, cabin etc.) and suspended high off a tree branch is the best idea. Whatever you do, don't feed them or try to get close-up photos of them and especially stay away from a mommy bear's cubs!

Other than that, there are just the pesky squirrels, racoons and mice. Don't feed them either and again, store food securely.

In the winter there's very little to bother the outdoor enthusiast, no matter what you hear about wolves and polar bears. It's highly unlikely you'll be camping anywhere near where they live.

Exploring National Parks

Thirty-seven National Parks exist in Canada in an attempt to protect and preserve the unique flora and fauna in those areas. As this book is written, there are plans to create more. Camping is allowed and sometimes canoes can be rented. Entrance fees vary from park to park. Banff is the oldest National Park, having opened in 1885. The most popular are probably Jasper, Banff, Cape Breton Highlands, Pacific Rim and the Rocky Mountain parks. Each province also runs its own system of parks.

Going to summer camp

A favourite pastime for Canadian children is to go to 'camp'. Some are specialised, such as equestrian, arts and crafts, gymnastics or sailing. Others are general outdoors camps that include canoe trips, arts and crafts, hiking, woodcrafts and swimming. Many of the general outdoors camps are girls-only or boys-only and most are sleepover camps where the kids stay overnight for a week or more.

Camps vary widely in terms of cost; the stay-away camps are usually the dearest. Kids who go back every summer sometimes opt to be counsellors in training (CITs) and then fully-fledged counsellors, but the pay is not outstanding (however, the leadership training is).

There are camps in the city, just outside the city and ones far, far away. There are day camps, overnight camps and camps for children with special needs. There are special camps for children from low-income families who otherwise would not be able to afford to go. Essentially, there is a camp for anyone who wants to go.

Patio time

It's pushing it a little to include patio culture under outdoor recreation, but Canadians like to think of it as such. Although Canada sees more cold than warm, its cafés, restaurants and bars are well equipped with patios for the summer months.

Canadians don't always wait until the summer to put them in use. As soon as the sun comes out and the snow starts melting, desperate Canucks will don whatever will keep them warm enough to be able to sit outside. When it finally does become warm, patios and sidewalk cafés thrive.

Many houses, and certainly most cottages, have porches, patios, balconies or decks for barbecues, sunbathing and parties. Canadian beer companies have long used fantasy patio culture in their commercials to promote their brand. They show beautiful people gathering in beautiful surroundings having a beautiful time all because of the beer they are drinking.

EXPLORING THE ARTS

Although Canada isn't hundreds of years old, it does have a lot to offer in the way of arts. Because it is so young there is a great deal of modern art and dance, and innovation in film and theatre. Most of the big cities have the typical fare of big musicals and plays, but smaller, independent productions are offered too. Even smaller towns and rural areas offer some form of theatre and it's often quite good.

Theatre

Many theatres struggle to stay alive monetarily, but nevertheless if you want to see a play there is much to choose from. Mainstream theatre, alternative theatre and large-scale musicals fill the marquees. Prices are across the board, from less than $20 for a play in a warehouse playhouse to $100 or more for a big name musical.

The famous Cirque du Soleil is a circus/theatre troupe that has found international fame with its amazing acrobatics and original acts.

The main theatre season is from November to May but in the summer there are dozens of festivals, both indoor and outdoor. Big cities and small towns alike hold music festivals (blues, jazz, folk, chamber music etc.) or offer theatre-in-the-park in the summertime. And then there are theatre offerings at the famous Stratford or Shaw festivals.

Music

Canadian musicians have done very well on the international stage, although some people don't know they're Canadian and mistake them for American.

Pop/rock/alternative

Okay, Celine Dion is not mistaken for being American very often. She is perhaps Canada's best known export. And maybe Bryan Adams and Nelly Furtado are known to be Canucks. Less identifiably Canadian are the Barenaked Ladies, Alanis Morissette, Sarah McLachlan, Jann Arden, Sum 41, Nickelback, Avril Lavigne, Kathleen Edwards, Hawksley Wortman, K-OS, Mobile and Our Lady Peace. This list is, of course, in no way exhaustive.

A couple of decades ago, Rush and The Guess Who also made it big. Newcomers arrive on the scene every week and time will tell whether they will be catapulted into fame like former unknown Alanis Morissette or the Barenaked Ladies. There are also names that are huge in Canada but relatively unknown beyond its borders. The Tragically Hip and Blue Rodeo are bands that are very popular with Canadians. They sell out wherever they go.

There are rock concerts all year long, but summer is when the concert season really heats up with outdoor venues and multi-act shows.

Country

Anne Murray is a household name and now Shania Twain is as well, although their interpretations of country music are very different. Country remains less popular in Canada than in the US, but it does continue to garner more fans every year. Other Canadian stars include kd Lang, Rita McNeil and Prairie Oyster.

Folk

This is probably the music for which Canadians are best known. Leonard Cohen, Joni Mitchell, Gordon Lightfoot and Neil Young are known throughout the world. Stars like Sarah McLachlan are lumped under pop music, but many feel her melodies are the 90s version of folk. Newcomers Kathleen Edwards and Sarah Harmer are reviving the genre.

Classical/opera/jazz

A number of cities have their own symphony orchestras. The name Glenn Gould is probably the best known among performers of classical music. Classical guitarist Liona Boyd is beloved for her music and voice. Canada might not have its own Vienna, but the Canadian Opera Company is known for the quality of its performances. In terms of jazz, Montreal's annual International Jazz Festival is world-renowned and other cities have followed suit. Canada is quite happy to claim jazz musician Oscar Peterson as its own.

Celtic

Based in the Atlantic Provinces, Celtic music is making a real comeback, as people seem to grow more nostalgic for their Irish and Scottish ancestry. The music is popular throughout the country as the Barra MacNeils, The Rankin Family, Natalie MacMaster and the Irish Descendants bring it a higher profile. Fiddler Ashley McIsaac is quite popular amongst the dance club crowd for marrying the traditional music with a dance beat/sound.

Dance

Modern dance abounds in Canada, but ballet is still a favourite. The National Ballet of Canada has been trying to reinvent itself lately, to mixed reviews, but it, along with the Royal Winnipeg Ballet and the Grands Ballets Canadiens, continues to enjoy international success.

Comedy

Canadians are known for their comedy. It's often joked that with our long winters, we have to have a sense of humour. A long list of Canadian comedians have made it big on the world stage, including Howie Mandel, Mike Myers, Rick Moranis, John Candy, Martin Short, Dan Ackroyd, Wayne and Schuster, Leslie Nielsen, Catherine O'Hara, Andrea Martin, Colin Mochrie, Jim Carey and Norm MacDonald, to name a few. Shows like *SCTV*, *Kids in the Hall* and *This Hour has 22 Minutes* have launched many of those comedians and others. Through the years, Canadian comedy careers have hit it big on New York's *Saturday Night Live*, and *In Living Colour*. And for the past 25 years, Montreal has hosted one of the biggest comedy festivals in the world: *Just for Laughs*.

Film

Films by the National Film Board seem to be better known outside Canada than within the country. The NFB creates animated, documentary and dramatic films. Canada does have a commercial film industry as well, but compared with the production power of its southern neighbour, Canadian cinema is small and relatively unknown. Some films, however, have become well known and/or internationally critically acclaimed (the two don't necessarily go hand in hand). *My American*

Cousin, Naked Lunch, Jesus of Montreal and *Night Zoo Water,* are well known outside Canadian borders as are many of Atom Egoyan's films (e.g. *The Sweet Hereafter* and *Felicity's Journey*). Unfortunately much of Canada's talent moves south. Director Norman Jewison, who directed such films as *Moonstruck* and *The Hurricane*, works in the United States, although he supports the Canadian industry in a financial and mentoring way. Screenwriter and director Paul Haggis (*Crash, Million Dollar Baby*) also works in Hollywood. Many actors find more opportunity and money down south after enduring relative anonymity in Canada.

However, many American production companies have preferred filming their productions on Canadian soil due to low production costs and the formerly low Canadian dollar. Both Toronto and Vancouver claim to be the 'Hollywood of the North' and Montreal is becoming popular for US film production too. But the rising Canadian dollar and new incentives south of the border are jeopardising the industry in Canada.

Most of the movies in the cinemas are American, but Canadian and international films can be seen in many of the independent theatres. American movies premiere in Canada at the same time as they first show in the US.

Many cities hold international film festivals. Toronto entertains the largest one, but Vancouver's and Montreal's are well attended too. Most festivals show a few mainstream upcoming movies, but the majority are independent productions that haven't been picked up by a distributor yet. During these festivals the streets are always crammed with limousines and people ogling for the stars to appear.

Native Indian art

Inuit art and Native Indian art are probably among Canada's most recognised art forms. They usually take the form of sculptures and carvings using materials like soapstone, ivory, bone, antler and wood. The subject and style of the art often depends on the geographic region in which the artist lives. Almost all work is done entirely by hand. If you find such art at a cheap price it's most likely a mass-produced copy. Native art can be very expensive.

More reasonably priced and perhaps more practical are the items of clothing the Inuit and Native artists create such as mukluks (moccasins), very thick knitted sweaters and parkas. They also do jewellery, bead work prints and paintings.

Literature

If Canadians are a little insecure about their lack of history when it comes to paintings or their international profile in film, one area where doubt should not exist is that of the writers Canada has produced.

Poetry

Who hasn't heard the poem *In Flanders Fields*? A Canadian soldier, John McCrae, wrote the moving poem in 1915 before he died in the war. Other well known poets are Leonard Cohen, Margaret Atwood and Gwendolyn McEwen. Dennis Lee is renowned for his poetry for children, found in his award-winning book, *Alligator Pie*.

Books

Alice Munro, Margaret Atwood, Robertson Davies, Mordecai Richler, Michael Ondaatje, Margaret Laurence, W O Mitchell, Farley Mowat, Carol Shields, Ann Marie MacDonald, Alistair MacLeod, David Adams Richards, June Callwood, W P Kinsella and Pierre Berton are just a sampling of the Canadian writers who have brought fame and pride to Canadian shores. These authors have written both full-length books and short stories, the latter being somewhat of a niche for Canadian writers.

Unfortunately Canadian publishing houses often struggle financially, which has made it difficult for up-and-coming writers to get backing to the same degree the well-established writers did when they started.

Festivals/readings

Promotion of Canadian and international literature is done through book festivals and public readings. Street festivals like Toronto's Word on the Street host all kinds of organisations from mainstream magazine companies to struggling academic journals to freedom of the press advocates. Many bookstores have started up in-house cafes and allow reading there without buying. Also, bookstores, both small and large host authors who read their works and those of others. Universities and independent bookstores also host such readings.

Painting

English and French Canadian artists date back to the 1700s. Much of the art was landscape painting. The Group of Seven was a group of seven artists whose style dominated Canadian art for 30 years (starting from just before WW1). Their work depicted eastern Canada. Emily Carr is also well known for her paintings of the west coast and Native Indian villages and totems. There continue to be many artists who have added to Canada's works, including modern and abstract.

The National Gallery in Ottawa is Canada's premier gallery, but there are art galleries and museums all across the country in major cities and small towns alike.

USING THE MEDIA

Perhaps due to Canada's perpetual inferiority complex or perhaps because of its multiculturalism (or because of both), international news is well covered in Canada. You will be surprised at how in touch with the world you will be. Even though Canadian news isn't front and centre in international papers, Canada does not retaliate in kind. Throughout the last recession, foreign bureaux were scaled back but things are bouncing back now. If you really want to read papers from home there are many news and magazine stores that sell international papers, albeit a day or two late. And, of course, there's always online papers and magazines if you get Internet access.

Newspapers

It's a tough time for newspapers in Canada and, in fact, in North America. For years the doomsday predictions that the Internet would kill newspapers seemed to be mistaken. But not so any more as readership and advertising revenues fall; some newspapers (community ones in particular) are folding or shrinking at the very least. Concentration of ownership hasn't helped matters, especially when the big corporations that own whole chains of newspapers get into financial trouble.

Canada has two national newspapers, the *Globe and Mail* and *The National Post.* The *Post* was created a decade ago by former media baron and former British lord, Conrad Black. But he sold it and all his other Canadian dailies and weeklies to the Winnipeg-based Asper family, who own Canwest Global Communications. Due to Canwest's current financial difficulties, the fate of the *Post* is unknown. The *Globe* is owned by CTV Globemedia. The principal shareholders are the Thompson family,

Torstar (which also owns the *Toronto Star* newspaper) and the Ontario Teachers' Pension Plan. CTV Globemedia also owns the Canadian Television Network (CTV). Major cities usually have more than one daily paper to choose from and smaller towns have their own dailies and/or weeklies as well. Alternative, independent weeklies are very popular in the big cities. News coverage is done with a good deal of objectivity, but more and more newspapers are becoming more overt in their ideologies.

Magazines

There are fewer Canadian magazines than there are American ones. Split-run magazines are those which originate in the US but that have some Canadian content, such as the Canadian edition of *Time*. But, Canadian magazines are of a high quality and there is still quite a variety to choose from, although it's hard for them to make money when competing with American magazines. Canada's oldest magazine, *Saturday Night*, is no longer published and a relaunch as a blog failed. However, new magazines do make a go of it from time to time, such as the *Walrus*, a Canadian attempt at its own version of America's *Atlantic Monthly*.

As well, there are many trade, speciality, fashion, news and literary magazines. Some of the mainstream and best-known ones are *Macleans, Flare, Chatelaine, Report on Business*.

Television

The Canadian Broadcasting Corporation (CBC) is the publicly-funded broadcaster that has stations all across the country doing national and regional coverage. It is also partly funded by commercials and this has been increasing due to government cutbacks. In addition to the CBC, there are several provincial public broadcasters, such as Knowledge in British Columbia, SCN in Saskatchewan and TVO and TFO in Ontario. The Canadian Television Network (CTV), the CBC's main competitor in terms of national coverage, is privately owned, as is the Global Television Network. Global was once just in southwestern Ontario, but it is now a national broadcaster, although not to the same degree as the CBC or CTV. Both CBC and CTV have 24-hour news channels in addition to their regular channels.

Until recently, Chum Media had eight local television stations across the country and 17 speciality stations. A major shakeup in Canada's television industry saw CTVglobemedia buy Chum Media's stations. The Canadian Radio-television

Telecommunications Commission (the CRTC, which regulates the television and radio industry) approved the deal when CTV agreed to sell Chum's Citytv stations to Rogers Telecommunications, but retain the A-Channel stations. Confused yet? Then, citing hard financial times, CTV went ahead and closed some of those A-Channel stations. The result is essentially fewer local stations serving their communities, something the CRTC was trying to avoid.

The CRTC also tries to enforce Canadian-content rules to ensure a certain amount of programming is Canadian. Right now the private broadcasters are lobbying to reduce the amount of Canadian content they have to show during prime-time evening hours. This despite some big hits recently, such as *Corner Gas* and *Being Erica*.

Shows that have done well that you may have seen in your own country are *The Littlest Hobo*, the *Degrassi* series, *Anne of Green Gables*, *The Road to Avonlea*, *Polka Dot Door*, *Due South*, *Fraggle Rock*, *Kids in the Hall*, *Little Mosque on the Prairie* and *Much Music*. CBC is notorious for its hard-hitting dramas and is also well known for its political satire comedy programmes.

However, the Canadian stations do import a great deal of American programming. In addition, Canadians have access through basic cable to many American channels including the main networks, and to North American speciality channels through satellite. Cable is relatively inexpensive compared with European countries. British dramas and sitcoms (Britcoms) are very popular and can be seen on TV Ontario, PBS (the American public broadcasting station), CBC (occasionally) and others. *Coronation Street* and *Eastenders* are both a season or two behind, however.

Canadian television also carries a variety of ethnic and culturally diverse programming and channels. OMNI TV is in BC, Manitoba and Ontario and carries shows in dozens of languages from Albanian, Romanian and Estonian, to Greek and German, to Cantonese and Punjabi. It also broadcasts news in dozens of languages. Digital cable and satellite television providers also offer ethnic channels from back home, whether you speak Arabic, Farsi, Italian, Tamil or one of more than two dozen languages.

Radio

Again, CBC is the national broadcaster on the radio with news, current affairs and music shows that represent all regions of Canada. CBC has both French and English stations as well as choices between information/talk stations and just classical music stations. Unlike its television counterpart, public radio has no commercials. After that it's up to the listener. Classical, jazz, multicultural, sports, rock, pop, alternative, dance, all-news and all-talk are just some of the radio station genres available in every major city. Those stations are owned by corporations (many were owned by Chum media and so are now owned by CTVglobemedia) that are focused on advertising revenue. Therefore, many stations are littered with commercials and have very repetitive music playlists. For some original sound you can try a student-run station. University radio often has a greater variety of music because their mandate is to appeal to all students. Canadian-content rules apply to radio as well but again, American music dominates. British music also gets its share of play, but often only the very big, mainstream names.

NIGHTLIFE

In the big cities there is plenty to do if you're looking for a little wining and dining. Restaurants offer all sorts of fare – no need to travel around the world for international cuisine. Pubs, bars, night clubs and comedy clubs usually cluster in downtown areas, but most suburbs have their own mini-selection too. Casinos are the latest rage with new ones being built left, right and centre by cash-strapped governments looking for revenue.

TAKING HOLIDAYS

Some public holidays are observed only in some provinces, but many are observed across the country. For people of religions other than Christianity, schools and employers must allow time off for religious observances that entail being at home or at a place of worship. Figure 13 gives the main holidays.

School summer holidays are from the end of June up to and including Labour Day (first Monday in September). For universities, exam periods usually finish at the end of April so university students often have four months off, usually to work to make money for the increasing tuition costs.

VISITING FAMOUS SITES

There is so much to see in Canada, whether you are just visiting, studying or actually living in the country. It is impossible to produce an exhaustive list, but there are some things that are simply must-sees.

Holiday	Date	Notes
New Year's Day	1 Jan.	
Valentine's Day*	14 Feb.	
Family Day	Third Monday in February	Ontario and Saskatchewan
St Patrick's Day*	17 Mar.	
Good Friday	Variable (April-May)	
Easter Monday	Variable (April-May)	All provinces, but day off only for government and elementary/secondary schools
Mother's Day	Second Sunday in May	
Victoria Day	Monday preceding 24 May	
Father's Day	Third Sunday in June	
Canada Day	1 July	
Civic Holiday	First Monday in August	Except Atlantic Provinces
Labour Day	First Monday in September	
Thanksgiving	Second Monday in October	
Halloween*	31 Oct.	
Remembrance Day	11 Nov.	All provinces, but day off only for banks and government
Christmas Day	25 Dec.	
Boxing Day	26 Dec.	

*No time off (except St Patrick's Day in Newfoundland). Celebrations only.

Fig. 13. The main public holidays.

In the west there are the Queen Charlotte Islands, Long Beach and, of course, the Rocky Mountains. Going to Banff, Jasper and Dinosaur National Park and attending the Calgary Stampede would make the most of any trip to Alberta. You can't understand how vast and flat the prairies are without driving across them. The C.N. Tower, still the tallest free-standing building in the world, Niagara Falls, Algonquin Provincial Park and the Parliament Buildings shouldn't be missed. Historic Quebec City is itself a wonderful site, as is Montreal with its mix of French and English culture. Newfoundland has Signal Hill and a ferry to France's island of Saint Pierre and Miquelon. New Brunswick offers the world's highest tides along the Bay of Fundy. Nova Scotia has the Bluenose II, Louisbourg and Cape Breton. A visit to tiny PEI would not be complete without a visit to the setting of the book *Anne of Green Gables* or the Confederation Room. The north is a haven for outdoor enthusiasts, but there's also Dawson City with its gold rush history.

SPEAKING THE LANGUAGE

English and French are the two official languages (but many immigrants speak their mother tongue at home and with friends). British English is the basis for Canadian

English and is evident in the spelling of words. It is hard to deny, however, that when spoken, Canadian English sounds much more like American English. To many it is indistinguishable but Canadians will tell you that it is only so to the untrained ear. The Canadian accent is more clipped and less drawled. Just listen for the 'ou' sound and you'll hear Canadians say 'out' and 'about' like 'oat' and 'aboat' while Americans drawl their 'ou' like an 'ow' sound.

Unlike most European countries, Canada does not have a whole host of dialects for each region. In Newfoundland, however, the accent is very distinct as is the vocabulary. The remaining Atlantic provinces have their share of inflections as do the Ottawa Valley and British Columbia. Canadians have developed their own words and Canadian dictionaries will reflect this by including the words. Of course, Canada's aboriginal people have dozens of languages, some which are thriving and others which are, sadly, dying out. And because of immigration, there are many foreign languages spoken in Canada. In 2006, 20 per cent of people said their mother tongue was something other than English or French. That being said, 98 per cent of people in Canada said they spoke one or both of the official languages. After English and French, the third largest language group is the Chinese languages.

If you learned French in France you will discover it is quite different from the French spoken in Canada, known as Quebecois (in Quebec) or Acadien (in New Brunswick, which is the only officially bilingual province). French Canadians will understand formal French, but you may take a little time to understand them. Many Francophones speak English as well, but in smaller towns and rural areas a majority speak French only. Federal government representatives and employees are supposed to be bilingual, although some are not.

KEEPING IN TOUCH

This chapter has been an attempt to educate on the more social aspects of Canadian life. Participating in the arts, sports or enjoying an evening out will help you meet other Canadians and feel more entrenched in a Canadian way of life. Social connections in Canada are also fostered through the telephone, much more so than in Europe and other countries because of cheap phone rates. You will most likely want to keep in touch with the people from where you came; traditional letters and mail is another method, but it is quickly being replaced by email.

Telephone

Welcome to the land of fierce long-distance rate competition. As the phone companies battle it out, the consumer benefits with lower and lower phone rates. In Canada there is a monthly fee for a basic phone line with additional charges for features like voicemail, call waiting and call display, but local calls are free – you can talk for as long as you like. Long-distance charges used to be high when there was a monopoly and Bell Canada was the only long distance provider. Now, with deregulation, you can pay as little as 5¢ a minute to the UK and 5¢ a minute for long-distance within Canada, depending on the long-distance provider you choose. A decent level of competition can be seen in the cellular phone industry. And now with the ability to make very cheap or even free international calls with Voice Over Internet Protocol (VOIP) on your computer, there is even more competition for your business than ever before.

Post and email

Canada Post is a Crown corporation and is often accused of being too expensive and inefficient, but it is reliable even if it's not too speedy. Letters within Canada can take three to five days, and overseas mail can take ten days to a couple of weeks depending on the destination. At the time of writing, a simple letter cost 54¢ to send within Canada, $1.65 for international destinations and 98¢ to the US. Canada Post has registered mail, special delivery and courier services as well. The corporation has seen a giant loss in letter business because of email. In 2007, nearly 73 per cent of Canadian households were connected to the Internet at home. Email, instant messaging and blogs have become common ways of communicating with friends, family and work colleagues. More than 19 million Canadians used the Internet for personal, non-business reasons in 2007. Internet cafés are common in every city and most companies equip their office staff with computers with Internet access.

Glossary

Anglophone. A person whose first language is English. Geographical areas can also be referred to as Anglophone.

Backpacking. A casual form of budget travel carrying one's belongings in a backpack (also known as a knapsack or rucksack). Often involves staying in hostels, finding temporary work and frequently moving to different cities and locations.

Canuck. The informal name for a Canadian, and especially, formerly, a French Canadian.

CEGEP. A junior college a person attends in Quebec after high school and before university.

Charter of Rights and Freedoms. An act entrenched in the Canadian Constitution that guarantees certain fundamental, democratic, mobility, legal, equality and language rights to the people of Canada.

Citizenship. All persons born in Canada are Canadian citizens at birth, with a few exceptions (one being the children of diplomats). Children born abroad to Canadian citizens are also automatically Canadian citizens. Landed immigrants can become Canadian citizens through a naturalisation process. Canadian citizens have the right to vote, run for office and to enter, remain in and leave Canada at their discretion. Only Canadian citizens can carry a Canadian passport.

Classifieds. Advertisements arranged under headings, such as 'rental accommodation', 'employment' and 'for sale' in a newspaper.

College. Post-secondary education, not as advanced as university.

Common law. Often called 'judge-made law', it relies on previous decisions made by the courts, called 'precedents'. Called 'common' because it applies to everyone, this law developed in England and is used in all provinces outside Quebec.

Confederation. Refers to the birth of Canada as a country on 1 July 1867 and also used to describe the events that led to Confederation.

Email. Electronic mail, or messages sent to and from individuals with addresses on the Internet system.

ESL. English as a second language.

Federal government. The government of Canada.

Football. A game played with an oval leather ball which is thrown, carried and kicked. Canadian football varies slightly from American football in that in the Canadian game there are three 'downs' (opportunity to get a touchdown, which amounts to 6 points) while in the US there are four 'downs'.

Francophone. Someone whose first language is French. Geographical areas can also be referred to as Francophone.

French Civil Code. Civil law relies on a written code of laws. Judges study the code to find the law that applies to the case at hand. Found in most European countries, it is also the law in Quebec.

GMAT. Graduate Management Admissions Test.

Governor General of Canada. Represents the Queen in Canada's federal government.

GRE. Graduate Record Exam.

Goods and Services Tax. (GST) A 7 per cent tax on most goods and services throughout Canada.

Health card. An identification card that enables individuals to use the public health care system.

High school. Post-secondary education, to be completed before college and/or university.

House of Commons. Elected body of Members of Parliament that fulfils much the same function as the House of Commons in Britain.

Humidex. A measure that combines 'humidity' and 'index'. Incorporated into the current air temperature (in the summer) to give a temperature reading of how hot it actually feels.

Igloo. A dome-shaped house of snow and ice.

Internet. The world-wide system of electronic communication via computer links.

Lieutenant Governor. Each province has a lieutenant governor who is appointed by the governor-general on the advice of the prime minister to be the Queen's official representative in the province. Duties are largely ceremonial.

LSAT. Law School Admissions Test.

MCAT. Medical School Admissions Test.

Medicare. Canada's national health insurance scheme carried out by the provinces with the goal of providing everyone with a similar level of medical care, regardless of their income.

Minister's Permit. The Minister of Immigration may issue a written permit authorising any person to come into or remain in Canada under special circumstances if that person cannot do so through ordinary methods.

Multiculturalism. The federal government's policy of recognising the customs and contributions of Canada's various ethnic groups.

Province. A geographical area within Canada (there are ten) that has some degree of self-government, much like English counties.

Résumé. Another term for a CV (Curriculum Vitae).

RRSP. Registered Retirement Saving Plan.

Sales tax. A tax added to the price of goods at the time of sale. Amount varies by province.

Senate. An appointed body that provides 'sober second thought' to proposed federal legislation, similar to the British House of Lords.

Social Insurance Number (SIN). A unique personal number required to work legally in Canada.

Skilled worker. An individual with a particular set of skills such as a trade or profession.

Soccer. The North American term for European football.

Social Security. The network of government programmes aimed at protecting the living standards of Canadians during periods of illness, injury, old age and unemployment.

SWAP. Student Work Abroad Program.

Territory. There are three territories in Canada, all of which are similar to the provinces in terms of having some degree of self-governance.

Visa Officer. The immigration official who deals with individual applications.

Wind-chill factor. A measure that takes into account the amount by which the wind cools the air in the winter. The resultant temperature measures how cold it really feels outside, not simply the air temperature alone.

Work permit. A visa issued by the Canadian High Commission that allows an individual to work in Canada for a specified period of time and for a particular employer.

Further Reading

ABOUT CANADA – GENERAL

National Geographic Countries Of The World: Canada, Brian Williams (National Geographic Adventure Press, 2007).

Canadian Global Almanac, 2005 Edition (John Wiley & Sons Ltd, 2005).

Canadians: A Portrait of a Country and Its People, Roy MacGregor (Viking Canada, 2007).

Canada and the British World: Culture, Migration and Identity, Phillip Buckner (UBC Press, 2006).

Culture Wise Canada: The Essential Guide to Culture, Customs & Business Etiquette, Graeme Chesters (Survival Books, Ltd, 2007).

The 2007 Annotated Immigration and Refugee Protection Act of Canada, Frank N. Marrocco and Henry M. Goslett (Thomson Carswell, 2006).

Canada In Afghanistan: The War So Far, Peter Pigott (Dundurn, 2007).

Canada and the Idea of North, Sherrill E. Grace (McGill-Queen's University Press, 2007).

Only In Canada You Say: A Treasury of Canadian Language, Katherine Barber (Oxford University Press, 2007).

HISTORY

The Story of Canada, Janet Lunn (Key Porter, 2007).

Canada's Prime Ministers: Macdonald to Trudeau – Portraits from the Dictionary of Canadian Biography, Réal Bélanger and Ramsay Cook (University of Toronto Press, 2007).

The Illustrated History of Canada, Craig Brown (Key Porter Books, 2007).

A Military History of Canada: Third Edition, Desmond Morton (McClelland & Stewart, 2007).

Victory At Vimy: Canada Comes of Age, April 9–12, 1917, Ted Barris (Thomas Allen Publishers, 2007).

Canadian History for Dummies, Will Ferguson (John Wiley & Sons, 2005).

The Canadian 100: The 100 Most Influential Canadians of the 20th Century, Jack Granatstein (McArthur & Co., 1998).

The Battles of The War of 1812: Adventures in Canadian History, Pierre Berton (Fifth House Books, 2006).

Klondike: The last great gold rush 1896–1899, Pierre Berton (McClelland & Stewart, 1994).

The National Dream: The great railway 1871–1881, Pierre Berton (McClelland & Stewart, 1989).

The Last Spike: The great railway 1881–1885, Pierre Berton (McClelland & Stewart, 1992).

EMPLOYMENT

Get the Right Job Right Now: Proven Tools, Tips and Technique From Canada's Career Coach, Alan Kearns (HarperCollins Canada, 2007).

The Canadian Hidden Job Market Directory, 6th Edition: Canada's Best Directory for Finding the Unadvertised Jobs, Kevin Makra (Sentor Media Inc., 2006).

The Canadian Student and Grad Job Directory, 12th Edition: Canada's Best Directory for Getting that Vital First Job, Kevin Makra (Sentor Media Inc., 2006).

Canadian Small Business Kit for Dummies, Margaret Kerr (John Wiley & Sons, 2007).

Starting a Successful Business in Canada, Jack D. James (Self-Counsel Press, 2006).

Canadian Directory of Search Firms (Mediacorp Canada Inc., 2005).

Who's Hiring (9th Edition): Canada's 5,000 Fastest-Growing Employers (Mediacorp Canada Inc., 2006).

Be Your Own Boss: The Insider's Guide to Buying a Small Business or Franchise In Canada, Douglas Gray (McGraw-Hill Ryerson Ltd, 2002).

EDUCATION

Multicultural Education Policies in Canada and the United States, Reva Joshee and Lauri Johnson (University of British Columbia Press, 2007).

Higher Education in Canada, Charles Beach (McGill-Queen's University Press, 2005).

State Support For Religioius Education: Canada Versus the United Nations, Anne F. Bayefsky (Brill Academic Publishers, 2006).

Foundations of Early Childhood Education: Learning Environments and Childcare In Canada, Beverlie Dietze (Pearson Foundation, 2006).

FINANCE AND ECONOMY

Tax Planning for You and Your Family 2007, Paul B. Hickey and Sandra Bussey (Thomson Carswell, 2006).

Tax Tips 2007 for Canadians For Dummies, Christie Henderson, Brian Quinlan, Suzanne Schultz and Leigh Vyn (John Wiley & Sons Canada Ltd, 2006).

Labour Market Economies, Dwayne Benjamin, Morley Gunderson and Thomas Lemieux (McGraw-Hill Ryerson Ltd, 2007).

History of Canadian Business, Tom Naylor (McGill-Queen's University Press, 2006).

History of the Canadian Economy, 4th Edition, Kenneth Norrie, Douglas Owram and J. C. Herbert Emery (Thomas Nelson, 2007).

Personal Finance for Canadians, Elliot J. Currie (Pearson Education Canada, 2007).

Personal Finance for Canadians for Dummies, Eric Tyson and Tony Martin (John Wiley & Sons, 2007).

TRAVEL/OUTDOOR

Canada Close Up: Canadian Festivals, Susan Hughes (Scholastic Canada Ltd, 2007).

Forgotten Highways: Wilderness Journeys Down the Historic Trails of the Canadian Rockies, Nickey L. Brink (Brindle & Glass Publishing, 2007).

Rough Guide to Canada (Rough Guides, 2007).

Fodor's Nova Scotia & Atlantic Canada, 10th Edition: With New Brunswick, Prince Edward Island and Newfoundland and Labrador (Fodor's Travel Publications, 2008).

Fodor's Canada, 28th Edition (Fodor's, 2006).

Fodor's Montreal and Quebec City 2007 (Fodor's, 2007).

Lonely Planet Canada, 9th Edition (Lonely Planet Publications, 2005).

Guide to Sea Kayaking in Lakes Huron, Erie and Ontario: The Best Day Trips and Tours, Sarah Ohmann (Globe Pequot Press, 2003).

Frommer's Canada: With the best hiking & outdoor adventures, Hilary Davidson, Paul Karr and Herbert Bailey Livesey (John Wiley & Sons, 2006).

CANADIAN MAGAZINES

Canadian Business, One Mount Pleasant Rd, 11th Floor, Toronto, ON, M4Y 2Y5. Tel; (416) 764-1200. www.canadianbusiness.com

Canadian Living, 25 Sheppard Avenue West, Suite 100, North York, ON, M2N 6S7. Tel: (416) 733-7600. www.canadianliving.com

Flare Magazine, One Mount Pleasant Rd, 8th Floor, Toronto, ON, M4Y 2Y5. Tel: (416) 764-2863. www.flare.com

Maclean's, One Mount Pleasant Rd, 11th Floor, Toronto, ON, M4Y 2Y5. Tel: (416) 764-1300. www.macleans.ca

Reader's Digest Canada, 1100 René-Lévesque Blvd W., Montreal, QC, H3B 5H5. Tel: (514) 940-0751. www.readersdigest.ca

Report on Business Magazine, 444 Front Street West, Toronto, ON, M5V 2S9. Tel: (416) 585-5499. www.theglobeandmail.com/robmagazine

Toronto Life, 111 Queen Street East, Suite 320, Toronto, ON, M5C 1S2. Tel: (416) 364-4433. www.torontolife.com

The Walrus Magazine, 19 Duncan Street, Toronto, ON, M5H 3H1. Tel: (416) 971-5004. www.walrusmagazine.ca

Useful Addresses

CANADIAN CONTACTS

Government/General

Canadian Bankers Association, Box 348, Commerce Court West, 199 Bay Street, 30th Floor, Toronto, ON, M5L 1G2. Tel: (416) 362-6092. Fax: (416) 362-7705. www.cba.ca

Canadian Firearms Centre, Ottawa, ON, K1A 1M6. Email: cfc-cafc@cfc-cafc.gc.ca (Website: www.cfc-cafc.gc.ca)

Canadian Food Inspection Agency (CFIA), Room 211 East, 59 Camelot Drive, Ottawa, ON, K1A 0Y9. Tel: (613) 225-2342. Animal Health Tel: (613) 225-2342. Fax: (613) 228-6631. www.inspection.gc.ca

Canada Revenue Agency, Public Affairs Branch, Connaught Building, 555 MacKenzie Avenue, 4th Floor, Ottawa, ON, K1A 0L5. Tel: (613) 957-3508 or 1-800-665-0354 (within Canada only). www.cra-arc.gc.ca

Ombudsman for Banking Services and Investments, PO Box 896, Station Adelaide, Toronto, ON, M5C 2K3. Tel: (416) 287-2877. Fax: (416) 225-4722. Email: ombudsman@obsi.ca (Website: www.obsi.ca)

Transport Canada, Place de Ville, Tower C, 330 Sparks Street, Ottawa, ON, K1A 0N5. Tel: (613) 990-2309. Vehicle Importation, Tel: (613) 998-8616. www.tc.gc.ca

Host programme 'service agencies'

Note: this is only a small selection; a full list can be found at: www.cic.gc.ca/english/newcomers/host.spo.asp

Association for New Canadians (St John's, NF). Tel: (709) 722-9680.

British Columbia and Manitoba have their own lists. For a full list of BC agencies go to: www.ag.gov.bc.ca/immigration/sam/agencies.htm

For more information on Manitoba settlement go to: http://www.gov.mb.ca/labour/immigrate/settlement/firstweeks.html

Calgary Catholic Immigration Centre. Tel: (403) 262-2006.

CultureLink (Toronto, ON). Tel: (416) 588-6288.

International Centre of Winnipeg. Tel: (204) 943-9158.

Kingston and District Immigration Services. Tel: (613) 548-3302.

London Cross-Cultural Learner Centre. Tel: (519) 432-1133.

Metropolitan Immigrant Settlement Association (Halifax, NS). Tel: (902) 423-3607.

Ministère des Relations avec les citoyens et de l'immigration (MRCI) (Montreal). Tel: (514) 864-9191.

MOSAIC (Vancouver, BC). Tel: (604) 254-9626.

Multicultural Association of Fredericton. Tel: (506) 455-7167.

Multicultural Council of Windsor-Essex County (Windsor, ON). Tel: (519) 255-1127.

Newcomer Information Centre, YMCA of Greater Toronto. Tel: (416) 928-6690.

New Home Immigration & Settlement (Edmonton, AB). Tel: (780) 456-4663.

North Shore Multicultural Society (Vancouver, BC). Tel: 604 988-2931.

Ottawa Carleton Immigrant Services Organization. Tel: (613) 725-5671.

Pacific Immigrant Resources Society (Vancouver, BC). Tel: (604) 298-0747.

PEI Association for Newcomers to Canada (Charlottetown). Tel: (902) 628-6009.

Regina Open Door Society. Tel: (306) 352-3500.

Saskatoon Open Door Society. Tel: (306) 653-4464.

Settlement & Integration Services Organization (Hamilton, ON). Tel: (905) 667-7484.

Housing

Canada Mortgage and Housing Corporation, 700 Montreal Road, Ottawa, ON, K1A 0P7. Tel: (613) 748-2000. Fax: (613) 748-2098. www.cmhc-schl.gc.ca

Canadian Real Estate Association, 200 Catherine St, 6th Floor, Ottawa, OK2P 2K9. Tel: (613) 237-7111. Fax: (613) 234-2567. www.crea.ca

Medical assessment information

Director, Health Programs (RNH), Citizenship and Immigration Canada, Jean Edmond Towers South, 14th Floor, 365 Laurier Avenue West, Ottawa, ON, K1A 1L1. Tel: (613) 941-5044. Fax: (613) 941-5043.

Business contacts

Business Development Bank of Canada, BDC Building, 5 Place Ville Marie, Suite 400, Montreal, PQ, H3B 5E7. Tel: (514) 283-5904. www.bdc.ca

The Canadian Chamber of Commerce, 360 Albert Street, Suite 420, Ottawa, ON, K1R 7X7. Tel: (613) 238-4000. Fax: (613) 238-7643. www.chamber.ca

Industry Canada, CD Howe Building, 235 Queen Street, Ottawa, ON, K1A 0H5. Tel: (613) 954-5031. www.ic.gc.ca

Credential assessment

Academic Credentials Assessment Service (Manitoba). Manitoba Labour and Immigration, Settlement & Labour Market Services Branch, 5th Floor, 213 Notre Dame Avenue, Winnipeg, MB, R3B 1N3. Tel: (204) 945-6300. Fax: (204) 948-2256. Email: immigratemanitoba@gov.mb.ca www.immigrate.manitoba.com

Canadian Information Centre for International Credentials, 95 St Clair Avenue West, Suite 1106, Toronto, ON, M4V 1N6. Tel: (416) 962-9725. Fax: (416) 962-2800. www.cicic.ca

Centre d'expertise sur les formations acquises hors du Québec (CEFAHQ), Ministère de l'Immigration et des Communautés culturelles (MICC), 255, boulevard Crémazie Est, 8e étage, Montréal, QC, H2M 1M2. Tel: (514) 864-9191. Fax: (514) 873-8701. Email: renseignements@micc.gouv.qc.ca (www.immigration-quebec.gouv.qc.ca/en/education/comparative-evaluation/index.htm)

Comparative Education Service, University of Toronto, 315 Bloor Street West, Toronto, ON, M5S 1A3 Canada. Tel: (416) 978-2190. Fax: (416) 978-7022. www.adm.utoronto.ca/contactus.htm

Foreign Credentials Referral Office, 365 Laurier Avenue West, Ottawa, ON, K1A 1L1. Email: credentials@cic.gc.ca (www.credentials.gc.ca)

International Credential Assessment Service of Canada, Ontario AgriCentre, 1, 100 Stone Rd West, Suite 303, Guelph, ON, N1G 5L3. Tel: (519) 763-7282. Fax: (519) 763-6964. Email: info@icascanada.ca (www.icascanada.ca)

International Credential Evaluation Service (ICES), 3700 Willingdon Avenue, Burnaby, BC, V5G 3H2. Tel: (604) 432-8800. Email: icesinfo@bcit.ca (www.bcit.ca/ices/)

International Qualifications Assessment Service (Alberta and Saskatchewan), 9th Floor, 108 Street Building, 9942–108 Street, Edmonton, AB, T5K 2J5 Tel: (780) 427-2655 Fax: (780) 422-9734. www.advancededucation.gov.ab.ca/iqas/iqas.asp

World Education Services-Canada (Ontario). 45 Charles Street East, Suite 700, Toronto, ON, M4Y 1S2. Tel: (416) 972-0070. Fax: (416) 972-9004. Email: ontario@wes.org (www.wes.org/ca/)

Employment contacts

Government

Human Resources and Social Development Canada, 5th Floor, Phase IV, 140 Promenade du Portqage, Gatineau, Québec, K1A 0J9. Tel: (819) 994-2603. Fax: (819) 953-7260. www.hrsdc.gc.ca

Agencies

Accu-Staff, 7755 Tecumseh Rd E., Windsor, ON, N8T 1G3. Tel: (519) 974-8888. Fax: (519) 974-6167. Email: www@accu-staff.com

Canadian Relocation Systems, 1–456 Gorge Road East, Victoria, BC, V8T 2W4. Tel: (250) 480-5543. E-mail: info@relocatecanada.com (www.relocatecanada.com)

Executrade, Suite 1600, Sun Life Plaza, 144-4 Avenue SW, Calgary, AB, T2P 3N4 Tel: (403) 252-5835. Fax: (403) 695-1795.

Multec Canada Ltd, Tel: (416) 244-2402. Fax: (416) 244-6883. www.multec.com

Robert W. Hort & Associates, Certified Placement Consultants, 225–620 Wilson Ave, Suite 230, Toronto, ON, M3K 1Z3. Tel: (416) 636-3933. Fax: (416) 636-8113. www.canadausemployment.com www.canadausemployment.co.uk www.canadausemployment.co.za

Attorney recruitment and placement

The Counsel Network, 1500 HSBC Building, 885 Georgia Street West, Vancouver, BC, V6Z 1G3. Tel: (604) 643-1755. Fax: (604) 575-9156. Email: headhunt.com. **Note**: offices in Calgary and Toronto as well.

Consultant firms

A. T. Kearney Executive Search, Box 68, Suite 2300, 20 Queen Street West, Toronto, ON, M5H 3R3. Tel: (416) 947-1990. Fax: (416) 947-0255. www.noinkinc.com

Education

Alberta Teachers' Association: http://www.teachers.ab.ca/

British Columbia College of Teachers: http://www.bcct.ca/default.aspx

Canadian Bureau for International Education, 220 Laurier Ave West, Suite 1550, Ottawa, ON, K1P 5Z9. Tel: (613) 237-4820. Fax: (613) 237-1073. www.cbie.ca/

The Canadian School Boards Association, L'Association Canadienne des commissions/conseils scolaires, Station D PO Box 2095, Ottawa, ON, K1P 5W31. Tel: (613) 235-3724. Fax: (613) 238-8434. E-mail: admin@cdnsba.org (www.cdnsba.org)

Ontario College of Teachers: http://www.oct.on.ca/

Society for Educational Visits & Exchanges in Canada, 57 Auriga Drive, Suite 201, Ottawa, ON, K2E 8B2. Tel: (613) 727-3832. www.sevec.ca

Teacher Certification information for all provinces: http://resource.educationcanada.com/certification.html

Newspapers

National

The Globe and Mail, 444 Front Street West, Toronto, ON, M5V 2S9. www.globeandmail.com

The National Post, 300–1450 Don Mills Road, Don Mills, ON, M3B 3R5. www.nationalpost.com

British Columbia

The Vancouver Sun, 200 Granville Street, Suite #1, Vancouver, BC, V6C 3N3. www.vancouversun.com

The Province, 200 Granville Street, Suite.#1, Vancouver BC, V6C 3N3. www.theprovince.com

The Times Colonist, Canadian Newspapers Co. Ltd, 2621 Douglas Street, Victoria, BC, V8T 4M2. www.timescolonist.com

Alberta

Calgary Herald, 215–16th Street S.E., P.O. Box 2400, Station M, Calgary, AB, T2P 0W8. www.calgaryherald.com

The Calgary Sun, 2615–12th Street N.E., Calgary, AB, T2E 7W9. www.calgarysun.com

The Edmonton Sun, #250, 4990–92nd Avenue, Edmonton, AB, T6B 3A1. www.edmontonsun.com

The Edmonton Journal, 10006 – 101 Street, Edmonton, AB, T5J 0S1. www.edmontonjournal.com

Saskatchewan

The Leader-Post, 1964 Park Street, Regina, SK, S4P 3G4. www.leaderpost.com
Star-Phoenix, 204 5th Avenue North, Saskatoon, SK, S7K 2P1.
  www.thestarphoenix.com

Manitoba

Winnipeg Free Press, 1355 Mountain Avenue, Winnipeg, MB, R2X 3B6.
  www.winnipegfreepress.com
The Winnipeg Sun, 1700 Church Avenue, Winnipeg, MB, R2X 3A2.
  www.winnipegsun.com

Ontario

The Toronto Star, 1 Yonge Street, Toronto, ON, M5E 1E6. www.thestar.com
The Toronto Sun, 333 King Street East, Toronto, ON, M5A 3X5.
  www.torontosun.com
Ottawa Sun, 6 Antares Drive, Phase III, Ottawa, ON, K2E 8A9. www.ottawasun.com
The Ottawa Citizen, 1101 Baxter Road, Ottawa, ON, K2C 3M4.
  www.ottawacitizen.com
Le Droit, 222–47 Clarence Street, Ottawa, ON, K1G 3J9.
  www.cyberpresse.ca/le-droit
Hamilton Spectator, 44 Frid Street, Hamilton, ON, L8N 3G3. www.thespec.com
The Whig-Standard, 6 Cataraqui St, Kingston, ON, K7L 4Z7. www.thewhig.com
The London Free Press, 369 York Street, London, ON, N6A 4G1. www.lfpress.com
The Windsor Star, 167 Ferry Strreet, Windsor, ON, N9A 4M5.
  www.windsorstar.com

Quebec

The Gazette, 1010 Ste. Catherine St West, Suite 200, Montreal, PQ, H3B 5L1.
  www.montrealgazette.com
Le Devoir, 2050 Rue de Bleury, Montreal, PQ, H3A 3M9. www.ledevoir.com
La Presse, 7 St-Jacob, Montreal, PQ, H2Y 1K9. www.cyberpresse.ca/actualities/
  regional/montreal
Le Journal de Montreal, 4545 Frontenac, Montreal, PQ, H2H 2R7.
  www.canoe.com/journaldemontreal
Le Journal de Quebec, 450 rue Bechard, Ville de Vanier, Quebec, PQ, G1M 2E9.
  www.lejournaldequebec.canoe.ca

Le Soleil, 410 blvd. Charest Is, CP 1547, Branch Terminus, Quebec, PQ, G1K 7J6 Canada. www.cyberpresse.ca/lesoleil

New Brunswick

Daily Gleaner, 12 Prospect Street, West Fredericton, NB, E3B 5A2. www.dailygleaner.canadaeast.com
The Telegraph-Journal, 210 Crown St, Saint John, NB, E2L 3V8. www.telegraphjournal.canadaeast.com
The Times & Transcript, 939 Main St, Moncton, NB, E1C 1G8. www.timesandtranscript.canadaeast.com

Newfoundland

The Evening Telegram, 1 Columbus Drive, PO Box 5970, St John's, NF, A1C 5X7. www.thetelegram.com

Nova Scotia

The Chronicle-Herald, 1650 Argyle Street, Halifax, NS, B3J 2T2. www.thechronicleherald.ca

Northwest Territories

Northern News Services Online: http://www.nnsl.com/index.php

The Yukon

The Whitehorse Star, 2149 2nd Avenue, Whitehorse, YT, Y1A 1C5. www.whitehorsestar.com

Nunavut

Nunatsiaq News, PO Box 8, Iqaluit, Nunavut X0A 0H0. www.nunatsiaq.com

INTERNATIONAL CONTACTS

Mailing addresses in brackets, if different from street address.

Embassies/Consulates

(For a complete list go to http://www.dfait-maeci.gc.ca/world/embassies/menu-en.asp)

The Canadian Embassy, Immigration Section, 35 Avenue Montaigne, 75008 Paris, France. Tel: 33-1-44-43-29-00.

The Canadian Embassy, Immigration Section, 19 Dong Zhi Men Wai Dajie, Chao Yang District, Beijing, 100600 China. Tel: 86-10-6532-3536.

The Canadian Embassy, Immigration Section, Kneza Milosa 75, 11000 Belgrade, Serbia and Montenegro. Tel: 381-11-306-3000, ext. 3341.

The Canadian Embassy, Immigration Section, Laurenzerberg 2, Vienna, 1010, Austria. Tel: 43-1-531-38-3000.

The Canadian Embassy, Immigration Section, Starokonyushenny Pereulok 23, Moscow 119002, Russia. Tel: 7-495-105-6090 or 7-495-105-6092.

The Canadian Embassy, Leipziger Platz 17, 10117 Berlin. Tel: 49-30-20-312-0.

The Canadian Embassy, Visa Section, 37-38 Akasaka 7-chome, Minato-ku, Tokyo, 107-8503, Japan. Tel: 81-3-5412-6200.

Consulate General of Canada, Immigration Section, 3000 HSBC Centre, 30th Floor, Buffalo, New York, 14203-2884, USA. Tel: 1-716-852-1247. (Note: also offices in Washington DC, Detroit, New York, L.A., Seattle.)

Consulate General of Canada, Immigration Section, Level 5, Quay West Bldg, 111 Harrington St, Sydney NSW, 2000, Australia. Tel: 61-02-9364-3000.
http://geo.international.gc.ca/asia/australia/about/menu-en.asp

Canadian High Commission, Macdonald House, 38 Grosvenor Street, London W1X 0AA. Tel: 0207 258 6600. Fax: 0207 258 6506. www.canada.org.uk
http://www.dfait-maeci.gc.ca/canada-europa/united_kingdom/menu-en.asp

Consulate General of Canada, Immigration Section, Tower One, Exchange Square, 12th Floor, 8 Connaught Place Central, Hong Kong (G.P.O. Box 11142), China. Tel: 852-2847-7555.

Canadian High Commission, Immigration Section, 1 George Street, #11-01 094145, (Robinson Road, PO Box 845, 901645) Singapore. Tel: 65-5854-5900.

Canadian High Commission, Immigration Section, 7/8 Shantipath, Chanakyapuri, (PO Box 5209), New Delhi, 110021 India. Tel: 91-11-4178-2000.

Business contacts

Canada/UK Chamber of Commerce, 38 Grosvenor Street, London W1K 4DP. Tel: (020) 7258-6578. www.canada-uk.org

Quebec Immigration

Bureau d'Immigration du Québec, Délégation générale du Québec 87/89, rue de la Boétie, 75008 Paris, France. Tel: 0-1-53-93-45-45. Fax: 0-1-53-93-45-40.

Bureau d'Immigration du Québec, Délégation générale du Québec, 46 avenue des Arts, 7ᵉ étage, 1000 Bruxelles, Belgium. Tel: 32-2-512-0036.

Police clearances

FBI Criminal Justice Information Services Division, SCU, Mod D-2, 1000 Custer Hollow Road, Clarksburg WV, 26306 USA.

Subject Access Office, Metropolitan Police, 10 The Broadway, London SW1H OBG, England.

Visa Clerk, Criminal Records Section, Level B3 NSW Police HQ, 1 Charles Street, Parramatta, NSW 2150, Australia.

Employment

The League for the Exchange of Commonwealth Teachers, Commonwealth House, 7 Lion Yard, Tremadoc Road, Clapham, London SW4 7NQ. Tel: 0870 770 2636. www.lect.org.uk

Labor Ready, Inc. (temporary manual labour), Customer Care Department, PO Box 2910, Tacoma, WA. Tel: (253) 383-9101. www.laborready.com

INTERNET CONTACTS

Canada Business	www.cbsc.org
Canadian Association of Professional Immigration Consultants	www.capic.ca
Canadian Technology Human Resource Board	www.cthrb.ca
Career Edge (Canada's Internship Organisation)	www.careeredge.ca
Citizenship and Immigration Canada	www.cic.gc.ca
Employment News	www.employmentnews.com
Government of Canada	www.gc.ca
Health Canada	www.hc-sc.gc.ca
Hire Immigrants	www.hireimmigrants.ca
Hire Immigrants Ottawa	www.hireimmigrantsottawa.ca
Human Resources and Skills Development Canada	www.hrsdc.gc.ca
	www.jobsetc.gc.ca
Migrate Canada	www.migratecanada.com
Niagara Region Employment Council	www.nrec.ca
Online Job Searches	www.monster.ca
	www.workopolis.ca
Ontario Settlement Portal	www.settlement.org
Quebec Immigration	www.immigration-quebec.
(main site is in French, but has links for both English and Spanish)	gouv.qc.ca

Service Canada Job Bank	www.jobbank.gc.ca
Society of Internet Professionals	www.sipgroup.org
Toronto Region Immigrant Employment Council	www.triec.ca
Waterloo Region Immigrant Employment Network	www.wrien.com

Provincial Governments

Alberta	www.gov.ab.ca
British Columbia	www.gov.bc.ca
Manitoba	www.gov.mb.ca
New Brunswick	www.gov.nb.ca
Newfoundland	www.gov.nf.ca
Northwest Territories	www.gov.nt.ca
Nova Scotia	www.gov.ns.ca
Nunavut	www.gov.nu.ca
Ontario	www.gov.on.ca
Prince Edward Island	www.gov.pe.ca
Quebec	www.gouv.qc.ca
Saskatchewan	www.gov.sk.ca
Yukon Territories	www.gov.yk.ca

Index

accommodation, 71–85
appliances, 81–2
arts and culture, 146–51
attitudes, 26–7

banking, 26
baseball, 143
basketball, 142
business contacts, 167–8, 173
business immigration, 47–8
business opportunities, 96–7
business visitors, 38
buying a house, 75–8

camp, 145
Canada Health Act, 53
Canadian Broadcasting Corporation, 12, 152
Canadian Pacific Railway, 11–12
cars, 132–5
    buying, 133
    importing, 132
    insuring and registering, 134
    leasing, 133–4
    motoring associations, 134–5
CEGEP, 108
child tax benefits, 60
citizenship, 48
climate, 22–4
clothing, 7
college system, 118–19
comedy, 148
condominiums, 78
Confederation, 11
Constitution Act, 12
Charter of Rights and Freedoms, 12
consultant firms, 169

correspondence courses, 120
cost of living, 25
cottage country, 143–4
courts, 20
cover letter, 91
credential assessment and advice, 87, 168
crime, 20, 120
customs, 82
CV see résumés

dance, 148
dangers, 144–5
dental services, 58
deportation, 49
discrimination, 78–9
disease, 56
doctors, 54–5
driving, 127–36
    drivers' licences, 131–2
    drunk driving, 130
    insurance, 134
    owning a war, 132–4
    pedestrians, 131
    rules of the road, 129–30
    speed limits, 130
drugs, 5

economy, 24–6, 164
    banking, 26
    finance, 164
    national debt, 26
    taxes, 63–8
education, 105–25
    funding, 105–6
elementary school, 106–7
email, 157

embassies/consulates, 172–3
employment, 85–103
  authorisation, 31, 34
  contacts, 169–70
  credential assessment, 87, 168
  insurance, 60–1
  interviews, 94–6
  qualifications, 86–7
  statistics, 89
  students, 101–2
employment agencies *see* placement
  agencies
English as a second language, 111
entrepreneurs, 48
expectations, 2
expenses, 25

family reunion, 44–7
famous Canadians, 147–9
famous sites, 154–5
films, 148
firearms, 5–6
football, 142–3
foreign students, 34
foreign workers, 34–9, 99
French as a second language, 111
French immersion, 110
fun, 139–57

gasoline, 135
general sales tax/Goods and Services Tax
  (GST), 65
geography, 20–2
glossary, 159–61
government, 18–19, 175
grades, 107

harassment, 98
harmonised sales tax, 66
health card, 56–7
health care, 51–8
  accountability, 58
  clinics, 56

dental services, 58
disease, 56
doctors, 54–5
eligibility and the health card, 56–7
hospitals, 55
insurance, 54
medicines, 57
numbers, 52–3
pregnancy, 58
public versus private, 53
high school, 108
history, 9–13, 162–3
hockey, 141–2
holidays, 98, 154
homesickness, 6
host program, 7, 166–7
household appliances, 81–2
housing, 71–85, 167
  buying, 75–8
  prices, 76
  renting, 72–5
  safety, 81
  subsidisation, 79

illegal immigration, 30
immigration, 29–49
  business, 47–8
  exemptions (work permits), 37
  family-based, 44–7
  fees, 48
  immigrant statistics, 16
  permanent residence, 39–40
  policy, 29
  provincial programmes, 43–4
  requirements, 31
  sponsorship, 44–7
  students, 34
  visitors' visas, 32
income tax, 63–5
Internet, 80
  contacts, 174
inventions, 13–14
investors, 47

job incentives, 88
job interviews, 94–6
job references, 94
justice system, 19–20

keeping in touch, 156–7
kindergarten, 107

labour market opinion, 35–6
    exemptions, 46–7
lacrosse, 140
language, 16, 40, 110, 111, 155–6
law, 19–20
legal system, 19–20
leisure and holidays, 154
literature, 150
live-in caregiver program, 102–3

magazines, 152, 164–5
mail, 157
media, 151–4
medical assessment information, 167
medical care *see* health
Medical Care Act, 51
medical inadmissability, 31
minimum wage, 88, 89
mortgages, 77
motor associations, 134–5
movies *see* films
multiculturalism, 3, 15
municipalities (revenue), 68
music, 146–7

national parks, 145
Native Indian art, 149
newspapers, 151–2, 170–2
nightlife, 154
Nunavut, 21

Old Age Security, 59
Olympics, 141
outdoor recreation, 143
overseas students *see* foreign students

painting, 151
patios, 145–6
pension plans, 59
permanent residence, 30, 39
pets, 4–5
placement agencies, 169
police clearances, 174
population, 17
post, 157
pre-school, 106–7
prescription drugs, 5, 57
private school, 108
professionals, 39
provincial government websites, 175
public school, 108

racism, 3
radio, 153–4
RCMP, 20
recreation, 139–57
regions, 21–2
Registered Retired Saving Plans, 64
relatives in Canada, 44–7
religion, 17
rent, 72–5
résumés, 91–4

sales tax, 66
schools, 105–12
    alternative, 110
    elementary, 106–7
    enrolling, 111
    facilities, 110–11
    high, 108
    kindergarten, 107
    pre-school, 106–7
    private, 108
    public, 108
    secondary *see* high
    separate, 110
school breaks, 111-12
school levels *see* grades
secondary school *see* high school

self-employment, 48
settlement funds, 42
sightseeing, 154–5
soccer, 142
social assistance, 61
Social Insurance Number, 86
social security, 58–9
    applying for, 61
speed limits, 130
sport, 139–43
student exchanges, 124
student loans, 114
student medical insurance, 123–4
student permit, 34
student visas, 34
Student Work Abroad, 101–2
summer camp see camp
Supreme Court of Canada, 20

taxation, 63–8
    deductions, 64
    rates, 64
telephone, 79–80, 157
television, 80, 152–3
temporary resident visa, 32
temporary work visa, 34–5, 99
temporary workers, 30, 34
theatre, 146
tipping, 68

TOEFL, 117
Trans Canada Highway, 129
Trans Canada Trail, 143
transportation, 135–6
travel, 127–8, 164

unemployment insurance see
    employment insurance
unemployment figures, 89
unions, 97–8
United Nations, 15
university, 112–18
    applying, 13
    books/supplies, 114
    housing, 115–16
    programmes, 112–13
    requirements, 116–17
    standards, 116–17
    tuition, 114
useful addresses, 166–75

visitor's visas, 32

weather, 22–4
welfare see social security
work experience, 40, 86–7, 94
workers' compensation, 61
working holiday programmes, 100–1